Financial Accounting

ACT 103

14th Edition

Carl S. Warren | Jim Reeve | Jonathan Duchac

CENGAGE Learning

Australia • Brazil • Japan • Korea • Mexico • Singapore • Spain • United Kingdom • United States

CENGAGE Learning

Financial Accounting, ACT 103, 14th Edition

Financial Accounting, 14th Edition
Carl S. Warren | Jim Reeve | Jonathan Duchac

For product information and technology assistance, contact us at
Cengage Learning Customer & Sales Support, 1-800-354-9706

For permission to use material from this text or product,
submit all requests online at **cengage.com/permissions**
Further permissions questions can be emailed to
permissionrequest@cengage.com

This book contains select works from existing Cengage Learning resources and was produced by Cengage Learning Custom Solutions for collegiate use. As such, those adopting and/or contributing to this work are responsible for editorial content accuracy, continuity and completeness.

ISBN: 978-1-337-03397-8

Cengage Learning
20 Channel Center Street
Boston, MA 02210
USA

Cengage Learning is a leading provider of customized learning solutions with office locations around the globe, including Singapore, the United Kingdom, Australia, Mexico, Brazil, and Japan. Locate your local office at: **www.international.cengage.com/region.**

Cengage Learning products are represented in Canada by Nelson Education, Ltd.

For your lifelong learning solutions, visit **www.cengage.com/custom.**

Visit our corporate website at **www.cengage.com.**

Printed in Mexico

About the Authors

Terry R. Spray InHisImage Studios

Carl S. Warren

Dr. Carl S. Warren is Professor Emeritus of Accounting at the University of Georgia, Athens. Dr. Warren has taught classes at the University of Georgia, University of Iowa, Michigan State University, and University of Chicago. Professor Warren focused his teaching efforts on principles of accounting and auditing. He received his Ph.D. from Michigan State University and his B.B.A. and M.A. from the University of Iowa. During his career, Dr. Warren published numerous articles in professional journals, including *The Accounting Review, Journal of Accounting Research, Journal of Accountancy, The CPA Journal,* and *Auditing: A Journal of Practice & Theory*. Dr. Warren has served on numerous committees of the American Accounting Association, the American Institute of Certified Public Accountants, and the Institute of Internal Auditors. He has also consulted with numerous companies and public accounting firms. Professor Warren is an avid handball player and has played in the World Handball Championships in Portland, Oregon, and Dublin, Ireland. He enjoys backpacking and recently took an eleven-day, ten-night trip in the Thorofare area of Yellowstone National Park. He has rafted the Grand Canyon and backpacked rim-to-rim. Professor Warren also enjoys fly fishing, skiing, golfing, and motorcycling.

Charles J. Garvey III / Garvey Photography

James M. Reeve

Dr. James M. Reeve is Professor Emeritus of Accounting and Information Management at the University of Tennessee. Professor Reeve taught on the accounting faculty for 25 years, after graduating with his Ph.D. from Oklahoma State University. His teaching efforts focused on undergraduate accounting principles and graduate education in the Master of Accountancy and Senior Executive MBA programs. Beyond this, Professor Reeve is also very active in the Supply Chain Certification program, which is a major executive education and research effort of the College. His research interests are varied and include work in managerial accounting, supply chain management, lean manufacturing, and information management. He has published over 40 articles in academic and professional journals, including the *Journal of Cost Management, Journal of Management Accounting Research, Accounting Review, Management Accounting Quarterly, Supply Chain Management Review,* and *Accounting Horizons*. He has consulted or provided training around the world for a wide variety of organizations, including Boeing, Procter & Gamble, Norfolk Southern, Hershey Foods, Coca-Cola, and Sony. When not writing books, Professor Reeve plays golf and is involved in faith-based activities.

© Ken Bennett

Jonathan Duchac

Dr. Jonathan Duchac is the Merrill Lynch and Co. Professor of Accounting and Director of International Programs at Wake Forest University. He holds a joint appointment at the Vienna University of Business and Economics in Vienna, Austria. Dr. Duchac currently teaches introductory and advanced courses in financial accounting and has received a number of awards during his career, including the Wake Forest University Outstanding Graduate Professor Award, the T.B. Rose Award for Instructional Innovation, and the University of Georgia Outstanding Teaching Assistant Award. In addition to his teaching responsibilities, Dr. Duchac has served as Accounting Advisor to Merrill Lynch Equity Research, where he worked with research analysts in reviewing and evaluating the financial reporting practices of public companies. He has testified before the U.S. House of Representatives, the Financial Accounting Standards Board, and the Securities and Exchange Commission and has worked with a number of major public companies on financial reporting and accounting policy issues. In addition to his professional interests, Dr. Duchac has served on the Board of Directors of The Special Children's School of Winston-Salem, a private, nonprofit developmental day school serving children with special needs. Dr. Duchac is an avid long-distance runner, mountain biker, and snow skier. His recent events include the Grandfather Mountain Marathon, the Black Mountain Marathon, the Shut-In Ridge Trail run, and NO MAAM (Nocturnal Overnight Mountain Bike Assault on Mount Mitchell).

Brief Contents

Contents

CHAPTER 12

Accounting for Partnerships and Limited Liability Companies

Boston Basketball Partners LLC

Boston Basketball Partners (BBP) LLC are the owners of the Boston Celtics NBA basketball franchise. The letters "LLC" stand for *limited liability company*. Unlike sole proprietorships illustrated in prior chapters, an LLC is a business form that normally has multiple owners. BBP LLC is led by Wic Grousbeck, a former venture fund manager from Boston, with the assistance of more than 15 other owners. Grousbeck called investing in the Celtics "a chance of a lifetime." Surprisingly, Grousbeck claims "money would not be the first priority." Even so, *Forbes* estimates the team is now worth $730 million, which is more than twice what BBP LLC originally paid, while ranking the Celtics as the fourth most valuable team in the NBA. So, Grousbeck must be doing something right. Grousbeck and his team have turned their venture capital skills toward the Celtics. Some of their innovations off the court include building a cable partnership, using technology to evaluate seat usage, and adding advertising sponsors. On the court, they pioneered the "three superstars to win" strategy with Rondo, Garnett, and Allen.

So why would BBP LLC choose the LLC form of organization?

The entity form chosen by a business has an important impact on the owners' legal liability, taxation, and ability to raise money. The four major forms of business entities discussed in this text are the proprietorship, partnership, limited liability company, and corporation. Proprietorships have been discussed in prior chapters. Partnerships and limited liability companies will be discussed in this chapter, and corporations will be introduced in the next chapter.

Learning Objectives

After studying this chapter, you should be able to: *Example Exercises*

OBJ 1 **Describe the characteristics of proprietorships, partnerships, and limited liability companies.**
Proprietorships, Partnerships, and Limited Liability Companies
- Proprietorships
- Partnerships
- Limited Liability Companies
- Comparing Proprietorships, Partnerships, and Limited Liability Companies

OBJ 2 **Describe and illustrate the accounting for forming a partnership and for dividing the net income and net loss of a partnership.**
Forming a Partnership and Dividing Income
- Forming a Partnership — EE 12-1
- Dividing Income — EE 12-2

OBJ 3 **Describe and illustrate the accounting for partner admission and withdrawal.**
Partner Admission and Withdrawal
- Admitting a Partner — EE 12-3
- Withdrawal of a Partner — EE 12-4
- Death of a Partner

OBJ 4 **Describe and illustrate the accounting for liquidating a partnership.**
Liquidating Partnerships
- Gain on Realization
- Loss on Realization — EE 12-5
- Loss on Realization—Capital Deficiency — EE 12-6

OBJ 5 **Prepare the statement of partnership equity.**
Statement of Partnership Equity

OBJ 6 **Analyze and interpret employee efficiency.**
Financial Analysis and Interpretation: Revenue per Employee — EE 12-7

At a Glance 12 Page 573

OBJ 1 Describe the characteristics of proprietorships, partnerships, and limited liability companies.

Proprietorships, Partnerships, and Limited Liability Companies

The four most common legal forms for organizing and operating a business are as follows:

- Proprietorship
- Corporation
- Partnership
- Limited liability company

In this section, the characteristics of proprietorships, partnerships, and limited liability companies are described. The characteristics of corporations are described in Chapter 13.

Proprietorships

A *proprietorship* is a company owned by a single individual. The most common proprietorships are professional service providers, such as lawyers, architects, realtors, and physicians.

Characteristics of proprietorships include the following:

- *Simple to form.* There are no legal restrictions or forms to file.
- *No limitation on legal liability.* The owner is personally liable for any debts or legal claims against the business. Thus, creditors can take the personal assets of the owner if the business debts exceed the owner's investment in the company.

The **Internal Revenue Service (IRS)** estimates that proprietorships file 70% of business tax returns, but earn only 5% of all business revenues.

- *Not taxable.* For federal income tax purposes, a proprietorship is not taxed. Instead, the proprietorship's income or loss is "passed through" to the owner's individual income tax return.[1]
- *Limited life.* When the owner dies or retires, the proprietorship ceases to exist.
- *Limited ability to raise capital (funds).* The ability to raise capital (funds) is limited to what the owner can provide from personal resources or through borrowing.

Partnerships

A **partnership** is an association of two or more persons who own and manage a business for profit.[2] Partnerships are less widely used than proprietorships.

Characteristics of a partnership include the following:

Note: A partnership is a nontaxable entity that has a limited life and unlimited liability.

- *Moderately complex to form.* A partnership is often formed with a partnership agreement. A **partnership agreement** includes matters such as amounts to be invested, limits on withdrawals, distributions of income and losses, and admission and withdrawal of partners. Thus, an attorney is often used in forming a partnership.
- *No limitation on legal liability.* The partners are personally liable for any debts or legal claims against the partnership. Therefore, creditors can take the personal assets of the partners if the business debts exceed the partners' investment in the business.
- *Not taxable.* For federal income tax purposes, a partnership is not taxed. Instead, the partnership's income or loss is "passed through" to the partners' individual income tax returns. However, partnerships must still report revenues, expenses, and income or loss annually to the Internal Revenue Service.
- *Limited life.* When a partner dies or retires, the partnership ceases to exist. Likewise, the admission of a new partner dissolves the old partnership, and a new partnership must be formed if operations are to continue.
- *Limited ability to raise capital (funds).* The ability to raise capital (funds) for the partnership is limited to what the partners can provide from personal resources or through borrowing.

In addition to those characteristics, some unique aspects of partnerships are:

- *Co-ownership of partnership property.* The property invested in a partnership by a partner becomes the joint property of all the partners. When a partnership is dissolved, each partner's share of the partnership assets is the balance in their capital account.
- *Mutual agency.* Each partner is an agent of the partnership and may act on behalf of the entire partnership. Thus, any liabilities created by one partner become liabilities of all the partners.
- *Participation in income.* Net income and net loss are distributed among the partners according to their partnership agreement. If the partnership agreement does not provide for distribution of income and losses, then income and losses are divided equally among the partners.

Business Connection

BREAKING UP IS HARD TO DO

Former partners of Adam Carolla filed court papers accusing the star of The Adam Carolla Show (adamcarolla.com) of a breach of their partnership agreement. They claimed the partnership agreement gave 30% ownership to Donny Misraje, 10% to Sandy Ganz, and 60% to Carolla. The suit alleges that Carolla began his popular podcast with the help of his partners at a time when future success of the venture was risky and unknown. The former partners claim to have given up jobs, invested money and equipment, and provided expertise to launch the show. Once the show achieved success, the former partners claim Carolla unfairly kicked them out of the partnership. The court will, in part, use the partnership agreement to help settle this dispute. A partnership agreement helps protect the interests of all parties to a business venture.

Source: Radar Staff, "Best Friend Sues Adam Carolla Over Hit Podcast Show," January 18, 2013.

[1] The proprietor's statement of income is included on Schedule C of the individual 1040 tax return.

[2] The definition of a partnership is included in the Uniform Partnership Act, which has been adopted by most states.

Limited Liability Companies

Many companies have joint ventures organized as LLCs. For example, **Walt Disney Company** has a 42% interest in **A&E Television Networks, LLC.**

A **limited liability company (LLC)** is a form of legal entity that provides limited liability to its owners but is treated as a partnership for tax purposes. Thus, the LLC organizational form is popular for small businesses.

Characteristics of an LLC include the following:

- *Moderately complex to form.* An LLC requires an agreement among the owners, who are called members. The *operating agreement* includes matters such as amounts to be invested, limits on withdrawals, distributions of income and losses, and admission and withdrawal of members. An attorney is normally used in forming an LCC.
- *Limited legal liability.* The members have *limited liability* even if they are active in the company. Thus, the members' personal assets are legally protected against creditor claims made against the LLC. That is, only the members' investments in the company are subject to claims of creditors.
- *Not taxable.* An LLC may elect to be treated as a partnership for tax purposes. In this way, income passes through the LLC and is taxed on the individual members' tax returns.[3]
- *Unlimited life.* Most LLC operating agreements specify continuity of life for the LLC, even when a member withdraws or new members join the LLC.
- *Moderate ability to raise capital (funds).* Because of their limited liability, LLCs are attractive to many investors, thus allowing for greater access to capital (funds) than is normally the case in a partnership.

An LLC may elect to operate as a *member-managed* or a *manager-managed* company. In a member-managed LLC, individual members may legally bind the LLC, like partners bind a partnership. In a manager-managed LLC, only authorized members may legally bind the LLC. Thus, in a manager-managed LLC, members may share in the income of the LLC without concern for managing the company.

Comparing Proprietorships, Partnerships, and Limited Liability Companies

Exhibit 1 summarizes the characteristics of proprietorships, partnerships, and limited liability companies.

EXHIBIT 1 **Characteristics of Proprietorships, Partnerships, and Limited Liability Companies**

Organizational Form	Complexity of Formation	Legal Liability	Taxation	Limitation on Life of Entity	Access to Capital
Proprietorship	Simple	No limitation	Nontaxable (pass-through) entity	Limited	Limited
Partnership	Moderate	No limitation	Nontaxable (pass-through) entity	Limited	Limited
Limited Liability Company	Moderate	Limited liability	Nontaxable (pass-through) entity by election	Unlimited	Moderate

Business Connection

ORGANIZATIONAL FORMS IN THE ACCOUNTING INDUSTRY

The four major accounting firms, **KPMG LLP**, **Ernst & Young**, **PricewaterhouseCoopers**, and **Deloitte & Touche**, all began as partnerships. This form was legally required due to the theory of mutual agency. That is, the partnership form was thought to create public trust by requiring all partners to be jointly liable and responsible for each other's judgments. In addition, investment in the partnerships was limited to practicing accountants. This prevented any pressures from outside investors affecting professional decisions.

As these firms grew and the risk increased, all of these firms were allowed to change, by law, to limited liability partnerships (LLPs). Thus, while remaining a partnership, the liability of the partners was limited to their investment in the firm. The LLP form is very similar to an LLC, except that investment is restricted to professionals.

[3] An LLC may also be taxed as a separate entity. However, doing so would remove these tax benefits, making this a less common election.

Forming a Partnership and Dividing Income

OBJ 2 Describe and illustrate the accounting for forming a partnership and for dividing the net income and net loss of a partnership.

Most of the day-to-day accounting for a partnership or an LLC is similar to that illustrated in earlier chapters. However, the formation, division of net income or net loss, dissolution, and liquidation of partnerships and LLCs give rise to unique transactions.

In the remainder of this chapter, the unique transactions for partnerships and LLCs are described and illustrated. The accounting for an LLC is the same as a partnership, except that the terms *member* and *members' equity* are used rather than *partner* or *owners' capital.* For this reason, the journal entries for an LLC are shown alongside the partnership entries.

Forming a Partnership

In forming a partnership, the investments of each partner are recorded in separate entries. The assets contributed by a partner are debited to the partnership asset accounts. If any liabilities are assumed by the partnership, the partnership liability accounts are credited. The partner's capital account is credited for the net amount.

To illustrate, assume that Joseph Stevens and Earl Foster, owners of competing hardware stores, agree to combine their businesses in a partnership. Stevens agrees to contribute the following:

Cash	$ 7,200	Office equipment	$2,500
Accounts receivable	16,300	Allowance for doubtful accounts	1,500
Merchandise inventory	28,700	Accounts payable	2,600
Store equipment	5,400		

The entry to record the assets and liabilities contributed by Stevens is as follows:

LLC		
Cash	*7,200*	
Accounts Receivable	*16,300*	
Merchandise Inventory	*28,700*	
Store Equipment	*5,400*	
Office Equipment	*2,500*	
Allowance for Doubtful Accounts		*1,500*
Accounts Payable		*2,600*
Joseph Stevens, Member Equity		*56,000*

Apr.	1	Cash		7,200	
		Accounts Receivable		16,300	
		Merchandise Inventory		28,700	
		Store Equipment		5,400	
		Office Equipment		2,500	
		Allowance for Doubtful Accounts			1,500
		Accounts Payable			2,600
		Joseph Stevens, Capital			56,000

In the preceding entry, the noncash assets are recorded at values agreed upon by the partners. These values are normally based on current market values. As a result, the book value of the assets contributed by the partners normally differs from that recorded by the new partnership.

To illustrate, the store equipment contributed by Stevens may have had a book value of $3,500 in Stevens' ledger (cost of $10,000 less accumulated depreciation of $6,500). However, the store equipment is recorded at its current market value of $5,400 in the preceding entry. The contributions of Foster would be recorded in an entry similar to the entry for Stevens.

Example Exercise 12-1 Journalize Partner's Original Investment

OBJ 1

Reese Howell contributed equipment, inventory, and $34,000 cash to a partnership. The equipment had a book value of $23,000 and a market value of $29,000. The inventory had a book value of $60,000, but only had a market value of $15,000, due to obsolescence. The partnership also assumed a $12,000 note payable owed by Howell that was used originally to purchase the equipment.

Provide the journal entry for Howell's contribution to the partnership.

(Continued)

Follow My Example 12-1

Cash	34,000	
Inventory	15,000	
Equipment	29,000	
Notes Payable		12,000
Reese Howell, Capital		66,000

Practice Exercises: PE 12-1A, PE 12-1B

Dividing Income

Income or losses of the partnership are divided as specified in the partnership agreement. If there is no specification or agreement, income and losses are divided equally.

Common methods of dividing partnership income are based on:

- Services of the partners
- Services and investments of the partners

Services of Partners One method of dividing partnership income is based on the services provided by each partner to the partnership. These services are often recognized by partner salary allowances. Such allowances reflect differences in partners' abilities and time devoted to the partnership. Since partners are not employees, such allowances are recorded as divisions of net income and are credited to the partners' capital accounts.

To illustrate, assume that the partnership agreement of Jennifer Stone and Crystal Mills provides for the following:

	Monthly Salary Allowance
Jennifer Stone	$5,000
Crystal Mills	4,000
Remaining net income:	Divided Equally

The division of income may be reported at the bottom of the partnership income statement. Using this format, the division of $150,000 of net income would be reported on the bottom of the partnership income statement as follows:

Net income			$150,000
Division of net income:			
	J. Stone	**C. Mills**	**Total**
Annual salary allowance (mo. × 12)	$60,000	$48,000	$108,000
Remaining income	21,000	21,000	42,000
Net income	$81,000	$69,000	$150,000

A closing entry is used to record the division of net income, even if the partners do not withdraw the amounts of their salary allowances. The entry for closing Income Summary and dividing net income is as follows:

LLC

Income Summary	*150,000*	
Jennifer Stone, Member Equity		*81,000*
Crystal Mills, Member Equity		*69,000*

Dec.	31	Income Summary	150,000	
		Jennifer Stone, Capital		81,000
		Crystal Mills, Capital		69,000

If Stone and Mills withdraw their salary allowances monthly, the withdrawals are debited to their drawing accounts. At the end of the year, the drawing account debit balances of $60,000 and $48,000 are then closed to the partners' capital accounts.

Services of Partners and Investments A partnership agreement may divide income based upon salary allowances, as discussed, and also based upon interest on capital balances of each partner. In this way, partners with more invested in the partnership are rewarded by receiving more of the partnership income. One such method of dividing partnership income would be as follows:

1. Partner salary allowances
2. Interest on capital investments
3. Any remaining income equally

To illustrate, assume that the partnership agreement for Stone and Mills provides for the following:

1.

	Monthly Salary Allowance
Jennifer Stone	$5,000
Crystal Mills	4,000

2. Interest of 12% on each partner's capital balance as of January 1.

Capital, Jennifer Stone, January 1	$160,000
Capital, Crystal Mills, January 1	120,000

3. Remaining income: Divided Equally

The $150,000 net income for the year is divided as follows:

Net income	$150,000
Division of net income:	

	J. Stone	C. Mills	Total
Annual salary allowance	$60,000	$48,000	$108,000
Interest allowance	19,200[1]	14,400[2]	33,600
Total	$79,200	$62,400	$141,600
Remaining income	4,200	4,200	8,400
Net income	$83,400	$66,600	$150,000

[1] 12% × $160,000
[2] 12% × $120,000

The entry for closing Income Summary and dividing net income is as follows:

LLC		
Income Summary	*150,000*	
Jennifer Stone, Member Equity		*83,400*
Crystal Mills, Member Equity		*66,600*

Dec.	31	Income Summary		150,000	
		Jennifer Stone, Capital			83,400
		Crystal Mills, Capital			66,600

Integrity, Objectivity, and Ethics in Business

TYRANNY OF THE MAJORITY

Some partnerships involve the contribution of money by one partner and the contribution of effort and expertise by another. This can create a conflict between the two partners, because one works and the other doesn't. Without a properly developed partnership agreement, the working partner could take income in the form of a salary allowance, leaving little for the investor partner. Thus, partnership agreements often require all partners to agree on salary allowances provided to working partners.

Allowances Exceed Net Income In the preceding example, the net income is $150,000. The total of the salary ($108,000) and interest ($33,600) allowances is $141,600. Thus, the net income exceeds the salary and interest allowances. In some cases, however, the net income may be less than the total of the allowances. In this case, the remaining net income to divide is a *negative* amount. This negative amount is divided among the partners as though it were a net loss.

To illustrate, assume the same salary and interest allowances as in the preceding example, but that the net income is $100,000. In this case, the total of the allowances of $141,600 exceeds the net income by $41,600 ($100,000 − $141,600). This amount is divided equally between Stone and Mills. Thus, $20,800 ($41,600 ÷ 2) is deducted from each partner's share of the allowances. The final division of net income between Stone and Mills is as follows:

Net income $100,000

Division of net income:

	J. Stone	C. Mills	Total
Annual salary allowance	$ 60,000	$48,000	$108,000
Interest allowance	19,200	14,400	33,600
Total	$ 79,200	$62,400	$141,600
Deduct excess of allowances over income	20,800	20,800	41,600
Net income[4]	$58,400	$41,600	$100,000

The entry for closing Income Summary and dividing net income is as follows:

LLC

Income Summary	*100,000*	
Jennifer Stone, Member Equity		*58,400*
Crystal Mills, Member Equity		*41,600*

Dec.	31	Income Summary		100,000	
		Jennifer Stone, Capital			58,400
		Crystal Mills, Capital			41,600

Example Exercise 12-2 Dividing Partnership Net Income

OBJ 2

Dynamic Exhibit

Steve Prince and Chelsy Bernard formed a partnership, dividing income as follows:

1. Annual salary allowance to Prince of $42,000.
2. Interest of 9% on each partner's capital balance on January 1.
3. Any remaining net income divided equally.

Prince and Bernard had $20,000 and $150,000 in their January 1 capital balances, respectively. Net income for the year was $240,000.

How much net income should be distributed to Prince and Bernard?

Follow My Example 12-2

	S. Prince	C. Bernard	Total
Annual salary allowance	$ 42,000	$ 0	$ 42,000
Interest allowance	1,800[1]	13,500[2]	15,300
Total	$ 43,800	$ 13,500	$ 57,300
Remaining income	91,350[3]	91,350	182,700
Net income	$135,150	$104,850	$240,000

[1] $20,000 × 9%
[2] $150,000 × 9%
[3] ($240,000 − $42,000 − $15,300) × 50%

Practice Exercises: PE 12-2A, PE 12-2B

[4] In the event of a net loss, the amount deducted from the total allowances would be the "excess of allowances over loss" or the sum of the net loss and the allowances, divided according to the sharing ratio.

Partner Admission and Withdrawal

OBJ 3 Describe and illustrate the accounting for partner admission and withdrawal.

Many partnerships provide for admitting new partners and for partner withdrawals by amending the existing partnership agreement. In this way, the company may continue operating without having to form a new partnership and prepare a new partnership agreement.

Admitting a Partner

As shown in Exhibit 2, a person may be admitted to a partnership by either of the following:

- Purchasing an interest from one or more of the existing partners
- Contributing assets to the partnership

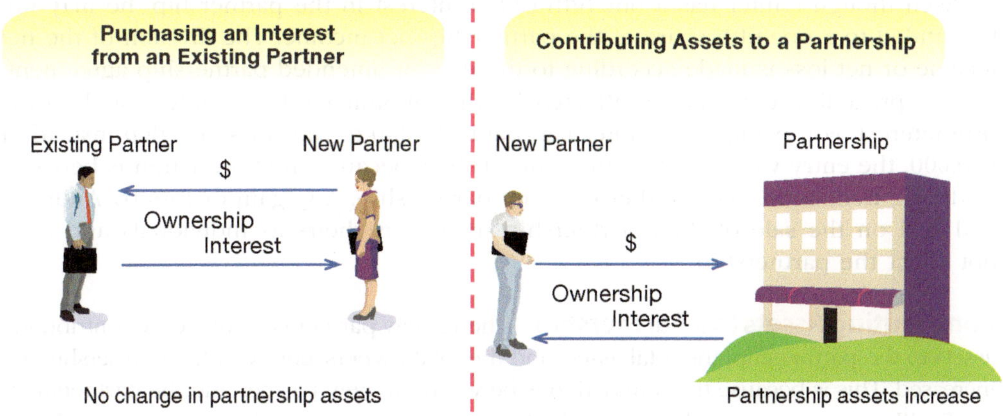

EXHIBIT 2

Two Methods for Admitting a Partner

When a new partner is admitted by *purchasing an interest* from one or more of the existing partners, the total assets and the total owners' equity of the partnership are not affected. The capital (equity) of the new partner is recorded by transferring capital (equity) from the existing partners.

When a new partner is admitted by *contributing assets* to the partnership, the total assets and the total owners' equity of the partnership are increased. The capital (equity) of the new partner is recorded as the amount of assets contributed to the partnership by the new partner.

Purchasing an Interest from Existing Partners

When a new partner is admitted by purchasing an interest from one or more of the existing partners, the transaction is between the new and existing partners acting as individuals. The admission of the new partner is recorded by transferring owners' equity amounts from the capital accounts of the selling partners to the capital account of the new partner.

To illustrate, assume that on June 1 Tom Andrews and Nathan Bell each sell one-fifth of their partnership equity of Bring It Consulting to Joe Canter for $10,000 in cash. On June 1, the partnership has net assets of $100,000 and both existing partners have capital balances of $50,000 each. This transaction is between Andrews, Bell, and Canter. The only entry required by Bring It Consulting is to record the transfer of capital (equity) from Andrews and Bell to Canter, as follows:

LLC

Tom Andrews, Member Equity	*10,000*	
Nathan Bell, Member Equity	*10,000*	
Joe Canter, Member Equity		*20,000*

June	1	Tom Andrews, Capital		10,000	
		Nathan Bell, Capital		10,000	
		Joe Canter, Capital			20,000

The effect of the transaction on the partnership accounts is as follows:

BRING IT CONSULTING

Partnership Accounts

Net Assets	
100,000	

Tom Andrews, Capital	
10,000	50,000

Joe Canter, Capital	
	20,000

Nathan Bell, Capital	
10,000	50,000

After Canter is admitted to Bring It Consulting, the total owners' equity is still $100,000. Canter has a one-fifth (20%) interest and a capital balance of $20,000. Andrews and Bell each own two-fifths (40%) interest and have capital balances of $40,000 each.

Even though Canter has a one-fifth (20%) interest in the partnership, he may not be entitled to a one-fifth share of the partnership net income. The division of the net income or net loss is made according to the new or amended partnership agreement.

The preceding entry is not affected by the amount paid by Canter for the one-fifth interest. For example, if Canter had paid $15,000 to Andrews and Bell instead of $10,000, the entry would still be the same. This is because the transaction is between Andrews, Bell, and Canter, rather than the partnership. Any gain or loss by Andrews and Bell on the sale of their partnership interest is theirs as individuals and does not affect the partnership.

Contributing Assets to a Partnership When a new partner is admitted by contributing assets to the partnership, the total assets and the total owners' equity of the partnership are increased. This is because the transaction is between the new partner and the partnership.

To illustrate, assume that instead of purchasing a one-fifth ownership in Bring It Consulting directly from Tom Andrews and Nathan Bell, Joe Canter contributes $20,000 cash to Bring It Consulting for ownership equity of $20,000. The entry to record this transaction is as follows:

LLC		
Cash	*20,000*	
Joe Canter, Member Equity		*20,000*

June	1	Cash	20,000	
		Joe Canter, Capital		20,000

The effect of the transaction on the partnership accounts is as follows:

BRING IT CONSULTING

Partnership Accounts

Net Assets	
100,000	
20,000	

Tom Andrews, Capital	
	50,000

Joe Canter, Capital	
	20,000

Nathan Bell, Capital	
	50,000

After the admission of Canter, the net assets and total owners' equity of Bring It Consulting increase to $120,000, of which Joe Canter has a $20,000 interest. In contrast, in the prior example, the net assets and total owners' equity of Bring It Consulting did not change from $100,000.

Revaluation of Assets Before a new partner is admitted, the balances of a partnership's asset accounts should be stated at current values. If necessary, the accounts should be adjusted. Any net adjustment (increase or decrease) in asset values is divided among the capital accounts of the existing partners, similar to the division of income.

To illustrate, assume that in the preceding example the balance of the merchandise inventory account is $14,000 and the current replacement value is $17,000. If Andrews and Bell share net income equally, the revaluation is recorded as follows:

LLC		
Merchandise Inventory	*3,000*	
Tom Andrews, Member Equity		*1,500*
Nathan Bell, Member Equity		*1,500*

June	1	Merchandise Inventory		3,000	
		Tom Andrews, Capital			1,500
		Nathan Bell, Capital			1,500

Failure to adjust the partnership accounts for current values before admission of a new partner may result in the new partner sharing in asset gains or losses that arose in prior periods.

Example Exercise 12-3 Revaluing and Contributing Assets to a Partnership

OBJ 3

Blake Nelson invested $45,000 in the Lawrence & Kerry partnership for ownership equity of $45,000. Prior to the investment, land was revalued to a market value of $260,000 from a book value of $200,000. Lynne Lawrence and Tim Kerry share net income in a 1:2 ratio.

a. Provide the journal entry for the revaluation of land.

b. Provide the journal entry to admit Nelson.

Follow My Example 12-3

a. Land	60,000	
Lynne Lawrence, Capital		20,000
Tim Kerry, Capital		40,000
[1] $60,000 × 1/3		
[2] $60,000 × 2/3		
b. Cash	45,000	
Blake Nelson, Capital		45,000

Practice Exercises: PE 12-3A, PE 12-3B

Partner Bonuses A new partner may pay existing partners a bonus to join a partnership. In other cases, existing partners may pay a new partner a bonus to join the partnership.

Bonuses are usually paid because of higher than normal profits the new or existing partners are expected to contribute in the future. For example, a new partner may bring special qualities or skills to the partnership. Celebrities such as actors, musicians, or sports figures often provide name recognition that is expected to increase a partnership's profits.

Partner bonuses are illustrated in Exhibit 3. Existing partners receive a bonus when the ownership interest received by the new partner is less than the amount paid. In

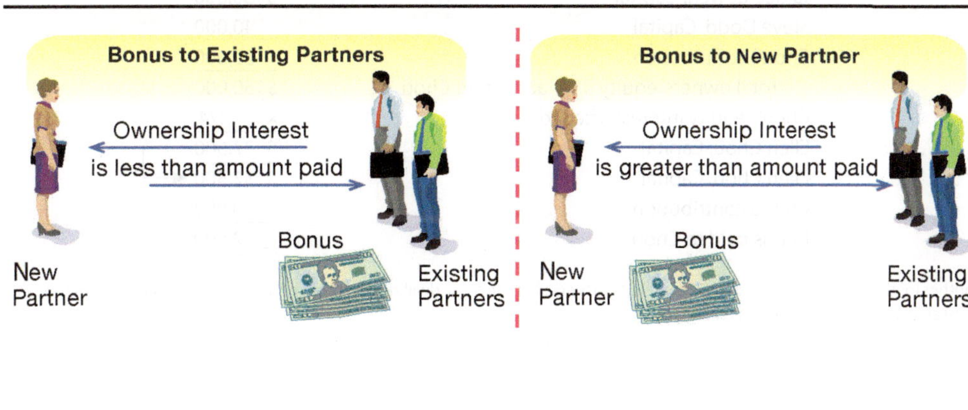

EXHIBIT 3

Partner Bonuses

contrast, the new partner receives a bonus when the ownership interest received by the new partner is greater than the amount paid.

To illustrate, assume that on March 1 the partnership of Marsha Jenkins and Helen Kramer is considering a new partner, Alex Diaz. After the assets of the partnership have been adjusted to current market values, the capital balances of Jenkins and Kramer are as follows:

Marsha Jenkins, Capital	$20,000
Helen Kramer, Capital	24,000
Total owners' equity *before* admitting Diaz	$44,000

Jenkins and Kramer agree to admit Diaz to the partnership for $31,000. In return, Diaz will receive a one-third equity in the partnership and will share equally with Jenkins and Kramer in partnership income or losses. In this case, Diaz is paying Jenkins and Kramer a $6,000 bonus to join the partnership, computed as follows:

Marsha Jenkins, Capital	$20,000
Helen Kramer, Capital	24,000
Diaz's contribution	31,000
Total owners' equity *after* admitting Diaz	$75,000
Diaz's equity interest after admission	× 1/3
Alex Diaz, Capital	$25,000
Diaz's contribution	$31,000
Alex Diaz, Capital	25,000
Bonus paid to Jenkins and Kramer	$ 6,000

The $6,000 bonus paid by Diaz increases Jenkins's and Kramer's capital accounts. It is distributed to the capital accounts of Jenkins and Kramer according to their income-sharing ratio.[5] Assuming that Jenkins and Kramer share profits and losses equally, the entry to record the admission of Diaz to the partnership is as follows:

LLC

Cash	*31,000*	
Alex Diaz, Member Equity		*25,000*
Marsha Jenkins, Member Equity		*3,000*
Helen Kramer, Member Equity		*3,000*

Mar.	1	Cash		31,000	
		Alex Diaz, Capital			25,000
		Marsha Jenkins, Capital			3,000
		Helen Kramer, Capital			3,000

Existing partners may agree to pay the new partner a bonus to join a partnership. To illustrate, assume that after adjusting assets to market values, the capital balances of Janice Cowen and Steve Dodd are as follows:

Janice Cowen, Capital	$ 80,000
Steve Dodd, Capital	40,000
Total owners' equity *before* admitting Chou	$120,000

Cowen and Dodd agree to admit Ellen Chou to the partnership on June 1 for an investment of $30,000. In return, Chou will receive a one-fourth equity interest in the partnership and will share in one-fourth of the profits and losses. In this case, Cowen and Dodd are paying Chou a $7,500 bonus to join the partnership, computed as follows:

Janice Cowen, Capital	$ 80,000
Steve Dodd, Capital	40,000
Chou's contribution	30,000
Total owners' equity *after* admitting Chou	$150,000
Chou's equity interest after admission	× 1/4
Ellen Chou, Capital	$ 37,500
Ellen Chou, Capital	$ 37,500
Chou's contribution	30,000
Bonus paid to Chou	$ 7,500

[5] Another method used to record the admission of partners attributes goodwill rather than a bonus to the partners. This method is discussed in advanced accounting textbooks.

The $7,500 bonus paid to Chou decreases Cowen's and Dodd's capital accounts. It is distributed to the capital accounts of Cowen and Dodd according to their income-sharing ratio. Assuming that the income-sharing ratio of Cowen and Dodd was 2:1 before the admission of Chou, the entry to record the admission of Chou to the partnership is as follows:

LLC

Cash	*30,000*	
Janice Cowen, Member Equity	*5,000*[1]	
Steve Dodd, Member Equity	*2,500*[2]	
Ellen Chou, Member Equity		*37,500*

June	1	Cash		30,000	
		Janice Cowen, Capital		5,000[1]	
		Steve Dodd, Capital		2,500[2]	
		Ellen Chou, Capital			37,500

[1] $7,500 × 2/3
[2] $7,500 × 1/3

Example Exercise 12-4 Partner Bonus

OBJ 3

Dynamic Exhibit

Lowman has a capital balance of $51,000 after adjusting assets to fair market value. Conrad contributes $24,000 to receive a 30% interest in a new partnership with Lowman.

Determine the amount and recipient of the partner bonus.

Follow My Example 12-4

Equity of Lowman	$51,000
Conrad's contribution	24,000
Total equity after admitting Conrad	$75,000
Conrad's equity interest	× 30%
Conrad's equity after admission	$22,500
Conrad's contribution	$24,000
Conrad's equity after admission	22,500
Bonus paid to Lowman	$ 1,500

Practice Exercises: PE 12-4A, PE 12-4B

Withdrawal of a Partner

A partner may retire or withdraw from a partnership. In such cases, the withdrawing partner's interest is normally sold to the:

- Existing partners or
- Partnership

If the *existing partners* purchase the withdrawing partner's interest, the purchase and sale of the partnership interest is between the partners as individuals. The only entry on the partnership's records is to debit the capital account of the partner withdrawing and to credit the capital account of the partner or partners buying the additional interest.

If the *partnership purchases* the withdrawing partner's interest, the assets and the owners' equity of the partnership are reduced by the purchase price. Before the purchase, the asset accounts should be adjusted to current values. The net amount of any adjustment should be divided among the capital accounts of the partners according to their income-sharing ratio.

The entry to record the purchase debits the capital account of the withdrawing partner and credits Cash for the amount of the purchase. If not enough partnership cash is available to pay the withdrawing partner, a liability may be created (credited) for the amount owed the withdrawing partner.

A partner generally cannot withdraw without permission of the remaining partners, nor can a partner be forced to withdraw by the other partners. In this sense, a partnership is like a marriage, "for better or for worse."

Death of a Partner

When a partner dies, the partnership accounts should be closed as of the date of death. The net income for the current period should then be determined and divided among the partners' capital accounts. The asset accounts should also be adjusted to current values and the amount of any adjustment divided among the capital accounts of the partners.

After the income is divided and any assets revalued, an entry is recorded to close the deceased partner's capital account. The entry debits the deceased partner's capital account for its balance and credits a liability account, which is payable to the deceased's estate. The remaining partner or partners may then decide to continue the business or liquidate it.

OBJ 4 Describe and illustrate the accounting for liquidating a partnership.

Liquidating Partnerships

When a partnership goes out of business, it sells the assets, pays the creditors, and distributes the remaining cash or other assets to the partners. This winding-up process is called the **liquidation** of the partnership. Although *liquidating* refers to the payment of liabilities, it includes the entire winding-up process.

When the partnership goes out of business and the normal operations are discontinued, the accounts should be adjusted and closed. The only accounts remaining open will be the asset, contra asset, liability, and owners' equity accounts.

The liquidation process is illustrated in Exhibit 4. The steps in the liquidation process are as follows:

Note: **In liquidation, cash is distributed to partners according to their capital balances.**

- Step 1. Sell the partnership assets. This step is called **realization.**
- Step 2. Distribute any gains or losses from realization to the partners based on their income-sharing ratio.
- Step 3. Pay the claims of creditors, using the cash from the step 1 realization.
- Step 4. Distribute the remaining cash to the partners based on the balances in their capital accounts.

EXHIBIT 4

Steps in Liquidating a Partnership

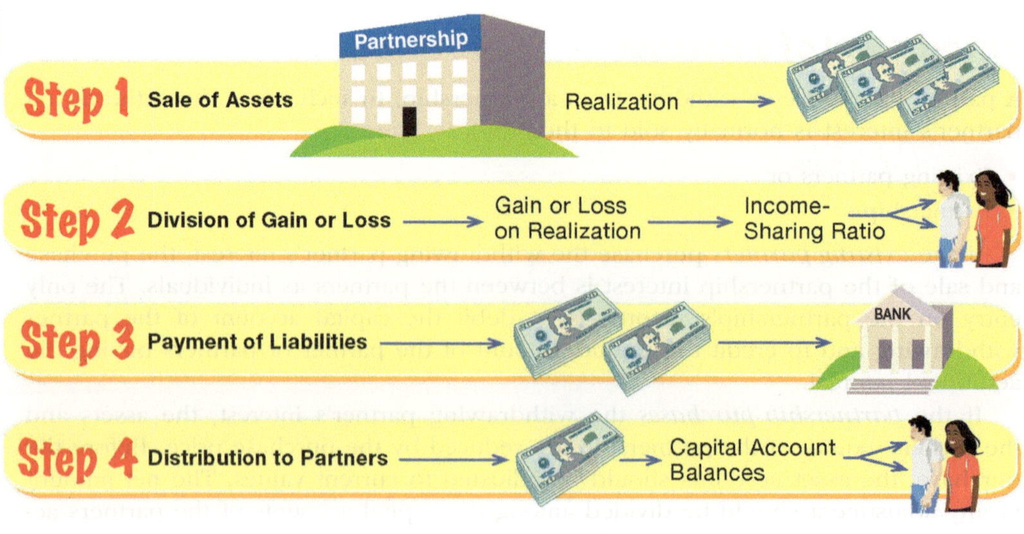

To illustrate, assume that Farley, Green, and Hall decide to liquidate their partnership. On April 9, after discontinuing business operations of the partnership and closing the accounts, the following trial balance is prepared:

Farley, Green, and Hall Post-Closing Trial Balance April 9, 2016		
	Debit Balances	**Credit Balances**
Cash	11,000	
Noncash Assets	64,000	
Liabilities		9,000
Jean Farley, Capital		22,000
Brad Green, Capital		22,000
Alice Hall, Capital		22,000
	75,000	75,000

Farley, Green, and Hall share income and losses in a ratio of 5:3:2 (50%, 30%, 20%). To simplify, assume that all noncash assets are sold in a single transaction and that all liabilities are paid at one time. In addition, Noncash Assets and Liabilities will be used as account titles in place of the various asset, contra asset, and liability accounts.

Gain on Realization

Assume that Farley, Green, and Hall sell all noncash assets for $72,000. Thus, a gain of $8,000 ($72,000 – $64,000) is realized. The partnership is liquidated during April as follows:

- Step 1. Sale of assets: $72,000 is realized from sale of all the noncash assets.
- Step 2. Division of gain: The gain of $8,000 is distributed to Farley, Green, and Hall in the income-sharing ratio of 5:3:2. Thus, the partner capital accounts are credited as follows:

Farley	$4,000 ($8,000 × 50%)
Green	2,400 ($8,000 × 30%)
Hall	1,600 ($8,000 × 20%)

- Step 3. Payment of liabilities: Creditors are paid $9,000.
- Step 4. Distribution of cash to partners: The remaining cash of $74,000 is distributed to the partners according to their capital balances as follows:

Farley	$26,000
Green	24,400
Hall	23,600

A **statement of partnership liquidation**, which summarizes the liquidation process, is shown in Exhibit 5.

EXHIBIT 5 **Statement of Partnership Liquidation: Gain on Realization**

	Farley, Green, and Hall Statement of Partnership Liquidation For Period April 10–30, 2016						
					Capital		
		Cash +	Noncash Assets =	Liabilities +	Farley (50%) +	Green (30%) +	Hall (20%)
	Balances before realization	$11,000	$64,000	$9,000	$22,000	$22,000	$22,000
Steps 1–2 →	Sale of assets and division of gain	+72,000	–64,000		+ 4,000	+ 2,400	+ 1,600
	Balances after realization	$83,000	$ 0	$9,000	$26,000	$24,400	$23,600
Step 3 →	Payment of liabilities	– 9,000		–9,000			
	Balances after payment of liabilities	$74,000	$ 0	$ 0	$26,000	$24,400	$23,600
Step 4 →	Cash distributed to partners	–74,000			–26,000	–24,400	–23,600
	Final balances	$ 0	$ 0	$ 0	$ 0	$ 0	$ 0

The entries to record the steps in the liquidating process are as follows:

Sale of assets (Step 1):

LLC

Account	Debit	Credit
Cash	*72,000*	
Noncash Assets		*64,000*
Gain on Realization		*8,000*

		Account		Debit	Credit
		Cash		72,000	
		Noncash Assets			64,000
		Gain on Realization			8,000

Division of gain (Step 2):

LLC

Account	Debit	Credit
Gain on Realization	*8,000*	
Jean Farley, Member Equity		*4,000*
Brad Green, Member Equity		*2,400*
Alice Hall, Member Equity		*1,600*

		Account		Debit	Credit
		Gain on Realization		8,000	
		Jean Farley, Capital			4,000
		Brad Green, Capital			2,400
		Alice Hall, Capital			1,600

Payment of liabilities (Step 3):

LLC

Account	Debit	Credit
Liabilities	*9,000*	
Cash		*9,000*

		Account		Debit	Credit
		Liabilities		9,000	
		Cash			9,000

Distribution of cash to partners (Step 4):

LLC

Account	Debit	Credit
Jean Farley, Member Equity	*26,000*	
Brad Green, Member Equity	*24,400*	
Alice Hall, Member Equity	*23,600*	
Cash		*74,000*

		Account		Debit	Credit
		Jean Farley, Capital		26,000	
		Brad Green, Capital		24,400	
		Alice Hall, Capital		23,600	
		Cash			74,000

As shown in Exhibit 5, *the cash is distributed to the partners based on the balances of their capital accounts.* These balances are determined after the gain on realization has been divided among the partners and the liabilities paid. *The income-sharing ratio should not be used as a basis for distributing the cash to partners.*

Loss on Realization

Assume that Farley, Green, and Hall sell all noncash assets for $44,000. Thus, a loss of $20,000 ($64,000 – $44,000) is realized. The liquidation of the partnership is as follows:

- Step 1. Sale of assets: $44,000 is realized from the sale of all the noncash assets.
- Step 2. Division of loss: The loss of $20,000 is distributed to Farley, Green, and Hall in the income-sharing ratio of 5:3:2. Thus, the partner capital accounts are debited as follows:

Farley	$10,000 ($20,000 × 50%)
Green	6,000 ($20,000 × 30%)
Hall	4,000 ($20,000 × 20%)

- Step 3. Payment of liabilities: Creditors are paid $9,000.

- Step 4. Distribution of cash to partners: The remaining cash of $46,000 is distributed to the partners according to their capital balances as follows:

Farley	$12,000
Green	16,000
Hall	18,000

The steps in liquidating the partnership are summarized in the statement of partnership liquidation shown in Exhibit 6.

EXHIBIT 6 **Statement of Partnership Liquidation: Loss on Realization**

Farley, Green, and Hall
Statement of Partnership Liquidation
For Period April 10–30, 2016

		Cash	+ Noncash Assets	= Liabilities	+ Capital Farley (50%)	+ Capital Green (30%)	+ Capital Hall (20%)
	Balances before realization	$11,000	$64,000	$9,000	$22,000	$22,000	$22,000
Steps 1–2 →	Sale of assets and division of loss	+44,000	−64,000		−10,000	− 6,000	− 4,000
	Balances after realization	$55,000	$ 0	$9,000	$12,000	$16,000	$18,000
Step 3 →	Payment of liabilities	− 9,000		−9,000			
	Balances after payment of liabilities	$46,000	$ 0	$ 0	$12,000	$16,000	$18,000
Step 4 →	Cash distributed to partners	−46,000			−12,000	−16,000	−18,000
	Final balances	$ 0	$ 0	$ 0	$ 0	$ 0	$ 0

The entries to liquidate the partnership are as follows:

Sale of assets (Step 1):

LLC		
Cash	*44,000*	
Loss on Realization	*20,000*	
Noncash Assets		*64,000*

Cash		44,000	
Loss on Realization		20,000	
Noncash Assets			64,000

Division of loss (Step 2):

LLC		
Jean Farley, Member Equity	*10,000*	
Brad Green, Member Equity	*6,000*	
Alice Hall, Member Equity	*4,000*	
Loss on Realization		*20,000*

Jean Farley, Capital		10,000	
Brad Green, Capital		6,000	
Alice Hall, Capital		4,000	
Loss on Realization			20,000

Payment of liabilities (Step 3):

LLC		
Liabilities	*9,000*	
Cash		*9,000*

Liabilities		9,000	
Cash			9,000

Distribution of cash to partners (Step 4):

LLC		
Jean Farley, Member Equity	*12,000*	
Brad Green, Member Equity	*16,000*	
Alice Hall, Member Equity	*18,000*	
Cash		*46,000*

	Jean Farley, Capital		12,000	
	Brad Green, Capital		16,000	
	Alice Hall, Capital		18,000	
	Cash			46,000

Example Exercise 12-5 Liquidating Partnerships

OBJ 4

Prior to liquidating their partnership, Todd and Gentry had capital accounts of $50,000 and $100,000, respectively. Prior to liquidation, the partnership had no other cash assets than what was realized from the sale of assets. These assets were sold for $220,000. The partnership had $20,000 of liabilities. Todd and Gentry share income and losses equally. Determine the amount received by Gentry as a final distribution from the liquidation of the partnership.

Follow My Example 12-5

Gentry's equity prior to liquidation		$100,000
Realization of asset sale	$220,000	
Book value of assets ($50,000 + $100,000 + $20,000)	170,000	
Gain on liquidation	$ 50,000	
Gentry's share of gain (50% × $50,000)		25,000
Gentry's cash distribution		$125,000

Practice Exercises: PE 12-5A, PE 12-5B

Loss on Realization—Capital Deficiency

The share of a loss on realization may be greater than the balance in a partner's capital account. The resulting debit balance in the capital account is called a **deficiency**. It represents a claim of the partnership against the partner.

To illustrate, assume that Farley, Green, and Hall sell all noncash assets for $10,000. Thus, a loss of $54,000 ($64,000 – $10,000) is realized. The liquidation of the partnership is as follows:

- Step 1. Sale of assets: $10,000 is realized from the sale of all the noncash assets.
- Step 2. Division of loss: The loss of $54,000 is distributed to Farley, Green, and Hall in the income-sharing ratio of 5:3:2. The partner capital accounts are debited as follows:

Farley	$27,000 ($54,000 × 50%)
Green	16,200 ($54,000 × 30%)
Hall	10,800 ($54,000 × 20%)

- Step 3. Payment of liabilities: Creditors are paid $9,000.
- Step 4. Distribution of cash to partners: The share of the loss allocated to Farley, $27,000 (50% x $54,000), exceeds the $22,000 balance in her capital account. This $5,000 deficiency represents an amount that Farley owes the partnership. Assuming that Farley pays the deficiency, the cash of $17,000 is distributed to the partners according to their capital balances as follows:

Farley	$ 0
Green	5,800
Hall	11,200

The steps in liquidating the partnership are summarized in the statement of partnership liquidation shown in Exhibit 7.

EXHIBIT 7 **Statement of Partnership Liquidation: Loss on Realization—Capital Deficiency**

Farley, Green, and Hall
Statement of Partnership Liquidation
For Period April 10–30, 2016

		Cash	+	Noncash Assets	=	Liabilities	+	Capital Farley (50%)	+	Capital Green (30%)	+	Capital Hall (20%)
	Balances before realization	$11,000		$64,000		$9,000		$22,000		$22,000		$22,000
Steps 1–2 →	Sale of assets and division of loss	+10,000		−64,000				−27,000		−16,200		−10,800
	Balances after realization	$21,000		$ 0		$9,000		$(5,000)		$ 5,800		$11,200
Step 3 →	Payment of liabilities	− 9,000				−9,000						
	Balances after payment of liabilities	$12,000		$ 0		$ 0		$(5,000)		$ 5,800		$11,200
Step 4 →	Receipt of deficiency	+ 5,000						+ 5,000				
	Balances	$17,000		$ 0		$ 0		$ 0		$ 5,800		$11,200
Step 4 →	Cash distributed to partners	−17,000								− 5,800		−11,200
	Final balances	$ 0		$ 0		$ 0		$ 0		$ 0		$ 0

The entries to liquidate the partnership are as follows:

Sale of assets (Step 1):

LLC		
Cash	*10,000*	
Loss on Realization	*54,000*	
Noncash Assets		*64,000*

	Debit	Credit
Cash	10,000	
Loss on Realization	54,000	
Noncash Assets		64,000

Division of loss (Step 2):

LLC		
Jean Farley, Member Equity	*27,000*	
Brad Green, Member Equity	*16,200*	
Alice Hall, Member Equity	*10,800*	
Loss on Realization		*54,000*

	Debit	Credit
Jean Farley, Capital	27,000	
Brad Green, Capital	16,200	
Alice Hall, Capital	10,800	
Loss on Realization		54,000

Payment of liabilities (Step 3):

LLC		
Liabilities	*9,000*	
Cash		*9,000*

	Debit	Credit
Liabilities	9,000	
Cash		9,000

Receipt of deficiency (Step 4):

LLC		
Cash	*5,000*	
Jean Farley, Member Equity		*5,000*

	Debit	Credit
Cash	5,000	
Jean Farley, Capital		5,000

Distribution of cash to partners (Step 4):

LLC		
Brad Green, Member Equity	*5,800*	
Alice Hall, Member Equity	*11,200*	
Cash		*17,000*

	Brad Green, Capital		5,800	
	Alice Hall, Capital		11,200	
	Cash			17,000

If the deficient partner does not pay the partnership the deficiency, there will not be sufficient partnership cash to pay the remaining partners in full. Any uncollected deficiency becomes a loss to the partnership and is divided among the remaining partners' capital balances based on their income-sharing ratio. The cash balance will then equal the sum of the capital account balances. The cash can then be distributed to the remaining partners, based on the balances of their capital accounts.

To illustrate, assume that in the preceding example Farley could not pay her deficiency. The deficiency would be allocated to Green and Hall based on their income-sharing ratio of 3:2. The remaining cash of $12,000 would then be distributed to Green ($2,800) and Hall ($9,200), computed as follows:

	Capital Balances *Before* Deficiency	Allocated (Deficiency)	Capital Balances *After* Deficiency
Farley	$ (5,000)	$ 5,000	$ 0
Green	5,800	(3,000)*	2,800
Hall	11,200	(2,000)**	9,200
Total	$12,000		$12,000

*$3,000 = ($5,000 × 3/5) or ($5,000 × 60%)
**$2,000 = ($5,000 × 2/5) or ($5,000 × 40%)

The entries to allocate Farley's deficiency and distribute the cash are as follows:

Allocation of deficiency (Step 4):

LLC		
Brad Green, Member Equity	*3,000*	
Alice Hall, Member Equity	*2,000*	
Jean Farley, Member Equity		*5,000*

	Brad Green, Capital		3,000	
	Alice Hall, Capital		2,000	
	Jean Farley, Capital			5,000

Distribution of cash to partners (Step 4):

LLC		
Brad Green, Member Equity	*2,800*	
Alice Hall, Member Equity	*9,200*	
Cash		*12,000*

	Brad Green, Capital		2,800	
	Alice Hall, Capital		9,200	
	Cash			12,000

Example Exercise 12-6 Liquidating Partnerships—Deficiency

OBJ 4

Prior to liquidating their partnership, Short and Bain had capital accounts of $20,000 and $80,000, respectively. The partnership assets were sold for $40,000. The partnership had no liabilities. Short and Bain share income and losses equally.

a. Determine the amount of Short's deficiency.
b. Determine the amount distributed to Bain, assuming Short is unable to satisfy the deficiency.

Follow My Example 12-6

a. Short's equity prior to liquidation		$ 20,000
Realization of asset sale	$ 40,000	
Book value of assets ($20,000 + $80,000)	100,000	
Loss on liquidation	$ 60,000	
Short's share of loss (50% × $60,000)		30,000
Short's deficiency		$(10,000)

b. $40,000 ($80,000 – $30,000 share of loss – $10,000 Short deficiency)

Practice Exercises: PE 12-6A, PE 12-6B

Statement of Partnership Equity

OBJ 5 Prepare the statement of partnership equity.

Reporting changes in partnership capital accounts is similar to that for a proprietorship. The primary difference is that there is a capital account for each partner. The changes in partner capital accounts for a period of time are reported in a **statement of partnership equity**.

Exhibit 8 illustrates a statement of partnership equity for Investors Associates, a partnership of Dan Cross and Kelly Baker. Each partner's capital account is shown as a separate column. The partner capital accounts may change due to capital additions, net income, or withdrawals.

EXHIBIT 8

Statement of Partnership Equity

Investors Associates
Statement of Partnership Equity
For the Year Ended December 31, 2016

	Dan Cross, Capital	Kelly Baker, Capital	Total Partnership Capital
Balance, January 1, 2016	$245,000	$365,000	$610,000
Capital additions	50,000		50,000
Net income for the year	40,000	80,000	120,000
Less partner withdrawals	(5,000)	(45,000)	(50,000)
Balance, December 31, 2016	$330,000	$400,000	$730,000

The equity reporting for an LLC is similar to that of a partnership. Instead of a statement of partnership capital, a statement of members' equity is prepared. The **statement of members' equity** reports the changes in member equity for a period. The statement is similar to Exhibit 8, except that the columns represent member equity rather than partner equity.

Financial Analysis and Interpretation: Revenue per Employee

OBJ 6 Analyze and interpret employee efficiency.

F·A·I

Many partnerships and LLCs operate as service-oriented enterprises. This is the case for many professions, such as medical, advertising, and accounting. The performance of such firms can be measured by the amount of net income per partner, as illustrated in this chapter. Another measure used to assess the performance of a service-oriented business is revenue per employee.

Revenue per employee is a measure of the efficiency of the business in generating revenues. It is computed as follows:

$$\text{Revenue per Employee} = \frac{\text{Revenue}}{\text{Number of Employees}}$$

In a partnership, the number of partners may be included with employees, or partners may be evaluated separately. Generally, the higher the revenue per employee, the more efficient the company is in generating revenue from its employees. In evaluating revenue per employee, changes over time as well as comparisons with industry peers or averages are often used.

To illustrate comparisons over time, assume Washburn & Lovett, CPAs, has the following information for two years:

	2017	2016
Revenues	$220,000,000	$180,000,000
Number of employees	1,600	1,500

For Washburn & Lovett, the revenue per employee ratio is computed for 2017 and 2016 as follows:

$$\text{Revenue per employee, 2017: } \frac{\$220{,}000{,}000}{1{,}600 \text{ employees}} = \$137{,}500 \text{ per employee}$$

$$\text{Revenue per employee, 2016: } \frac{\$180{,}000{,}000}{1{,}500 \text{ employees}} = \$120{,}000 \text{ per employee}$$

Washburn & Lovett increased revenues by $40,000,000 ($220,000,000 – $180,000,000), or 22.2% ($40,000,000 ÷ $180,000,000) from 2016 to 2017. The number of employees increased by 100, or 6.7% (100 employees ÷ 1,500 employees) between the two years. Thus, the firm increased revenues at a rate faster than the increase in employees. As a result, the revenue per employee improved from $120,000 to $137,500 between the two years, suggesting improved efficiency in generating revenues.

To illustrate comparison within an industry, the revenue per employee for **Starbucks** and **McDonald's** for a recent year are as computed as follows:

$$\text{Starbucks: } \frac{\$13{,}299{,}500{,}000}{160{,}000 \text{ employees}} = \$83{,}122 \text{ per employee}$$

$$\text{McDonald's: } \frac{\$27{,}567{,}000{,}000}{440{,}000 \text{ employees}} = \$62{,}652 \text{ per employee}$$

Starbucks is able to generate more revenues per employee than is McDonald's. Many factors may explain this difference, including relative employee efficiency, extent of part-time workforce, and product pricing.

Example Exercise 12-7 Revenue per Employee

OBJ 6

AccuTax, CPAs earned $4,200,000 during 2016 using 20 employees. During 2017, the firm grew revenues to $4,560,000 and expanded the staff to 24 employees.

a. Determine the revenue per employee for each year.
b. Interpret the results.

Follow My Example 12-7

a. $$\text{2016: } \frac{\$4{,}200{,}000}{20 \text{ employees}} = \$210{,}000 \text{ per employee}$$

$$\text{2017: } \frac{\$4{,}560{,}000}{24 \text{ employees}} = \$190{,}000 \text{ per employee}$$

b. While AccuTax grew revenues by $360,000 ($4,560,000 – $4,200,000), or 8.6% ($360,000 ÷ $4,200,000), the number of employees expanded by 4, or 20% (4/20). The growth in revenue was less than the growth in the number of employees; thus, the revenue per employee declined between the two years. The firm was less efficient in generating revenues from its employees in 2017.

Practice Exercises: PE 12-7A, PE 12-7B

At a Glance 12

OBJ 1 Describe the characteristics of proprietorships, partnerships, and limited liability companies.

Key Points The advantages and disadvantages of proprietorships, partnerships, and limited liability companies are summarized in Exhibit 1.

Learning Outcomes	Example Exercises	Practice Exercises
• Identify the advantages and disadvantages of proprietorships, partnerships, and limited liability companies.		

OBJ 2 Describe and illustrate the accounting for forming a partnership and for dividing the net income and net loss of a partnership.

Key Points When a partnership is formed, accounts are debited for contributed assets and credited for assumed liabilities, and the partner's capital account is credited for the net amount. The net income of a partnership may be divided among the partners on the basis of services rendered, interest earned on the capital account balance, and the income-sharing ratio.

Learning Outcomes	Example Exercises	Practice Exercises
• Journalize the initial formation of a partnership and establish partner capital.	**EE12-1**	**PE12-1A, 12-1B**
• Determine and journalize the income distributed to each partner.	**EE12-2**	**PE12-2A, 12-2B**

OBJ 3 Describe and illustrate the accounting for partner admission and withdrawal.

Key Points Partnership assets should be restated to current values prior to the admission or withdrawal of a partner. A new partner may be admitted into a partnership by either purchasing an interest from an existing partner or by purchasing an interest directly from the partnership.

Learning Outcomes	Example Exercises	Practice Exercises
• Prepare for partner admission by revaluing assets to approximate current values.	**EE12-3**	**PE12-3A, 12-3B**
• Distinguish between partner admission through purchase from an existing partner or purchase from the partnership.	**EE12-3**	**PE12-3A, 12-3B**
• Determine partner bonuses.	**EE12-4**	**PE12-4A, 12-4B**

OBJ 4 Describe and illustrate the accounting for liquidating a partnership.

Key Points A partnership is liquidated by the (1) sale of partnership assets (realization), (2) distribution of gain or loss on realization to the partners, (3) payments to creditors, and (4) distribution of the remaining cash to partners according to their capital account balances. A partner may be deficient when the amount of loss distribution exceeds the capital balance.

Learning Outcomes	Example Exercises	Practice Exercises
• Apply the four steps of liquidating a partnership for either gain or loss on realization.	EE12-5	PE12-5A, 12-5B
• Apply the four steps of partnership liquidation when there is a partner deficiency.	EE12-6	PE12-6A, 12-6B

OBJ 5 Prepare the statement of partnership equity.

Key Points A statement of partnership equity reports the changes in partnership equity from capital additions, net income, and withdrawals.

Learning Outcomes	Example Exercises	Practice Exercises
• Prepare a statement of partnership equity.		

OBJ 6 Analyze and interpret employee efficiency.

Key Points The revenue per employee ratio is calculated as the total annual revenues divided by the total employees. This ratio measures the total revenue earned by each employee and, thus, is a measure of the efficiency of each employee in revenue terms. The ratio is often used to measure efficiency trends over time and across similar firms.

Learning Outcomes	Example Exercises	Practice Exercises
• Analyze and interpret the revenue per employee ratio.	EE12-7	PE12-7A, 12-7B

Key Terms

deficiency (568)
limited liability company (LLC) (554)
liquidation (564)
partnership (553)
partnership agreement (553)
realization (564)
revenue per employee (571)
statement of members' equity (571)
statement of partnership equity (571)
statement of partnership liquidation (565)

Illustrative Problem

Radcliffe, Sonders, and Towers, who share in income and losses in the ratio of 2:3:5, decided to discontinue operations as of April 30, 2016, and liquidate their partnership. After the accounts were closed on April 30, 2016, the following trial balance was prepared:

Radcliffe, Sonders, and Towers
Post-Closing Trial Balance
April 30, 2016

	Debit Balances	Credit Balances
Cash	5,900	
Noncash Assets	109,900	
Liabilities		26,800
Radcliffe, Capital		14,600
Sonders, Capital		27,900
Towers, Capital		46,500
	115,800	115,800

Between May 1 and May 18, the noncash assets were sold for $27,400, and the liabilities were paid.

Instructions

1. Assuming that the partner with the capital deficiency pays the entire amount owed to the partnership, prepare a statement of partnership liquidation.
2. Journalize the entries to record (a) the sale of the assets, (b) the division of loss on the sale of the assets, (c) the payment of the liabilities, (d) the receipt of the deficiency, and (e) the distribution of cash to the partners.

Solution

1.

Radcliffe, Sonders, and Towers
Statement of Partnership Liquidation
For Period May 1–18, 2016

							Capital				
	Cash	+	Noncash Assets	=	Liabilities	+	Radcliffe (20%)	+	Sonders (30%)	+	Towers (50%)
Balances before realization	$ 5,900		$109,900		$26,800		$14,600		$27,900		$46,500
Sale of assets and division of loss	+27,400		−109,900				−16,500		−24,750		−41,250
Balances after realization	$33,300		$ 0		$26,800		$ (1,900)		$ 3,150		$ 5,250
Payment of liabilities	−26,800				−26,800						
Balances after payment of liabilities	$ 6,500		$ 0		$ 0		$ (1,900)		$ 3,150		$ 5,250
Receipt of deficiency	+ 1,900						+ 1,900				
Balances	$ 8,400		$ 0		$ 0		$ 0		$ 3,150		$ 5,250
Cash distributed to partners	− 8,400								− 3,150		− 5,250
Final balances	$ 0		$ 0		$ 0		$ 0		$ 0		$ 0

2.a.

		Cash	27,400	
		Loss on Realization	82,500	
		Noncash Assets		109,900

b.

		Radcliffe, Capital	16,500	
		Sonders, Capital	24,750	
		Towers, Capital	41,250	
		Loss on Realization		82,500

c.

		Liabilities	26,800	
		Cash		26,800

d.

		Cash	1,900	
		Radcliffe, Capital		1,900

e.

		Sonders, Capital	3,150	
		Towers, Capital	5,250	
		Cash		8,400

Discussion Questions

1. What are the main advantages of (a) proprietorships, (b) partnerships, and (c) limited liability companies?

2. What are the disadvantages of a partnership over a limited liability company form of organization for a profit-making business?

3. Emilio Alvarez and Graciela Zavala joined together to form a partnership. Is it possible for them to lose a greater amount than the amount of their investment in the partnership? Explain.

4. What are the major features of a partnership agreement for a partnership, or an operating agreement for a limited liability company?

5. Josiah Barlow, Patty DuMont, and Owen Maholic are contemplating the formation of a partnership. According to the partnership agreement, Barlow is to invest $60,000 and devote one-half time, DuMont is to invest $40,000 and devote three-fourths time, and Maholic is to make no investment and devote full time. Would Maholic be correct in assuming

that, since he is not contributing any assets to the firm, he is risking nothing? Explain.

6. During the current year, Marsha Engles withdrew $4,000 monthly from the partnership of Engles and Cox Water Management Consultants. Is it possible that her share of partnership net income for the current year might be more or less than $48,000? Explain.
7. a. What accounts are debited and credited to record a partner's cash withdrawal in lieu of salary?

   b. The articles of partnership provide for a salary allowance of $6,000 per month to partner C. If C withdrew only $4,000 per month, would this affect the division of the partnership net income?

   c. At the end of the fiscal year, what accounts are debited and credited to record the division of net income among partners?
8. Explain the difference between the admission of a new partner to a partnership (a) by purchase of an interest from another partner and (b) by contribution of assets to the partnership.
9. Why is it important to state all partnership assets in terms of current prices at the time of the admission of a new partner?
10. Why might a partnership pay a bonus to a newly admitted partner?

Practice Exercises

EE 12-1 *p. 555* SHOW ME HOW

PE 12-1A Journalizing partner's original investment — OBJ. 2

Catrina Santana contributed a patent, accounts receivable, and $23,000 cash to a partnership. The patent had a book value of $8,000. However, the technology covered by the patent appeared to have significant market potential. Thus, the patent was appraised at $85,000. The accounts receivable control account was $38,000, with an allowance for doubtful accounts of $2,000. The partnership also assumed a $10,000 account payable owed to a Santana supplier.

Provide the journal entry for Santana's contribution to the partnership.

EE 12-1 *p. 555* SHOW ME HOW

PE 12-1B Journalizing partner's original investment — OBJ. 2

Austin Fisher contributed land, inventory, and $36,000 cash to a partnership. The land had a book value of $120,000 and a market value of $175,000. The inventory had a book value of $50,000 and a market value of $42,000. The partnership also assumed a $35,000 note payable owed by Fisher that was used originally to purchase the land.

Provide the journal entry for Fisher's contribution to the partnership.

EE 12-2 *p. 558* SHOW ME HOW

PE 12-2A Dividing partnership net income — OBJ. 2

Han Lee and Monica Andrews formed a partnership, dividing income as follows:

1. Annual salary allowance to Lee of $32,000.
2. Interest of 4% on each partner's capital balance on January 1.
3. Any remaining net income divided to Lee and Andrews, 2:1.

Lee and Andrews had $80,000 and $150,000, respectively, in their January 1 capital balances. Net income for the year was $64,000.

How much net income should be distributed to Lee and Andrews?

EE 12-2 *p. 558* SHOW ME HOW

PE 12-2B Dividing partnership net income — OBJ. 2

John Prado and Ayana Nicks formed a partnership, dividing income as follows:

1. Annual salary allowance to Prado, $10,000 and Nicks, $28,000.
2. Interest of 5% on each partner's capital balance on January 1.
3. Any remaining net income divided equally.

(Continued)

Prado and Nicks had $20,000 and $50,000, respectively, in their January 1 capital balances. Net income for the year was $30,000.

How much net income should be distributed to Prado and Nicks?

EE 12-3 p. 561

SHOW ME HOW

PE 12-3A Revaluing and contributing assets to a partnership **OBJ. 3**

Aasif Safar purchased one-half of Michael Thorton's interest in the Vale and Thorton partnership for $34,000. Prior to the investment, land was revalued to a market value of $150,000 from a book value of $80,000. Tony Vale and Michael Thorton share net income equally. Thorton had a capital balance of $28,000 prior to these transactions.

a. Provide the journal entry for the revaluation of land.

b. Provide the journal entry to admit Safar.

EE 12-3 p. 561

SHOW ME HOW

PE 12-3B Revaluing and contributing assets to a partnership **OBJ. 3**

Demarco Lee invested $60,000 in the Camden and Sayler partnership for ownership equity of $60,000. Prior to the investment, equipment was revalued to a market value of $39,000 from a book value of $30,000. Kevin Camden and Chloe Sayler share net income in a 2:1 ratio.

a. Provide the journal entry for the revaluation of equipment.

b. Provide the journal entry to admit Lee.

EE 12-4 p. 563

SHOW ME HOW

PE 12-4A Partner bonus **OBJ. 3**

Bellows has a capital balance of $200,000 after adjusting assets to fair market value. Rodriguez contributes $340,000 to receive a 60% interest in a new partnership with Bellows.

Determine the amount and recipient of the partner bonus.

EE 12-4 p. 563

SHOW ME HOW

PE 12-4B Partner bonus **OBJ. 3**

Hiro has a capital balance of $75,000 after adjusting assets to fair market value. Marone contributes $20,000 to receive a 40% interest in a new partnership with Hiro.

Determine the amount and recipient of the partner bonus.

EE 12-5 p. 568

SHOW ME HOW

PE 12-5A Liquidating partnerships **OBJ. 4**

Prior to liquidating their partnership, Parker and Xi had capital accounts of $40,000 and $75,000, respectively. Prior to liquidation, the partnership had no cash assets other than what was realized from the sale of assets. These partnership assets were sold for $155,000. The partnership had $10,000 of liabilities. Parker and Xi share income and losses equally. Determine the amount received by Parker as a final distribution from liquidation of the partnership.

EE 12-5 p. 568

SHOW ME HOW

PE 12-5B Liquidating partnerships **OBJ. 4**

Prior to liquidating their partnership, Manning and Adamo had capital accounts of $240,000 and $150,000, respectively. Prior to liquidation, the partnership had no cash assets other than what was realized from the sale of assets. These partnership assets were sold for $410,000. The partnership had $80,000 of liabilities. Manning and Adamo share income and losses equally. Determine the amount received by Manning as a final distribution from liquidation of the partnership.

EE 12-6 p. 570

SHOW ME HOW

PE 12-6A Liquidating partnerships—deficiency **OBJ. 4**

Prior to liquidating their partnership, Wakefield and Barns had capital accounts of $105,000 and $55,000, respectively. The partnership assets were sold for $40,000. The partnership had no liabilities. Wakefield and Barns share income and losses equally.

a. Determine the amount of Barns' deficiency.

b. Determine the amount distributed to Wakefield, assuming Barns is unable to satisfy the deficiency.

EE 12-6 p. 570

PE 12-6B Liquidating partnerships—deficiency **OBJ. 4**

SHOW ME HOW

Prior to liquidating their partnership, Bonilla and Perez had capital accounts of $185,000 and $245,000, respectively. The partnership assets were sold for $30,000. The partnership had no liabilities. Bonilla and Perez share income and losses equally.

a. Determine the amount of Bonilla's deficiency.

b. Determine the amount distributed to Perez, assuming Bonilla is unable to satisfy the deficiency.

EE 12-7 p. 572

F·A·I

PE 12-7A Revenue per employee **OBJ. 6**

SHOW ME HOW

Niles and Cohen, CPAs earned $12,375,000 during 2016 using 75 employees. During 2017, the firm grew revenues to $15,400,000 and expanded the staff to 88 employees.

a. Determine the revenue per employee for each year.

b. Interpret the results.

EE 12-7 p. 572

F·A·I

PE 12-7B Revenue per employee **OBJ. 6**

SHOW ME HOW

Eclipse Architects earned $1,800,000 during 2016 using 12 employees. During 2017, the firm reduced revenues to $1,440,000 and reduced the staff to nine employees.

a. Determine the revenue per employee for each year.

b. Interpret the results.

Exercises

EX 12-1 Recording partner's original investment **OBJ. 2**

SHOW ME HOW

LaTasha Nabors and Chelsey Rollins decide to form a partnership by combining the assets of their separate businesses. Nabors contributes the following assets to the partnership: cash, $24,000; accounts receivable with a face amount of $160,000 and an allowance for doubtful accounts of $4,200; merchandise inventory with a cost of $92,000; and equipment with a cost of $136,000 and accumulated depreciation of $45,000.

The partners agree that $6,000 of the accounts receivable are completely worthless and are not to be accepted by the partnership, that $4,800 is a reasonable allowance for the uncollectibility of the remaining accounts, that the merchandise inventory is to be recorded at the current market price of $104,300, and that the equipment is to be valued at $84,500.

Journalize the partnership's entry to record Nabor's investment.

EX 12-2 Recording partner's original investment **OBJ. 2**

SHOW ME HOW

Melissa Myers and Hugo Hernandez form a partnership by combining assets of their former businesses. The following balance sheet information is provided by Myers, sole proprietorship:

Cash		$ 75,000
Accounts receivable	$135,000	
Less: Allowance for doubtful accounts	7,200	127,800
Land		215,000
Equipment	$ 78,000	
Less: Accumulated depreciation—equipment	41,000	37,000
Total assets		$454,800
Accounts payable		$ 24,800
Notes payable		84,000
Melissa Myers, capital		346,000
Total liabilities and owner's equity		$454,800

(Continued)

Myers obtained appraised values for the land and equipment as follows:

Land	$300,000
Equipment	32,700

An analysis of the accounts receivable indicated that the allowance for doubtful accounts should be increased to $9,200.

Journalize the partnership's entry for Myers' investment.

EX 12-3 Dividing partnership income — OBJ. 2

✔ b. Taylor, $187,500

SHOW ME HOW

Brittany Taylor and Piper Albright formed a partnership, investing $210,000 and $70,000, respectively. Determine their participation in the year's net income of $250,000 under each of the following independent assumptions: (a) no agreement concerning division of net income; (b) divided in the ratio of original capital investment; (c) interest at the rate of 5% allowed on original investments and the remainder divided in the ratio of 2:3; (d) salary allowances of $30,000 and $40,000, respectively, and the balance divided equally; (e) allowance of interest at the rate of 5% on original investments, salary allowances of $30,000 and $40,000, respectively, and the remainder divided equally.

EX 12-4 Dividing partnership income — OBJ. 2

✔ c. Taylor, $43,300

SHOW ME HOW

Determine the income participation of Taylor and Albright, according to each of the five assumptions as to income division listed in Exercise 12-3, if the year's net income is $96,000.

EX 12-5 Dividing partnership net loss — OBJ. 2

Leigh Meadows and Luke Kowalski formed a partnership in which the partnership agreement provided for salary allowances of $35,000 and $25,000, respectively. Determine the division of a $30,000 net loss for the current year, assuming remaining income or losses are shared equally by the two partners.

EX 12-6 Negotiating income-sharing ratio — OBJ. 2

Sixty-year-old Wanda Davis retired from her computer consulting business in Boston and moved to Florida. There she met 27-year-old Ava Jain, who had just graduated from Eldon Community College with an associate degree in computer science. Wanda and Ava formed a partnership called D&J Computer Consultants. Wanda contributed $50,000 for startup costs and devoted one-half time to the business. Ava devoted full time to the business. The monthly drawings were $2,500 for Wanda and $5,000 for Ava.

At the end of the first year of operations, the two partners disagreed on the division of net income. Wanda reasoned that the division should be equal. Although she devoted only one-half time to the business, she contributed all of the startup funds. Ava reasoned that the income-sharing ratio should be 2:1 in her favor because she devoted full time to the business and her monthly drawings were twice those of Wanda.

a. Can you identify any flaws in the partners' reasoning regarding the income-sharing ratio?

b. How could an income-sharing agreement resolve this dispute?

EX 12-7 Dividing LLC income — OBJ. 2

✔ a. Farley, $86,800

Martin Farley and Ashley Clark formed a limited liability company with an operating agreement that provided a salary allowance of $40,000 and $30,000 to each member, respectively. In addition, the operating agreement specified an income-sharing ratio of 3:2. The two members withdrew amounts equal to their salary allowances.

a. Determine the division of $148,000 net income for the year.

b. Provide journal entries to close the (1) income summary and (2) drawing accounts for the two members.

c. If the net income were less than the sum of the salary allowances, how would income be divided between the two members of the LLC?

EX 12-8 LLC net income and statement of members' equity — OBJ. 2, 5

✔ a. Sanders, $138,500

Marvel Media, LLC, has three members: WLKT Partners, Madison Sanders, and Observer Newspaper, LLC. On January 1, 2016, the three members had equity of $200,000, $40,000, and $160,000, respectively. WLKT Partners contributed an additional $50,000 to Marvel Media, LLC, on June 1, 2016. Madison Sanders received an annual salary allowance of $55,000 during 2016. The members' equity accounts are also credited with 10% interest on each member's January 1 capital balance. Any remaining income is to be shared in the ratio of 4:3:3 among the three members. The net income for Marvel Media, LLC, for 2016 was $360,000. Amounts equal to the salary and interest allowances were withdrawn by the members.

a. Determine the division of income among the three members.

b. Prepare the journal entry to close the net income and withdrawals to the individual member equity accounts.

c. Prepare a statement of members' equity for 2016.

d. What are the advantages of an income-sharing agreement for the members of this LLC?

EX 12-9 Partner income and withdrawal journal entries — OBJ. 2

The notes to the annual report for **KPMG LLP** (U.K.) indicated the following policies regarding the partners' capital:

> The allocation of profits to those who were partners during the financial year occurs following the finalization of the annual financial statements. During the year, partners receive monthly drawings and, from time to time, additional profit distributions. Both the monthly drawings and profit distributions represent payments on account of current-year profits and are reclaimable from partners until profits have been allocated.

Assume that the partners draw £50 million per month for 2016 and the net income for the year is £740 million. Journalize the partner capital and partner drawing control accounts in the following requirements:

a. Provide the journal entry for the monthly partner drawing for January.

b. Provide the journal entry to close the income summary account at the end of the year.

c. Provide the journal entry to close the drawing account at the end of the year.

d. Why would partner drawings be considered "reclaimable" until profits have been allocated?

EX 12-10 Admitting new partners — OBJ. 3

SHOW ME HOW

Hope Abrams and Crystal Santori are partners who share in the income equally and have capital balances of $180,000 and $62,500, respectively. Abrams, with the consent of Santori, sells one-third of her interest to David Cruz. What entry is required by the partnership if the sales price is (a) $60,000? (b) $80,000?

EX 12-11 Admitting new partners who buy an interest and contribute assets — OBJ. 3

✔ b. Henry, $112,000

SHOW ME HOW

The capital accounts of Trent Henry and Paul Chavez have balances of $140,000 and $90,000, respectively. LeAnne Gilbert and Jen Faber are to be admitted to the partnership. Gilbert buys one-fifth of Henry's interest for $30,000 and one-fourth of Chavez's interest for $20,000. Faber contributes $75,000 cash to the partnership, for which she is to receive an ownership equity of $75,000.

a. Journalize the entries to record the admission of (1) Gilbert and (2) Faber.

b. What are the capital balances of each partner after the admission of the new partners?

EX 12-12 Admitting new partner who contributes assets — OBJ. 3

✔ b. Neel, $35,000

After the tangible assets have been adjusted to current market prices, the capital accounts of Brad Paulson and Drew Webster have balances of $45,000 and $60,000, respectively.

(Continued)

Austin Neel is to be admitted to the partnership, contributing $30,000 cash to the partnership, for which he is to receive an ownership equity of $35,000. All partners share equally in income.

a. Journalize the entry to record the admission of Neel, who is to receive a bonus of $5,000.

b. What are the capital balances of each partner after the admission of the new partner?

c. Why are tangible assets adjusted to current market prices, prior to admitting a new partner?

EX 12-13 Admitting new partner with bonus **OBJ. 3**

Cody Jenkins and Jun Ito formed a partnership to provide landscaping services. Jenkins and Ito shared profits and losses equally. After all the tangible assets have been adjusted to current market prices, the capital accounts of Cody Jenkins and Jun Ito have balances of $72,000 and $38,000, respectively. Valeria Solano has expertise with using the computer to prepare landscape designs, cost estimates, and renderings. Jenkins and Ito deem these skills useful; thus, Solano is admitted to the partnership at a 30% interest for a purchase price of $30,000.

a. Determine the recipient and amount of the partner bonus.

b. Provide the journal entry to admit Solano into the partnership.

c. Why would a bonus be paid in this situation?

EX 12-14 Admitting a new LLC member with bonus **OBJ. 3**

✔ b. (2) Bonus paid to Lin, $7,500

Alert Medical, LLC, consists of two doctors, Abrams and Lipscomb, who share in all income and losses according to a 2:3 income-sharing ratio. Dr. Lin has been asked to join the LLC. Prior to admitting Lin, the assets of Alert Medical were revalued to reflect their current market values. The revaluation resulted in medical equipment being increased by $40,000. Prior to the revaluation, the equity balances for Abrams and Lipscomb were $154,000 and $208,000, respectively.

a. Provide the journal entry for the asset revaluation.

b. Provide the journal entry for the bonus under the following independent situations:

1. Lin purchased a 30% interest in Alert Medical, LLC, for $228,000.
2. Lin purchased a 25% interest in Alert Medical, LLC, for $124,000.

EX 12-15 Admitting new partner with bonus **OBJ. 3**

✔ b. (1) Bonus paid to Ortiz, $9,600

L. Bowers and V. Lipscomb are partners in Elegant Event Consultants. Bowers and Lipscomb share income equally. M. Ortiz will be admitted to the partnership. Prior to the admission, equipment was revalued downward by $8,000. The capital balances of each partner are $96,000 and $40,000, respectively, prior to the revaluation.

a. Provide the journal entry for the asset revaluation.

b. Provide the journal entry for Ortiz's admission under the following independent situations:

1. Ortiz purchased a 20% interest for $20,000.
2. Ortiz purchased a 30% interest for $60,000.

EX 12-16 Partner bonuses, statement of partners' equity **OBJ. 2, 3, 5**

✔ Dennis Overton, Capital, Dec. 31, 2016, $226,400

The partnership of Angel Investor Associates began operations on January 1, 2016, with contributions from two partners as follows:

Dennis Overton	$180,000
Ben Testerman	120,000

The following additional partner transactions took place during the year:

1. In early January, Randy Campbell is admitted to the partnership by contributing $75,000 cash for a 20% interest.

2. Net income of $150,000 was earned in 2016. In addition, Dennis Overton received a salary allowance of $40,000 for the year. The three partners agree to an income-sharing ratio equal to their capital balances after admitting Campbell.
3. The partners' withdrawals are equal to half of the increase in their capital balances from salary allowance and income.

Prepare a statement of partnership equity for the year ended December 31, 2016.

EX 12-17 Withdrawal of partner — OBJ. 3

SHOW ME HOW

Justin Marley is to retire from the partnership of Marley and Associates as of March 31, the end of the current fiscal year. After closing the accounts, the capital balances of the partners are as follows: Justin Marley, $140,000; Cherrie Ford, $70,000; and LaMarcus Rollins, $60,000. They have shared net income and net losses in the ratio of 3:2:2. The partners agree that the merchandise inventory should be increased by $15,500, and the allowance for doubtful accounts should be increased by $1,500. Marley agrees to accept a note for $100,000 in partial settlement of his ownership equity. The remainder of his claim is to be paid in cash. Ford and Rollins are to share equally in the net income or net loss of the new partnership.

Journalize the entries to record (a) the adjustment of the assets to bring them into agreement with current market prices and (b) the withdrawal of Marley from the partnership.

EX 12-18 Statement of members' equity, admitting new member — OBJ. 2, 3, 5

✔ a. 3:7

The statement of members' equity for Bonanza, LLC, follows:

Bonanza, LLC
Statement of Members' Equity
For the Years Ended December 31, 2016 and 2017

	Idaho Properties, LLC, Member Equity	Silver Streams, LLC, Member Equity	Thomas Dunn, Member Equity	Total Members' Equity
Members' equity, January 1, 2016	$273,000	$307,000		$ 580,000
Net income	57,000	133,000		190,000
Members' equity, December 31, 2016	$330,000	$440,000		$ 770,000
Dunn contribution, January 1, 2017	3,000	7,000	$220,000	230,000
Net income	62,500	137,500	50,000	250,000
Less member withdrawals	(32,000)	(48,000)	(40,000)	(120,000)
Members' equity, December 31, 2017	$363,500	$536,500	$230,000	$1,130,000

a. What was the income-sharing ratio in 2016?
b. What was the income-sharing ratio in 2017?
c. How much cash did Thomas Dunn contribute to Bonanza, LLC, for his interest?
d. Why do the member equity accounts of Idaho Properties, LLC, and Silver Streams, LLC, have positive entries for Thomas Dunn's contribution?
e. What percentage interest of Bonanza did Thomas Dunn acquire?
f. Why are withdrawals less than net income?

EX 12-19 Distribution of cash upon liquidation — OBJ. 4

✔ a. $11,000 loss

Hewitt and Patel are partners, sharing gains and losses equally. They decide to terminate their partnership. Prior to realization, their capital balances are $28,000 and $18,000, respectively. After all noncash assets are sold and all liabilities are paid, there is a cash balance of $35,000.

a. What is the amount of a gain or loss on realization?
b. How should the gain or loss be divided between Hewitt and Patel?
c. How should the cash be divided between Hewitt and Patel?

✔ Oliver, $30,000

EX 12-20 Distribution of cash upon liquidation **OBJ. 4**

David Oliver and Umar Ansari, with capital balances of $28,000 and $35,000, respectively, decide to liquidate their partnership. After selling the noncash assets and paying the liabilities, there is $67,000 of cash remaining. If the partners share income and losses equally, how should the cash be distributed?

✔ b. $97,500

EX 12-21 Liquidating partnerships—capital deficiency **OBJ. 4**

Lewis, Zapata, and Fowler share equally in net income and net losses. After the partnership sells all assets for cash, divides the losses on realization, and pays the liabilities, the balances in the capital accounts are as follows: Lewis, $73,500 Cr.; Zapata, $41,000 Cr.; Fowler, $17,000 Dr.

a. What term is applied to the debit balance in Fowler's capital account?

b. What is the amount of cash on hand?

c. Journalize the transaction that must take place for Lewis and Zapata to receive cash in the liquidation process equal to their capital account balances.

✔ a. Bray, $550

EX 12-22 Distribution of cash upon liquidation **OBJ. 4**

Bray, Lincoln, and Mapes arranged to import and sell orchid corsages for a university dance. They agreed to share equally the net income or net loss of the venture. Bray and Lincoln advanced $225 and $300 of their own respective funds to pay for advertising and other expenses. After collecting for all sales and paying creditors, the partnership has $1,500 in cash.

a. How should the money be distributed?

b. Assuming that the partnership has only $300 instead of $1,500, do any of the three partners have a capital deficiency? If so, how much?

EX 12-23 Liquidating partnerships—capital deficiency **OBJ. 4**

Nettles, King, and Tanaka are partners sharing income 3:2:1. After the firm's loss from liquidation is distributed, the capital account balances were: Nettles, $15,000 Dr.; King, $46,000 Cr.; and Tanaka, $71,000 Cr. If Nettles is personally bankrupt and unable to pay any of the $15,000, what will be the amount of cash received by King and Tanaka upon liquidation?

EX 12-24 Statement of partnership liquidation **OBJ. 4, 5**

SHOW ME HOW

After closing the accounts on July 1, prior to liquidating the partnership, the capital account balances of Gold, Porter, and Sims are $55,000, $45,000, and $20,000, respectively. Cash, noncash assets, and liabilities total $56,000, $96,000, and $32,000, respectively. Between July 1 and July 29, the noncash assets are sold for $90,000, the liabilities are paid, and the remaining cash is distributed to the partners. The partners share net income and loss in the ratio of 3:2:1. Prepare a statement of partnership liquidation for the period July 1–29, 2016.

EX 12-25 Statement of LLC liquidation **OBJ. 4, 5**

Lester, Torres, and Hearst are members of Arcadia Sales, LLC, sharing income and losses in the ratio of 2:2:1, respectively. The members decide to liquidate the limited liability company. The members' equity prior to liquidation and asset realization on August 1, 2016, are as follows:

Lester	$ 49,000
Torres	61,000
Hearst	27,000
Total	$137,000

In winding up operations during the month of August, noncash assets with a book value of $146,000 are sold for $158,000, and liabilities of $35,000 are satisfied. Prior to realization, Arcadia Sales has a cash balance of $26,000.

a. Prepare a statement of LLC liquidation.

b. Provide the journal entry for the final cash distribution to members.

c. What is the role of the income- and loss-sharing ratio in liquidating a LLC?

EX 12-26 Partnership entries and statement of partners' equity OBJ. 2, 5

✔ b. Alvarez, Capital, Dec. 31, $54,000

The capital accounts of Angel Alvarez and Emma Allison have balances of $47,000 and $73,000, respectively, on January 1, 2016, the beginning of the fiscal year. On March 10, Alvarez invested an additional $8,000. During the year, Alvarez and Allison withdrew $32,000 and $39,000, respectively, and net income for the year was $62,000. The articles of partnership make no reference to the division of net income.

a. Journalize the entries to close (1) the income summary account and (2) the drawing accounts.

b. Prepare a statement of partnership equity for the current year for the partnership of Alvarez and Allison.

EX 12-27 Revenue per professional staff OBJ. 6

F·A·I

The accounting firm of Deloitte & Touche is the largest international accounting firm in the world as ranked by total revenues. For two recent years, Deloitte & Touche reported the following for its U.S. operations:

	Current Year	Previous Year
Revenue (in billions)	$13.1	$11.9
Number of professional staff (including partners)	46,243	41,187

a. For the current and previous years, determine the revenue per professional staff.

b. Interpret the trend between the two years.

EX 12-28 Revenue per employee OBJ. 6

F·A·I

Superior Cleaning Services, LLC, provides cleaning services for office buildings. The firm has 10 members in the LLC, which did not change between 2016 and 2017. During 2017, the business terminated two commercial contracts. The following revenue and employee information is provided:

	2017	2016
Revenues (in thousands)	$16,200	$18,400
Number of employees (excluding members)	150	200

a. For 2017 and 2016, determine the revenue per employee (excluding members).

b. Interpret the trend between the two years.

Problems: Series A

PR 12-1A Entries and balance sheet for partnership OBJ. 2

✔ 3. Keene net income, $41,900

General Ledger

SHOW ME HOW

On March 1, 2016, Eric Keene and Abigail McKee form a partnership. Keene agrees to invest $21,100 in cash and merchandise inventory valued at $55,900. McKee invests certain business assets at valuations agreed upon, transfers business liabilities, and contributes sufficient cash to bring her total capital to $60,000. Details regarding the book values of the business assets and liabilities, and the agreed valuations, follow:

(Continued)

	McKee's Ledger Balance	Agreed-Upon Valuation
Accounts Receivable	$18,900	$18,000
Allowance for Doubtful Accounts	1,200	1,500
Equipment	83,500	54,900
Accumulated Depreciation—Equipment	29,800	
Accounts Payable	15,000	15,000
Notes Payable (current)	36,000	36,000

The partnership agreement includes the following provisions regarding the division of net income: interest on original investments at 10%, salary allowances of $22,500 (Keene) and $30,400 (McKee), and the remainder equally.

Instructions

1. Journalize the entries to record the investments of Keene and McKee in the partnership accounts.
2. Prepare a balance sheet as of March 1, 2016, the date of formation of the partnership of Keene and McKee.
3. After adjustments and the closing of revenue and expense accounts at February 28, 2017, the end of the first full year of operations, the income summary account has a credit balance of $90,000, and the drawing accounts have debit balances of $28,000 (Keene) and $30,400 (McKee). Journalize the entries to close the income summary account and the drawing accounts at February 28, 2017.

PR 12-2A Dividing partnership income — OBJ. 2

✔ 1. f. Morrison net income, $40,400

SHOW ME HOW

Morrison and Amato have decided to form a partnership. They have agreed that Morrison is to invest $150,000 and that Amato is to invest $50,000. Morrison is to devote one-half time to the business and Amato is to devote full time. The following plans for the division of income are being considered:

a. Equal division.
b. In the ratio of original investments.
c. In the ratio of time devoted to the business.
d. Interest of 12% on original investments and the remainder equally.
e. Interest of 12% on original investments, salary allowances of $30,000 to Morrison and $64,000 to Amato, and the remainder equally.
f. Plan (e), except that Amato is also to be allowed a bonus equal to 20% of the amount by which net income exceeds the total salary allowances.

Instructions

For each plan, determine the division of the net income under each of the following assumptions: (1) net income of $105,000 and (2) net income of $180,000. Present the data in tabular form, using the following columnar headings:

	$105,000		$180,000	
Plan	Morrison	Amato	Morrison	Amato

PR 12-3A Financial statements for partnership — OBJ. 2, 5

✔ 2. Dec. 31 capital—Yost, $125,000

The ledger of Tyler Lambert and Jayla Yost, attorneys-at-law, contains the following accounts and balances after adjustments have been recorded on December 31, 2016:

Lambert and Yost
Trial Balance
December 31, 2016

	Debit Balances	Credit Balances
Cash	34,000	
Accounts Receivable	47,800	
Supplies	2,000	
Land	120,000	
Building	157,500	
Accumulated Depreciation—Building		67,200
Office Equipment	63,600	
Accumulated Depreciation—Office Equipment		21,700
Accounts Payable		27,900
Salaries Payable		5,100
Tyler Lambert, Capital		135,000
Tyler Lambert, Drawing	50,000	
Jayla Yost, Capital		88,000
Jayla Yost, Drawing	60,000	
Professional Fees		395,300
Salary Expense	154,500	
Depreciation Expense—Building	15,700	
Property Tax Expense	12,000	
Heating and Lighting Expense	8,500	
Supplies Expense	6,000	
Depreciation Expense—Office Equipment	5,000	
Miscellaneous Expense	3,600	
	740,200	740,200

The balance in Yost's capital account includes an additional investment of $10,000 made on April 10, 2016.

Instructions

1. Prepare an income statement for 2016, indicating the division of net income. The partnership agreement provides for salary allowances of $45,000 to Lambert and $54,700 to Yost, allowances of 10% on each partner's capital balance at the beginning of the fiscal year, and equal division of the remaining net income or net loss.
2. Prepare a statement of partnership equity for 2016.
3. Prepare a balance sheet as of the end of 2016.

✔ 3. Total assets, $326,300

General Ledger

PR 12-4A Admitting new partner — OBJ. 3

Musa Moshref and Shaniqua Hollins have operated a successful firm for many years, sharing net income and net losses equally. Taylor Anderson is to be admitted to the partnership on July 1 of the current year, in accordance with the following agreement:

a. Assets and liabilities of the old partnership are to be valued at their book values as of June 30, except for the following:
   - Accounts receivable amounting to $2,500 are to be written off, and the allowance for doubtful accounts is to be increased to 5% of the remaining accounts.
   - Merchandise inventory is to be valued at $76,600.
   - Equipment is to be valued at $155,700.

b. Anderson is to purchase $70,000 of the ownership interest of Hollins for $75,000 cash and to contribute another $45,000 cash to the partnership for a total ownership equity of $115,000.

(Continued)

The post-closing trial balance of Moshref and Hollins as of June 30 is as follows:

Moshref and Hollins
Post-Closing Trial Balance
June 30, 2016

	Debit Balances	Credit Balances
Cash	8,000	
Accounts Receivable	42,500	
Allowance for Doubtful Accounts		1,600
Merchandise Inventory	72,000	
Prepaid Insurance	3,000	
Equipment	180,500	
Accumulated Depreciation—Equipment		43,100
Accounts Payable		21,300
Notes Payable (current)		35,000
Musa Moshref, Capital		120,000
Shaniqua Hollins, Capital		85,000
	306,000	306,000

Instructions

1. Journalize the entries as of June 30 to record the revaluations, using a temporary account entitled Asset Revaluations. The balance in the accumulated depreciation account is to be eliminated. After journalizing the revaluations, close the balance of the asset revaluations account to the capital accounts of Musa Moshref and Shaniqua Hollins.
2. Journalize the additional entries to record Anderson's entrance to the partnership on July 1, 2016.
3. Present a balance sheet for the new partnership as of July 1, 2016.

PR 12-5A Statement of partnership liquidation

OBJ. 4

After the accounts are closed on February 3, 2016, prior to liquidating the partnership, the capital accounts of William Gerloff, Joshua Chu, and Courtney Jewett are $19,300, $4,500, and $22,300, respectively. Cash and noncash assets total $5,200 and $55,900, respectively. Amounts owed to creditors total $15,000. The partners share income and losses in the ratio of 2:1:1. Between February 3 and February 28, the noncash assets are sold for $34,300, the partner with the capital deficiency pays the deficiency to the partnership, and the liabilities are paid.

Instructions

1. Prepare a statement of partnership liquidation, indicating (a) the sale of assets and division of loss, (b) the payment of liabilities, (c) the receipt of the deficiency (from the appropriate partner), and (d) the distribution of cash.
2. Assume the partner with the capital deficiency declares bankruptcy and is unable to pay the deficiency. Journalize the entries to (a) allocate the partner's deficiency and (b) distribute the remaining cash.

PR 12-6A Statement of partnership liquidation

OBJ. 4

On November 1, 2016, the firm of Sails, Welch, and Greenberg decided to liquidate their partnership. The partners have capital balances of $58,000, $72,000, and $10,000, respectively. The cash balance is $32,000, the book values of noncash assets total $128,000, and liabilities total $20,000. The partners share income and losses in the ratio of 2:2:1.

Instructions

1. Prepare a statement of partnership liquidation, covering the period November 1–30, 2016, for each of the following independent assumptions:
   a. All of the noncash assets are sold for $156,000 in cash, the creditors are paid, and the remaining cash is distributed to the partners.

b. All of the noncash assets are sold for $55,000 in cash, the creditors are paid, the partner with the debit capital balance pays the amount owed to the firm, and the remaining cash is distributed to the partners.

2. Assume the partner with the capital deficiency in part (b) declares bankruptcy and is unable to pay the deficiency. Journalize the entries to (a) allocate the partner's deficiency and (b) distribute the remaining cash.

Problems: Series B

PR 12-1B Entries and balance sheet for partnership — OBJ. 2

✔ 3. Lang net income, $63,400

General Ledger

SHOW ME HOW

On April 1, 2015, Whitney Lang and Eli Capri form a partnership. Lang agrees to invest $18,000 cash and merchandise inventory valued at $50,000. Capri invests certain business assets at valuations agreed upon, transfers business liabilities, and contributes sufficient cash to bring his total capital to $120,000. Details regarding the book values of the business assets and liabilities, and the agreed valuations, follow:

	Capri's Ledger Balance	Agreed-Upon Balance
Accounts Receivable	$45,700	$43,400
Allowance for Doubtful Accounts	3,200	3,500
Merchandise Inventory	31,500	28,900
Equipment	89,500	63,400
Accumulated Depreciation—Equipment	19,000	
Accounts Payable	23,400	23,400
Notes Payable (current)	15,000	15,000

The partnership agreement includes the following provisions regarding the division of net income: interest of 10% on original investments, salary allowances of $36,000 (Lang) and $22,000 (Capri), and the remainder equally.

Instructions

1. Journalize the entries to record the investments of Lang and Capri in the partnership accounts.
2. Prepare a balance sheet as of April 1, 2015, the date of formation of the partnership of Lang and Capri.
3. After adjustments and the closing of revenue and expense accounts at March 31, 2016, the end of the first full year of operations, the income summary account has a credit balance of $118,000, and the drawing accounts have debit balances of $40,000 (Lang) and $30,000 (Capri). Journalize the entries to close the income summary account and the drawing accounts at March 31, 2016.

PR 12-2B Dividing partnership income — OBJ. 2

✔ 1. f. Howell net income, $254,550

SHOW ME HOW

Dylan Howell and Demond Nickles have decided to form a partnership. They have agreed that Howell is to invest $50,000 and that Nickles is to invest $75,000. Howell is to devote full time to the business, and Nickles is to devote one-half time. The following plans for the division of income are being considered:

a. Equal division.

b. In the ratio of original investments.

c. In the ratio of time devoted to the business.

d. Interest of 10% on original investments and the remainder in the ratio of 3:2.

e. Interest of 10% on original investments, salary allowances of $38,000 to Howell and $19,000 to Nickles, and the remainder equally.

f. Plan (e), except that Howell is also to be allowed a bonus equal to 20% of the amount by which net income exceeds the total salary allowances.

(Continued)

Instructions

For each plan, determine the division of the net income under each of the following assumptions: (1) net income of $420,000 and (2) net income of $150,000. Present the data in tabular form, using the following columnar headings:

	$420,000		$150,000	
Plan	**Howell**	**Nickles**	**Howell**	**Nickles**

PR 12-3B Financial statements for partnerships — OBJ. 2, 5

✔ 2. Dec. 31 capital—Xue, $179,100

The ledger of Camila Ramirez and Ping Xue, attorneys-at-law, contains the following accounts and balances after adjustments have been recorded on December 31, 2016:

Ramirez and Xue
Trial Balance
December 31, 2016

	Debit Balances	Credit Balances
Cash	70,300	
Accounts Receivable	33,600	
Supplies	5,800	
Land	128,000	
Building	175,000	
Accumulated Depreciation—Building		80,000
Office Equipment	42,000	
Accumulated Depreciation—Office Equipment		25,300
Accounts Payable		12,400
Salaries Payable		10,000
Camila Ramirez, Capital		125,000
Camila Ramirez, Drawing	35,000	
Ping Xue, Capital		155,000
Ping Xue, Drawing	50,000	
Professional Fees		555,300
Salary Expense	384,900	
Depreciation Expense—Building	12,900	
Heating and Lighting Expense	10,500	
Depreciation Expense—Office Equipment	6,300	
Property Tax Expense	3,200	
Supplies Expense	3,000	
Miscellaneous Expense	2,500	
	963,000	963,000

The balance in Xue's capital account includes an additional investment of $20,000 made on May 5, 2016.

Instructions

1. Prepare an income statement for the current fiscal year, indicating the division of net income. The partnership agreement provides for salary allowances of $50,000 to Ramirez and $65,000 to Xue, allowances of 12% on each partner's capital balance at the beginning of the fiscal year, and equal division of the remaining net income or net loss.
2. Prepare a statement of partnership equity for 2016.
3. Prepare a balance sheet as of the end of 2016.

✔ 3. Total assets, $173,900

General Ledger

PR 12-4B Admitting new partner — OBJ. 3

Brian Caldwell and Adriana Estrada have operated a successful firm for many years, sharing net income and net losses equally. Kris Mays is to be admitted to the partnership on September 1 of the current year, in accordance with the following agreement:

a. Assets and liabilities of the old partnership are to be valued at their book values as of August 31, except for the following:
   - Accounts receivable amounting to $1,500 are to be written off, and the allowance for doubtful accounts is to be increased to 5% of the remaining accounts.
   - Merchandise inventory is to be valued at $46,800.
   - Equipment is to be valued at $64,500.

b. Mays is to purchase $26,000 of the ownership interest of Estrada for $30,000 cash and to contribute $32,000 cash to the partnership for a total ownership equity of $58,000.

The post-closing trial balance of Caldwell and Estrada as of August 31 follows:

Caldwell and Estrada
Post-Closing Trial Balance
August 31, 2016

	Debit Balances	Credit Balances
Cash	12,300	
Accounts Receivable	19,500	
Allowance for Doubtful Accounts		600
Merchandise Inventory	42,500	
Prepaid Insurance	1,200	
Equipment	67,500	
Accumulated Depreciation—Equipment		15,500
Accounts Payable		8,900
Notes Payable (current)		15,000
Brian Caldwell, Capital		55,000
Adriana Estrada, Capital		48,000
	143,000	143,000

Instructions

1. Journalize the entries as of August 31 to record the revaluations, using a temporary account entitled Asset Revaluations. The balance in the accumulated depreciation account is to be eliminated. After journalizing the revaluations, close the balance of the asset revaluations account to the capital accounts of Brian Caldwell and Adriana Estrada.
2. Journalize the additional entries to record Mays' entrance to the partnership on September 1, 2016.
3. Present a balance sheet for the new partnership as of September 1, 2016.

PR 12-5B Statement of partnership liquidation

OBJ. 4

After the accounts are closed on April 10, 2016, prior to liquidating the partnership, the capital accounts of Zach Fairchild, Austin Lowes, and Amber Howard are $42,000, $7,500, and $36,500, respectively. Cash and noncash assets total $23,500 and $84,500, respectively. Amounts owed to creditors total $22,000. The partners share income and losses in the ratio of 1:1:2. Between April 10 and April 30, the noncash assets are sold for $48,500, the partner with the capital deficiency pays the deficiency to the partnership, and the liabilities are paid.

Instructions

1. Prepare a statement of partnership liquidation, indicating (a) the sale of assets and division of loss, (b) the payment of liabilities, (c) the receipt of the deficiency (from the appropriate partner), and (d) the distribution of cash.
2. Assume the partner with the capital deficiency declares bankruptcy and is unable to pay the deficiency. Journalize the entries to (a) allocate the partner's deficiency and (b) distribute the remaining cash.

PR 12-6B Statement of partnership liquidation — OBJ. 4

On August 3, 2016, the firm of Chapelle, Rock, and Pryor decided to liquidate their partnership. The partners have capital balances of $14,000, $102,000, and $86,000, respectively. The cash balance is $65,000, the book values of noncash assets total $167,000, and liabilities total $30,000. The partners share income and losses in the ratio of 1:2:2.

Instructions

1. Prepare a statement of partnership liquidation, covering the period August 3–29, 2016, for each of the following independent assumptions:
   a. All of the noncash assets are sold for $217,000 in cash, the creditors are paid, and the remaining cash is distributed to the partners.
   b. All of the noncash assets are sold for $72,000 in cash, the creditors are paid, the partner with the debit capital balance pays the amount owed to the firm, and the remaining cash is distributed to the partners.
2. Assume the partner with the capital deficiency in part (b) declares bankruptcy and is unable to pay the deficiency. Journalize the entries to (a) allocate the partner's deficiency and (b) distribute the remaining cash.

Cases & Projects

CP 12-1 Partnership agreement

Taye Barrow, M.D., and James Robbins, M.D., are sole owners of two medical practices that operate in the same medical building. The two doctors agree to combine assets and liabilities of the two businesses to form a partnership. The partnership agreement calls for dividing income equally between the two doctors. After several months, the following conversation takes place between the two doctors:

Barrow: I've noticed that your patient load has dropped over the last couple of months. When we formed our partnership, we were seeing about the same number of patients per week. However, now our patient records show that you have been seeing about half as many patients as I have. Are there any issues that I should be aware of?

Robbins: There's nothing going on. When I was working on my own, I was really putting in the hours. One of the reasons I formed this partnership was to enjoy life a little more and scale back a little bit.

Barrow: I see. Well, I find that I'm working as hard as I did when I was on my own, yet making less than I did previously. Essentially, you're sharing in half of my billings and I'm sharing in half of yours. Since you are working much less than I am, I end up on the short end of the bargain.

Robbins: Well, I don't know what to say. An agreement is an agreement. The partnership is based on a 50/50 split. That's what a partnership is all about.

Barrow: If that's so, then it applies equally well on the effort end of the equation as on the income end.

Discuss whether Robbins is acting in an ethical manner. How could Barrow renegotiate the partnership agreement to avoid this dispute?

CP 12-2 Dividing partnership income

Terry Willard and Jasmine Hill decide to form a partnership. Willard will contribute $300,000 to the partnership, while Hill will contribute only $30,000. However, Hill will be responsible for running the day-to-day operations of the partnership, which are anticipated to require about 45 hours per week. In contrast, Willard will only work five hours per week for the partnership. The two partners are attempting to determine a formula for dividing partnership net income. Willard believes the partners should divide income in the ratio of 7:3, favoring Willard, since Willard provides the majority of the capital. Hill believes the income should be divided 7:3, favoring Hill, since Hill provides the majority of effort in running the partnership business.

How would you advise the partners in developing a method for dividing income?

CP 12-3 Revenue per employee

F·A·I

The following table shows key operating statistics for the four largest public accounting firms:

	U.S. Net Revenues (in millions)	No. of Partners
Deloitte & Touche	$13,067	2,949
PwC	9,552	2,350
Ernst & Young	8,200	2,500
KPMG	5,753	1,775

Source: The 2013 *Accounting Today* Top 100 Firms.

a. Determine the revenue per partner for each firm. Round to the nearest dollar.

b. Interpret the differences between the firms in terms of your answer in (a) and the table information.

CP 12-4 Partnership agreement

General Ledger

Lindsey Wilson has agreed to invest $200,000 into an LLC with Lacy Lovett and Justin Lassiter. Lovett and Lassiter will not invest any money but will provide effort and expertise to the LLC. Lovett and Lassiter have agreed that the net income of the LLC should be divided so that Wilson is to receive a 10% preferred return on her capital investment prior to any remaining income being divided equally among the partners. In addition, Lovett and Lassiter have suggested that the operating agreement be written so that all matters are settled by majority vote, with each partner having a one-third voting interest in the LLC. If you were providing Lindsey Wilson counsel, what might you suggest in forming the final agreement?

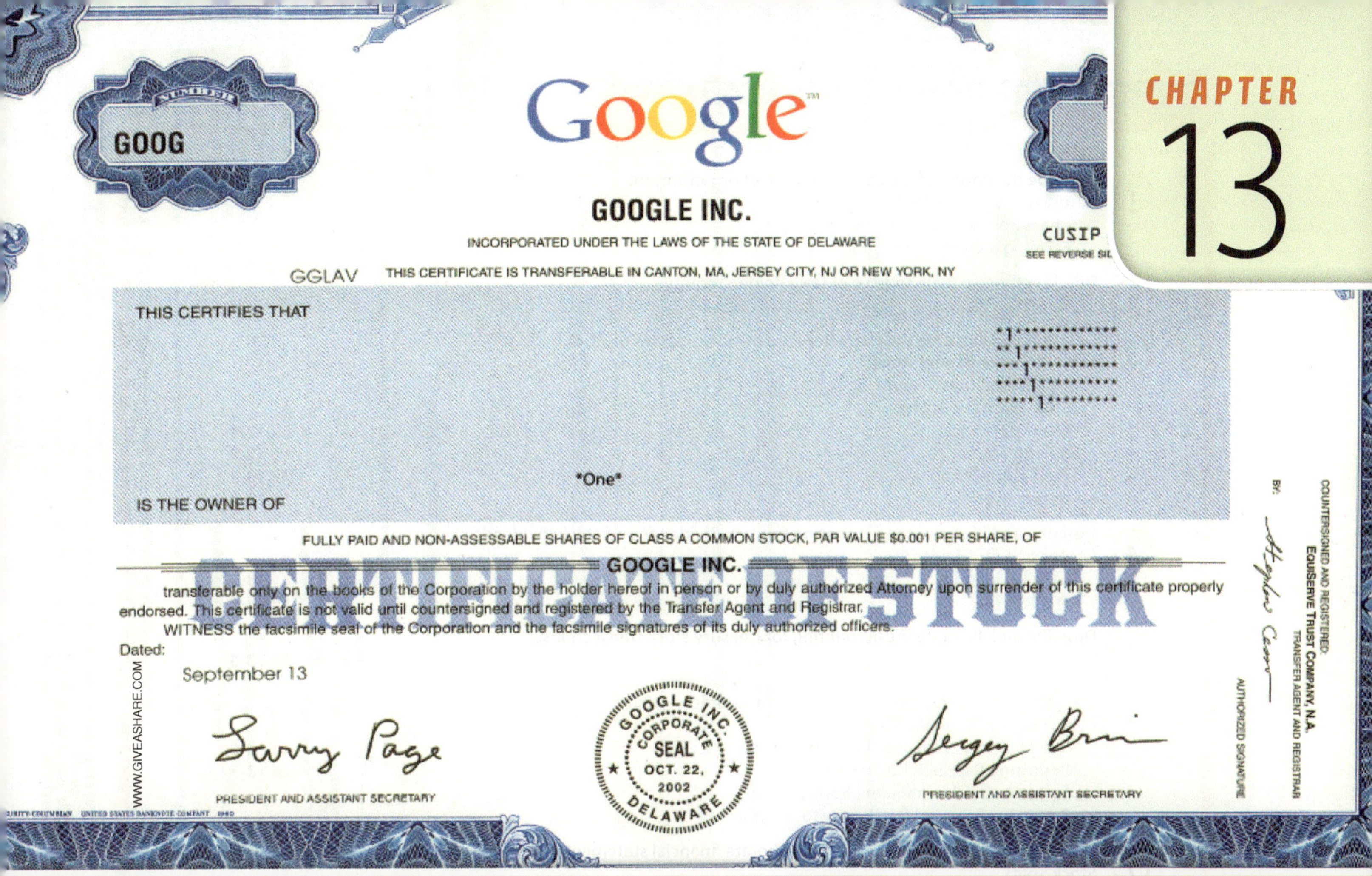

CHAPTER 13

Corporations: Organization, Stock Transactions, and Dividends

Google

If you purchase a share of stock from **Google**, you own a small interest in the company. You may request a Google stock certificate as an indication of your ownership.

Google is one of the most visible companies on the Internet. Many of us cannot visit the Web without using Google to power a search or to retrieve our e-mail using Google's gmail. Yet Google's Internet tools are free to online browsers. Google generates most of its revenue through online advertising.

Purchasing a share of stock from Google may be a great gift idea for the "hard-to-shop-for person." However, a stock certificate represents more than just a picture that you can frame. In fact, the stock certificate is a document that reflects legal ownership of the future financial prospects of Google. In addition, as a shareholder, it represents your claim against the assets and earnings of the corporation.

If you are purchasing Google stock as an investment, you should analyze Google's financial statements and management's plans for the future. For example, Google first offered its stock to the public on August 19, 2004, for $100 per share. Google's stock recently sold for more than $1,000 per share, even though it pays no dividends. In addition, Google recently expanded into developing and offering free software platforms for mobile devices such as cell phones. For example, your cell phone may use Google's Android™ operating system. So, should you purchase Google stock?

This chapter describes and illustrates the nature of corporations, including the accounting for stock and dividends. This discussion will aid you in making decisions such as whether or not to buy stock in a company.

Learning Objectives

After studying this chapter, you should be able to: — *Example Exercises*

At a Glance 13 Page 617

OBJ 1 Describe the nature of the corporate form of organization.

Nature of a Corporation

Most large businesses are organized as corporations. As a result, corporations generate more than 90% of the total business dollars in the United States. In contrast, most small businesses are organized as proprietorships, partnerships, or limited liability companies.

Characteristics of a Corporation

A corporation was defined in the Dartmouth College case of 1819, in which Chief Justice Marshall of the U.S. Supreme Court stated: "A corporation is an artificial being, invisible, intangible, and existing only in contemplation of the law."

A *corporation* is a legal entity, distinct and separate from the individuals who create and operate it. As a legal entity, a corporation may acquire, own, and dispose of property in its own name. It may also incur liabilities and enter into contracts. Most importantly, it can sell shares of ownership, called **stock**. This characteristic gives corporations the ability to raise large amounts of capital.

The **stockholders** or *shareholders* who own the stock own the corporation. They can buy and sell stock without affecting the corporation's operations or continued existence. Corporations whose shares of stock are traded in public markets are called *public corporations*. Corporations whose shares are not traded publicly are usually owned by a small group of investors and are called *nonpublic* or *private corporations*.

The stockholders of a corporation have *limited liability*. This means that creditors usually may not go beyond the assets of the corporation to satisfy their claims. Thus, the financial loss that a stockholder may suffer is limited to the amount invested.

The stockholders control a corporation by electing a *board of directors*. This board meets periodically to establish corporate policies. It also selects the chief executive officer (CEO) and other major officers to manage the corporation's day-to-day affairs. Exhibit 1 shows the organizational structure of a corporation.

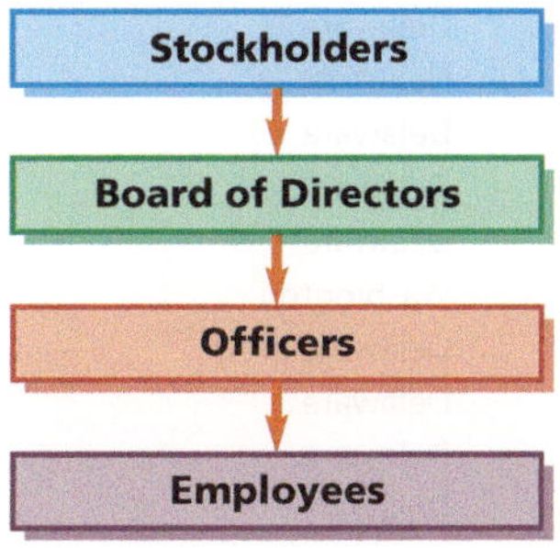

EXHIBIT 1

Organizational Structure of a Corporation

As a separate entity, a corporation is subject to taxes. For example, corporations must pay federal income taxes on their income.[1] Thus, corporate income that is distributed to stockholders in the form of *dividends* has already been taxed. In turn, stockholders must pay income taxes on the dividends they receive. This *double taxation* of corporate earnings is a major disadvantage of the corporate form. The advantages and disadvantages of the corporate form are listed in Exhibit 2.

Note:
Corporations have a separate legal existence, transferable units of ownership, and limited stockholder liability.

EXHIBIT 2 **Advantages and Disadvantages of the Corporate Form**

Advantages	Explanation
Separate legal existence	A corporation exists separately from its owners.
Continuous life	A corporation's life is separate from its owners; therefore, it exists indefinitely.
Raising large amounts of capital	The corporate form is suited for raising large amounts of money from shareholders.
Ownership rights are easily transferable	A corporation sells shares of ownership, called *stock*. The stockholders of a public company can transfer their shares of stock to other stockholders through stock markets, such as the New York Stock Exchange.
Limited liability	A corporation's creditors usually may not go beyond the assets of the corporation to satisfy their claims. Thus, the financial loss that a stockholder may suffer is limited to the amount invested.
Disadvantages	**Explanation**
Owner is separate from management	Stockholders control management through a board of directors. The board of directors should represent shareholder interests; however, the board is often more closely tied to management than to shareholders. As a result, the board of directors and management may not always behave in the best interests of stockholders.
Double taxation of dividends	As a separate legal entity, a corporation is subject to taxation. Thus, net income distributed as dividends will be taxed once at the corporation level, and then again at the individual level.
Regulatory costs	Corporations must satisfy many requirements, such as those required by the Sarbanes-Oxley Act.

Forming a Corporation

The first step in forming a corporation is to file an *application of incorporation* with the state. State incorporation laws differ, and corporations often organize in those states with the more favorable laws. For this reason, more than half of the largest companies are incorporated in Delaware. Exhibit 3 lists some corporations, their states of incorporation, and the location of their headquarters.

After the application of incorporation has been approved, the state grants a *charter* or *articles of incorporation*. The articles of incorporation formally create the corporation.[2] The corporate management and board of directors then prepare a set of *bylaws*, which are the rules and procedures for conducting the corporation's affairs.

[1] A majority of states also require corporations to pay income taxes.

[2] The articles of incorporation may also restrict a corporation's activities in certain areas, such as owning certain types of real estate, conducting certain types of business activities, or purchasing its own stock.

EXHIBIT 3

Examples of Corporations and their States of Incorporation

Corporation	State of Incorporation	Headquarters
Caterpillar	Delaware	Peoria, IL
Delta Air Lines	Delaware	Atlanta, GA
The Dow Chemical Company	Delaware	Midland, MI
Google	Delaware	Mountain View, CA
General Electric Company	New York	Fairfield, CT
The Home Depot	Delaware	Atlanta, GA
Kellogg Company	Delaware	Battle Creek, MI
R.J. Reynolds Tobacco Company	Delaware	Winston-Salem, NC
Starbucks Corporation	Washington	Seattle, WA
Sun Microsystems, Inc.	Delaware	Palo Alto, CA
3M	Delaware	St. Paul, MN
The Washington Post Company	Delaware	Washington, D.C.
Whirlpool Corporation	Delaware	Benton Harbor, MI

Costs may be incurred in organizing a corporation. These costs include legal fees, taxes, state incorporation fees, license fees, and promotional costs. Such costs are debited to an expense account entitled *Organizational Expenses.*

To illustrate, a corporation's organizing costs of $8,500 on January 5 are recorded as follows:

Jan.	5	Organizational Expenses	8,500	
		Cash		8,500
		Paid costs of organizing the corporation.		

OBJ 2 Describe the two main sources of stockholders' equity.

Stockholders' Equity

The owners' equity in a corporation is called **stockholders' equity**, *shareholders' equity, shareholders' investment,* or *capital.* On the balance sheet, stockholders' equity is reported by its following two main sources, as shown in Exhibit 4:

- Capital contributed to the corporation by the stockholders, called **paid-in capital** or *contributed capital.*
- Net income retained in the business, called **retained earnings**.

EXHIBIT 4

Sources of Stockholders' Equity

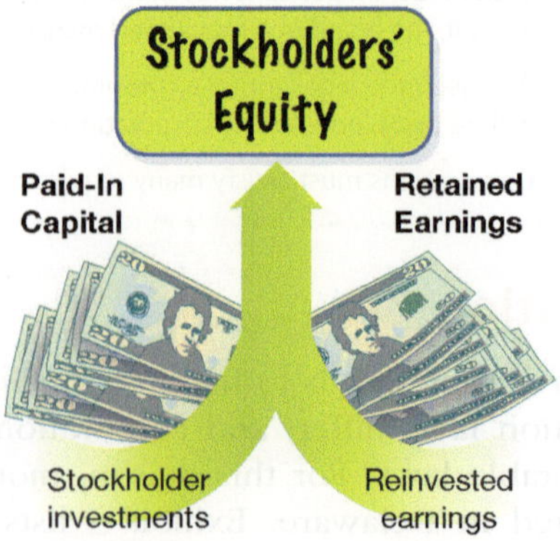

A Stockholders' Equity section of a balance sheet follows:[3]

Stockholders' Equity

Paid-in capital:		
Common stock	$330,000	
Retained earnings	80,000	
Total stockholders' equity		$410,000

[3] The reporting of stockholders' equity is further discussed and illustrated later in this chapter.

The paid-in capital contributed by the stockholders is recorded in separate accounts for each class of stock. If there is only one class of stock, the account is entitled *Common Stock* or *Capital Stock*.

Retained earnings is a corporation's cumulative net income that has not been distributed as dividends. **Dividends** are distributions of a corporation's earnings to stockholders. Sometimes retained earnings that are not distributed as dividends are referred to in the financial statements as *earnings retained for use in the business* and *earnings reinvested in the business*.

Net income increases retained earnings, while a net loss and dividends decrease retained earnings. The net increase or decrease in retained earnings for a period is recorded by the following closing entries:

1. The balance of Income Summary (the net income or net loss) is transferred to Retained Earnings. For net income, Income Summary is debited and Retained Earnings is credited. For a net loss, Retained Earnings is debited and Income Summary is credited.
2. The balance of the dividends account, which is similar to the drawing account for a proprietorship, is transferred to Retained Earnings. Retained Earnings is debited and Dividends is credited for the balance of the dividends account.

Most companies generate net income. In addition, most companies do not pay out all of their net income in dividends. As a result, Retained Earnings normally has a credit balance. However, in some cases, a debit balance in Retained Earnings may occur. A debit balance in Retained Earnings is called a **deficit**. Such a balance results from accumulated net losses. In the Stockholders' Equity section, a deficit is deducted from paid-in capital in determining total stockholders' equity.

The balance of Retained Earnings does not represent surplus cash or cash left over for dividends. This is because cash generated from operations is normally used to improve or expand operations. As cash is used, its balance decreases; however, the balance of the retained earnings account is unaffected. As a result, over time the balance in Retained Earnings becomes less and less related to the balance of Cash.

Paid-In Capital from Issuing Stock

OBJ 3 Describe and illustrate the characteristics of stock, classes of stock, and entries for issuing stock.

The two main sources of stockholders' equity are paid-in capital (or contributed capital) and retained earnings. The main source of paid-in capital is from issuing stock.

Characteristics of Stock

The number of shares of stock that a corporation is *authorized* to issue is stated in its charter. The term *issued* refers to the shares issued to the stockholders. A corporation may reacquire some of the stock that it has issued. The stock remaining in the hands of stockholders is then called **outstanding stock**. The relationship between authorized, issued, and outstanding stock is shown in Exhibit 5.

Upon request, corporations may issue stock certificates to stockholders to document their ownership. Printed on a stock certificate is the name of the company, the name of

EXHIBIT 5

Authorized, Issued, and Outstanding Stock

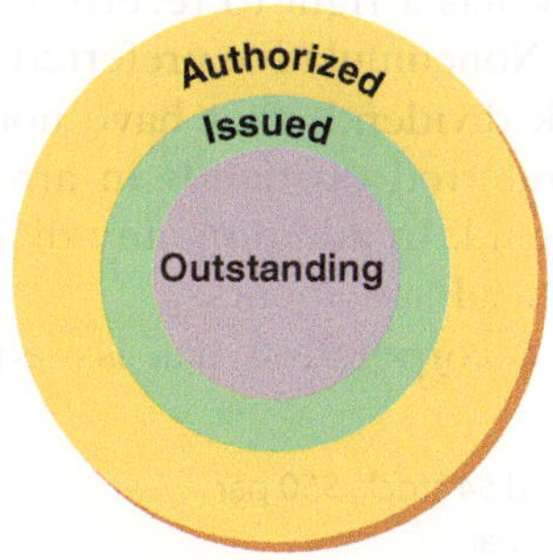

Number of shares authorized, issued, and outstanding

the stockholder, and the number of shares owned. The stock certificate may also indicate a dollar amount assigned to each share of stock, called **par value**. Stock may be issued without par, in which case it is called *no-par stock*. In some states, the board of directors of a corporation is required to assign a *stated value* to no-par stock.

Corporations have limited liability, and thus, creditors have no claim against stockholders' personal assets. To protect creditors, however, some states require corporations to maintain a minimum amount of paid-in capital. This minimum amount, called *legal capital,* usually includes the par or stated value of the shares issued.

The major rights that accompany ownership of a share of stock are as follows:

- The right to vote in matters concerning the corporation.
- The right to share in distributions of earnings.
- The right to share in assets upon liquidation.

These stock rights normally vary with the class of stock.

Classes of Stock

Dynamic Exhibit

Note:
The two primary classes of paid-in capital are common stock and preferred stock.

When only one class of stock is issued, it is called **common stock**. Each share of common stock has equal rights.

A corporation may also issue one or more classes of stock with various preference rights such as a preference to dividends. Such a stock is called a **preferred stock**. The dividend rights of preferred stock are stated either as dollars per share or as a percent of par. For example, a $50 par value preferred stock with a $4 per share dividend may be described as either:[4]

preferred $4 stock, $50 par
or
preferred 8% stock, $50 par

As shown in Exhibit 6, preferred stockholders have first rights (preference) to any dividends, and thus, they have a greater chance of receiving dividends than common stockholders. However, since dividends are normally based on earnings, a corporation cannot guarantee dividends even to preferred stockholders.

EXHIBIT 6

Dividend Preferences

The payment of dividends is authorized by the corporation's board of directors. When authorized, the directors are said to have *declared* a dividend.

Cumulative preferred stock has a right to receive regular dividends that were not declared (paid) in prior years. Noncumulative preferred stock does not have this right.

Cumulative preferred stock dividends that have not been paid in prior years are said to be **in arrears**. Any preferred dividends in arrears must be paid before any common stock dividends are paid. In addition, any dividends in arrears are normally disclosed in notes to the financial statements.

To illustrate, assume that a corporation has issued the following preferred and common stock:

1,000 shares of cumulative preferred $4 stock, $50 par
4,000 shares of common stock, $15 par

[4] In some cases, preferred stock may receive additional dividends if certain conditions are met. Such stock, called *participating preferred stock*, is not often issued.

The corporation was organized on January 1, 2014, and paid no dividends in 2014 and 2015. In 2016, the corporation paid $22,000 in dividends, of which $12,000 was paid to preferred stockholders and $10,000 was paid to common stockholders, computed as follows:

Total dividends paid		$22,000
Preferred stockholders:		
2014 dividends in arrears (1,000 shares × $4)	$4,000	
2015 dividends in arrears (1,000 shares × $4)	4,000	
2016 dividend (1,000 shares × $4)	4,000	
Total preferred dividends paid		(12,000)
Dividends available to common stockholders		$10,000

As a result, preferred stockholders received $12.00 per share ($12,000 ÷ 1,000 shares) in dividends, while common stockholders received $2.50 per share ($10,000 ÷ 4,000 shares).

In addition to dividend preference, preferred stock may be given preferences to assets if the corporation goes out of business and is liquidated. However, claims of creditors must be satisfied first. Preferred stockholders are next in line to receive any remaining assets, followed by the common stockholders.

Example Exercise 13-1 Dividends per Share

OBJ 3

Sandpiper Company has 20,000 shares of cumulative preferred 1% stock of $100 par and 100,000 shares of $50 par common stock. The following amounts were distributed as dividends:

Year 1	$10,000
Year 2	45,000
Year 3	80,000

Determine the dividends per share for preferred and common stock for each year.

Follow My Example 13-1

	Year 1	Year 2	Year 3
Amount distributed	$10,000	$45,000	$80,000
Preferred dividend (20,000 shares)	10,000	30,000*	20,000
Common dividend (100,000 shares)	$ 0	$15,000	$60,000
*($10,000 + $20,000)			
Dividends per share:			
Preferred stock	$0.50	$1.50	$1.00
Common stock	None	$0.15	$0.60

Practice Exercises: PE 13-1A, PE 13-1B

Issuing Stock

Dynamic Exhibit

A separate account is used for recording the amount of each class of stock issued to investors in a corporation. For example, assume that a corporation is authorized to issue 10,000 shares of $100 par preferred stock and 100,000 shares of $20 par common stock. The corporation issued 5,000 shares of preferred stock and 50,000 shares of common stock at par for cash. The corporation's entry to record the stock issue is as follows:[5]

		Cash	1,500,000	
		Preferred Stock		500,000
		Common Stock		1,000,000
		Issued preferred stock and common stock at par for cash.		

Stock is often issued by a corporation at a price other than its par. The price at which stock is sold depends on a variety of factors, such as the following:

- The financial condition, earnings record, and dividend record of the corporation.
- Investor expectations of the corporation's potential earning power.
- General business and economic conditions and expectations.

If stock is issued (sold) for a price that is more than its par, the stock has been sold at a **premium**. For example, if common stock with a par of $50 is sold for $60 per share, the stock has sold at a premium of $10.

If stock is issued (sold) for a price that is less than its par, the stock has been sold at a **discount**. For example, if common stock with a par of $50 is sold for $45 per share, the stock has sold at a discount of $5. Many states do not permit stock to be sold at a discount. In other states, stock may be sold at a discount in only unusual cases. Because stock is rarely sold at a discount, it is not illustrated.

In order to distribute dividends, financial statements, and other reports, a corporation must keep track of its stockholders. Large public corporations normally use a financial institution, such as a bank, for this purpose.[6] In such cases, the financial institution is referred to as a *transfer agent* or *registrar*.

Premium on Stock

When stock is issued at a premium, Cash is debited for the amount received. Common Stock or Preferred Stock is credited for the par amount. The excess of the amount paid over par is part of the paid-in capital. An account entitled *Paid-In Capital in Excess of Par* is credited for this amount.

To illustrate, assume that Caldwell Company issues 2,000 shares of $50 par preferred stock for cash at $55. The entry to record this transaction is as follows:

		Cash	110,000	
		Preferred Stock		100,000
		Paid-In Capital in Excess of Par—Preferred Stock		10,000
		Issued $50 par preferred stock at $55.		

When stock is issued in exchange for assets other than cash, such as land, buildings, and equipment, the assets acquired are recorded at their fair market value. If this value cannot be determined, the fair market price of the stock issued is used.

To illustrate, assume that a corporation acquired land with a fair market value that cannot be determined. In exchange, the corporation issued 10,000 shares of its

[5] The accounting for investments in stocks from the point of view of the investor is discussed in Chapter 15.

[6] Small corporations may use a subsidiary ledger, called a *stockholders ledger*. in this case, the stock accounts (Preferred Stock and Common Stock) are controlling accounts for the subsidiary ledger.

$10 par common stock. If the stock has a market price of $12 per share, the transaction is recorded as follows:

		Land	120,000	
		Common Stock		100,000
		Paid-In Capital in Excess of Par		20,000
		Issued $10 par common stock, valued at $12 per share, for land.		

No-Par Stock

In most states, no-par preferred and common stock may be issued. When no-par stock is issued, Cash is debited and Common Stock is credited for the proceeds. As no-par stock is issued over time, this entry is the same even if the issuing price varies.

To illustrate, assume that on January 9, a corporation issues 10,000 shares of no-par common stock at $40 a share. On June 27, the corporation issues an additional 1,000 shares at $36. The entries to record these issuances of the no-par stock are as follows:

Jan.	9	Cash	400,000	
		Common Stock		400,000
		Issued 10,000 shares of no-par common stock at $40.		
June	27	Cash	36,000	
		Common Stock		36,000
		Issued 1,000 shares of no-par common stock at $36.		

In some states, no-par stock may be assigned a *stated value per share*. The stated value is recorded like a par value. Any excess of the proceeds over the stated value is credited to *Paid-In Capital in Excess of Stated Value.*

To illustrate, assume that in the preceding example the no-par common stock is assigned a stated value of $25. The issuance of the stock on January 9 and June 27 is recorded as follows:

Jan.	9	Cash	400,000	
		Common Stock		250,000
		Paid-In Capital in Excess of Stated Value		150,000
		Issued 10,000 shares of no-par common stock at $40; stated value, $25.		
June	27	Cash	36,000	
		Common Stock		25,000
		Paid-In Capital in Excess of Stated Value		11,000
		Issued 1,000 shares of no-par common stock at $36; stated value, $25.		

Business Connection

GOOGLE INC.

Some excepts from Google's bylaws follow:

ARTICLE I—CORPORATE OFFICES

1.1 REGISTERED OFFICE.

The registered office of Google Inc. shall be fixed in the corporation's certificate of incorporation. ...

1.2 OTHER OFFICES.

The corporation's Board of Directors (the "Board") may at any time establish other offices at any place or places where the corporation is qualified to do business.

ARTICLE II—MEETINGS OF STOCKHOLDERS

2.2 ANNUAL MEETING.

The annual meeting of stockholders shall be held each year on a date and at a time designated by the Board. At the annual meeting, directors shall be elected and any other proper business may be transacted.

2.4 NOTICE OF STOCKHOLDERS' MEETINGS.

All notices of meetings of stockholders shall be sent ... not less than ten (10) nor more than sixty (60) days before the date of the meeting to each stockholder entitled to vote at such meeting. ... The notice shall specify the place, if any, date and hour of the meeting, the means of remote communication, if any, by which stockholders and proxy holders may be deemed to be present in person and vote at such meeting. ...

2.8 ADMINISTRATION OF THE MEETING.

Meetings of stockholders shall be presided over by the chairman of the Board. ...

ARTICLE V—OFFICERS

5.1 OFFICERS.

The officers of the corporation shall be a chief executive officer, one or more presidents (at the discretion of the Board), a chairman of the Board and a secretary. The corporation may also have, at the discretion of the Board, a vice chairman of the Board, a chief financial officer, a treasurer, one or more vice presidents, one or more assistant vice presidents, one or more assistant treasurers, one or more assistant secretaries, and any such other officers as may be appointed in accordance with the provisions of these bylaws.

5.6 CHAIRMAN OF THE BOARD.

The chairman of the Board shall be a member of the Board and, if present, preside at meetings of the Board. ...

5.7 CHIEF EXECUTIVE OFFICER.

Subject to the control of the Board, ... the chief executive officer shall, together with the president or presidents of the corporation, have general supervision, direction, and control of the business and affairs of the corporation. ... The chief executive officer shall ... preside at all meetings of the stockholders.

5.11 CHIEF FINANCIAL OFFICER.

The chief financial officer shall keep and maintain ... adequate and correct books and records of accounts of the properties and business transactions of the corporation, including accounts of its assets, liabilities, receipts, disbursements, gains, losses, capital, retained earnings and shares. ...

5.12 TREASURER.

The treasurer shall deposit all moneys and other valuables in the name and to the credit of the corporation. ...

Source: http://investor.google.com/corporate/bylaws.html

Example Exercise 13-2 Entries for Issuing Stock (OBJ 3)

On March 6, Limerick Corporation issued for cash 15,000 shares of no-par common stock at $30. On April 13, Limerick issued at par 1,000 shares of preferred 4% stock, $40 par for cash. On May 19, Limerick issued for cash 15,000 shares of 4%, $40 par preferred stock at $42.

Journalize the entries to record the March 6, April 13, and May 19 transactions.

Follow My Example 13-2

Date	Account	Debit	Credit
Mar. 6	Cash	450,000	
	Common Stock		450,000
	(15,000 shares × $30).		
Apr. 13	Cash	40,000	
	Preferred Stock		40,000
	(1,000 shares × $40).		
May 19	Cash	630,000	
	Preferred Stock		600,000
	Paid-In Capital in Excess of Par		30,000
	(15,000 shares × $42).		

Practice Exercises: PE 13-2A, PE 13-2B

Accounting for Dividends

OBJ 4 Describe and illustrate the accounting for cash dividends and stock dividends.

When a board of directors declares a cash dividend, it authorizes the distribution of cash to stockholders. When a board of directors declares a stock dividend, it authorizes the distribution of its stock. In both cases, declaring a dividend reduces the retained earnings of the corporation.[7]

Cash Dividends

A cash distribution of earnings by a corporation to its shareholders is a **cash dividend**. Although dividends may be paid in other assets, cash dividends are the most common.

Three conditions for a cash dividend are as follows:

- Sufficient retained earnings
- Sufficient cash
- Formal action by the board of directors

International Connection

IFRS IFRS FOR SMEs

In 2010, the International Accounting Standards Board (IASB) issued a set of accounting standards specifically designed for small- and medium-sized enterprises (SMEs) called International Financial Reporting Standards (IFRS) for SMEs. SMEs in the United States are private companies and such small corporations that they do not report to the Securities and Exchange Commission (SEC). IFRS for SMEs consist of only 230 pages, compared to 2,700 pages for full IFRS. These standards are designed to be cost effective for SMEs. Thus, IFRS for SMEs require fewer disclosures and contain no industry-specific standards or exceptions.

The American Institute of CPAs (AICPA) has accepted IFRS for SMEs as part of U.S. generally accepted accounting principles (GAAP) for private companies not reporting to the SEC. If users, such as bankers and investors, accept these financial statements, IFRS for SMEs may become popular in the United States.*

*Differences between U.S. GAAP and IFRS are further discussed and illustrated in Appendix D.

There must be a sufficient (large enough) balance in Retained Earnings to declare a cash dividend. That is, the balance of Retained Earnings must be large enough so that the dividend does not create a debit balance in the retained earnings account. However, a large Retained Earnings balance does not mean that there is cash available to pay dividends. This is because the balances of Cash and Retained Earnings are often unrelated.

Even if there are sufficient retained earnings and cash, a corporation's board of directors is not required to pay dividends. Nevertheless, many corporations pay quarterly cash dividends to make their stock more attractive to investors. *Special* or *extra dividends* may also be paid when a corporation experiences higher than normal profits.

Three dates included in a dividend announcement are as follows:

1. Date of declaration
2. Date of record
3. Date of payment

Microsoft Corporation declared a dividend of $0.28 per share on November 19, 2013, to common stockholders of record as of February 20, 2014, payable on March 13, 2014.

The *date of declaration* is the date the board of directors formally authorizes the payment of the dividend. On this date, the corporation incurs the liability to pay the amount of the dividend.

The *date of record* is the date the corporation uses to determine which stockholders will receive the dividend. During the period of time between the date of declaration and

[7] In rare cases, when a corporation is reducing its operations or going out of business, a dividend may be a distribution of paid-in capital. Such a dividend is called a *liquidating dividend.*

the date of record, the stock price is quoted as selling *with-dividends*. This means that any investors purchasing the stock before the date of record will receive the dividend.

The *date of payment* is the date the corporation will pay the dividend to the stockholders who owned the stock on the date of record. During the period of time between the record date and the payment date, the stock price is quoted as selling *ex-dividends*. This means that since the date of record has passed, any new investors will not receive the dividend.

To illustrate, assume that on October 1, Hiber Corporation declares the following cash dividends with a date of record of November 10 and a date of payment of December 2:

	Dividend per Share	Total Dividends
Preferred stock, $100 par, 5,000 shares outstanding	$2.50	$12,500
Common stock, $10 par, 100,000 shares outstanding	$0.30	30,000
Total		$42,500

On October 1, the declaration date, Hiber Corporation records the following entry:

Declaration Date

Oct.	1	Cash Dividends	42,500	
		Cash Dividends Payable		42,500
		Declared cash dividends.		

Date of Record

On November 10, the date of record, no entry is necessary. This date merely determines which stockholders will receive the dividends.

On December 2, the date of payment, Hiber Corporation records the payment of the dividends as follows:

Date of Payment

Dec.	2	Cash Dividends Payable	42,500	
		Cash		42,500
		Paid cash dividends.		

At the end of the accounting period, the balance in Cash Dividends will be transferred to Retained Earnings as part of the closing process. This closing entry debits Retained Earnings and credits Cash Dividends for the balance of the cash dividends account. If the cash dividends have not been paid by the end of the period, Cash Dividends Payable will be reported on the balance sheet as a current liability.

Example Exercise 13-3 Entries for Cash Dividends

OBJ 4

The important dates in connection with a cash dividend of $75,000 on a corporation's common stock are February 26, March 30, and April 2. Journalize the entries required on each date.

Follow My Example 13-3

Feb. 26	Cash Dividends	75,000	
	Cash Dividends Payable		75,000
Mar. 30	No entry required.		
Apr. 2	Cash Dividends Payable	75,000	
	Cash		75,000

Practice Exercises: PE 13-3A, PE 13-3B

Integrity, Objectivity, and Ethics in Business

THE PROFESSOR WHO KNEW TOO MUCH

A major Midwestern university released a quarterly "American Customer Satisfaction Index" based on its research of customers of popular U.S. products and services. Before the release of the index to the public, the professor in charge of the research bought and sold stocks of some of the companies in the report. The professor was quoted as saying that he thought it was important to test his theories of customer satisfaction with "real" [his own] money.

Is this proper or ethical? Apparently, the dean of the Business School didn't think so. In a statement to the press, the dean stated: "I have instructed anyone affiliated with the (index) not to make personal use of information gathered in the course of producing the quarterly index, prior to the index's release to the general public, and they [the researchers] have agreed."

Sources: Jon E. Hilsenrath and Dan Morse, "Researcher Uses Index to Buy, Short Stocks," *The Wall Street Journal*, February 18, 2003; and Jon E. Hilsenrath, "Satisfaction Theory: Mixed Results," *The Wall Street Journal*, February 19, 2003.

Stock Dividends

A **stock dividend** is a distribution of shares of stock to stockholders. Stock dividends are normally declared only on common stock and issued to common stockholders.

A stock dividend affects only stockholders' equity. Specifically, the amount of the stock dividend is transferred from Retained Earnings to Paid-In Capital. The amount transferred is normally the fair value (market price) of the shares issued in the stock dividend.[8]

To illustrate, assume that the stockholders' equity accounts of Hendrix Corporation as of December 15 are as follows:

Common Stock, $20 par (2,000,000 shares issued)	$40,000,000
Paid-In Capital in Excess of Par—Common Stock	9,000,000
Retained Earnings	26,600,000

On December 15, Hendrix Corporation declares a stock dividend of 5% or 100,000 shares (2,000,000 shares × 5%) to be issued on January 10 to stockholders of record on December 31. The market price of the stock on December 15 (the date of declaration) is $31 per share.

The entry to record the stock dividend is as follows:

Dec.	15	Stock Dividends		3,100,000	
		Stock Dividends Distributable			2,000,000
		Paid-In Capital in Excess of Par—Common Stock			1,100,000
		Declared 5% (100,000 shares) stock dividend on $20 par common stock with a market price of $31 per share.			

After the preceding entry is recorded, Stock Dividends will have a debit balance of $3,100,000. Like cash dividends, the stock dividends account is closed to Retained Earnings at the end of the accounting period. This closing entry debits Retained Earnings and credits Stock Dividends.

At the end of the period, the *stock dividends distributable* and *paid-in capital in excess of par—common stock* accounts are reported in the Paid-In Capital section of the balance sheet. Thus, the effect of the preceding stock dividend is to transfer $3,100,000 of retained earnings to paid-in capital.

[8] The use of fair market value is justified as long as the number of shares issued for the stock dividend is small (less than 25% of the shares outstanding).

On January 10, the stock dividend is distributed to stockholders by issuing 100,000 shares of common stock. The issuance of the stock is recorded by the following entry:

Jan.	10	Stock Dividends Distributable		2,000,000	
		Common Stock			2,000,000
		Issued stock as stock dividend.			

A stock dividend does not change the assets, liabilities, or total stockholders' equity of a corporation. Likewise, a stock dividend does not change an individual stockholder's proportionate interest (equity) in the corporation.

To illustrate, assume a stockholder owns 1,000 of a corporation's 10,000 shares outstanding. If the corporation declares a 6% stock dividend, the stockholder's proportionate interest will not change, computed as follows:

	Before **Stock Dividend**	***After*** **Stock Dividend**
Total shares issued	10,000	10,600 [10,000 + (10,000 × 6%)]
Number of shares owned	1,000	1,060 [1,000 + (1,000 × 6%)]
Proportionate ownership	10% (1,000 ÷ 10,000)	10% (1,060 ÷ 10,600)

Example Exercise 13-4 Entries for Stock Dividends OBJ 4

Vienna Highlights Corporation has 150,000 shares of $100 par common stock outstanding. On June 14, Vienna Highlights declared a 4% stock dividend to be issued August 15 to stockholders of record on July 1. The market price of the stock was $110 per share on June 14.

Journalize the entries required on June 14, July 1, and August 15.

Follow My Example 13-4

June 14	Stock Dividends (150,000 × 4% × $110)	660,000	
	Stock Dividends Distributable (6,000 × $100)		600,000
	Paid-In Capital in Excess of Par—Common Stock ($660,000 – $600,000)		60,000
July 1	No entry required.		
Aug. 15	Stock Dividends Distributable	600,000	
	Common Stock		600,000

Practice Exercises: PE 13-4A, PE 13-4B

OBJ 5 Describe and illustrate the accounting for treasury stock transactions.

Treasury Stock Transactions

Treasury stock is stock that a corporation has issued and then reacquired. A corporation may reacquire (purchase) its own stock for a variety of reasons, including the following:

- To provide shares for resale to employees
- To reissue as bonuses to employees, or
- To support the market price of the stock

The 2012 edition of *Accounting Trends & Techniques* indicated that 68.2% of the companies surveyed reported treasury stock.

Dynamic Exhibit

The *cost method* is normally used for recording the purchase and resale of treasury stock.[9] Using the cost method, *Treasury Stock* is debited for the cost (purchase price) of the stock. When the stock is resold, Treasury Stock is credited for its cost. Any difference between the cost and the selling price is debited or credited to *Paid-In Capital from Sale of Treasury Stock.*

[9] Another method that is infrequently used, called the *par value method*, is discussed in advanced accounting texts.

To illustrate, assume that a corporation has the following paid-in capital on January 1:

Common stock, $25 par (20,000 shares authorized and issued)	$500,000
Excess of issue price over par	150,000
	$650,000

On February 13, the corporation purchases 1,000 shares of its common stock at $45 per share. The entry to record the purchase of the treasury stock is as follows:

Feb.	13	Treasury Stock	45,000	
		Cash		45,000
		Purchased 1,000 shares of treasury stock at $45.		

On April 29, the corporation sells 600 shares of the treasury stock for $60. The entry to record the sale is as follows:

Apr.	29	Cash	36,000	
		Treasury Stock		27,000
		Paid-In Capital from Sale of Treasury Stock		9,000
		Sold 600 shares of treasury stock at $60.		

A sale of treasury stock may result in a decrease in paid-in capital. To the extent that Paid-In Capital from Sale of Treasury Stock has a credit balance, it is debited for any such decrease. Any remaining decrease is then debited to the retained earnings account.

To illustrate, assume that on October 4, the corporation sells the remaining 400 shares of treasury stock for $40 per share. The entry to record the sale is as follows:

Oct.	4	Cash	16,000	
		Paid-In Capital from Sale of Treasury Stock	2,000	
		Treasury Stock		18,000
		Sold 400 shares of treasury stock at $40.		

The preceding October 4 entry decreases paid-in capital by $2,000. Because Paid-In Capital from Sale of Treasury Stock has a credit balance of $9,000, the entire $2,000 was debited to Paid-In Capital from Sale of Treasury Stock.

No dividends (cash or stock) are paid on the shares of treasury stock. To do so would result in the corporation earning dividend revenue from itself.

Example Exercise 13-5 Entries for Treasury Stock

OBJ 5

On May 3, Buzz Off Corporation reacquired 3,200 shares of its common stock at $42 per share. On July 22, Buzz Off sold 2,000 of the reacquired shares at $47 per share. On August 30, Buzz Off sold the remaining shares at $40 per share.

Journalize the transactions of May 3, July 22, and August 30.

Follow My Example 13-5

May 3	Treasury Stock (3,200 × $42)	134,400	
	Cash		134,400
July 22	Cash (2,000 × $47)	94,000	
	Treasury Stock (2,000 × $42)		84,000
	Paid-In Capital from Sale of Treasury Stock [2,000 × ($47 – $42)]		10,000
Aug. 30	Cash (1,200 × $40)	48,000	
	Paid-In Capital from Sale of Treasury Stock [1,200 × ($42 – $40)]	2,400	
	Treasury Stock (1,200 × $42)		50,400

Practice Exercises: PE 13-5A, PE 13-5B

OBJ 6 Describe and illustrate the reporting of stockholders' equity.

Reporting Stockholders' Equity

As with other sections of the balance sheet, alternative terms and formats may be used in reporting stockholders' equity. Also, changes in retained earnings and paid-in capital may be reported in separate statements or notes to the financial statements.

Stockholders' Equity on the Balance Sheet

Exhibit 7 shows two methods for reporting stockholders' equity for the December 31, 2016, balance sheet for Telex Inc.

- Method 1. Each class of stock is reported, followed by its related paid-in capital accounts. Retained earnings is then reported followed by a deduction for treasury stock.
- Method 2. The stock accounts are reported, followed by the paid-in capital reported as a single item, Additional paid-in capital. Retained earnings is then reported followed by a deduction for treasury stock.

EXHIBIT 7 **Stockholders' Equity Section of a Balance Sheet**

Telex Inc.
Balance Sheet
December 31, 2016

Stockholders' Equity

Paid-in capital:				Method 1
Preferred 10% stock, $50 par (2,000 shares authorized and issued)	$100,000			
Excess of issue price over par	10,000	$ 110,000		
Common stock, $20 par (50,000 shares authorized, 45,000 shares issued)	$900,000			
Excess of issue price over par	190,000	1,090,000		
From sale of treasury stock		2,000		
Total paid-in capital			$1,202,000	
Retained earnings			350,000	
Total			$1,552,000	
Deduct treasury stock (600 shares at cost)			27,000	
Total stockholders' equity			$1,525,000	
Contributed capital:				Method 2
Preferred 10% stock, $50 par (2,000 shares authorized and issued)		$ 100,000		
Common stock, $20 par (50,000 shares authorized, 45,000 shares issued)		900,000		
Additional paid-in capital		202,000		
Total contributed capital			$1,202,000	
Retained earnings			350,000	
Total			$1,552,000	
Deduct treasury stock (600 shares at cost)			27,000	
Total stockholders' equity			$1,525,000	

Significant changes in stockholders' equity during a period may also be presented in a statement of stockholders' equity or in the notes to the financial statements. The statement of stockholders' equity is illustrated later in this section.

Relevant rights and privileges of the various classes of stock outstanding should also be reported.[10] Examples include dividend and liquidation preferences, conversion rights, and redemption rights. Such information may be disclosed on the face of the balance sheet or in the notes to the financial statements.

Example Exercise 13-6 Reporting Stockholders' Equity

OBJ 6

Using the following accounts and balances, prepare the Stockholders' Equity section of the balance sheet. Forty thousand shares of common stock are authorized, and 5,000 shares have been reacquired.

Common Stock, $50 par	$1,500,000
Paid-In Capital from Sale of Treasury Stock	44,000
Paid-In Capital in Excess of Par	160,000
Retained Earnings	4,395,000
Treasury Stock	120,000

Follow My Example 13-6

Stockholders' Equity

Paid-in capital:		
Common stock, $50 par		
(40,000 shares authorized, 30,000 shares issued)	$1,500,000	
Excess of issue price over par	160,000	$1,660,000
From sale of treasury stock		44,000
Total paid-in capital		$1,704,000
Retained earnings		4,395,000
Total		$6,099,000
Deduct treasury stock (5,000 shares at cost)		120,000
Total stockholders' equity		$5,979,000

Practice Exercises: PE 13-6A, PE 13-6B

Reporting Retained Earnings

Changes in retained earnings may be reported using one of the following:

- Separate retained earnings statement
- Combined income and retained earnings statement
- Statement of stockholders' equity

Changes in retained earnings may be reported in a separate retained earnings statement. When a separate **retained earnings statement** is prepared, the beginning balance of retained earnings is reported. The net income is then added (or net loss is subtracted) and any dividends are subtracted to arrive at the ending retained earnings for the period.

To illustrate, a retained earnings statement for Telex Inc. is shown in Exhibit 8.

EXHIBIT 8

Retained Earnings Statement

Telex Inc.
Retained Earnings Statement
For the Year Ended December 31, 2016

Retained earnings, January 1, 2016			$245,000
Net income		$180,000	
Less dividends:			
Preferred stock dividends	$10,000		
Common stock dividends	65,000	75,000	
Increase in retained earnings			105,000
Retained earnings, December 31, 2016			$350,000

[10] *FASB Accounting Standards Codification*, Section 505-10-50.

Changes in retained earnings may also be reported in combination with the income statement. This format emphasizes net income as the connecting link between the income statement and ending retained earnings. Because this format is not often used, we do not illustrate it.

Changes in retained earnings may also be reported in a statement of stockholders' equity. An example of reporting changes in retained earnings in a statement of stockholders' equity for Telex Inc. is shown in Exhibit 9.

Example Exercise 13-7 Retained Earnings Statement

OBJ 6

Dry Creek Cameras Inc. reported the following results for the year ending March 31, 2016:

Retained earnings, April 1, 2015	$3,338,500
Net income	461,500
Cash dividends declared	80,000
Stock dividends declared	120,000

Prepare a retained earnings statement for the fiscal year ended March 31, 2016.

Follow My Example 13-7

Dry Creek Cameras Inc.
Retained Earnings Statement
For the Year Ended March 31, 2016

Retained earnings, April 1, 2015		$3,338,500
Net income	$461,500	
Less dividends declared	200,000	
Increase in retained earnings		261,500
Retained earnings, March 31, 2016		$3,600,000

Practice Exercises: PE 13-7A, PE 13-7B

Restrictions The use of retained earnings for payment of dividends may be restricted by action of a corporation's board of directors. Such **restrictions**, sometimes called *appropriations,* remain part of the retained earnings.

Restrictions of retained earnings are classified as:

- *Legal.* State laws may require a restriction of retained earnings.

  Example: States may restrict retained earnings by the amount of treasury stock purchased. In this way, legal capital cannot be used for dividends.

- *Contractual.* A corporation may enter into contracts that require restrictions of retained earnings.

  Example: A bank loan may restrict retained earnings so that money for repaying the loan cannot be used for dividends.

- *Discretionary.* A corporation's board of directors may restrict retained earnings voluntarily.

  Example: The board may restrict retained earnings and, thus, limit dividend distributions so that more money is available for expanding the business.

Restrictions of retained earnings must be disclosed in the financial statements. Such disclosures are usually included in the notes to the financial statements.

Prior Period Adjustments An error may arise from a mathematical mistake or from a mistake in applying accounting principles. Such errors may not be discovered within the same period in which they occur. In such cases, the effect of the error should not affect the current period's net income. Instead, the correction of the error, called a **prior period adjustment**, is reported in the retained earnings statement. Such corrections are reported as an adjustment to the beginning balance of retained earnings.[11]

[11] Prior period adjustments are illustrated in advanced texts.

Statement of Stockholders' Equity

When the only change in stockholders' equity is due to net income or net loss and dividends, a retained earnings statement is sufficient. However, when a corporation also has changes in stock and paid-in capital accounts, a **statement of stockholders' equity** is normally prepared.

A statement of stockholders' equity is normally prepared in a columnar format. Each column is a major stockholders' equity classification. Changes in each classification are then described in the left-hand column. Exhibit 9 illustrates a statement of stockholders' equity for Telex Inc.

EXHIBIT 9 **Statement of Stockholders' Equity**

Telex Inc.
Statement of Stockholders' Equity
For the Year Ended December 31, 2016

	Preferred Stock	Common Stock	Additional Paid-In Capital	Retained Earnings	Treasury Stock	Total
Balance, January 1, 2016	$100,000	$850,000	$177,000	$245,000	$(17,000)	$1,355,000
Net income				180,000		180,000
Dividends on preferred stock				(10,000)		(10,000)
Dividends on common stock				(65,000)		(65,000)
Issuance of additional common stock		50,000	25,000			75,000
Purchase of treasury stock					(10,000)	(10,000)
Balance, December 31, 2016	$100,000	$900,000	$202,000	$350,000	$(27,000)	$1,525,000

Reporting Stockholders' Equity for Mornin' Joe

Mornin' Joe reports stockholders' equity in its balance sheet. Mornin' Joe also includes a retained earnings statement and statement of stockholders' equity in its financial statements.

The Stockholders' Equity section of Mornin' Joe's balance sheet as of December 31, 2016, follows:

Mornin' Joe
Balance Sheet
December 31, 2016

Stockholders' Equity

Paid-in capital:		
Preferred 10% stock, $50 par (6,000 shares authorized and issued)	$ 300,000	
Excess of issue price over par	50,000	$ 350,000
Common stock, $20 par (50,000 shares authorized, 45,000 shares issued)	$ 900,000	
Excess of issue price over par	1,450,000	2,350,000
Total paid-in capital		$2,700,000
Retained earnings		1,200,300
Total		$3,900,300
Deduct treasury stock (1,000 shares at cost)		46,000
Total stockholders' equity		$3,854,300
Total liabilities and stockholders' equity		$6,169,700

Mornin' Joe's retained earnings statement for the year ended December 31, 2016, is as follows:

Mornin' Joe
Retained Earnings Statment
For the Year Ended December 31, 2016

Retained earnings, January 1, 2016			$ 852,700
Net income		$421,600	
Less dividends:			
Preferred stock	$30,000		
Common stock	44,000	74,000	
Increase in retained earnings			347,600
Retained earnings, December 31, 2016			$1,200,300

The statement of stockholders' equity for Mornin' Joe follows:

Mornin' Joe
Statement of Stockholders' Equity
For the Year Ended December 31, 2016

	Preferred Stock	Common Stock	Additional Paid-In Capital	Retained Earnings	Treasury Stock	Total
Balance, January 1, 2016	$300,000	$800,000	$1,325,000	$ 852,700	$(36,000)	$3,241,700
Net income				421,600		421,600
Dividends on preferred stock				(30,000)		(30,000)
Dividends on common stock				(44,000)		(44,000)
Issuance of additional common stock		100,000	175,000			275,000
Purchase of treasury stock					(10,000)	(10,000)
Balance, December 31, 2016	$300,000	$900,000	$1,500,000	$1,200,300	$(46,000)	$3,854,300

OBJ 7 Describe the effect of stock splits on corporate financial statements.

Dynamic Exhibit

Stock Splits

A **stock split** is a process by which a corporation reduces the par or stated value of its common stock and issues a proportionate number of additional shares. A stock split applies to all common shares including the unissued, issued, and treasury shares.

A major objective of a stock split is to reduce the market price per share of the stock. This attracts more investors and broadens the types and numbers of stockholders.

To illustrate, assume that Rojek Corporation has 10,000 shares of $100 par common stock outstanding with a current market price of $150 per share. The board of directors declares the following stock split:

1. Each common shareholder will receive 5 shares for each share held. This is called a 5-for-l stock split. As a result, 50,000 shares (10,000 shares × 5) will be outstanding.
2. The par of each share of common stock will be reduced to $20 ($100÷5).

The par value of the common stock outstanding is $1,000,000 both before and after the stock split as shown in Exhibit 10 and computed as follows:

	Before Split	After Split
Number of shares	10,000	50,000
Par value per share	× $100	× $20
Total	$1,000,000	$1,000,000

In addition, each Rojek Corporation shareholder owns the same total par amount of stock before and after the stock split. For example, a stockholder who owned 4 shares of $100 par stock before the split (total par of $400) would own 20 shares of

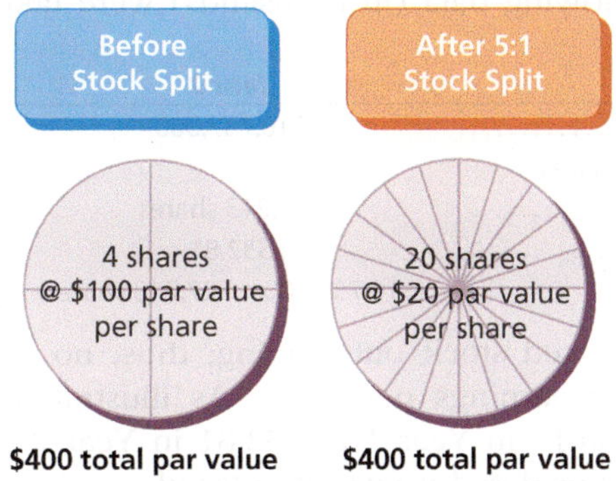

EXHIBIT 10

Stock Split: Before and After

$20 par stock after the split (total par of $400). Only the number of shares and the par value per share have changed.

Because there are more shares outstanding after the stock split, the market price of the stock should decrease. For example, in the preceding example, there would be 5 times as many shares outstanding after the split. Thus, the market price of the stock would be expected to fall from $150 to about $30 ($150 ÷ 5).

Stock splits do not require a journal entry because only the par (or stated) value and number of shares outstanding have changed. However, the details of stock splits are normally disclosed in the notes to the financial statements.

Note:
A stock split does not require a journal entry.

Business Connection

BUFFETT ON STOCK SPLITS

Warren E. Buffett, chairman and chief executive officer of Berkshire Hathaway Inc., opposes stock splits on the basis that they add no value to the company. Since its inception, Berkshire Hathaway has never declared a stock split on its primary (Class A) common stock. As a result, Berkshire Hathaway's Class A common stock sells well above $170,000 per share, which is the most expensive stock on the New York Stock Exchange. Such a high price doesn't bother Buffet because he believes that high stock prices attract more sophisticated and long-term investors and discourage stock speculators and short-term investors.

In contrast, Microsoft Corporation has split its stock nine times since it went public in 1986. As a result, one share of Microsoft purchased in 1986 is equivalent to 288 shares today, which would be worth more than $10,000.

Financial Analysis and Interpretation: Earnings per Share

OBJ 8 Describe and illustrate the use of earnings per share in evaluating a company's profitability.

F·A·I

Net income is often used by investors and creditors in evaluating a company's profitability. However, net income by itself is difficult to use in comparing companies of different sizes. Also, trends in net income may be difficult to evaluate if there have been significant changes in a company's stockholders' equity. Thus, the profitability of companies is often expressed as earnings per share.

Earnings per common share (EPS), sometimes called *basic earnings per share,* is the net income per share of common stock outstanding during a period.[12] Corporations whose stock is traded in a public market must report earnings per common share on their income statements.

Earnings per share is computed as follows:

$$\text{Earnings per Share} = \frac{\text{Net Income} - \text{Preferred Dividends}}{\text{Average Number of Common Shares Outstanding}}$$

If a company has preferred stock outstanding, any preferred dividends are subtracted from net income. This is because the numerator represents only those earnings available to the common shareholders.

[12] For complex capital structures, earnings per share assuming dilution may also be reported as described in Chapter 17.

To illustrate, the following data (in thousands) were taken from recent financial statements of Google:

	Year 2	Year 1
Net income	$10,737,000	$9,737,000
Average number of common shares outstanding	327,213 shares	322,778 shares
Earnings per share	$32.81	$30.17
	($10,737,000 ÷ 327,213 shares)	($9,737,000 ÷ 322,778 shares)

Google had no preferred stock outstanding; thus, no preferred dividends were subtracted in computing earnings per share. As illustrated, Google's earnings per share increased from $30.17 in Year 1 to $32.81 in Year 2. An increase in earnings per share is generally considered a favorable trend.

Earnings per share can be used to compare two companies with different net incomes. For example, the following data (in millions) were taken from a recent year's financial statements for Goldman Sachs Group, Inc., and Wells Fargo & Company:

	Goldman Sachs	Wells Fargo
Net income	$7,475	$18,897
Preferred dividends	$183	$898
Average number of common shares outstanding	516.1 shares	5,287.6 shares

Goldman Sachs:

$$\text{Earnings per Share} = \frac{\text{Net Income} - \text{Preferred Dividends}}{\text{Average Number of Common Shares Outstanding}} = \frac{\$7{,}475 - \$183}{516.1 \text{ shares}} = \frac{\$7{,}292}{516.1 \text{ shares}} = \$14.13$$

Wells Fargo:

$$\text{Earnings per Share} = \frac{\text{Net Income} - \text{Preferred Dividends}}{\text{Average Number of Common Shares Outstanding}} = \frac{\$18{,}897 - \$898}{5{,}287.6 \text{ shares}} = \frac{\$17{,}999}{5{,}287.6 \text{ shares}} = \$3.40$$

Based on earnings per share, Goldman Sachs is more profitable than Wells Fargo.

Example Exercise 13-8 Earnings per Share

OBJ 8

Financial statement data for years ending December 31 for Finnegan Company follows:

	2016	2015
Net income	$350,000	$195,000
Preferred dividends	$20,000	$15,000
Average number of common shares outstanding	75,000 shares	50,000 shares

a. Determine earnings per share for 2016 and 2015.

b. Does the change in the earnings per share from 2015 to 2016 indicate a favorable or an unfavorable trend?

Follow My Example 13-8

a.

2016:

$$\text{Earnings per Share} = \frac{\text{Net Income} - \text{Preferred Dividends}}{\text{Average Number of Common Shares Outstanding}} = \frac{\$350{,}000 - \$20{,}000}{75{,}000 \text{ shares}} = \frac{\$330{,}000}{75{,}000 \text{ shares}} = \$4.40$$

2015:

$$\text{Earnings per Share} = \frac{\text{Net Income} - \text{Preferred Dividends}}{\text{Average Number of Common Shares Outstanding}} = \frac{\$195{,}000 - \$15{,}000}{50{,}000 \text{ shares}} = \frac{\$180{,}000}{50{,}000 \text{ shares}} = \$3.60$$

b. The increase in the earnings per share from $3.60 to $4.40 indicates a favorable trend in the company's profitability.

Practice Exercises: PE 13-8A, PE 13-8B

At a Glance 13

OBJ 1 Describe the nature of the corporate form of organization.

Key Points Corporations have a separate legal existence, transferable units of stock, unlimited life, and limited stockholders' liability. The advantages and disadvantages of the corporate form are summarized in Exhibit 2. Costs incurred in organizing a corporation are debited to Organizational Expenses.

Learning Outcomes	Example Exercises	Practice Exercises
• Describe the characteristics of corporations.		
• List the advantages and disadvantages of the corporate form.		
• Prepare a journal entry for the costs of organizing a corporation.		

OBJ 2 Describe the two main sources of stockholders' equity.

Key Points The two main sources of stockholders' equity are (1) capital contributed by the stockholders and others, called *paid-in capital*, and (2) net income retained in the business, called *retained earnings*. Stockholders' equity is reported in a corporation balance sheet according to these two sources.

Learning Outcomes	Example Exercises	Practice Exercises
• Describe what is meant by paid-in capital.		
• Describe what is meant by net income retained in the business.		
• Prepare a simple Stockholders' Equity section of the balance sheet.		

OBJ 3 Describe and illustrate the characteristics of stock, classes of stock, and entries for issuing stock.

Key Points The main source of paid-in capital is from issuing common and preferred stock. Stock issued at par is recorded by debiting Cash and crediting the class of stock issued for its par amount. Stock issued for more than par is recorded by debiting Cash, crediting the class of stock for its par, and crediting Paid-In Capital in Excess of Par for the difference. When no-par stock is issued, the entire proceeds are credited to the stock account. No-par stock may be assigned a stated value per share, and the excess of the proceeds over the stated value may be credited to Paid-In Capital in Excess of Stated Value.

Learning Outcomes	Example Exercises	Practice Exercises
• Describe the characteristics of common and preferred stock including rights to dividends.	**EE13-1**	**PE13-1A, 13-1B**
• Journalize the entry for common and preferred stock issued at par.	**EE13-2**	**PE13-2A, 13-2B**
• Journalize the entry for common and preferred stock issued at more than par.	**EE13-2**	**PE13-2A, 13-2B**
• Journalize the entry for issuing no-par stock.	**EE13-2**	**PE13-2A, 13-2B**

OBJ 4 Describe and illustrate the accounting for cash dividends and stock dividends.

Key Points The entry to record a declaration of cash dividends debits Dividends and credits Dividends Payable. When a stock dividend is declared, Stock Dividends is debited for the fair value of the stock to be issued. Stock Dividends Distributable is credited for the par or stated value of the common stock to be issued. The difference between the fair value of the stock and its par or stated value is credited to Paid-In Capital in Excess of Par—Common Stock. When the stock is issued on the date of payment, Stock Dividends Distributable is debited and Common Stock is credited for the par or stated value of the stock issued.

Learning Outcomes	Example Exercises	Practice Exercises
• Journalize the entries for the declaration and payment of cash dividends.	**EE13-3**	**PE13-3A, 13-3B**
• Journalize the entries for the declaration and payment of stock dividends.	**EE13-4**	**PE13-4A, 13-4B**

OBJ 5 Describe and illustrate the accounting for treasury stock transactions.

Key Points When a corporation buys its own stock, the cost method of accounting is normally used. Treasury Stock is debited for its cost, and Cash is credited. If the stock is resold, Treasury Stock is credited for its cost and any difference between the cost and the selling price is normally debited or credited to Paid-In Capital from Sale of Treasury Stock.

Learning Outcomes	Example Exercises	Practice Exercises
• Define treasury stock.		
• Describe the accounting for treasury stock.		
• Journalize entries for the purchase and sale of treasury stock.	**EE13-5**	**PE13-5A, 13-5B**

OBJ 6 Describe and illustrate the reporting of stockholders' equity.

Key Points Two alternatives for reporting stockholders' equity are shown in Exhibit 7. Changes in retained earnings are reported in a retained earnings statement, as shown in Exhibit 8. Restrictions to retained earnings should be disclosed. Any prior period adjustments are reported in the retained earnings statement. Changes in stockholders' equity may be reported on a statement of stockholders' equity, as shown in Exhibit 9.

Learning Outcomes	Example Exercises	Practice Exercises
• Prepare the Stockholders' Equity section of the balance sheet.	**EE13-6**	**PE13-6A, 13-6B**
• Prepare a retained earnings statement.	**EE13-7**	**PE13-7A, 13-7B**
• Describe retained earnings restrictions and prior period adjustments.		
• Prepare a statement of stockholders' equity.		

OBJ 7

Describe the effect of stock splits on corporate financial statements.

Key Points When a corporation reduces the par or stated value of its common stock and issues a proportionate number of additional shares, a stock split has occurred. There are no changes in the balances of any accounts, and no entry is required for a stock split.

Learning Outcomes	Example Exercises	Practice Exercises
• Define and give an example of a stock split.		
• Describe the accounting for and effects of a stock split on the financial statements.		

OBJ 8

Describe and illustrate the use of earnings per share in evaluating a company's profitability.

Key Points The profitability of companies is often expressed as earnings per share. Earnings per share is computed by subtracting preferred dividends from net income and dividing by the average number of common shares outstanding.

Learning Outcomes	Example Exercises	Practice Exercises
• Describe the use of earnings per share in evaluating a company's profitability.		
• Compute and interpret earnings per share.	EE13-8	PE13-8A, 13-8B

Key Terms

cash dividend (605)
common stock (600)
cumulative preferred stock (600)
deficit (599)
discount (602)
dividends (599)
earnings per common share (EPS) (615)
in arrears (600)
outstanding stock (599)
paid-in capital (598)
par value (600)
preferred stock (600)
premium (602)
prior period adjustments (612)
restrictions (612)
retained earnings (598)
retained earnings statement (611)
statement of stockholders' equity (613)
stock (596)
stock dividend (607)
stock split (614)
stockholders (596)
stockholders' equity (598)
treasury stock (608)

Illustrative Problem

Altenburg Inc. is a lighting fixture wholesaler located in Arizona. During its current fiscal year, ended December 31, 2016, Altenburg Inc. completed the following selected transactions:

Feb. 3. Purchased 2,500 shares of its own common stock at $26, recording the stock at cost. (Prior to the purchase, there were 40,000 shares of $20 par common stock outstanding.)

May 1. Declared a semiannual dividend of $1 on the 10,000 shares of preferred stock and a $0.30 dividend on the common stock to stockholders of record on May 31, payable on June 15.

June 15. Paid the cash dividends.

Sept. 23. Sold 1,000 shares of treasury stock at $28, receiving cash.

Nov. 1. Declared semiannual dividends of $1 on the preferred stock and $0.30 on the common stock. In addition, a 5% common stock dividend was declared on the common stock outstanding, to be capitalized at the fair market value of the common stock, which is estimated at $30.

Dec. 1. Paid the cash dividends and issued the certificates for the common stock dividend.

Instructions

Journalize the entries to record the transactions for Altenburg Inc.

Solution

2016					
Feb.	3	Treasury Stock		65,000	
		Cash			65,000
May	1	Cash Dividends		21,250	
		Cash Dividends Payable			21,250
		(10,000 × $1) + [(40,000 – 2,500) × $0.30].			
June	15	Cash Dividends Payable		21,250	
		Cash			21,250
Sept.	23	Cash		28,000	
		Treasury Stock			26,000
		Paid-In Capital from Sale of Treasury Stock			2,000
Nov.	1	Cash Dividends		21,550	
		Cash Dividends Payable			21,550
		(10,000 × $1) + [(40,000 – 1,500) × $0.30].			
	1	Stock Dividends		57,750*	
		Stock Dividends Distributable			38,500
		Paid-In Capital in Excess of Par—Common Stock			19,250
		*(40,000 – 1,500) × 5% × $30.			
Dec.	1	Cash Dividends Payable		21,550	
		Stock Dividends Distributable		38,500	
		Cash			21,550
		Common Stock			38,500

Discussion Questions

1. Of two corporations organized at approximately the same time and engaged in competing businesses, one issued $80 par common stock, and the other issued $1 par common stock. Do the par designations provide any indication as to which stock is preferable as an investment? Explain.
2. A stockbroker advises a client to "buy preferred stock. … With that type of stock, … [you] will never have to worry about losing the dividends." Is the broker right?
3. A corporation with both preferred stock and common stock outstanding has a substantial credit balance in its retained earnings account at the beginning of the current fiscal year. Although net income for the current year is sufficient to pay the preferred dividend of $150,000 each quarter and a common dividend of $90,000 each quarter, the board of directors declares dividends only on the preferred stock. Suggest possible reasons for passing the dividends on the common stock.
4. An owner of 2,500 shares of Simmons Company common stock receives a stock dividend of 50 shares.
   a. What is the effect of the stock dividend on the stockholder's proportionate interest (equity) in the corporation?
   b. How does the total equity of 2,550 shares compare with the total equity of 2,500 shares before the stock dividend?
5. a. Where should a declared but unpaid cash dividend be reported on the balance sheet?
   b. Where should a declared but unissued stock dividend be reported on the balance sheet?
6. A corporation reacquires 60,000 shares of its own $10 par common stock for $3,000,000, recording it at cost.
   a. What effect does this transaction have on revenue or expense of the period?
   b. What effect does it have on stockholders' equity?
7. The treasury stock in Discussion Question 6 is resold for $3,750,000.
   a. What is the effect on the corporation's revenue of the period?
   b. What is the effect on stockholders' equity?
8. What are the three classifications of restrictions of retained earnings, and how are such restrictions normally reported on the financial statements?
9. Indicate how prior period adjustments would be reported on the financial statements presented only for the current period.
10. What is the primary purpose of a stock split?

Practice Exercises

EE 13-1 *p. 601*

SHOW ME HOW

PE 13-1A Dividends per share **OBJ. 3**

National Furniture Company has 25,000 shares of cumulative preferred 2% stock, $75 par and 200,000 shares of $10 par common stock. The following amounts were distributed as dividends:

Year 1	$25,000
Year 2	88,000
Year 3	95,500

Determine the dividends per share for preferred and common stock for each year.

EE 13-1 p. 601

SHOW ME HOW

PE 13-1B Dividends per share OBJ. 3

Zero Calories Company has 16,000 shares of cumulative preferred 1% stock, $40 par and 80,000 shares of $150 par common stock. The following amounts were distributed as dividends:

Year 1	$ 21,600
Year 2	4,000
Year 3	100,800

Determine the dividends per share for preferred and common stock for each year.

EE 13-2 p. 604

SHOW ME HOW

PE 13-2A Entries for issuing stock OBJ. 3

On August 26, Mountain Realty Inc. issued for cash 120,000 shares of no-par common stock (with a stated value of $5) at $8. On October 1, Mountain Realty Inc. issued at par value 40,000 shares of preferred 1% stock, $10 par for cash. On November 30, Mountain Realty Inc. issued for cash 18,000 shares of preferred 1% stock, $10 par at $13.

Journalize the entries to record the August 26, October 1, and November 30 transactions.

EE 13-2 p. 604

SHOW ME HOW

PE 13-2B Entries for issuing stock OBJ. 3

On January 22, Zentric Corporation issued for cash 180,000 shares of no-par common stock at $4. On February 14, Zentric Corporation issued at par value 44,000 shares of preferred 2% stock, $55 par for cash. On August 30, Zentric Corporation issued for cash 9,000 shares of preferred 2% stock, $55 par at $60.

Journalize the entries to record the January 22, February 14, and August 30 transactions.

EE 13-3 p. 606

SHOW ME HOW

PE 13-3A Entries for cash dividends OBJ. 4

The declaration, record, and payment dates in connection with a cash dividend of $710,000 on a corporation's common stock are June 15, August 10, and September 15. Journalize the entries required on each date.

EE 13-3 p. 606

SHOW ME HOW

PE 13-3B Entries for cash dividends OBJ. 4

The declaration, record, and payment dates in connection with a cash dividend of $480,000 on a corporation's common stock are February 1, March 18, and May 1. Journalize the entries required on each date.

EE 13-4 p. 608

SHOW ME HOW

PE 13-4A Entries for stock dividends OBJ. 4

Olde Wine Corporation has 250,000 shares of $40 par common stock outstanding. On February 15, Olde Wine Corporation declared a 2% stock dividend to be issued May 2 to stockholders of record on March 27. The market price of the stock was $52 per share on February 15.

Journalize the entries required on February 15, March 27, and May 2.

EE 13-4 p. 608

SHOW ME HOW

PE 13-4B Entries for stock dividends OBJ. 4

Antique Buggy Corporation has 820,000 shares of $35 par common stock outstanding. On June 8, Antique Buggy Corporation declared a 5% stock dividend to be issued August 12 to stockholders of record on July 13. The market price of the stock was $63 per share on June 8.

Journalize the entries required on June 8, July 13, and August 12.

EE 13-5 p. 609

SHOW ME HOW

PE 13-5A Entries for treasury stock OBJ. 5

On January 31, Wilderness Resorts Inc. reacquired 22,500 shares of its common stock at $31 per share. On April 20, Wilderness Resorts sold 12,800 of the reacquired shares at $40 per share. On October 4, Wilderness Resorts sold the remaining shares at $28 per share.

Journalize the transactions of January 31, April 20, and October 4.

SHOW ME HOW

EE 13-5 p. 609

PE 13-5B Entries for treasury stock **OBJ. 5**

On May 27, Hydro Clothing Inc. reacquired 75,000 shares of its common stock at $8 per share. On August 3, Hydro Clothing sold 54,000 of the reacquired shares at $11 per share. On November 14, Hydro Clothing sold the remaining shares at $7 per share.

Journalize the transactions of May 27, August 3, and November 14.

SHOW ME HOW

EE 13-6 p. 611

PE 13-6A Reporting stockholders' equity **OBJ. 6**

Using the following accounts and balances, prepare the Stockholders' Equity section of the balance sheet. Two hundred fifty thousand shares of common stock are authorized, and 17,500 shares have been reacquired.

Common Stock, $60 par	$12,000,0000
Paid-In Capital from Sale of Treasury Stock	320,000
Paid-In Capital in Excess of Par—Common Stock	3,200,000
Retained Earnings	18,500,000
Treasury Stock	1,137,500

SHOW ME HOW

EE 13-6 p. 611

PE 13-6B Reporting stockholders' equity **OBJ. 6**

Using the following accounts and balances, prepare the Stockholders' Equity section of the balance sheet. Five-hundred thousand shares of common stock are authorized, and 40,000 shares have been reacquired.

Common Stock, $120 par	$48,000,000
Paid-In Capital from Sale of Treasury Stock	4,500,000
Paid-In Capital in Excess of Par—Common Stock	6,400,000
Retained Earnings	63,680,000
Treasury Stock	5,200,000

SHOW ME HOW

EE 13-7 p. 612

PE 13-7A Retained earnings statement **OBJ. 6**

Rockwell Inc. reported the following results for the year ended June 30, 2016:

Retained earnings, July 1, 2015	$3,900,000
Net income	714,000
Cash dividends declared	100,000
Stock dividends declared	50,000

Prepare a retained earnings statement for the fiscal year ended June 30, 2016.

SHOW ME HOW

EE 13-7 p. 612

PE 13-7B Retained earnings statement **OBJ. 6**

Noric Cruises Inc. reported the following results for the year ended October 31, 2016:

Retained earnings, November 1, 2015	$12,400,000
Net income	2,350,000
Cash dividends declared	175,000
Stock dividends declared	300,000

Prepare a retained earnings statement for the fiscal year ended October 31, 2016.

SHOW ME HOW

EE 13-8 p. 616

F·A·I

PE 13-8A Earnings per share **OBJ. 8**

Financial statement data for the years ended December 31 for Dovetail Corporation follows:

	2016	2015
Net income	$448,750	$376,000
Preferred dividends	$40,000	$40,000
Average number of common shares outstanding	75,000 shares	60,000 shares

a. Determine the earnings per share for 2016 and 2015.

b. Does the change in the earnings per share from 2015 to 2016 indicate a favorable or an unfavorable trend?

EE 13-8 p. 616 F·A·I

SHOW ME HOW

PE 13-8B Earnings per share **OBJ. 8**

Financial statement data for the years ended December 31 for Black Bull Inc. follows:

	2016	2015
Net income	$2,485,700	$1,538,000
Preferred dividends	$50,000	$50,000
Average number of common shares outstanding	115,000 shares	80,000 shares

a. Determine the earnings per share for 2016 and 2015.

b. Does the change in the earnings per share from 2015 to 2016 indicate a favorable or an unfavorable trend?

Exercises

✔ Preferred stock, 1st year: $2.25

SHOW ME HOW

EX 13-1 Dividends per share **OBJ. 3**

Triple Z Inc., a developer of radiology equipment, has stock outstanding as follows: 12,000 shares of cumulative preferred 2% stock, $150 par and 50,000 shares of $10 par common. During its first four years of operations, the following amounts were distributed as dividends: first year, $27,000; second year, $60,000; third year, $80,000; fourth year, $90,000. Calculate the dividends per share on each class of stock for each of the four years.

✔ Preferred stock, 1st year: $0.90

EX 13-2 Dividends per share **OBJ. 3**

Lightfoot Inc., a software development firm, has stock outstanding as follows: 40,000 shares of cumulative preferred 1% stock, $125 par, and 100,000 shares of $150 par common. During its first four years of operations, the following amounts were distributed as dividends: first year, $36,000; second year, $58,000; third year, $75,000; fourth year, $124,000. Calculate the dividends per share on each class of stock for each of the four years.

SHOW ME HOW

EX 13-3 Entries for issuing par stock **OBJ. 3**

On April 20, Gallatin County Rocks Inc., a marble contractor, issued for cash 75,000 shares of $45 par common stock at $54, and on August 7, it issued for cash 20,000 shares of preferred stock, $10 par at $12.

a. Journalize the entries for April 20 and August 7.

b. What is the total amount invested (total paid-in capital) by all stockholders as of August 7?

SHOW ME HOW

EX 13-4 Entries for issuing no-par stock **OBJ. 3**

On May 15, Helena Carpet Inc., a carpet wholesaler, issued for cash 750,000 shares of no-par common stock (with a stated value of $1.50) at $4, and on June 30, it issued for cash 17,500 shares of preferred stock, $50 par at $60.

a. Journalize the entries for May 15 and June 30, assuming that the common stock is to be credited with the stated value.

b. What is the total amount invested (total paid-in capital) by all stockholders as of June 30?

SHOW ME HOW

EX 13-5 Issuing stock for assets other than cash **OBJ. 3**

On July 11, American Lift Corporation, a wholesaler of hydraulic lifts, acquired land in exchange for 5,000 shares of $5 par common stock with a current market price of $32. Journalize the entry to record the transaction.

EX 13-6 Selected stock transactions **OBJ. 3**

Alpha Sounds Corp., an electric guitar retailer, was organized by Michele Kirby, Paul Glenn, and Gretchen Northway. The charter authorized 1,000,000 shares of common stock with a par of $1. The following transactions affecting stockholders' equity were completed during the first year of operations:

a. Issued 100,000 shares of stock at par to Paul Glenn for cash.

b. Issued 3,000 shares of stock at par to Michele Kirby for promotional services provided in connection with the organization of the corporation, and issued 45,000 shares of stock at par to Michele Kirby for cash.

c. Purchased land and a building from Gretchen Northway in exchange for stock issued at par. The building is mortgaged for $180,000 for 20 years at 6%, and there is accrued interest of $5,200 on the mortgage note at the time of the purchase. It is agreed that the land is to be priced at $60,000 and the building at $225,000 and that Gretchen Northway's equity will be exchanged for stock at par. The corporation agreed to assume responsibility for paying the mortgage note and the accrued interest.

Journalize the entries to record the transactions.

EX 13-7 Issuing stock **OBJ. 3**

Willow Creek Nursery, with an authorization of 75,000 shares of preferred stock and 200,000 shares of common stock, completed several transactions involving its stock on October 1, the first day of operations. The trial balance at the close of the day follows:

Cash	3,780,000	
Land	840,000	
Buildings	2,380,000	
Preferred 1% Stock, $80 par		2,800,000
Paid-In Capital in Excess of Par—Preferred Stock		420,000
Common Stock, $30 par		3,600,000
Paid-In Capital in Excess of Par—Common Stock		180,000
	7,000,000	7,000,000

All shares within each class of stock were sold at the same price. The preferred stock was issued in exchange for the land and buildings.

Journalize the two entries to record the transactions summarized in the trial balance.

EX 13-8 Issuing stock **OBJ. 3**

SHOW ME HOW

Occupational Products Inc., a wholesaler of office products, was organized on March 1 of the current year, with an authorization of 25,000 shares of preferred 2% stock, $100 par and 500,000 shares of $10 par common stock. The following selected transactions were completed during the first year of operations:

Mar. 1. Issued 220,000 shares of common stock at par for cash.

1. Issued 500 shares of common stock at par to an attorney in payment of legal fees for organizing the corporation.

May 31. Issued 70,000 shares of common stock in exchange for land, buildings, and equipment with fair market prices of $150,000, $560,000 and $165,000 respectively.

July 1. Issued 18,000 shares of preferred stock at $110 for cash.

Journalize the transactions.

EX 13-9 Entries for cash dividends **OBJ. 4**

SHOW ME HOW

The declaration, record, and payment dates in connection with a cash dividend of $135,000 on a corporation's common stock are January 12, March 13, and April 12. Journalize the entries required on each date.

EX 13-10 Entries for stock dividends **OBJ. 4**

✔ b. (1) $3,000,000
(3) $36,500,000

SHOW ME HOW

Senior Life Co. is an HMO for businesses in the Portland area. The following account balances appear on the balance sheet of Senior Life Co.: Common stock (800,000 shares authorized; 500,000 shares issued), $4 par, $2,000,000; Paid-in capital in excess of par—common stock, $1,000,000; and Retained earnings, $33,500,000. The board of directors declared a 2% stock dividend when the market price of the stock was $13 a share. Senior Life Co. reported no income or loss for the current year.

a. Journalize the entries to record (1) the declaration of the dividend, capitalizing an amount equal to market value, and (2) the issuance of the stock certificates.

b. Determine the following amounts before the stock dividend was declared: (1) total paid-in capital, (2) total retained earnings, and (3) total stockholders' equity.

c. Determine the following amounts after the stock dividend was declared and closing entries were recorded at the end of the year: (1) total paid-in capital, (2) total retained earnings, and (3) total stockholders' equity.

✔ b. $170,000 credit

SHOW ME HOW

EX 13-11 Treasury stock transactions **OBJ. 5**

Mystic Lake Inc. bottles and distributes spring water. On July 9 of the current year, Mystic Lake reacquired 40,000 shares of its common stock at $44 per share. On September 22, Mystic Lake Inc. sold 30,000 of the reacquired shares at $50 per share. The remaining 10,000 shares were sold at $43 per share on November 23.

a. Journalize the transactions of July 9, September 22, and November 23.

b. What is the balance in Paid-In Capital from Sale of Treasury Stock on December 31 of the current year?

c. For what reasons might Mystic Lake have purchased the treasury stock?

✔ b. $57,000 credit

SHOW ME HOW

EX 13-12 Treasury stock transactions **OBJ. 5, 6**

Lawn Smart Inc. develops and produces spraying equipment for lawn maintenance and industrial uses. On May 29 of the current year, Lawn Smart Inc. reacquired 18,000 shares of its common stock at $20 per share. On August 11, 13,500 of the reacquired shares were sold at $24 per share, and on October 30, 3,000 of the reacquired shares were sold at $21.

a. Journalize the transactions of May 29, August 11, and October 30.

b. What is the balance in Paid-In Capital from Sale of Treasury Stock on December 31 of the current year?

c. What is the balance in Treasury Stock on December 31 of the current year?

d. How will the balance in Treasury Stock be reported on the balance sheet?

✔ b. $55,500 credit

EX 13-13 Treasury stock transactions **OBJ. 5, 6**

Biscayne Bay Water Inc. bottles and distributes spring water. On May 14 of the current year, Biscayne Bay Water Inc. reacquired 23,500 shares of its common stock at $75 per share. On September 6, Biscayne Bay Water Inc. sold 14,000 of the reacquired shares at $81 per share. The remaining 9,500 shares were sold at $72 per share on November 30.

a. Journalize the transactions of May 14, September 6, and November 30.

b. What is the balance in Paid-In Capital from Sale of Treasury Stock on December 31 of the current year?

c. Where will the balance in Paid-In Capital from Sale of Treasury Stock be reported on the balance sheet?

d. For what reasons might Biscayne Bay Water Inc. have purchased the treasury stock?

✔ Total paid-in capital, $13,615,000

EX 13-14 Reporting paid-in capital **OBJ. 6**

The following accounts and their balances were selected from the unadjusted trial balance of Point Loma Group Inc., a freight forwarder, at October 31, the end of the current fiscal year:

Common Stock, no par, $14 stated value	$ 4,480,000
Paid-In Capital from Sale of Treasury Stock	45,000
Paid-In Capital in Excess of Par—Preferred Stock	210,000
Paid-In Capital in Excess of Stated Value—Common Stock	480,000
Preferred 2% Stock, $120 par	8,400,000
Retained Earnings	39,500,000

Prepare the Paid-In Capital portion of the Stockholders' Equity section of the balance sheet using Method 1 of Exhibit 7. There are 375,000 shares of common stock authorized and 85,000 shares of preferred stock authorized.

EX 13-15 Stockholders' Equity section of balance sheet OBJ. 6

✔ Total stockholders' equity, $23,676,000

The following accounts and their balances appear in the ledger of Goodale Properties Inc. on June 30 of the current year:

Common Stock, $45 par	$ 3,060,000
Paid-In Capital from Sale of Treasury Stock	115,000
Paid-In Capital in Excess of Par—Common Stock	272,000
Retained Earnings	20,553,000
Treasury Stock	324,000

Prepare the Stockholders' Equity section of the balance sheet as of June 30. Eighty thousand shares of common stock are authorized, and 9,000 shares have been reacquired.

EX 13-16 Stockholders' Equity section of balance sheet OBJ. 6

✔ Total stockholders' equity, $89,100,000

Specialty Auto Racing Inc. retails racing products for BMWs, Porsches, and Ferraris. The following accounts and their balances appear in the ledger of Specialty Auto Racing Inc. on July 31, the end of the current year:

Common Stock, $36 par	$10,080,000
Paid-In Capital from Sale of Treasury Stock—Common	340,000
Paid-In Capital in Excess of Par—Common Stock	420,000
Paid-In Capital in Excess of Par—Preferred Stock	384,000
Preferred 1% Stock, $150 par	7,200,000
Retained Earnings	71,684,000
Treasury Stock—Common	1,008,000

Fifty thousand shares of preferred and 300,000 shares of common stock are authorized. There are 24,000 shares of common stock held as treasury stock.

Prepare the Stockholders' Equity section of the balance sheet as of July 31, the end of the current year using Method 1 of Exhibit 7.

EX 13-17 Retained earnings statement OBJ. 6

✔ Retained earnings, January 31, $64,210,000

SHOW ME HOW

Sumter Pumps Corporation, a manufacturer of industrial pumps, reports the following results for the year ended January 31, 2016:

Retained earnings, February 1, 2015	$59,650,000
Net income	8,160,000
Cash dividends declared	1,000,000
Stock dividends declared	2,600,000

Prepare a retained earnings statement for the fiscal year ended January 31, 2016.

EX 13-18 Stockholders' Equity section of balance sheet OBJ. 6

✔ Corrected total stockholders' equity, $122,800,000

List the errors in the following Stockholders' Equity section of the balance sheet prepared as of the end of the current year:

Stockholders' Equity

Paid-in capital:		
Preferred 2% stock, $80 par		
(125,000 shares authorized and issued)	$10,000,000	
Excess of issue price over par	500,000	$ 10,500,000
Retained earnings		96,700,000
Treasury stock (75,000 shares at cost)		1,755,000
Dividends payable		430,000
Total paid-in capital		$ 109,385,000
Common stock, $20 par (1,000,000 shares authorized, 825,000 shares issued)		17,655,000
Organizing costs		300,000
Total stockholders' equity		$127,340,000

✔ Total stockholders' equity, Dec. 31, $21,587,000

EX 13-19 Statement of stockholders' equity **OBJ. 6**

The stockholders' equity T accounts of I-Cards Inc. for the fiscal year ended December 31, 2016, are as follows. Prepare a statement of stockholders' equity for the fiscal year ended December 31, 2016.

COMMON STOCK

			Jan. 1	Balance	4,800,000
			Apr. 14	Issued 30,000 shares	1,200,000
			Dec. 31	Balance	6,000,000

PAID-IN CAPITAL IN EXCESS OF PAR

			Jan. 1	Balance	960,000
			Apr. 14	Issued 30,000 shares	300,000
			Dec. 31	Balance	1,260,000

TREASURY STOCK

Aug. 7	Purchased 12,000 shares	552,000			

RETAINED EARNINGS

Mar. 31	Dividend	69,000	Jan. 1	Balance	11,375,000
June 30	Dividend	69,000	Dec. 31	Closing (net income)	3,780,000
Sept. 30	Dividend	69,000			
Dec. 31	Dividend	69,000	Dec. 31	Balance	14,879,000

EX 13-20 Effect of stock split **OBJ. 7**

SHOW ME HOW

Copper Grill Restaurant Corporation wholesales ovens and ranges to restaurants throughout the Southwest. Copper Grill Restaurant Corporation, which had 50,000 shares of common stock outstanding, declared a 3-for-1 stock split.

a. What will be the number of shares outstanding after the split?

b. If the common stock had a market price of $210 per share before the stock split, what would be an approximate market price per share after the split?

EX 13-21 Effect of cash dividend and stock split **OBJ. 4, 7**

Indicate whether the following actions would (+) increase, (–) decrease, or (0) not affect Indigo Inc.'s total assets, liabilities, and stockholders' equity:

	Assets	Liabilities	Stockholders' Equity
(1) Authorizing and issuing stock certificates in a stock split	______	______	______
(2) Declaring a stock dividend	______	______	______
(3) Issuing stock certificates for the stock dividend declared in (2)	______	______	______
(4) Declaring a cash dividend	______	______	______
(5) Paying the cash dividend declared in (4)	______	______	______

EX 13-22 Selected dividend transactions, stock split **OBJ. 4, 7**

Selected transactions completed by Canyon Ferry Boating Corporation during the current fiscal year are as follows:

Jan. 8. Split the common stock 2 for 1 and reduced the par from $80 to $40 per share. After the split, there were 150,000 common shares outstanding.

Apr. 30. Declared semiannual dividends of $0.75 on 18,000 shares of preferred stock and $0.28 on the common stock payable on July 1.

July 1. Paid the cash dividends.

Oct. 31. Declared semiannual dividends of $0.75 on the preferred stock and $0.14 on the common stock (before the stock dividend). In addition, a 5% common stock dividend was declared on the common stock outstanding. The fair market value of the common stock is estimated at $52.

Dec. 31. Paid the cash dividends and issued the certificates for the common stock dividend.

Journalize the transactions.

EX 13-23 EPS **OBJ. 8**

F·A·I

Junkyard Arts, Inc., had earnings of $316,000 for 2016. The company had 40,000 shares of common stock outstanding during the year. In addition, the company issued 15,000 shares of $50 par value preferred stock on January 9, 2016. The preferred stock has a dividend of $1.60 per share. There were no transactions in either common or preferred stock during 2016.

Determine the basic earnings per share for Junkyard Arts.

EX 13-24 EPS **OBJ. 8**

F·A·I

Pacific Gas and Electric Company is a large gas and electric utility operating in northern and central California. Three recent years of financial data for Pacific Gas and Electric Company are as follows:

	Fiscal Years Ended (in millions)		
	Year 3	**Year 2**	**Year 1**
Net income	$830	$858	$1,113
Preferred dividends	$14	$14	$14
Average number of common shares outstanding	424	401	382

a. Determine the earnings per share for fiscal Year 3, Year 2, and Year 1. Round to the nearest cent.

b. Evaluate the growth in earnings per share for the three years in comparison to the growth in net income for the three years.

EX 13-25 EPS **OBJ. 8**

F·A·I

For a recent year, **OfficeMax** and **Staples** are two companies competing in the retail office supply business. OfficeMax had a net income of $34,894,000, while Staples had a net loss of $210,706,000. OfficeMax had preferred stock of $28,726,000 with preferred dividends of $2,123,000. Staples had no preferred stock. The average outstanding common shares for each company were as follows:

	Average Number of Common Shares Outstanding
OfficeMax	85,881,000
Staples	669,479,000

a. Determine the earnings per share for each company. Round to the nearest cent.

b. Evaluate the relative profitability of the two companies.

Problems: Series A

PR 13-1A Dividends on preferred and common stock

OBJ. 3

✔ 1. Common dividends in 2013: $36,000

SHOW ME HOW

Sunbird Theatre Inc. owns and operates movie theaters throughout Florida and Georgia. Sunbird Theatre Inc. has declared the following annual dividends over a six-year period: 2011, $20,000; 2012, $36,000; 2013, $70,000; 2014, $90,000; 2015, $100,000 and 2016, $150,000. During the entire period ended December 31 of each year, the outstanding stock of the company was composed of 100,000 shares of cumulative, preferred 1% stock, $30 par, and 400,000 shares of common stock, $20 par.

Instructions

1. Calculate the total dividends and the per-share dividends declared on each class of stock for each of the six years. There were no dividends in arrears on January 1, 2011. Summarize the data in tabular form, using the following column headings:

		Preferred Dividends		Common Dividends	
Year	Total Dividends	Total	Per Share	Total	Per Share
2011	$ 20,000				
2012	36,000				
2013	70,000				
2014	90,000				
2015	102,000				
2016	150,000				

2. Calculate the average annual dividend per share for each class of stock for the six-year period.
3. Assuming a market price per share of $37.50 for the preferred stock and $30.00 for the common stock, calculate the average annual percentage return on initial shareholders' investment, based on the average annual dividend per share (a) for preferred stock and (b) for common stock.

PR 13-2A Stock transactions for corporate expansion

OBJ. 3

General Ledger

On December 1 of the current year, the following accounts and their balances appear in the ledger of Latte Corp., a coffee processor:

Preferred 2% Stock, $50 par (250,000 shares authorized, 80,000 shares issued)	$ 4,000,000
Paid-In Capital in Excess of Par—Preferred Stock	560,000
Common Stock, $35 par (1,000,000 shares authorized, 400,000 shares issued)	14,000,000
Paid-In Capital in Excess of Par—Common Stock	1,200,000
Retained Earnings	180,000,000

At the annual stockholders' meeting on March 31, the board of directors presented a plan for modernizing and expanding plant operations at a cost of approximately $11,000,000. The plan provided (a) that a building, valued at $3,375,000, and the land on which it is located, valued at $1,500,000, be acquired in accordance with preliminary negotiations by the issuance of 125,000 shares of common stock, (b) that 40,000 shares of the unissued preferred stock be issued through an underwriter, and (c) that the corporation borrow $4,000,000. The plan was approved by the stockholders and accomplished by the following transactions:

May 11. Issued 125,000 shares of common stock in exchange for land and a building, according to the plan.

20. Issued 40,000 shares of preferred stock, receiving $52 per share in cash.

31. Borrowed $4,000,000 from Laurel National, giving a 5% mortgage note.

Instructions

Journalize the entries to record the May transactions.

✔ f. Cash dividends, $243,000

General Ledger

SHOW ME HOW

PR 13-3A Selected stock transactions

OBJ. 3, 4, 5

The following selected accounts appear in the ledger of EJ Construction Inc. at the beginning of the current fiscal year:

Preferred 1% Stock, $50 par (100,000 shares authorized, 80,000 shares issued)	$ 4,000,000
Paid-In Capital in Excess of Par—Preferred Stock	175,000
Common Stock, $3 par (5,000,000 shares authorized, 2,000,000 shares issued)	6,000,000
Paid-In Capital in Excess of Par—Common Stock	1,500,000
Retained Earnings	32,350,000

During the year, the corporation completed a number of transactions affecting the stockholders' equity. They are summarized as follows:

a. Issued 500,000 shares of common stock at $8, receiving cash.

b. Issued 10,000 shares of preferred 1% stock at $60.

c. Purchased 50,000 shares of treasury common for $7 per share.

d. Sold 20,000 shares of treasury common for $9 per share.

e. Sold 5,000 shares of treasury common for $6 per share.

f. Declared cash dividends of $0.50 per share on preferred stock and $0.08 per share on common stock.

g. Paid the cash dividends.

Instructions

Journalize the entries to record the transactions. Identify each entry by letter.

✔ 4. Total stockholders' equity, $44,436,200

General Ledger

PR 13-4A Entries for selected corporate transactions

OBJ. 3, 4, 5, 6

Morrow Enterprises Inc. manufactures bathroom fixtures. The stockholders' equity accounts of Morrow Enterprises Inc., with balances on January 1, 2016, are as follows:

Common Stock, $20 stated value (500,000 shares authorized, 375,000 shares issued)	$ 7,500,000
Paid-In Capital in Excess of Stated Value—Common Stock	825,000
Retained Earnings	33,600,000
Treasury Stock (25,000 shares, at cost)	450,000

The following selected transactions occurred during the year:

Jan. 22. Paid cash dividends of $0.08 per share on the common stock. The dividend had been properly recorded when declared on December 1 of the preceding fiscal year for $28,000.

Apr. 10. Issued 75,000 shares of common stock for $24 per share.

June 6. Sold all of the treasury stock for $26 per share.

July 5. Declared a 4% stock dividend on common stock, to be capitalized at the market price of the stock, which is $25 per share.

Aug. 15. Issued the certificates for the dividend declared on July 5.

Nov. 23. Purchased 30,000 shares of treasury stock for $19 per share.

Dec. 28. Declared a $0.10-per-share dividend on common stock.

31. Closed the credit balance of the income summary account, $1,125,000.

31. Closed the two dividends accounts to Retained Earnings.

(Continued)

Instructions

1. Enter the January 1 balances in T accounts for the stockholders' equity accounts listed. Also prepare T accounts for the following: Paid-In Capital from Sale of Treasury Stock; Stock Dividends Distributable; Stock Dividends; Cash Dividends.
2. Journalize the entries to record the transactions, and post to the eight selected accounts.
3. Prepare a retained earnings statement for the year ended December 31, 2016.
4. Prepare the Stockholders' Equity section of the December 31, 2016, balance sheet.

PR 13-5A Entries for selected corporate transactions — OBJ. 3, 4, 5, 7

✔ Oct. 1, cash dividends, $202,800

General Ledger

Selected transactions completed by Primo Discount Corporation during the current fiscal year are as follows:

Jan. 9. Split the common stock 3 for 1 and reduced the par from $75 to $25 per share. After the split, there were 1,200,000 common shares outstanding.

Feb. 28. Purchased 40,000 shares of the corporation's own common stock at $28, recording the stock at cost.

May 1. Declared semiannual dividends of $0.80 on 75,000 shares of preferred stock and $0.12 on the common stock to stockholders of record on June 1, payable on July 10.

July 10. Paid the cash dividends.

Sept. 7. Sold 30,000 shares of treasury stock at $34, receiving cash.

Oct. 1. Declared semiannual dividends of $0.80 on the preferred stock and $0.12 on the common stock (before the stock dividend). In addition, a 2% common stock dividend was declared on the common stock outstanding. The fair market value of the common stock is estimated at $36.

Dec. 1. Paid the cash dividends and issued the certificates for the common stock dividend.

Instructions

Journalize the transactions.

Problems: Series B

PR 13-1B Dividends on preferred and common stock — OBJ. 3

✔ 1. Common dividends in 2013: $25,000

SHOW ME HOW

Yosemite Bike Corp. manufactures mountain bikes and distributes them through retail outlets in California, Oregon, and Washington. Yosemite Bike Corp. has declared the following annual dividends over a six-year period ended December 31 of each year: 2011, $24,000; 2012, $10,000; 2013, $126,000; 2014, $100,000; 2015, $125,000; and 2016, $125,000. During the entire period, the outstanding stock of the company was composed of 25,000 shares of cumulative preferred 2% stock, $90 par, and 100,000 shares of common stock, $4 par.

Instructions

1. Determine the total dividends and the per-share dividends declared on each class of stock for each of the six years. There were no dividends in arrears on January 1, 2011. Summarize the data in tabular form, using the following column headings:

		Preferred Dividends		Common Dividends	
Year	**Total Dividends**	**Total**	**Per Share**	**Total**	**Per Share**
2011	$ 24,000				
2012	10,000				
2013	126,000				
2014	100,000				
2015	125,000				
2016	125,000				

2. Determine the average annual dividend per share for each class of stock for the six-year period.
3. Assuming a market price of $100 for the preferred stock and $5 for the common stock, calculate the average annual percentage return on initial shareholders' investment, based on the average annual dividend per share (a) for preferred stock and (b) for common stock.

PR 13-2B Stock transaction for corporate expansion **OBJ. 3**

General Ledger

Pulsar Optics produces medical lasers for use in hospitals. The accounts and their balances appear in the ledger of Pulsar Optics on April 30 of the current year as follows:

Preferred 1% Stock, $120 par (300,000 shares authorized, 36,000 shares issued)	$ 4,320,000
Paid-In Capital in Excess of Par—Preferred Stock	180,000
Common Stock, $15 par (2,000,000 shares authorized, 1,400,000 shares issued)	21,000,000
Paid-In Capital in Excess of Par—Common Stock	3,500,000
Retained Earnings	78,000,000

At the annual stockholders' meeting on August 5, the board of directors presented a plan for modernizing and expanding plant operations at a cost of approximately $9,000,000. The plan provided (a) that the corporation borrow $1,500,000, (b) that 20,000 shares of the unissued preferred stock be issued through an underwriter, and (c) that a building, valued at $4,150,000, and the land on which it is located, valued at $800,000, be acquired in accordance with preliminary negotiations by the issuance of 300,000 shares of common stock. The plan was approved by the stockholders and accomplished by the following transactions:

Oct. 9. Borrowed $1,500,000 from St. Peter City Bank, giving a 4% mortgage note.
17. Issued 20,000 shares of preferred stock, receiving $126 per share in cash.
28. Issued 300,000 shares of common stock in exchange for land and a building, according to the plan.

Instructions

Journalize the entries to record the October transactions.

PR 13-3B Selected stock transactions **OBJ. 3, 4, 5**

✔ f. Cash dividends, $234,775

General Ledger

SHOW ME HOW

Diamondback Welding & Fabrication Corporation sells and services pipe welding equipment in Illinois. The following selected accounts appear in the ledger of Diamondback Welding & Fabrication Corporation at the beginning of the current fiscal year:

Preferred 2% Stock, $80 par (100,000 shares authorized, 60,000 shares issued)	$ 4,800,000
Paid-In Capital in Excess of Par—Preferred Stock	210,000
Common Stock, $9 par (3,000,000 shares authorized, 1,750,000 shares issued)	15,750,000
Paid-In Capital in Excess of Par—Common Stock	1,400,000
Retained Earnings	52,840,000

During the year, the corporation completed a number of transactions affecting the stockholders' equity. They are summarized as follows:

a. Purchased 87,500 shares of treasury common for $8 per share.
b. Sold 55,000 shares of treasury common for $11 per share.
c. Issued 20,000 shares of preferred 2% stock at $84.
d. Issued 400,000 shares of common stock at $13, receiving cash.

(Continued)

e. Sold 18,000 shares of treasury common for $7.50 per share.

f. Declared cash dividends of $1.60 per share on preferred stock and $0.05 per share on common stock.

g. Paid the cash dividends.

Instructions

Journalize the entries to record the transactions. Identify each entry by letter.

PR 13-4B Entries for selected corporate transactions — OBJ. 3, 4, 5, 6

✔ 4. Total stockholders' equity, $11,262,432

General Ledger

Nav-Go Enterprises Inc. produces aeronautical navigation equipment. The stockholders' equity accounts of Nav-Go Enterprises Inc., with balances on January 1, 2016, are as follows:

Common Stock, $5 stated value (900,000 shares authorized, 620,000 shares issued)	$3,100,000
Paid-In Capital in Excess of Stated Value—Common Stock	1,240,000
Retained Earnings	4,875,000
Treasury Stock (48,000 shares, at cost)	288,000

The following selected transactions occurred during the year:

Jan. 15. Paid cash dividends of $0.06 per share on the common stock. The dividend had been properly recorded when declared on December 1 of the preceding fiscal year for $34,320.

Mar. 15. Sold all of the treasury stock for $6.75 per share.

Apr. 13. Issued 200,000 shares of common stock for $8 per share.

June 14. Declared a 3% stock dividend on common stock, to be capitalized at the market price of the stock, which is $7.50 per share.

July 16. Issued the certificates for the dividend declared on June 14.

Oct. 30. Purchased 50,000 shares of treasury stock for $6 per share.

Dec. 30. Declared a $0.08-per-share dividend on common stock.

31. Closed the credit balance of the income summary account, $775,000.

31. Closed the two dividends accounts to Retained Earnings.

Instructions

1. Enter the January 1 balances in T accounts for the stockholders' equity accounts listed. Also prepare T accounts for the following: Paid-In Capital from Sale of Treasury Stock; Stock Dividends Distributable; Stock Dividends; Cash Dividends.
2. Journalize the entries to record the transactions, and post to the eight selected accounts.
3. Prepare a retained earnings statement for the year ended December 31, 2016.
4. Prepare the Stockholders' Equity section of the December 31, 2016, balance sheet.

PR 13-5B Entries for selected corporate transactions — OBJ. 3, 4, 5, 7

✔ Sept. 1, Cash dividends, $95,200

General Ledger

West Yellowstone Outfitters Corporation manufactures and distributes leisure clothing. Selected transactions completed by West Yellowstone Outfitters during the current fiscal year are as follows:

Jan. 15. Split the common stock 4 for 1 and reduced the par from $120 to $30 per share. After the split, there were 800,000 common shares outstanding.

Mar. 1. Declared semiannual dividends of $0.25 on 100,000 shares of preferred stock and $0.07 on the 800,000 shares of $30 par common stock to stockholders of record on March 31, payable on April 30.

Apr. 30. Paid the cash dividends.

May 31. Purchased 60,000 shares of the corporation's own common stock at $32, recording the stock at cost.

Aug. 17. Sold 40,000 shares of treasury stock at $38, receiving cash.

Sept. 1. Declared semiannual dividends of $0.25 on the preferred stock and $0.09 on the common stock (before the stock dividend). In addition, a 1% common stock dividend was declared on the common stock outstanding, to be capitalized at the fair market value of the common stock, which is estimated at $40.

Oct. 31. Paid the cash dividends and issued the certificates for the common stock dividend.

Instructions

Journalize the transactions.

Cases & Projects

CP 13-1 Board of directors' actions

Bernie Ebbers, the CEO of WorldCom, a major telecommunications company, was having personal financial troubles. Ebbers pledged a large stake of his WorldCom stock as security for some personal loans. As the price of WorldCom stock sank, Ebbers' bankers threatened to sell his stock in order to protect their loans. To avoid having his stock sold, Ebbers asked the board of directors of WorldCom to loan him nearly $400 million of corporate assets at 2.5% interest to pay off his bankers. The board agreed to lend him the money.

Comment on the decision of the board of directors in this situation.

CP 13-2 Ethics and professional conduct in business

Lou Hoskins and Shirley Crothers are organizing Red Lodge Metals Unlimited Inc. to undertake a high-risk gold-mining venture in Canada. Lou and Shirley tentatively plan to request authorization for 400,000,000 shares of common stock to be sold to the general public. Lou and Shirley have decided to establish par of $0.03 per share in order to appeal to a wide variety of potential investors. Lou and Shirley feel that investors would be more willing to invest in the company if they received a large quantity of shares for what might appear to be a "bargain" price.

Discuss whether Lou and Shirley are behaving in a professional manner.

CP 13-3 Issuing stock

Epstein Engineering Inc. began operations on January 5, 2016, with the issuance of 500,000 shares of $80 par common stock. The sole stockholders of Epstein Engineering Inc. are Barb Abrams and Dr. Amber Epstein, who organized Epstein Engineering Inc.

(Continued)

with the objective of developing a new flu vaccine. Dr. Epstein claims that the flu vaccine, which is nearing the final development stage, will protect individuals against 90% of the flu types that have been medically identified. To complete the project, Epstein Engineering Inc. needs $25,000,000 of additional funds. The local banks have been unwilling to loan the funds because of the lack of sufficient collateral and the riskiness of the business.

The following is a conversation between Barb Abrams, the chief executive officer of Epstein Engineering Inc., and Amber Epstein, the leading researcher:

Barb: What are we going to do? The banks won't loan us any more money, and we've got to have $25 million to complete the project. We are so close! It would be a disaster to quit now. The only thing I can think of is to issue additional stock. Do you have any suggestions?

Amber: I guess you're right. But if the banks won't loan us any more money, how do you think we can find any investors to buy stock?

Barb: I've been thinking about that. What if we promise the investors that we will pay them 5% of sales until they have received an amount equal to what they paid for the stock?

Amber: What happens when we pay back the $25 million? Do the investors get to keep the stock? If they do, it'll dilute our ownership.

Barb: How about, if after we pay back the $25 million, we make them turn in their stock for $120 per share? That's one and one-half times what they paid for it, plus they would have already gotten all their money back. That's a $120 profit per share for the investors.

Amber: It could work. We get our money, but don't have to pay any interest, dividends, or the $80 per share until we start generating sales. At the same time, the investors could get their money back plus $120 per share profit.

Barb: We'll need current financial statements for the new investors. I'll get our accountant working on them and contact our attorney to draw up a legally binding contract for the new investors. Yes, this could work.

In late 2016, the attorney and the various regulatory authorities approved the new stock offering, and 312,500 shares of common stock were privately sold to new investors at the stock's par of $80.

In preparing financial statements for 2016, Barb Abrams and Dan Fisher, the controller for Epstein Engineering Inc., have the following conversation:

Dan: Barb, I've got a problem.

Barb: What's that, Dan?

Dan: Issuing common stock to raise that additional $25 million was a great idea. But . . .

Barb: But what?

Dan: I've got to prepare the 2016 annual financial statements, and I am not sure how to classify the common stock.

Barb: What do you mean? It's common stock.

Dan: I'm not so sure. I called the auditor and explained how we are contractually obligated to pay the new stockholders 5% of sales until $80 per share is paid. Then, we may be obligated to pay them $120 per share.

Barb: So . . .

Dan: So the auditor thinks that we should classify the additional issuance of $25 million as debt, not stock! And, if we put the $25 million on the balance sheet as debt, we will violate our other loan agreements with the banks. And, if these agreements are violated, the banks may call in all our debt immediately. If they do that, we are in deep trouble. We'll probably have to file for bankruptcy. We just don't have the cash to pay off the banks.

1. Discuss the arguments for and against classifying the issuance of the $25 million of stock as debt.
2. What do you think might be a practical solution to this classification problem?

CP 13-4 Interpret stock exchange listing

F·A·I

The following stock exchange data for Microsoft Corporation were taken from the Yahoo! Finance Web site on November 29, 2013:

Microsoft Corporation (MSFT)

Last Trade:	38.13	Prev. Clos:	37.60
Trade Time:	1:00 PM EST	1y Target Est:	36.32
		Day's Range:	37.82–38.29
		52wk Range:	26.26–38.29
		Volume:	22,090,428
		Div & Yield:	1.12 (3.00%)

a. If you owned 500 shares of Mircosoft, what amount would you receive as a quarterly dividend?

b. Compute the percentage increase in price from the Previous Close to the Last Trade. Round to two decimal places.

c. What is Microsoft's percentage change in market price from the 52-week low to the Last Trade on November 29, 2013? Round to one decimal place.

d. If you bought 500 shares of Microsoft at the Last Trade price on November 29, 2013, how much would it cost, and who gets the money?

CP 13-5 Dividends

Motion Designs Inc. has paid quarterly cash dividends since 2005. These dividends have steadily increased from $0.05 per share to the latest dividend declaration of $0.50 per share. The board of directors would like to continue this trend and is hesitant to suspend or decrease the amount of quarterly dividends. Unfortunately, sales dropped sharply in the fourth quarter of 2016 because of worsening economic conditions and increased competition. As a result, the board is uncertain as to whether it should declare a dividend for the last quarter of 2016.

On October 1, 2016, Motion Designs Inc. borrowed $4,000,000 from Valley National Bank to use in modernizing its retail stores and to expand its product line in reaction to its competition. The terms of the 10-year, 6% loan require Motion Designs Inc. to:

a. Pay monthly interest on the last day of the month.

b. Pay $400,000 of the principal each October 1, beginning in 2017.

c. Maintain a current ratio (current assets ÷ current liabilities) of 2.

d. Maintain a minimum balance (a compensating balance) of $100,000 in its Valley National Bank account.

(Continued)

On December 31, 2016, $1,000,000 of the $4,000,000 loan had been disbursed in modernization of the retail stores and in expansion of the product line. Motion Designs Inc.'s balance sheet as of December 31, 2016, follows:

Motion Designs Inc.
Balance Sheet
December 31, 2016

Assets			
Current assets:			
Cash		$ 250,000	
Marketable securities		3,000,000	
Accounts receivable	$ 800,000		
Less allowance for doubtful accounts	50,000	750,000	
Merchandise inventory		2,980,000	
Prepaid expenses		20,000	
Total current assets			$ 7,000,000
Property, plant, and equipment:			
Land		$1,500,000	
Buildings	$5,050,000		
Less accumulated depreciation	1,140,000	3,910,000	
Equipment	$3,320,000		
Less accumulated depreciation	730,000	2,590,000	
Total property, plant, and equipment			8,000,000
Total assets			$15,000,000
Liabilities			
Current liabilities:			
Accounts payable	$ 1,590,000		
Notes payable (Valley National Bank)	400,000		
Salaries payable	10,000		
Total current liabilities		$2,000,000	
Long-term liabilities:			
Notes payable (Valley National Bank)		3,600,000	
Total liabilities			$ 5,600,000
Stockholders' Equity			
Paid-in capital:			
Common stock, $25 par (200,000 shares authorized, 180,000 shares issued)	$ 4,500,000		
Excess of issue price over par	270,000		
Total paid-in capital		$4,770,000	
Retained earnings		4,630,000	
Total stockholders' equity			9,400,000
Total liabilities and stockholders' equity			$15,000,000

The board of directors is scheduled to meet January 10, 2017, to discuss the results of operations for 2016 and to consider the declaration of dividends for the fourth quarter of 2016. The chairman of the board has asked for your advice on the declaration of dividends.

1. What factors should the board consider in deciding whether to declare a cash dividend?
2. The board is considering the declaration of a stock dividend instead of a cash dividend. Discuss the issuance of a stock dividend from the point of view of (a) a stockholder and (b) the board of directors.

CP 13-6 Profiling a corporation

Group Project

Internet Project

Select a public corporation you are familiar with or which interests you. Using the Internet, develop a short (1 to 2 pages) profile of the corporation. Include in your profile the following information:

1. Name of the corporation.
2. State of incorporation.
3. Nature of its operations.
4. Total assets for the most recent balance sheet.
5. Total revenues for the most recent income statement.
6. Net income for the most recent income statement.
7. Classes of stock outstanding.
8. Market price of the stock outstanding.
9. High and low price of the stock for the past year.
10. Cash dividends paid for each share of stock during the past year.

In groups of three or four, discuss each corporate profile. Select one of the corporations, assuming that your group has $100,000 to invest in its stock. Summarize why your group selected the corporation it did and how financial accounting information may have affected your decision. Keep track of the performance of your corporation's stock for the remainder of the term.

Note: Most major corporations maintain "home pages" on the Internet. This home page provides a variety of information on the corporation and often includes the corporation's financial statements. In addition, the New York Stock Exchange Web site (www.nyse.com) includes links to the home pages of many listed companies that can be assessed by clicking on "Listings Directory." Financial statements can also be accessed using EDGAR, the electronic archives of financial statements filed with the Securities and Exchange Commission (SEC).

SEC documents can also be retrieved using the EdgarScan™ service at www.sec.gov/edgar/searchedgar/companysearch.html. To obtain annual report information, key in a company name in the appropriate space. Edgar will list the reports available to you for the company you've selected. Select the most recent annual report filing, identified as a 10-K or 10-K405.

CHAPTER 14

Long-Term Liabilities: Bonds and Notes

Dick's Sporting Goods

Most of us don't have enough money in our bank accounts to buy a house or a car by simply writing a check. Just imagine if you had to save the entire purchase price of a house before you could buy it! To help us make these types of purchases, banks will typically lend us the money, as long as we agree to repay the loan with interest in smaller future payments. Loans such as this, or long-term debt, allow us to purchase assets such as houses and cars today, which benefit us over the long term.

The use of debt can also help a business reach its objectives. Most businesses have to borrow money in order to acquire assets that they will use to generate income. For example, in 1948 Dick Stack borrowed $300 from his grandmother to start a sporting goods store in Binghamton, New York. Over the years the business grew, and in the early 1990s, **Dick's Sporting Goods** used long-term debt to transform itself from a small business to a Fortune 500 company with more than 450 stores across the United States.

While debt can help companies like Dick's Sporting Goods grow to achieve financial success, too much debt can be a financial burden that may even lead to bankruptcy. Just like individuals, businesses must manage debt wisely. In this chapter, we will discuss the nature of, accounting for, and analysis of, long-term debt.

Learning Objectives

After studying this chapter, you should be able to: | *Example Exercises*

OBJ	Objective	Example Exercises
1	**Compute the potential impact of long-term borrowing on earnings per share.** Financing Corporations	EE 14-1
2	**Describe the characteristics and terminology of bonds payable.** Nature of Bonds Payable Bond Characteristics and Terminology Proceeds from Issuing Bonds	
3	**Journalize entries for bonds payable.** Accounting for Bonds Payable Bonds Issued at Face Amount Bonds Issued at a Discount Amortizing a Bond Discount Bonds Issued at a Premium Amortizing a Bond Premium Bond Redemption	 EE 14-2 EE 14-3 EE 14-4 EE 14-5 EE 14-6 EE 14-7
4	**Describe and illustrate the accounting for installment notes.** Installment Notes Issuing an Installment Note Annual Payments	 EE 14-8
5	**Describe and illustrate the reporting of long-term liabilities, including bonds and notes payable.** Reporting Long-Term Liabilities	
6	**Describe and illustrate how the number of times interest charges are earned is used to evaluate a company's financial condition.** Financial Analysis and Interpretation: Number of Times Interest Charges Are Earned	EE 14-9

At a Glance 14 Page 664

OBJ 1 Compute the potential impact of long-term borrowing on earnings per share.

Financing Corporations

Corporations finance their operations using the following sources:

- Short-term debt, such as purchasing goods or services on account.
- Long-term debt, such as issuing bonds or notes payable.
- Equity, such as issuing common or preferred stock.

Short-term debt, including the purchase of goods and services on account and the issuance of short-term notes payable, was discussed in Chapter 11. Issuing equity in the form of common or preferred stock was discussed in Chapter 13. This chapter focuses on the use of long-term debt such as bonds and notes payable to finance a company's operations.

A **bond** is a form of an interest-bearing note. Like a note, a bond requires periodic interest payments, with the face amount to be repaid at the maturity date. For example, a 12% bond requires the company issuing the bond to pay 12% interest on the face amount of the bonds every year. As creditors of the corporation, bondholder claims on the corporation's assets rank ahead of stockholders.

One of the main factors that influences the decision to issue debt or equity is the effect that various financing alternatives will have on earnings per share. **Earnings per share (EPS)** measures the income earned by each share of common stock. It is computed as follows:[1]

$$\text{Earnings per Share} = \frac{\text{Net Income} - \text{Preferred Dividends}}{\text{Number of Common Shares Outstanding}}$$

[1] Earnings per share is also discussed in the *Financial Analysis and Interpretation* section of Chapter 13 and in Chapter 17.

To illustrate the effects that issuing debt can have on earnings per share, consider the following alternative plans for financing Boz Corporation, a $4,000,000 company:

	Plan 1		Plan 2		Plan 3	
	Amount	**Percent**	**Amount**	**Percent**	**Amount**	**Percent**
Issue 12% bonds	—	0%	—	0%	$2,000,000	50%
Issue preferred 9% stock, $50 par value	—	0	$2,000,000	50	1,000,000	25
Issue common stock, $10 par value	$4,000,000	100	2,000,000	50	1,000,000	25
Total amount of financing	$4,000,000	100%	$4,000,000	100%	$4,000,000	100%

The company must choose one of these plans. Each plan finances some of the corporation's operations by issuing common stock. However, the percentage financed by common stock varies from 100% (Plan 1) to 25% (Plan 3).

Assume the following data for Boz Corporation:

- Earnings before interest and income taxes are $800,000.
- The tax rate is 40%.
- All bonds or stocks are issued at their par or face amount.

The effect of the preceding financing plans on Boz's net income and earnings per share is shown in Exhibit 1.

EXHIBIT 1

Effect of Alternative Financing Plans—$800,000 Earnings

Dynamic Exhibit

	Plan 1	Plan 2	Plan 3
12% bonds	—	—	$2,000,000
Preferred 9% stock, $50 par	—	$2,000,000	1,000,000
Common stock, $10 par	$4,000,000	2,000,000	1,000,000
Total	$4,000,000	$4,000,000	$4,000,000
Earnings before interest and income tax	$ 800,000	$ 800,000	$ 800,000
Deduct interest on bonds	—	—	240,000[a]
Income before income tax	$ 800,000	$ 800,000	$ 560,000
Deduct income tax	320,000[b]	320,000[b]	224,000[b]
Net income	$ 480,000	$ 480,000	$ 336,000
Dividends on preferred stock	—	180,000[c]	90,000[c]
Available for dividends on common stock	$ 480,000	$ 300,000	$ 246,000
Shares of common stock outstanding	÷ 400,000[d]	÷ 200,000[d]	÷ 100,000[d]
Earnings per share on common stock	$ 1.20	$ 1.50	$ 2.46

[a] $2,000,000 bonds × 12%
[b] Income before income tax × 40%
[c] Preferred stock × 9%
[d] Common stock ÷ $10 par value per share

Exhibit 1 indicates that when earnings are strong, Plan 3 has the highest earnings per share, making it the most attractive for common shareholders. This is because the company is generating more than enough net income to cover the bond interest. If the estimated earnings are more than $800,000, the difference between the earnings per share to common stockholders under Plans 1 and 3 is even greater.[2]

Lower earnings, however, have the opposite effect. If earnings are reduced to $440,000, as illustrated in Exhibit 2, Plans 1 and 2 become more attractive to common stockholders. This is because more of the company's earnings are being used to pay bond interest, leaving less net income attributable to common stockholders.

[2] The higher earnings per share under Plan 3 is due to a finance concept known as *leverage*. This concept is discussed further in Chapter 17.

EXHIBIT 2

Effect of Alternative Financing Plans—$440,000 Earnings

Dynamic Exhibit

	Plan 1	Plan 2	Plan 3
12% bonds	—	—	$2,000,000
Preferred 9% stock, $50 par	—	$2,000,000	1,000,000
Common stock, $10 par	$4,000,000	2,000,000	1,000,000
Total	$4,000,000	$4,000,000	$4,000,000
Earnings before interest and income tax	$ 440,000	$ 440,000	$ 440,000
Deduct interest on bonds	—	—	240,000
Income before income tax	$ 440,000	$ 440,000	$ 200,000
Deduct income tax	176,000	176,000	80,000
Net income	$ 264,000	$ 264,000	$ 120,000
Dividends on preferred stock	—	180,000	90,000
Available for dividends on common stock	$ 264,000	$ 84,000	$ 30,000
Shares of common stock outstanding	÷ 400,000	÷ 200,000	÷ 100,000
Earnings per share on common stock	$ 0.66	$ 0.42	$ 0.30

In addition to earnings per share, the corporation should consider other factors in deciding among the financing plans. For example, if bonds are issued, the interest and the face value of the bonds at maturity must be paid. If these payments are not made, the bondholders could seek court action and force the company into bankruptcy. In contrast, a corporation is not legally obligated to pay dividends on preferred or common stock.

Example Exercise 14-1 Alternative Financing Plans

OBJ 1

Gonzales Co. is considering the following alternative plans for financing its company:

	Plan 1	Plan 2
Issue 10% bonds (at face value)	—	$2,000,000
Issue common stock, $10 par	$3,000,000	1,000,000

Income tax is estimated at 40% of income.

Determine the earnings per share of common stock under the two alternative financing plans, assuming income before bond interest and income tax is $750,000.

Follow My Example 14-1

	Plan 1	Plan 2
Earnings before bond interest and income tax	$750,000	$750,000
Deduct interest on bonds	0	200,000[2]
Income before income tax	$750,000	$550,000
Deduct income tax	300,000[1]	220,000[3]
Net income	$450,000	$330,000
Dividends on preferred stock	0	0
Available for dividends on common stock	$450,000	$330,000
Shares of common stock outstanding	÷300,000	÷100,000
Earnings per share on common stock	$ 1.50	$ 3.30

[1]$750,000 × 40% [2]$2,000,000 × 10% [3]$550,000 × 40%

Practice Exercises: PE 14-1A, PE 14-1B

OBJ 2 Describe the characteristics and terminology of bonds payable.

Nature of Bonds Payable

Corporate bonds normally differ in face amount, interest rates, interest payment dates, and maturity dates. Bonds also differ in other ways such as whether corporate assets are pledged in support of the bonds.

Bond Characteristics and Terminology

A bond issue is normally divided into a number of individual bonds. The face amount of each bond is called the *principal*. This is the amount that must be repaid on the dates the bonds mature. The principal is usually $1,000, or a multiple of $1,000. The interest on bonds may be payable annually, semiannually, or quarterly. Most bonds pay interest semiannually.

The underlying contract between the company issuing bonds and the bondholders is called a **bond indenture**. This contract can be written in different ways, depending on the financing needs of the company. The two most common types of bonds are term bonds and serial bonds. When all bonds of an issue mature at the same time, they are called *term bonds*. If the bonds mature over several dates, they are called *serial bonds*. For example, one-tenth of an issue of $1,000,000 bonds, or $100,000, may mature 16 years from the issue date, another $100,000 in the 17th year, and so on.

There are also a variety of more complicated bond structures. For example, *convertible bonds* may be exchanged for shares of common stock, and *callable bonds* may be redeemed by the corporation prior to maturity. These bonds are discussed in intermediate and advanced accounting texts.

Proceeds from Issuing Bonds

When a corporation issues bonds, the proceeds received for the bonds depend on:

- The face amount of the bonds, which is the amount due at the maturity date.
- The interest rate on the bonds.
- The market rate of interest for similar bonds.

The face amount and the interest rate on the bonds are identified in the bond indenture. The interest rate to be paid on the face amount of the bond is called the **contract rate** or *coupon rate*.

The **market rate of interest**, sometimes called the **effective rate of interest**, is the rate determined from sales and purchases of similar bonds. The market rate of interest is affected by a variety of factors, including investors' expectations of current and future economic conditions.

By comparing the market and contract rates of interest, it can be determined whether the bonds will sell for more than, less than, or at their face amount, as shown in Exhibit 3.

EXHIBIT 3 **Issuing Bonds at a Discount, at Face Amount, and at a Premium**

If: Market Rate > Contract Rate

Less than $1,000

Then: Selling Price < Face Amount

Sold at a DISCOUNT

If: Market Rate = Contract Rate

$1,000

Then: Selling Price = Face Amount

Sold at FACE AMOUNT

If: Market Rate < Contract Rate

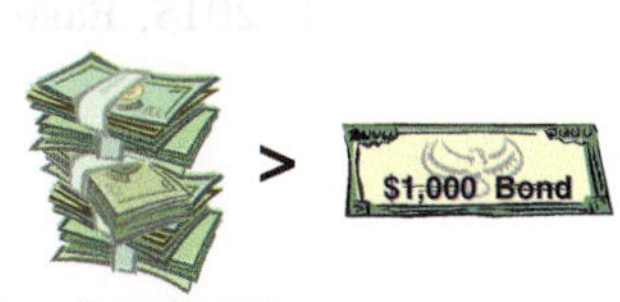

More than $1,000

Then: Selling Price > Face Amount

Sold at a PREMIUM

If the market rate equals the contract rate, bonds will sell at the **face amount**.

If the market rate is greater than the contract rate, the bonds will sell for less than their face value. The face amount of the bonds less the selling price is called a **discount**. A bond sells at a discount because buyers are not willing to pay the full face amount for bonds with a contract rate that is lower than the market rate.

Dow Chemical Company's 9.00% bonds, maturing in 2021, sold for 129.97 on February 26, 2013.

If the market rate is less than the contract rate, the bonds will sell for more than their face value. The selling price of the bonds less the face amount is called a **premium**. A bond sells at a premium because buyers are willing to pay more than the face amount for bonds with a contract rate that is higher than the market rate.

The price of a bond is quoted as a percentage of the bond's face value. For example, a $1,000 bond quoted at 98 could be purchased or sold for $980 ($1,000 × 0.98). Likewise, bonds quoted at 109 could be purchased or sold for $1,090 ($1,000 × 1.09).

Business Connection

U.S. GOVERNMENT DEBT

Like many corporations, the U.S. government issues debt to finance its operations. The debt is issued by the U.S. Treasury Department in the form of U.S. Treasury bills, notes, and bonds, which have the following characteristics:

	Issued at	Interest Paid	Maturity
U.S. Treasury bills	Discount	None	1 year or less
U.S. Treasury notes	Face value	Semiannual	1 to 10 years
U.S. Treasury bonds	Face value	Semiannual	10 years or more

At the end of 2013, total U.S. government debt issued by the federal government was estimated to be $17,548 billion. The Congressional Budget Office estimated that this amount would grow to $21,325 billion by 2017.

Source: Historical Tables: Budget of the U.S. Government, Fiscal Year 2013, U.S. Office of Management and Budget.

OBJ 3 Journalize entries for bonds payable.

Accounting for Bonds Payable

Bonds may be issued at their face amount, a discount, or a premium. When bonds are issued at less or more than their face amount, the discount or premium must be amortized over the life of the bonds. At the maturity date, the face amount must be repaid. In some situations, a corporation may redeem bonds before their maturity date by repurchasing them from investors.

Bonds Issued at Face Amount

If the market rate of interest is equal to the contract rate of interest, the bonds will sell for their face amount or at a price of 100. To illustrate, assume that on January 1, 2015, Eastern Montana Communications Inc. issued the following bonds:

Face amount	$100,000
Contract rate of interest	12%
Interest paid semiannually on June 30 and December 31.	
Term of bonds	5 years
Market rate of interest	12%

Since the contract rate of interest and the market rate of interest are the same, the bonds will sell at their face amount. The entry to record the issuance of the bonds is as follows:

Date		Description	Post. Ref.	Debit	Credit
2015 Jan.	1	Cash		100,000	
		Bonds Payable			100,000
		Issued $100,000 bonds payable at face amount.			

Every six months (on June 30 and December 31) after the bonds are issued, interest of $6,000 ($100,000 × 12% × ½ year) is paid. The first interest payment on June 30, 2015, is recorded as follows:

2015				
June	30	Interest Expense	6,000	
		Cash		6,000
		Paid six months' interest on bonds.		

At the maturity date, the payment of the principal of $100,000 is recorded as follows:

2019				
Dec.	31	Bonds Payable	100,000	
		Cash		100,000
		Paid bond principal at maturity date.		

Example Exercise 14-2 Issuing Bonds at Face Amount

OBJ 3

On January 1, the first day of the fiscal year, a company issues a $1,000,000, 6%, five-year bond that pays semiannual interest of $30,000 ($1,000,000 × 6% × ½ year), receiving cash of $1,000,000. Journalize the entries to record (a) the issuance of the bonds at their face amount, (b) the first interest payment on June 30, and (c) the payment of the principal on the maturity date.

Follow My Example 14-2

a.		
Cash	1,000,000	
Bonds Payable		1,000,000
b.		
Interest Expense	30,000	
Cash		30,000
c.		
Bonds Payable	1,000,000	
Cash		1,000,000

Practice Exercises: PE 14-2A, PE 14-2B

Bonds Issued at a Discount

If the market rate of interest is greater than the contract rate of interest, the bonds will sell for less than their face amount. This is because investors are not willing to pay the full face amount for bonds that pay a lower contract rate of interest than the rate they could earn on similar bonds (market rate). The difference between the face amount and the selling price of the bonds is the bond discount.[3]

Note:

Bonds will sell at a discount when the market rate of interest is higher than the contract rate.

To illustrate, assume that on January 1, 2015, Western Wyoming Distribution Inc. issued the following bonds:

Face amount	$100,000
Contract rate of interest	12%
Interest paid semiannually on June 30 and December 31.	
Term of bonds	5 years
Market rate of interest	13%

[3] The price that investors are willing to pay for the bonds depends on present value concepts. Present value concepts, including the computation of bond prices, are described and illustrated in Appendix 1 at the end of this chapter.

Because the contract rate of interest is less than the market rate of interest, the bonds will sell at less than their face amount. Assuming the bonds sell for $96,406, the entry to record the issuance of the bonds is as follows:

2015 Jan.	1	Cash		96,406	
		Discount on Bonds Payable		3,594	
		Bonds Payable			100,000
		Issued $100,000 bonds at discount.			

The $96,406 is the amount investors are willing to pay for bonds that have a lower contract rate of interest (12%) than the market rate (13%). The discount is the market's way of adjusting the contract rate of interest to the higher market rate of interest.

The account, Discount on Bonds Payable, is a contra account to Bonds Payable and has a normal debit balance. It is subtracted from Bonds Payable to determine the carrying amount (or book value) of the bonds payable. The **carrying amount** of bonds payable is the face amount of the bonds less any unamortized discount or plus any unamortized premium. Thus, after the preceding entry, the carrying amount of the bonds payable is $96,406 ($100,000 − $3,594).

Example Exercise 14-3 Issuing Bonds at a Discount

OBJ 3

On the first day of the fiscal year, a company issues a $1,000,000, 6%, five-year bond that pays semiannual interest of $30,000 ($1,000,000 × 6% × ½), receiving cash of $936,420. Journalize the entry to record the issuance of the bonds.

Follow My Example 14-3

Cash	936,420	
Discount on Bonds Payable	63,580	
Bonds Payable		1,000,000

Practice Exercises: PE 14-3A, PE 14-3B

Amortizing a Bond Discount

Every period, a portion of the bond discount must be reduced and added to interest expense to reflect the passage of time. This process, called **amortization**, increases the contract rate of interest on a bond to the market rate of interest that existed on the date the bonds were issued. The entry to amortize a bond discount is as follows:

		Interest Expense		XXX	
		Discount on Bonds Payable			XXX

The preceding entry may be made annually as an adjusting entry, or it may be combined with the semiannual interest payment. In the latter case, the entry would be as follows:

		Interest Expense		XXX	
		Discount on Bonds Payable			XXX
		Cash (amount of semiannual interest)			XXX

The two methods of computing the amortization of a bond discount are:

- *Straight-line method*
- *Effective interest rate method,* sometimes called the *interest method*

The **effective interest rate method** is required by generally accepted accounting principles. However, the straight-line method may be used if the results do not differ significantly from the interest method. The straight-line method is used in this chapter. The effective interest rate method is described and illustrated in Appendix 2 at the end of this chapter.

The straight-line method provides equal amounts of amortization each period. To illustrate, amortization of the Western Wyoming Distribution bond discount of $3,594 is computed as follows:

Discount on bonds payable	$3,594
Term of bonds	5 years
Semiannual amortization	$359.40 ($3,594 ÷ 10 periods)

The combined entry to record the first interest payment and the amortization of the discount is as follows:

2015					
June	30	Interest Expense		6,359.40	
		Discount on Bonds Payable			359.40
		Cash			6,000.00
		Paid semiannual interest and amortized 1/10 of bond discount.			

The preceding entry is made on each interest payment date. Thus, the amount of the semiannual interest expense on the bonds ($6,359.40) remains the same over the life of the bonds.

The effect of the discount amortization is to increase the interest expense from $6,000.00 to $6,359.40 on every semiannual interest payment date. In effect, this increases the contract rate of interest from 12% to a rate of interest that approximates the market rate of 13%. In addition, as the discount is amortized, the carrying amount of the bonds increases until it equals the face amount of the bonds on the maturity date.

Example Exercise 14-4 Discount Amortization

OBJ 3

Using the bond from Example Exercise 14-3, journalize the first interest payment and the amortization of the related bond discount.

Follow My Example 14-4

Interest Expense	36,358	
Discount on Bonds Payable		6,358
Cash		30,000
Paid interest and amortized the bond discount ($63,580 ÷ 10).		

Practice Exercises: PE 14-4A, PE 14-4B

Bonds Issued at a Premium

If the market rate of interest is less than the contract rate of interest, the bonds will sell for more than their face amount. This is because investors are willing to pay more for bonds that pay a higher contract rate of interest than the rate they could earn on similar bonds (market rate).

Note:
Bonds will sell at a premium when the market rate of interest is less than the contract rate.

To illustrate, assume that on January 1, 2015, Northern Idaho Transportation Inc. issued the following bonds:

Face amount	$100,000
Contract rate of interest	12%
Interest paid semiannually on June 30 and December 31.	
Term of bonds	5 years
Market rate of interest	11%

Because the contract rate of interest is more than the market rate of interest, the bonds will sell for more than their face amount. Assuming the bonds sell for $103,769, the entry to record the issuance of the bonds is as follows:

2015				
Jan.	1	Cash	103,769	
		Bonds Payable		100,000
		Premium on Bonds Payable		3,769
		Issued $100,000 bonds at a premium.		

The $3,769 premium is the extra amount investors are willing to pay for bonds that have a higher contract rate of interest (12%) than the market rate (11%). The premium is the market's way of adjusting the contract rate of interest to the lower market rate of interest.

The account, Premium on Bonds Payable, has a normal credit balance. It is added to Bonds Payable to determine the carrying amount (or book value) of the bonds payable. Thus, after the preceding entry, the carrying amount of the bonds payable is $103,769 ($100,000 + $3,769).

Example Exercise 14-5 Issuing Bonds at a Premium

OBJ 3

On the first day of the fiscal year, a company issues a $2,000,000, 12%, five-year bond that pays semiannual interest of $120,000 ($2,000,000 × 12% × ½), receiving cash of $2,154,440. Journalize the bond issuance.

Follow My Example 14-5

Cash	2,154,440	
Premium on Bonds Payable		154,440
Bonds Payable		2,000,000

Practice Exercises: PE 14-5A, PE 14-5B

Amortizing a Bond Premium

Like bond discounts, a bond premium must be amortized over the life of the bond. The amortization of a bond premium decreases the contract rate of interest on a bond to the market rate of interest that existed on the date the bonds were issued. The amortization can be computed using either the straight-line or the effective interest rate method. The entry to amortize a bond premium is as follows:

		Premium on Bonds Payable	XXX	
		Interest Expense		XXX

The preceding entry may be made annually as an adjusting entry, or it may be combined with the semiannual interest payment. In the latter case, it would be:

		Interest Expense	XXX	
		Premium on Bonds Payable	XXX	
		Cash (amount of semiannual interest)		XXX

To illustrate, amortization of the preceding premium of $3,769 is computed as follows using the straight-line method:

Premium on bonds payable	$3,769
Term of bonds	5 years
Semiannual amortization	$376.90 ($3,769 ÷ 10 periods)

The combined entry to record the first interest payment and the amortization of the premium is as follows:

2015				
June	30	Interest Expense	5,623.10	
		Premium on Bonds Payable	376.90	
		Cash		6,000.00
		Paid semiannual interest and amortized 1/10 of bond premium.		

The preceding entry is made on each interest payment date. Thus, the amount of the semiannual interest expense ($5,623.10) on the bonds remains the same over the life of the bonds.

The effect of the premium amortization is to decrease the interest expense from $6,000.00 to $5,623.10. In effect, this decreases the rate of interest from 12% to a rate of interest that approximates the market rate of 11%. In addition, as the premium is amortized, the carrying amount of the bonds decreases until it equals the face amount of bonds on the maturity date.

Example Exercise 14-6 Premium Amortization

OBJ 3

Using the bond from Example Exercise 14-5, journalize the first interest payment and the amortization of the related bond premium.

Follow My Example 14-6

Interest Expense	104,556	
Premium on Bonds Payable	15,444	
Cash		120,000
Paid interest and amortized the bond premium ($154,440 ÷ 10).		

Practice Exercises: PE 14-6A, PE 14-6B

Business Connection

BOND RATINGS

When purchasing bonds, investors are very interested in understanding how likely it is that the bond issuer will be able to repay the bond principal and associated interest. To help them assess this likelihood, independent rating agencies review and grade the financial condition of companies that issue bonds. For example, the **Standard & Poor's** rating agency rates bonds on a scale from D (lowest) to AAA (highest). Bonds with a rating of BBB- or higher are called *investment grade* because they are issued by companies in sound financial condition and are considered to be reasonably safe investments. Bonds issued by companies in relatively weak financial condition receive ratings below BBB-, reflecting the higher potential for default or nonpayment. These lesser quality bonds are referred to as *non-investment grade* or *junk* bonds. The market rate of interest on junk bonds is much higher than the market rate on investment grade bonds, which compensates bond investors for junk bonds' higher risk of default.

Bond Redemption

A corporation may redeem or call bonds before they mature. This is often done when the market rate of interest declines below the contract rate of interest. In such cases, the corporation may issue new bonds at a lower interest rate and use the proceeds to redeem the original bond issue.

Callable bonds can be redeemed by the issuing corporation within the period of time and at the price stated in the bond indenture. Normally, the call price is above the face value. A corporation may also redeem its bonds by purchasing them on the open market.[4]

A corporation usually redeems its bonds at a price different from the carrying amount (or book value) of the bonds. A gain or loss may be realized on a bond redemption as follows:

- A *gain* is recorded if the price paid for redemption is below the bond carrying amount.
- A *loss* is recorded if the price paid for the redemption is above the carrying amount.

Gains and losses on the redemption of bonds are reported in the *Other income (loss)* section of the income statement.

To illustrate, assume that on June 30, 2015, a corporation has the following bond issue:

Face amount of bonds	$100,000
Premium on bonds payable	4,000

On June 30, 2015, the corporation redeemed one-fourth ($25,000) of these bonds in the market for $24,000. The entry to record the redemption is as follows:

Date		Description	Post. Ref.	Debit	Credit
2015 June	30	Bonds Payable		25,000	
		Premium on Bonds Payable		1,000	
		Cash			24,000
		Gain on Redemption of Bonds			2,000
		Redeemed $25,000 bonds for $24,000.			

In the preceding entry, only the portion of the premium related to the redeemed bonds ($4,000 × 25% = $1,000) is written off. The difference between the carrying amount of the bonds redeemed, $26,000 ($25,000 + $1,000), and the redemption price, $24,000, is recorded as a gain.

Assume that the corporation calls the remaining $75,000 of outstanding bonds, which are held by a private investor, for $79,500 on July 1, 2015. The entry to record the redemption is as follows:

Date		Description	Post. Ref.	Debit	Credit
2015 July	1	Bonds Payable		75,000	
		Premium on Bonds Payable		3,000	
		Loss on Redemption of Bonds		1,500	
		Cash			79,500
		Redeemed $75,000 bonds for $79,500.			

Example Exercise 14-7 Redemption of Bonds Payable

OBJ 3

A $500,000 bond issue on which there is an unamortized discount of $40,000 is redeemed for $475,000. Journalize the redemption of the bonds.

[4] Some bond indentures require the corporation issuing the bonds to transfer cash to a special cash fund, called a *sinking fund,* over the life of the bond. Such funds help assure investors that there will be adequate cash to pay the bonds at their maturity date.

Follow My Example 14-7

Bonds Payable	500,000	
Loss on Redemption of Bonds	15,000	
Discount on Bonds Payable		40,000
Cash		475,000

Practice Exercises: PE 14-7A, PE 14-7B

Installment Notes

OBJ 4 Describe and illustrate the accounting for installment notes.

Corporations often finance their operations by issuing bonds payable. As an alternative, corporations may issue a different kind of notes payable called installment notes. An **installment note** is a debt that requires the borrower to make equal periodic payments to the lender for the term of the note. Unlike bonds, each note payment includes the following:

- Payment of a portion of the amount initially borrowed, called the *principal*
- Payment of interest on the outstanding balance

At the end of the note's term, the principal will have been repaid in full.

Installment notes are often used to purchase specific assets such as equipment, and are often secured by the purchased asset. When a note is secured by an asset, it is called a **mortgage note**. If the borrower fails to pay a mortgage note, the lender has the right to take possession of the pledged asset and sell it to pay off the debt. Mortgage notes are typically issued by an individual bank.

Individuals typically use mortgage notes when buying a house or car.

Issuing an Installment Note

When an installment note is issued, an entry is recorded debiting Cash and crediting Notes Payable. To illustrate, assume that Lewis Company issues the following installment note to City National Bank on January 1, 2015:

Principal amount of note	$24,000
Interest rate	6%
Term of note	5 years
Annual payments	$5,698[5]

The entry to record the issuance of the note is as follows:

2015 Jan.	1	Cash		24,000	
		Notes Payable			24,000
		Issued installment note for cash.			

Annual Payments

The preceding note payable requires Lewis Company to repay the principal and interest in equal payments of $5,698 beginning December 31, 2015, for each of the next five years. Unlike bonds, however, each installment note payment includes an interest and principal component.

The interest portion of an installment note payment is computed by multiplying the interest rate by the carrying amount (book value) of the note at the beginning of the period. The principal portion of the payment is then computed as the difference between the total installment note payment (cash paid) and the interest component. These computations are illustrated in Exhibit 4 (rounded to the nearest dollar).

[5] The amount of the annual payment is calculated by using the present value concepts discussed in Appendix 1 at the end of this chapter. The annual payment of $5,698 is computed by dividing the $24,000 loan amount by the present value of an annuity of $1 for five periods at 6% (4.21236) from Exhibit 10 (rounded to the nearest dollar).

EXHIBIT 4 **Amortization of Installment Notes**

For the Year Ending	A January 1 Carrying Amount	B Note Payment (cash paid)	C Interest Expense (6% of January 1 Note Carrying Amount)	D Decrease in Notes Payable (B – C)	E December 31 Carrying Amount (A – D)
December 31, 2015	$24,000	$ 5,698	$ 1,440 (6% of $24,000)	$ 4,258	$19,742
December 31, 2016	19,742	5,698	1,185 (6% of $19,742)	4,513	15,229
December 31, 2017	15,229	5,698	914 (6% of $15,229)	4,784	10,445
December 31, 2018	10,445	5,698	627 (6% of $10,445)	5,071	5,374
December 31, 2019	5,374	5,698	324* (6% of $5,374)	5,374	0
		$28,490	**$4,490**	**$24,000**	

*Rounded ($5,374 – $5,698).

1. The January 1, 2015, carrying value (Column A) equals the amount borrowed from the bank. The January 1 balance in the following years equals the December 31 balance from the prior year.
2. The note payment (Column B) remains constant at $5,698, the annual cash payment required by the bank.
3. The interest expense (Column C) is computed at 6% of the installment note carrying amount at the beginning of each year. As a result, the interest expense decreases each year.
4. Notes payable decreases each year by the amount of the principal repayment (Column D). The principal repayment is computed by subtracting the interest expense (Column C) from the total payment (Column B). The principal repayment (Column D) increases each year as the interest expense decreases (Column C).
5. The carrying amount on December 31 (Column E) of the note decreases from $24,000, the initial amount borrowed, to $0 at the end of the five years.

The entry to record the first payment on December 31, 2015, is as follows:

2015				
Dec.	31	Interest Expense	1,440	
		Notes Payable	4,258	
		Cash		5,698
		Paid principal and interest on installment note.		

The entry to record the second payment on December 31, 2016, is as follows:

2016				
Dec.	31	Interest Expense	1,185	
		Notes Payable	4,513	
		Cash		5,698
		Paid principal and interest on installment note.		

As the prior entries show, the cash payment is the same in each year. The interest and principal repayment, however, change each year. This is because the carrying amount (book value) of the note decreases each year as principal is repaid, which decreases the interest component the next period.

The entry to record the final payment on December 31, 2019, is as follows:

2019				
Dec.	31	Interest Expense	324	
		Notes Payable	5,374	
		Cash		5,698
		Paid principal and interest on installment note.		

After the final payment, the carrying amount on the note is zero, indicating that the note has been paid in full. Any assets that secure the note would then be released by the bank.

Example Exercise 14-8 Journalizing Installment Notes

OBJ 3

On the first day of the fiscal year, a company issues a $30,000, 10%, five-year installment note that has annual payments of $7,914. The first note payment consists of $3,000 of interest and $4,914 of principal repayment.

a. Journalize the entry to record the issuance of the installment note.

b. Journalize the first annual note payment.

Follow My Example 14-8

a.

Cash	30,000	
Notes Payable		30,000

b.

Interest Expense	3,000	
Notes Payable	4,914	
Cash		7,914

Practice Exercises: PE 14-8A, PE 14-8B

Integrity, Objectivity, and Ethics in Business

THE RATINGS GAME

In February 2013, the United States Justice Department filed a lawsuit against the three main credit rating agencies **(Moody's, Standard & Poor's,** and **Fitch)** for inflating their ratings on highly risk bond issuances between 2004 and 2007. During this time period, the three ratings agencies gave their highest rating (AAA) to debt securities that were, in fact, highly risky. During the financial crisis of 2008, most of these bonds experienced significant drops in value, leaving investors with huge losses. The Justice Department lawsuit alleges that the ratings agencies were aware of the high risks associated with these bonds but inflated their ratings because of the large fee they received for providing a rating on these bonds. At the time of this writing, the lawsuit was pending.

Source: "U.S. vs. S&P: The Rating Game," *The Chicago Tribune*, February 6, 2013.

Reporting Long-Term Liabilities

OBJ 5 Describe and illustrate the reporting of long-term liabilities, including bonds and notes payable.

Bonds payable and notes payable are reported as liabilities on the balance sheet. Any portion of the bonds or notes that is due within one year is reported as a current liability. Any remaining bonds or notes are reported as a long-term liability.

Any unamortized premium is reported as an addition to the face amount of the bonds. Any unamortized discount is reported as a deduction from the face amount of the bonds. A description of the bonds and notes should also be reported either on the face of the financial statements or in the accompanying notes.

The reporting of bonds and notes payable for **Mornin' Joe** follows:

Mornin' Joe
Balance Sheet
December 31, 2016

Current liabilities:		
Accounts payable	$133,000	
Notes payable (current portion)	200,000	
Salaries and wages payable	42,000	
Payroll taxes payable	16,400	
Interest payable	40,000	
Total current liabilities		$ 431,400
Long-term liabilities:		
Bonds payable, 8%, due December 31, 2030	$500,000	
Less unamortized discount	16,000	$ 484,000
Notes payable		1,400,000
Total long-term liabilities		$1,884,000
Total liabilities		$2,315,400

OBJ 6 Describe and illustrate how the number of times interest charges are earned is used to evaluate a company's financial condition.

F·A·I

Financial Analysis and Interpretation: Number of Times Interest Charges Are Earned

As we have discussed, the assets of a company are subject to the (1) claims of creditors and (2) the rights of owners. As creditors, bondholders are primarily concerned with the company's ability to make its periodic interest payments and repay the face amount of the bonds at maturity.

Analysts assess the risk that bondholders will not receive their interest payments by computing the **number of times interest charges are earned** during the year as follows:

$$\text{Number of Times Interest Charges Are Earned} = \frac{\text{Income Before Income Tax} + \text{Interest Expense}}{\text{Interest Expense}}$$

This ratio computes the number of times interest payments could be paid out of current period earnings, measuring the company's ability to make its interest payments. Because interest payments reduce income tax expense, the ratio is computed using income before tax.

To illustrate, the following data were taken from a recent annual report of The Coca-Cola Company (in thousands):

Interest expense	$ 733,000
Income before income tax	14,243,000

The number of times interest charges are earned for The Coca-Cola Company is computed as follows:

$$\text{Number of Times Interest Charges Are Earned} = \frac{\$14,243,000 + \$733,000}{\$733,000} = 20.43$$

Compare this to the number of times interest charges are earned for United Continental Holdings (an airline), and Verizon Communications (a telecommunications company) which follow (in thousands):

	Coca-Cola	United Continental	Verizon Communications
Interest expense	$733,000	$783,000	$2,523,000
Income before income tax expense	$14,243,000	$250,000	$12,684,000
Number of times interest charges are earned	20.43	1.32	6.03

Coca-Cola's number of times interest charges are earned is 20.43, indicating that the company generates enough income before taxes to pay (cover) its interest payments 20.43 times. As a result, debtholders have extremely good protection in the event of an earnings decline. Compare this to United Continental, which only generates enough income before taxes to pay (cover) its interest payments 1.32 times. A small decrease in United Continental's earnings could jeopardize the payment of interest. Verizon Communications falls in between, with a ratio of 6.03.

Example Exercise 14-9 Number of Times Interest Charges Are Earned

OBJ 6

Harris Industries reported the following on the company's income statement in 2016 and 2015:

	2016	2015
Interest expense	$ 200,000	$180,000
Income before income tax expense	1,000,000	720,000

a. Determine the number of times interest charges were earned for 2016 and 2015.
b. Is the number of times interest charges are earned improving or declining?

Follow My Example 14-9

a. 2016:

Number of times interest charges are earned: $\frac{\$1{,}000{,}000 + \$200{,}000}{\$200{,}000} = 6.0$

2015:

Number of times interest charges are earned: $\frac{\$720{,}000 + \$180{,}000}{\$180{,}000} = 5.0$

b. The number of times interest charges are earned has increased from 5.0 in 2015 to 6.0 in 2016. Thus, the debtholders have improved confidence in the company's ability to make its interest payments.

Practice Exercises: PE 14-9A, PE 14-9B

APPENDIX 1

Present Value Concepts and Pricing Bonds Payable

When a corporation issues bonds, the price that investors are willing to pay for the bonds depends on the following:

- The face amount of the bonds, which is the amount due at the maturity date.
- The periodic interest to be paid on the bonds.
- The market rate of interest.

An investor determines how much to pay for the bonds by computing the present value of the bond's future cash receipts, using the market rate of interest. A bond's future cash receipts include its face value at maturity and the periodic interest payments.

Present Value Concepts

The concept of present value is based on the time value of money. The *time value of money concept* recognizes that cash received today is worth more than the same amount of cash to be received in the future.

To illustrate, what would you rather have: $1,000 today or $1,000 one year from now? You would rather have the $1,000 today because it could be invested to earn interest. For example, if the $1,000 could be invested to earn 10% per year, the $1,000 will accumulate to $1,100 ($1,000 plus $100 interest) in one year. In this sense, you can think of the $1,000 in hand today as the **present value** of $1,100 to be received a year from today. This present value is illustrated in Exhibit 5.

EXHIBIT 5 **Present Value and Future Value**

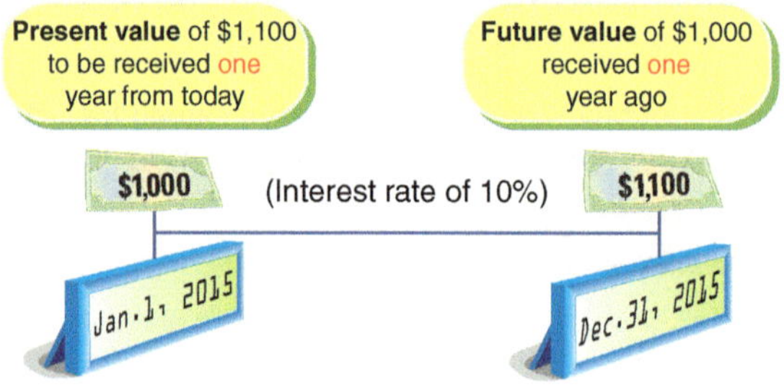

A related concept to present value is **future value**. To illustrate, using the preceding example illustrated in Exhibit 5, the $1,100 to be received on December 31, 2015, is the *future value* of $1,000 on January 1, 2015, assuming an interest rate of 10%.

Present Value of an Amount To illustrate the present value of an amount, assume that $1,000 is to be received in one year. If the market rate of interest is 10%, the present value of the $1,000 is $909.09 ($1,000 ÷ 1.10). This present value is illustrated in Exhibit 6.

EXHIBIT 6 **Present Value of an Amount to Be Received in One Year**

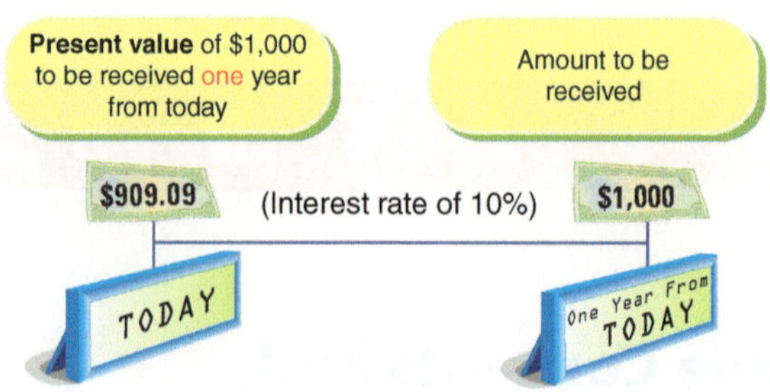

If the $1,000 is to be received in two years, with interest of 10% compounded at the end of the first year, the present value is $826.45 ($909.09 ÷ 1.10).[6] This present value is illustrated in Exhibit 7.

[6] Note that the future value of $826.45 in two years, at an interest rate of 10% compounded annually, is $1,000.

EXHIBIT 7 **Present Value of an Amount to Be Received in Two Years**

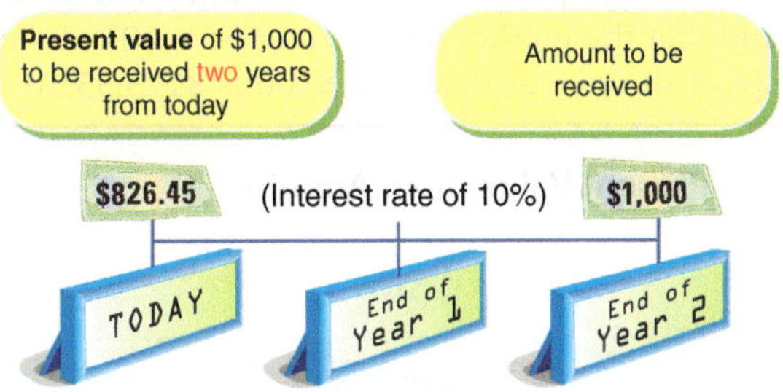

The present value of an amount to be received in the future can be determined by a series of divisions as illustrated in Exhibits 5, 6, and 7. In practice, however, it is easier to use a table of present values.

Spreadsheet software and business calculators have built-in present value functions that can also be used to calculate present values.

The *present value of $1* table is used to find the present value factor for $1 to be received after a number of periods in the future. The amount to be received is then multiplied by this factor to determine its present value.

To illustrate, Exhibit 8 is a partial table of the present value of $1.[7] Exhibit 8 indicates that the present value of $1 to be received in two years with a market rate of interest of 10% a year is 0.82645. Multiplying $1,000 to be received in two years by 0.82645 yields $826.45 ($1,000 × 0.82645). This amount is the same amount computed earlier. In Exhibit 8, the Periods column represents the number of compounding periods, and the percentage columns represent the compound interest rate per period. Thus, the present value factor from Exhibit 8 for 12% for five years is 0.56743. If the interest is compounded semiannually, the interest rate is 6% (12% ÷ 2), and the number of periods is 10 (5 years × 2 times per year). Thus, the present value factor from Exhibit 8 for 6% and 10 periods is 0.55839.

EXHIBIT 8 **Present Value of $1 at Compound Interest**

Periods	4%	4½%	5%	5½%	6%	6½%	7%	10%	11%	12%	13%
1	0.96154	0.956940	0.95238	0.94787	0.94340	0.93897	0.93458	0.90909	0.90090	0.89286	0.88496
2	0.92456	0.915730	0.90703	0.89845	0.89000	0.88166	0.87344	0.82645	0.81162	0.79719	0.78315
3	0.88900	0.876300	0.86384	0.85161	0.83962	0.82785	0.81630	0.75131	0.73119	0.71178	0.69305
4	0.85480	0.838560	0.82270	0.80722	0.79209	0.77732	0.76290	0.68301	0.65873	0.63552	0.61332
5	0.82193	0.802450	0.78353	0.76513	0.74726	0.72988	0.71299	0.62092	0.59345	0.56743	0.54276
6	0.79031	0.767900	0.74622	0.72525	0.70496	0.68533	0.66634	0.56447	0.53464	0.50663	0.48032
7	0.75992	0.734830	0.71068	0.68744	0.66506	0.64351	0.62275	0.51316	0.48166	0.45235	0.42506
8	0.73069	0.703190	0.67684	0.65160	0.62741	0.60423	0.58201	0.46651	0.43393	0.40388	0.37616
9	0.70259	0.672900	0.64461	0.61763	0.59190	0.56735	0.54393	0.42410	0.39092	0.36061	0.33288
10	0.67556	0.643930	0.61391	0.58543	0.55839	0.53273	0.50835	0.38554	0.35218	0.32197	0.29459

Some additional examples using Exhibit 8 follow:

	Number of Periods	Interest Rate	Present Value of $1 Factor from Exhibit 8
10% for *two* years compounded *annually*	2	10%	0.82645
10% for *two* years compounded *semiannually*	4	5%	0.82270
10% for *three* years compounded *semiannually*	6	5%	0.74622
12% for *five* years compounded *semiannually*	10	6%	0.55839

[7] To simplify the illustrations and homework assignments, the tables presented in this chapter are limited to 10 periods for a small number of interest rates, and the amounts are carried to only five decimal places. Computer programs and business function calculators can be used to determine present values for any number of interest rates, decimal places, or periods. More complete interest tables are presented in Appendix A of the text.

Present Value of the Periodic Receipts A series of equal cash receipts spaced equally in time is called an **annuity**. The **present value of an annuity** is the sum of the present values of each cash receipt. To illustrate, assume that $100 is to be received annually for two years and that the market rate of interest is 10%. Using Exhibit 8, the present value of the receipt of the two amounts of $100 is $173.55, as shown in Exhibit 9.

EXHIBIT 9 **Present Value of an Annuity**

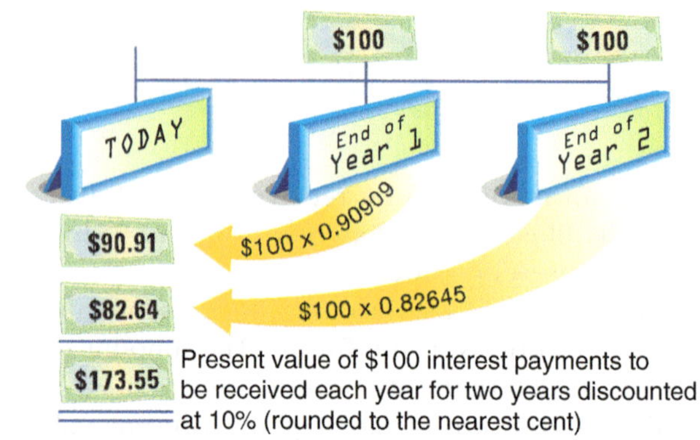

Instead of using present value of $1 tables to determine the present value of each cash flow separately, such as in Exhibit 8, the present value of an annuity can be computed in a single step. Using a value from the *present value of an annuity of $1* table in Exhibit 10, the present value of the entire annuity can be calculated by multiplying the equal cash payment times the appropriate present value of an annuity of $1.

EXHIBIT 10 **Present Value of an Annuity of $1 at Compound Interest**

Periods	4%	4½%	5%	5½%	6%	6½%	7%	10%	11%	12%	13%
1	0.96154	0.95694	0.95238	0.94787	0.94340	0.93897	0.93458	0.90909	0.90090	0.89286	0.88496
2	1.88609	1.87267	1.85941	1.84632	1.83339	1.82063	1.80802	1.73554	1.71252	1.69005	1.66810
3	2.77509	2.74896	2.72325	2.69793	2.67301	2.64848	2.62432	2.48685	2.44371	2.40183	2.36115
4	3.62990	3.58753	3.54595	3.50515	3.46511	3.42580	3.38721	3.16987	3.10245	3.03735	2.97447
5	4.45182	4.38998	4.32948	4.27028	4.21236	4.15568	4.10020	3.79079	3.69590	3.60478	3.51723
6	5.24214	5.15787	5.07569	4.99553	4.91732	4.84101	4.76654	4.35526	4.23054	4.11141	3.99755
7	6.00205	5.89270	5.78637	5.68297	5.58238	5.48452	5.38929	4.86842	4.71220	4.56376	4.42261
8	6.73274	6.59589	6.46321	6.33457	6.20979	6.08875	5.97130	5.33493	5.14612	4.96764	4.79677
9	7.43533	7.26879	7.10782	6.95220	6.80169	6.65610	6.51523	5.75902	5.53705	5.32825	5.13166
10	8.11090	7.91272	7.72173	7.53763	7.36009	7.18883	7.02358	6.14457	5.88923	5.65022	5.42624

To illustrate, the present value of $100 to be received at the end of each of the next two years at 10% compound interest per period is $173.55 ($100 × 1.73554). This amount is the same amount computed previously using the present value of $1.

Pricing Bonds

The selling price of a bond is the sum of the present values of:

- The face amount of the bonds due at the maturity date
- The periodic interest to be paid on the bonds

The market rate of interest is used to compute the present value of both the face amount and the periodic interest.

To illustrate the pricing of bonds, assume that Southern Utah Communications Inc. issued the following bond on January 1, 2015:

Face amount	$100,000
Contract rate of interest	12%
Interest paid semiannually on June 30 and December 31.	
Term of bonds	5 years

Market Rate of Interest of 12% Assuming a market rate of interest of 12%, the bonds would sell for their face amount. As shown by the following present value computations, the bonds would sell for $100,000:

Present value of face amount of $100,000 due in five years, at 12% compounded semiannually: $100,000 × 0.55839 (present value of $1 for 10 periods at 6% from Exhibit 8)	$ 55,839
Present value of 10 semiannual interest payments of $6,000, at 12% compounded semiannually: $6,000 × 7.36009 (present value of an annuity of $1 for 10 periods at 6% from Exhibit 10)	44,161
Total present value of bonds	$100,000

Market Rate of Interest of 13% Assuming a market rate of interest of 13%, the bonds would sell at a discount. As shown by the following present value computations, the bonds would sell for $96,406:[8]

Present value of face amount of $100,000 due in five years, at 13% compounded semiannually: $100,000 × 0.53273 (present value of $1 for 10 periods at 6½% from Exhibit 8)	$53,273
Present value of 10 semiannual interest payments of $6,000, at 13% compounded semiannually: $6,000 × 7.18883 (present value of an annuity of $1 for 10 periods at 6½% from Exhibit 10)	43,133
Total present value of bonds	$96,406

Market Rate of Interest of 11% Assuming a market rate of interest of 11%, the bonds would sell at a premium. As shown by the following present value computations, the bonds would sell for $103,769:

Present value of face amount of $100,000 due in five years, at 11% compounded semiannually: $100,000 × 0.58543 (present value of $1 for 10 periods at 5½% from Exhibit 8)	$ 58,543
Present value of 10 semiannual interest payments of $6,000, at 11% compounded semiannually: $6,000 × 7.53763 (present value of an annuity of $1 for 10 periods at 5½% from Exhibit 10)	45,226
Total present value of bonds	$103,769

As shown, the selling price of the bond varies with the present value of the bond's face amount at maturity, interest payments, and the market rate of interest.

APPENDIX 2

Effective Interest Rate Method of Amortization

The effective interest rate method of amortization provides for a constant *rate* of interest over the life of the bonds. As the discount or premium is amortized, the carrying amount of the bonds changes. As a result, interest expense also changes each period. This is in contrast to the straight-line method, which provides for a constant *amount* of interest expense each period.

[8] Some corporations issue bonds called *zero-coupon bonds* that provide for only the payment of the face amount at maturity. Such bonds sell for large discounts. In this example, such a bond would sell for $53,273, which is the present value of the face amount.

The interest rate used in the effective interest rate method of amortization, sometimes called the *interest method*, is the market rate on the date the bonds are issued. The carrying amount of the bonds is multiplied by this interest rate to determine the interest expense for the period. The difference between the interest expense and the interest payment is the amount of discount or premium to be amortized for the period.

Amortization of Discount by the Interest Method

To illustrate, the following data taken from the chapter illustration of issuing bonds at a discount are used:

Face value of 12%, five-year bonds, interest compounded semiannually....................	$100,000
Present value of bonds at effective (market) rate of interest of 13%	96,406
Discount on bonds payable..	$ 3,594

Exhibit 11 illustrates the interest method for the preceding bonds. Exhibit 11 begins with six columns. The first column is not lettered. The remaining columns are lettered A through E. The exhibit was then prepared as follows:

- Step 1. List the interest payments dates in the first column, which for the preceding bond are 10 interest payment dates (semiannual interest over five years). Also, list on the first line the initial amount of discount in Column D and the initial carrying amount (selling price) of the bonds in Column E.
- Step 2. List in Column A the semiannual interest payments, which for the preceding bond are $6,000 ($100,000 × 6%).
- Step 3. Compute the interest expense in Column B by multiplying the bond carrying amount at the beginning of each period times 6½%, which is the semiannual effective interest (market) rate (13% ÷ 2).
- Step 4. In Column C, compute the discount to be amortized each period by subtracting the interest payment in Column A ($6,000) from the interest expense for the period shown in Column B.
- Step 5. Compute the remaining unamortized discount by subtracting the amortized discount in Column C for the period from the unamortized discount at the beginning of the period in Column D.
- Step 6. Compute the bond carrying amount at the end of the period by subtracting the unamortized discount at the end of the period in Column D from the face amount of the bonds ($100,000).

Steps 3–6 are repeated for each interest payment.

EXHIBIT 11 **Amortization of Discount on Bonds Payable**

Interest Payment Date	A Interest Paid (6% of Face Amount)	B Interest Expense (6½% of Bond Carrying Amount)	C Discount Amortization (B – A)	D Unamortized Discount (D – C)	E Bond Carrying Amount ($100,000 – D)
				$3,594	$ 96,406
June 30, 2015	$6,000	$6,266 (6½% of $96,406)	$266	3,328	96,672
Dec. 31, 2015	6,000	6,284 (6½% of $96,672)	284	3,044	96,956
June 30, 2016	6,000	6,302 (6½% of $96,956)	302	2,742	97,258
Dec. 31, 2016	6,000	6,322 (6½% of $97,258)	322	2,420	97,580
June 30, 2017	6,000	6,343 (6½% of $97,580)	343	2,077	97,923
Dec. 31, 2017	6,000	6,365 (6½% of $97,923)	365	1,712	98,288
June 30, 2018	6,000	6,389 (6½% of $98,288)	389	1,323	98,677
Dec. 31, 2018	6,000	6,414 (6½% of $98,677)	414	909	99,091
June 30, 2019	6,000	6,441 (6½% of $99,091)	441	468	99,532
Dec. 31, 2019	6,000	6,470 (6½% of $99,532)	468*	—	100,000

*Cannot exceed unamortized discount.

As shown in Exhibit 11, the interest expense increases each period as the carrying amount of the bond increases. Also, the unamortized discount decreases each period to zero at the maturity date. Finally, the carrying amount of the bonds increases from $96,406 to $100,000 (the face amount) at maturity.

The entry to record the first interest payment on June 30, 2015, and the related discount amortization is as follows:

2015				
June	30	Interest Expense	6,266	
		Discount on Bonds Payable		266
		Cash		6,000
		Paid semiannual interest and amortized bond discount for 1/2 year.		

If the amortization is recorded only at the end of the year, the amount of the discount amortized on December 31, 2015, would be $550. This is the sum of the first two semiannual amortization amounts ($266 and $284) from Exhibit 11.

Amortization of Premium by the Interest Method

To illustrate, the following data taken from the chapter illustration of issuing bonds at a premium are used:

Present value of bonds at effective (market) rate of interest of 11%	$103,769
Face value of 12%, five-year bonds, interest compounded semiannually	100,000
Premium on bonds payable	$ 3,769

Exhibit 12 illustrates the interest method for the preceding bonds. Exhibit 12 begins with six columns. The first column is not lettered. The remaining columns are lettered A through E. The exhibit was then prepared as follows:

- Step 1. List the number of interest payments in the first column, which for the preceding bond are 10 interest payments (semiannual interest over five years). Also, list on the first line the initial amount of premium in Column D and the initial carrying amount of the bonds in Column E.
- Step 2. List in Column A the semiannual interest payments, which for the preceding bond are $6,000 ($100,000 × 6%).

EXHIBIT 12 **Amortization of Premium on Bonds Payable**

Interest Payment Date	A Interest Paid (6% of Face Amount)	B Interest Expense (5½% of Bond Carrying Amount)	C Premium Amortization (A – B)	D Unamortized Premium (D – C)	E Bond Carrying Amount ($100,000 + D)
				$3,769	$103,769
June 30, 2015	$6,000	$5,707 (5½% of $103,769)	$293	3,476	103,476
Dec. 31, 2015	6,000	5,691 (5½% of $103,476)	309	3,167	103,167
June 30, 2016	6,000	5,674 (5½% of $103,167)	326	2,841	102,841
Dec. 31, 2016	6,000	5,656 (5½% of $102,841)	344	2,497	102,497
June 30, 2017	6,000	5,637 (5½% of $102,497)	363	2,134	102,134
Dec. 31, 2017	6,000	5,617 (5½% of $102,134)	383	1,751	101,751
June 30, 2018	6,000	5,596 (5½% of $101,751)	404	1,347	101,347
Dec. 31, 2018	6,000	5,574 (5½% of $101,347)	426	921	100,921
June 30, 2019	6,000	5,551 (5½% of $100,921)	449	472	100,472
Dec. 31, 2019	6,000	5,526 (5½% of $100,472)	472*	—	100,000

*Cannot exceed unamortized premium.

- Step 3. Compute the interest expense in Column B by multiplying the bond carrying amount at the beginning of each period times 5½%, which is the semiannual effective interest (market) rate (11% ÷ 2).
- Step 4. In Column C, compute the premium to be amortized each period by subtracting the interest expense for the period shown in Column B from the interest payment in Column A ($6,000).
- Step 5. Compute the remaining unamortized premium by subtracting the amortized premium in Column C for the period from the unamortized premium at the beginning of the period in Column D.
- Step 6. Compute the bond carrying amount at the end of the period by adding the unamortized premium at the end of the period in Column D to the face amount of the bonds ($100,000).

Steps 3–6 are repeated for each interest payment.

As shown in Exhibit 12, the interest expense decreases each period as the carrying amount of the bond decreases. Also, the unamortized premium decreases each period to zero at the maturity date. Finally, the carrying amount of the bonds decreases from $103,769 to $100,000 (the face amount) at maturity.

The entry to record the first interest payment on June 30, 2015, and the related premium amortization is as follows:

2015					
June	30	Interest Expense		5,707	
		Premium on Bonds Payable		293	
		Cash			6,000
		Paid semiannual interest and amortized bond premium for ½ year.			

If the amortization is recorded only at the end of the year, the amount of the premium amortized on December 31, 2015, would be $602. This is the sum of the first two semiannual amortization amounts ($293 and $309) from Exhibit 12.

At a Glance 14

OBJ 1 Compute the potential impact of long-term borrowing on earnings per share.

Key Points Corporations can finance their operations by issuing short-term debt, long-term debt, or equity. One of the many factors that influence a corporation's decision on whether it should issue long-term debt or equity is the effect each alternative has on earnings per share.

Learning Outcomes	Example Exercises	Practice Exercises
• Define the concept of a bond.		
• Calculate and compare the effect of alternative long-term financing plans on earnings per share.	EE14-1	PE14-1A, 14-1B

OBJ 2 Describe the characteristics and terminology of bonds payable.

Key Points A corporation that issues bonds enters into a contract, or bond indenture.

When a corporation issues bonds, the price that buyers are willing to pay for the bonds depends on (1) the face amount of the bonds, (2) the periodic interest to be paid on the bonds, and (3) the market rate of interest.

Learning Outcomes	Example Exercises	Practice Exercises
• Define the characteristics of a bond.		
• Describe the various types of bonds.		
• Describe the factors that determine the price of a bond.		

OBJ 3 Journalize entries for bonds payable.

Key Points The journal entry for issuing bonds payable debits Cash and credits Bonds Payable. Any difference between the face amount of the bonds and the selling price is debited to Discount on Bonds Payable or credited to Premium on Bonds Payable when the bonds are issued. The discount or premium on bonds payable is amortized to interest expense over the life of the bonds.

At the maturity date, the entry to record the repayment of the face value of a bond is a debit to Bonds Payable and a credit to Cash.

When a corporation redeems bonds before they mature, Bonds Payable is debited for the face amount of the bonds, the premium (discount) on bonds payable account is debited (credited) for its unamortized balance, Cash is credited, and any gain or loss on the redemption is recorded.

Learning Outcomes	Example Exercises	Practice Exercises
• Journalize the issuance of bonds at face value and the payment of periodic interest.	**EE14-2**	**PE14-2A, 14-2B**
• Journalize the issuance of bonds at a discount.	**EE14-3**	**PE14-3A, 14-3B**
• Journalize the amortization of a bond discount.	**EE14-4**	**PE14-4A, 14-4B**
• Journalize the issuance of bonds at a premium.	**EE14-5**	**PE14-5A, 14-5B**
• Journalize the amortization of a bond premium.	**EE14-6**	**PE14-6A, 14-6B**
• Describe bond redemptions.		
• Journalize the redemption of bonds payable	**EE14-7**	**PE14-7A, 14-7B**

OBJ 4 Describe and illustrate the accounting for installment notes.

Key Points An installment note requires the borrower to make equal periodic payments to the lender for the term of the note. Unlike bonds, the annual payment in an installment note consists of both principal and interest. The journal entry for the annual payment debits Interest Expense and Notes Payable and credits Cash for the amount of the payment. After the final payment, the carrying amount on the note is zero.

Learning Outcomes	Example Exercises	Practice Exercises
• Define the characteristics of an installment note.		
• Journalize the issuance of installment notes.	**EE14-8**	**PE14-8A, 14-8B**
• Journalize the annual payment for an installment note.		

OBJ 5

Describe and illustrate the reporting of long-term liabilities, including bonds and notes payable.

Key Points Bonds payable and notes payable are usually reported as long-term liabilities. If the balance sheet date is within one year, they are reported as current liabilities. A discount on bonds should be reported as a deduction from the related bonds payable. A premium on bonds should be reported as an addition to related bonds payable.

Learning Outcome	Example Exercises	Practice Exercises
• Illustrate the balance sheet presentation of bonds payable and notes payable.		

OBJ 6

Describe and illustrate how the number of times interest charges are earned is used to evaluate a company's financial condition.

Key Points The number of times interest charges are earned measures the risk to bondholders that a company will not be able to make its interest payments. It is computed by dividing income before income tax plus interest expense by interest expense. This ratio measures the number of times interest payments could be paid (covered) by current period earnings.

Learning Outcomes	Example Exercises	Practice Exercises
• Describe and compute the number of times interest charges are earned.	EE14-9	PE14-9A, 14-9B
• Interpret the number of times interest charges are earned.		

Key Terms

amortization (648)
annuity (660)
bond (642)
bond indenture (645)
carrying amount (648)
contract rate (645)
discount (645)
earnings per share (EPS) (642)
effective interest rate method (648)
effective rate of interest (645)
face amount (645)
future value (658)
installment note (653)
market rate of interest (645)
mortgage notes (653)
number of times interest charges are earned (656)
premium (646)
present value (658)
present value of annuity (660)

Illustrative Problem

The fiscal year of Russell Inc., a manufacturer of acoustical supplies, ends December 31. Selected transactions for the period 2015 through 2022, involving bonds payable issued by Russell Inc., are as follows:

2015

June 30. Issued $2,000,000 of 25-year, 7% callable bonds dated June 30, 2015, for cash of $1,920,000. Interest is payable semiannually on June 30 and December 31.

Dec. 31. Paid the semiannual interest on the bonds. The bond discount is amortized annually in a separate journal entry.

31. Recorded straight-line amortization of $1,600 of discount on the bonds.

31. Closed the interest expense account.

2016

June 30. Paid the semiannual interest on the bonds. The bond discount is amortized annually in a separate journal entry.

Dec. 31. Paid the semiannual interest on the bonds. The bond discount is amortized annually in a separate journal entry.

31. Recorded straight-line amortization of $3,200 of discount on the bonds.

31. Closed the interest expense account.

2022

June 30. Recorded the redemption of the bonds, which were called at 101.5. The balance in the bond discount account is $57,600 after the payment of interest and amortization of discount have been recorded. (Record the redemption only.)

Instructions

1. Journalize entries to record the preceding transactions.
2. Determine the amount of interest expense for 2015 and 2016.
3. Determine the carrying amount of the bonds as of December 31, 2016.

Solution

1.

Date		Description	Debit	Credit
2015 June	30	Cash	1,920,000	
		Discount on Bonds Payable	80,000	
		Bonds Payable		2,000,000
Dec.	31	Interest Expense	70,000	
		Cash		70,000
	31	Interest Expense	1,600	
		Discount on Bonds Payable		1,600
		Amortization of discount from July 1 to December 31.		
	31	Income Summary	71,600	
		Interest Expense		71,600
2016 June	30	Interest Expense	70,000	
		Cash		70,000
Dec.	31	Interest Expense	70,000	
		Cash		70,000
	31	Interest Expense	3,200	
		Discount on Bonds Payable		3,200
		Amortization of discount from January 1 to December 31.		
	31	Income Summary	143,200	
		Interest Expense		143,200
2022 June	30	Bonds Payable	2,000,000	
		Loss on Redemption of Bonds Payable	87,600	
		Discount on Bonds Payable		57,600
		Cash		2,030,000

2. a. 2015: $71,600 = $70,000 + $1,600

   b. 2016: $143,200 = $70,000 + $70,000 + $3,200

3.

Initial carrying amount of bonds	$1,920,000
Discount amortized on December 31, 2015	1,600
Discount amortized on December 31, 2016	3,200
Carrying amount of bonds, December 31, 2016	$1,924,800

Discussion Questions

1. Describe the two distinct obligations incurred by a corporation when issuing bonds.
2. Explain the meaning of each of the following terms as they relate to a bond issue: (a) convertible, and (b) callable.
3. If you asked your broker to purchase for you a 12% bond when the market interest rate for such bonds was 11%, would you expect to pay more or less than the face amount for the bond? Explain.
4. A corporation issues $26,000,000 of 9% bonds to yield interest at the rate of 7%. (a) Was the amount of cash received from the sale of the bonds greater or less than $26,000,000? (b) Identify the following amounts as they relate to the bond issue: (1) face amount, (2) market or effective rate of interest, (3) contract rate of interest, and (4) maturity amount.
5. If bonds issued by a corporation are sold at a discount, is the market rate of interest greater or less than the contract rate?
6. The following data relate to a $2,000,000, 8% bond issued for a selected semiannual interest period:

Bond carrying amount at beginning of period	$2,125,000
Interest paid during period	160,000
Interest expense allocable to the period	148,750

   (a) Were the bonds issued at a discount or at a premium? (b) What is the unamortized amount of the discount or premium account at the beginning of the period? (c) What account was debited to amortize the discount or premium?
7. Bonds Payable has a balance of $5,000,000 and Discount on Bonds Payable has a balance of $150,000. If the issuing corporation redeems the bonds at 98, is there a gain or loss on the bond redemption?
8. What is a mortgage note?
9. Fleeson Company needs additional funds to purchase equipment for a new production facility and is considering either issuing bonds payable or borrowing the money from a local bank in the form of an installment note. How does an installment note differ from a bond payable?
10. In what section of the balance sheet would a bond payable be reported if: (a) it is payable within one year and (b) it is payable beyond one year?

Practice Exercises

EE 14-1 p. 644 **PE 14-1A Alternative financing plans** **OBJ. 1**

SHOW ME HOW

Owen Co. is considering the following alternative financing plans:

	Plan 1	Plan 2
Issue 7% bonds (at face value)	$5,000,000	$3,400,000
Issue preferred $1 stock, $20 par	—	3,600,000
Issue common stock, $25 par	5,000,000	3,000,000

Income tax is estimated at 40% of income.

Determine the earnings per share of common stock, assuming income before bond interest and income tax is $750,000.

SHOW ME HOW

EE 14-1 p. 644

PE 14-1B Alternative financing plans **OBJ. 1**

Brower Co. is considering the following alternative financing plans:

	Plan 1	Plan 2
Issue 10% bonds (at face value)	$4,000,000	$2,500,000
Issue preferred $2.50 stock, $25 par	—	3,000,000
Issue common stock, $10 par	4,000,000	2,500,000

Income tax is estimated at 40% of income.

Determine the earnings per share of common stock, assuming income before bond interest and income tax is $2,000,000.

SHOW ME HOW

EE 14-2 p. 647

PE 14-2A Issuing bonds at face amount **OBJ. 3**

On January 1, the first day of the fiscal year, a company issues a $500,000, 5%, 10-year bond that pays semiannual interest of $12,500 ($500,000 × 5% × ½ year), receiving cash of $500,000. Journalize the entries to record (a) the issuance of the bonds, (b) the first interest payment on June 30, and (c) the payment of the principal on the maturity date.

SHOW ME HOW

EE 14-2 p. 647

PE 14-2B Issuing bonds at face amount **OBJ. 3**

On January 1, the first day of the fiscal year, a company issues a $800,000, 4%, 10-year bond that pays semiannual interest of $16,000 ($800,000 × 4% × ½ year), receiving cash of $800,000. Journalize the entries to record (a) the issuance of the bonds, (b) the first interest payment on June 30, and (c) the payment of the principal on the maturity date.

SHOW ME HOW

EE 14-3 p. 648

PE 14-3A Issuing bonds at a discount **OBJ. 3**

On the first day of the fiscal year, a company issues a $1,200,000, 9%, five-year bond that pays semiannual interest of $54,000 ($1,200,000 x 9% x ½), receiving cash of $1,153,670. Journalize the bond issuance.

SHOW ME HOW

EE 14-3 p. 648

PE 14-3B Issuing bonds at a discount **OBJ. 3**

On the first day of the fiscal year, a company issues a $3,000,000, 11%, five-year bond that pays semiannual interest of $165,000 ($3,000,000 x 11% x ½), receiving cash of $2,889,599. Journalize the bond issuance.

SHOW ME HOW

EE 14-4 p. 649

PE 14-4A Discount amortization **OBJ. 3**

Using the bond from Practice Exercise 14-3A, journalize the first interest payment and the amortization of the related bond discount. Round to the nearest dollar.

SHOW ME HOW

EE 14-4 p. 649

PE 14-4B Discount amortization **OBJ. 3**

Using the bond from Practice Exercise 14-3B, journalize the first interest payment and the amortization of the related bond discount. Round to the nearest dollar.

SHOW ME HOW

EE 14-5 p. 650

PE 14-5A Issuing bonds at a premium **OBJ. 3**

On the first day of the fiscal year, a company issues a $2,000,000, 8%, five-year bond that pays semiannual interest of $80,000 ($2,000,000 x 8% x ½), receiving cash of $2,170,604. Journalize the bond issuance.

SHOW ME HOW

EE 14-5 p. 650

PE 14-5B Issuing bonds at a premium **OBJ. 3**

On the first day of the fiscal year, a company issues an $8,000,000, 11%, five-year bond that pays semiannual interest of $440,000 ($8,000,000 x 11% x ½), receiving cash of $8,308,869. Journalize the bond issuance.

EE 14-6 p. 651

PE 14-6A Premium amortization OBJ. 3

SHOW ME HOW

Using the bond from Practice Exercise 14-5A, journalize the first interest payment and the amortization of the related bond premium. Round to the nearest dollar.

EE 14-6 p. 651

PE 14-6B Premium amortization OBJ. 3

SHOW ME HOW

Using the bond from Practice Exercise 14-5B, journalize the first interest payment and the amortization of the related bond premium. Round to the nearest dollar.

EE 14-7 p. 652

PE 14-7A Redemption of bonds payable OBJ. 3

SHOW ME HOW

A $1,500,000 bond issue on which there is an unamortized discount of $70,100 is redeemed for $1,455,000. Journalize the redemption of the bonds.

EE 14-7 p. 652

PE 14-7B Redemption of bonds payable OBJ. 3

SHOW ME HOW

A $500,000 bond issue on which there is an unamortized premium of $67,000 is redeemed for $490,000. Journalize the redemption of the bonds.

EE 14-8 p. 655

PE 14-8A Journalizing installment notes OBJ. 4

SHOW ME HOW

On the first day of the fiscal year, a company issues $65,000, 6%, five-year installment notes that have annual payments of $15,431. The first note payment consists of $3,900 of interest and $11,531 of principal repayment.

a. Journalize the entry to record the issuance of the installment notes.

b. Journalize the first annual note payment.

EE 14-8 p. 655

PE 14-8B Journalizing installment notes OBJ. 4

SHOW ME HOW

On the first day of the fiscal year, a company issues $45,000, 8%, six-year installment notes that have annual payments of $9,734. The first note payment consists of $3,600 of interest and $6,134 of principal repayment.

a. Journalize the entry to record the issuance of the installment notes.

b. Journalize the first annual note payment.

EE 14-9 p. 657

F·A·I

PE 14-9A Number of times interest charges are earned OBJ. 6

SHOW ME HOW

Berry Company reported the following on the company's income statement in 2016 and 2015:

	2016	2015
Interest expense	$ 320,000	$ 300,000
Income before income tax expense	3,200,000	3,600,000

a. Determine the number of times interest charges are earned for 2016 and 2015. Round to one decimal place.

b. Is the number of times interest charges are earned improving or declining?

EE 14-9 p. 657

F·A·I

PE 14-9B Number of times interest charges are earned OBJ. 6

SHOW ME HOW

Averill Products Inc. reported the following on the company's income statement in 2016 and 2015:

	2016	2015
Interest expense	$ 440,000	$ 400,000
Income before income tax expense	5,544,000	4,400,000

a. Determine the number of times interest charges are earned for 2016 and 2015. Round to one decimal place.

b. Is the number of times interest charges are earned improving or declining?

Exercises

✔ a. $1.64

SHOW ME HOW

EX 14-1 Effect of financing on earnings per share — OBJ. 1

Domanico Co., which produces and sells biking equipment, is financed as follows:

Bonds payable, 8% (issued at face amount)	$10,000,000
Preferred 5% stock, $10 par	10,000,000
Common stock, $20 par	10,000,000

Income tax is estimated at 40% of income.

Determine the earnings per share of common stock, assuming that the income before bond interest and income tax is (a) $10,500,000, (b) $11,800,000, and (c) $13,000,000.

EX 14-2 Evaluate alternative financing plans — OBJ. 1

Based on the data in Exercise 14-1, what factors other than earnings per share should be considered in evaluating these alternative financing plans?

EX 14-3 Corporate financing — OBJ. 1

The financial statements for **Nike, Inc.**, are presented in Appendix C at the end of the text. What is the major source of financing for Nike?

EX 14-4 Bond price — OBJ. 3

United States Steel's 7.375% bonds due in 2020 were reported as selling for 103.00.

Were the bonds selling at a premium or at a discount? Why is United States Steel able to sell its bonds at this price?

SHOW ME HOW

EX 14-5 Entries for issuing bonds — OBJ. 3

Gabriel Co. produces and distributes semiconductors for use by computer manufacturers. Gabriel Co. issued $600,000 of 10-year, 8% bonds on May 1 of the current year at face value, with interest payable on May 1 and November 1. The fiscal year of the company is the calendar year. Journalize the entries to record the following selected transactions for the current year:

May 1. Issued the bonds for cash at their face amount.

Nov. 1. Paid the interest on the bonds.

Dec. 31. Recorded accrued interest for two months.

✔ b. $2,122,340

SHOW ME HOW

EX 14-6 Entries for issuing bonds and amortizing discount by straight-line method — OBJ. 2, 3

On the first day of its fiscal year, Pretender Company issued $18,500,000 of five-year, 10% bonds to finance its operations of producing and selling home improvement products. Interest is payable semiannually. The bonds were issued at a market (effective) interest rate of 12%, resulting in Pretender Company receiving cash of $17,138,298.

a. Journalize the entries to record the following:
   1. Issuance of the bonds.
   2. First semiannual interest payment. The bond discount is combined with the semiannual interest payment. (Round your answer to the nearest dollar.)
   3. Second semiannual interest payment. The bond discount is combined with the semiannual interest payment. (Round your answer to the nearest dollar.)

b. Determine the amount of the bond interest expense for the first year.

c. Explain why the company was able to issue the bonds for only $17,138,298 rather than for the face amount of $18,500,000.

SHOW ME HOW

EX 14-7 Entries for issuing bonds and amortizing premium by straight-line method OBJ. 2, 3

Lerner Corporation wholesales repair products to equipment manufacturers. On April 1, 2016, Lerner Corporation issued $12,000,000 of five-year, 8% bonds at a market (effective) interest rate of 6%, receiving cash of $13,023,576. Interest is payable semiannually on April 1 and October 1. Journalize the entries to record the following:

a. Issuance of bonds on April 1, 2016.

b. First interest payment on October 1, 2016, and amortization of bond premium for six months, using the straight-line method. (Round to the nearest dollar.)

c. Explain why the company was able to issue the bonds for $13,023,576 rather than for the face amount of $12,000,000.

SHOW ME HOW

EX 14-8 Entries for issuing and calling bonds; loss OBJ. 3

Adele Corp., a wholesaler of music equipment, issued $22,000,000 of 20-year, 7% callable bonds on March 1, 2016 at their face amount, with interest payable on March 1 and September 1. The fiscal year of the company is the calendar year. Journalize the entries to record the following selected transactions:

2016

Mar. 1. Issued the bonds for cash at their face amount.

Sept. 1. Paid the interest on the bonds.

2020

Sept. 1. Called the bond issue at 102, the rate provided in the bond indenture. (Omit entry for payment of interest.)

SHOW ME HOW

EX 14-9 Entries for issuing and calling bonds; gain OBJ. 3

Emil Corp. produces and sells wind-energy-driven engines. To finance its operations, Emil Corp. issued $15,000,000 of 20-year, 9% callable bonds on May 1, 2016 at their face amount, with interest payable on May 1 and November 1. The fiscal year of the company is the calendar year. Journalize the entries to record the following selected transactions:

2016

May 1. Issued the bonds for cash at their face amount.

Nov. 1. Paid the interest on the bonds.

2022

Nov. 1. Called the bond issue at 96, the rate provided in the bond indenture. (Omit entry for payment of interest.)

SHOW ME HOW

EX 14-10 Entries for installment note transactions OBJ. 4

On the first day of the fiscal year, Shiller Company borrowed $85,000 by giving a seven-year, 7% installment note to Soros Bank. The note requires annual payments of $15,772, with the first payment occurring on the last day of the fiscal year. The first payment consists of interest of $5,950 and principal repayment of $9,822.

a. Journalize the entries to record the following:
   1. Issued the installment note for cash on the first day of the fiscal year.
   2. Paid the first annual payment on the note.

b. Explain how the notes payable would be reported on the balance sheet at the end of the first year.

SHOW ME HOW

EX 14-11 Entries for installment note transactions **OBJ. 4**

On January 1, 2016, Hebron Company issued a $175,000, five-year, 8% installment note to Ventsam Bank. The note requires annual payments of $43,380, beginning on December 31, 2016. Journalize the entries to record the following:

2016

Jan. 1. Issued the note for cash at its face amount.

Dec. 31. Paid the annual payment on the note, which consisted of interest of $14,000 and principal of $29,830.

2019

Dec. 31. Paid the annual payment on the note, included $6,253 of interest. The remainder of the payment reduced the principal balance on the note.

SHOW ME HOW

EX 14-12 Entries for installment note transactions **OBJ. 4**

On January 1, 2016, Bryson Company obtained a $147,750, four-year, 7% installment note from Campbell Bank. The note requires annual payments of $43,620, beginning on December 31, 2016.

a. Prepare an amortization table for this installment note, similar to the one presented in Exhibit 4.

b. Journalize the entries for the issuance of the note and the four annual note payments.

c. Describe how the annual note payment would be reported in the 2016 income statement.

EX 14-13 Reporting bonds **OBJ. 5**

At the beginning of the current year, two bond issues (Simmons Industries 7% 20-year bonds and Hunter Corporation 8% 10-year bonds) were outstanding. During the year, the Simmons Industries bonds were redeemed and a significant loss on the redemption of bonds was reported as an extraordinary item on the income statement. At the end of the year, the Hunter Corporation bonds were reported as a noncurrent liability. The maturity date on the Hunter Corporation bonds was early in the following year.

Identify the flaws in the reporting practices related to the two bond issues.

EX 14-14 Number of times interest charges are earned **OBJ. 6**

F·A·I

The following data were taken from recent annual reports of Southwest Airlines, which operates a low-fare airline service to more than 50 cities in the United States:

	Current Year	Preceding Year
Interest expense	$147,000,000	$194,000,000
Income before income tax	685,000,000	323,000,000

a. Determine the number of times interest charges are earned for the current and preceding years. Round to one decimal place.

b. What conclusions can you draw?

EX 14-15 Number of times interest charges are earned **OBJ. 6**

F·A·I

Loomis, Inc. reported the following on the company's income statement in 2016 and 2015:

	2016	2015
Interest expense	$ 13,500,000	$ 16,000,000
Income before income tax expense	310,500,000	432,000,000

a. Determine the number of times interest charges were earned for 2016 and 2015. Round to one decimal place.

b. Is the number of times interest charges are earned improving or declining?

EX 14-16 Number of times interest charges are earned **OBJ. 6**

F·A·I

Iacouva Company reported the following on the company's income statement for 2016 and 2015:

	2016	2015
Interest expense	$5,000,000	$5,000,000
Income before income tax	3,500,000	6,000,000

a. Determine the number of times interest charges are earned for 2016 and 2015. Round to one decimal place.

b. What conclusions can you draw?

Appendix 1
EX 14-17 Present value of amounts due

Tommy John is going to receive $1,000,000 in three years. The current market rate of interest is 10%.

a. Using the present value of $1 table in Exhibit 8, determine the present value of this amount compounded annually.

b. Why is the present value less than the $1,000,000 to be received in the future?

Appendix 1
EX 14-18 Present value of an annuity

Determine the present value of $200,000 to be received at the end of each of four years, using an interest rate of 7%, compounded annually, as follows:

a. By successive computations, using the present value table in Exhibit 8.

b. By using the present value table in Exhibit 10.

c. Why is the present value of the four $200,000 cash receipts less than the $800,000 to be received in the future?

Appendix 1
EX 14-19 Present value of an annuity

✔ $40,395,063

On January 1, 2016, you win $50,000,000 in the state lottery. The $50,000,000 prize will be paid in equal installments of $6,250,000 over eight years. The payments will be made on December 31 of each year, beginning on December 31, 2016. If the current interest rate is 5%, determine the present value of your winnings. Use the present value tables in Appendix A.

Appendix 1
EX 14-20 Present value of an annuity

Assume the same data as in Exercise 14–19, except that the current interest rate is 12%. Will the present value of your winnings using an interest rate of 12% be more than the present value of your winnings using an interest rate of 5%? Why or why not?

Appendix 1
EX 14-21 Present value of bonds payable; discount

Pinder Co. produces and sells high-quality video equipment. To finance its operations, Pinder Co. issued $25,000,000 of five-year, 7% bonds, with interest payable semiannually, at a market (effective) interest rate of 9%. Determine the present value of the bonds payable, using the present value tables in Exhibits 8 and 10. Round to the nearest dollar.

Appendix 1
EX 14-22 Present value of bonds payable; premium

✔ $45,323,443

Moss Co. issued $42,000,000 of five-year, 11% bonds, with interest payable semiannually, at a market (effective) interest rate of 9%. Determine the present value of the bonds payable using the present value tables in Exhibits 8 and 10. Round to the nearest dollar.

Appendix 2

EX 14-23 Amortize discount by interest method

✔ b. $3,923,959

On the first day of its fiscal year, Ebert Company issued $50,000,000 of 10-year, 7% bonds to finance its operations. Interest is payable semiannually. The bonds were issued at a market (effective) interest rate of 9%, resulting in Ebert Company receiving cash of $43,495,895. The company uses the interest method.

a. Journalize the entries to record the following:
   1. Sale of the bonds.
   2. First semiannual interest payment, including amortization of discount. Round to the nearest dollar.
   3. Second semiannual interest payment, including amortization of discount. Round to the nearest dollar.

b. Compute the amount of the bond interest expense for the first year.

c. Explain why the company was able to issue the bonds for only $43,495,895 rather than for the face amount of $50,000,000.

Appendix 2

EX 14-24 Amortize premium by interest method

✔ b. $1,662,619

Shunda Corporation wholesales parts to appliance manufacturers. On January 1, 2016, Shunda Corporation issued $22,000,000 of five-year, 9% bonds at a market (effective) interest rate of 7%, receiving cash of $23,829,684. Interest is payable semiannually. Shunda Corporation's fiscal year begins on January 1. The company uses the interest method.

a. Journalize the entries to record the following:
   1. Sale of the bonds.
   2. First semiannual interest payment, including amortization of premium. Round to the nearest dollar.
   3. Second semiannual interest payment, including amortization of premium. Round to the nearest dollar.

b. Determine the bond interest expense for the first year.

c. Explain why the company was able to issue the bonds for $23,829,684 rather than for the face amount of $22,000,000.

Appendix 1 and Appendix 2

EX 14-25 Compute bond proceeds, amortizing premium by interest method, and interest expense

✔ a. $37,702,483

✔ c. $225,620

Ware Co. produces and sells motorcycle parts. On the first day of its fiscal year, Ware Co. issued $35,000,000 of five-year, 12% bonds at a market (effective) interest rate of 10%, with interest payable semiannually. Compute the following, presenting figures used in your computations:

a. The amount of cash proceeds from the sale of the bonds. Use the tables of present values in Exhibits 8 and 10. Round to the nearest dollar.

b. The amount of premium to be amortized for the first semiannual interest payment period, using the interest method. Round to the nearest dollar.

c. The amount of premium to be amortized for the second semiannual interest payment period, using the interest method. Round to the nearest dollar.

d. The amount of the bond interest expense for the first year.

Appendix 1 and Appendix 2

EX 14-26 Compute bond proceeds, amortizing discount by interest method, and interest expense

✔ a. $71,167,524

✔ b. $670,051

Boyd Co. produces and sells aviation equipment. On the first day of its fiscal year, Boyd Co. issued $80,000,000 of five-year, 9% bonds at a market (effective) interest rate of 12%, with interest payable semiannually. Compute the following, presenting figures used in your computations:

(Continued)

a. The amount of cash proceeds from the sale of the bonds. Use the tables of present values in Exhibits 8 and 10. Round to the nearest dollar.

b. The amount of discount to be amortized for the first semiannual interest payment period, using the interest method. Round to the nearest dollar.

c. The amount of discount to be amortized for the second semiannual interest payment period, using the interest method. Round to the nearest dollar.

d. The amount of the bond interest expense for the first year.

Problems: Series A

PR 14-1A Effect of financing on earnings per share — OBJ. 1

✔ 1. Plan 3: $1.44

Three different plans for financing an $18,000,000 corporation are under consideration by its organizers. Under each of the following plans, the securities will be issued at their par or face amount, and the income tax rate is estimated at 40% of income:

	Plan 1	Plan 2	Plan 3
8% Bonds	—	—	$ 9,000,000
Preferred 4% stock, $20 par	—	$ 9,000,000	4,500,000
Common stock, $10 par	$18,000,000	9,000,000	4,500,000
Total	$18,000,000	$18,000,000	$18,000,000

Instructions

1. Determine the earnings per share of common stock for each plan, assuming that the income before bond interest and income tax is $2,100,000.
2. Determine the earnings per share of common stock for each plan, assuming that the income before bond interest and income tax is $1,050,000.
3. Discuss the advantages and disadvantages of each plan.

PR 14-2A Bond discount, entries for bonds payable transactions — OBJ. 2, 3

✔ 3. $1,232,685

General Ledger

SHOW ME HOW

On July 1, 2016, Merideth Industries Inc. issued $28,500,000 of 10-year, 8% bonds at a market (effective) interest rate of 9%, receiving cash of $26,646,292. Interest on the bonds is payable semiannually on December 31 and June 30. The fiscal year of the company is the calendar year.

Instructions

1. Journalize the entry to record the amount of cash proceeds from the issuance of the bonds on July 1, 2016.
2. Journalize the entries to record the following:
   a. The first semiannual interest payment on December 31, 2016, and the amortization of the bond discount, using the straight-line method. (Round to the nearest dollar.)
   b. The interest payment on June 30, 2017, and the amortization of the bond discount, using the straight-line method. (Round to the nearest dollar.)
3. Determine the total interest expense for 2016.
4. Will the bond proceeds always be less than the face amount of the bonds when the contract rate is less than the market rate of interest?
5. (Appendix 1) Compute the price of $26,646,292 received for the bonds by using the present value tables in Appendix A at the end of the text. (Round to the nearest dollar.)

PR 14-3A Bond premium, entries for bonds payable transactions — OBJ. 2, 3

✔ 3. $2,600,141

General Ledger

Saverin Inc. produces and sells outdoor equipment. On July 1, 2016, Saverin Inc. issued $62,500,000 of 10-year, 9% bonds at a market (effective) interest rate of 8%, receiving cash of $66,747,178. Interest on the bonds is payable semiannually on December 31 and June 30. The fiscal year of the company is the calendar year.

Instructions

1. Journalize the entry to record the amount of cash proceeds from the issuance of the bonds on July 1, 2016.
2. Journalize the entries to record the following:
   a. The first semiannual interest payment on December 31, 2016, and the amortization of the bond premium, using the straight-line method. (Round to the nearest dollar.)
   b. The interest payment on June 30, 2017, and the amortization of the bond premium, using the straight-line method. (Round to the nearest dollar.)
3. Determine the total interest expense for 2016.
4. Will the bond proceeds always be greater than the face amount of the bonds when the contract rate is greater than the market rate of interest?
5. (Appendix 1) Compute the price of 66,747,178 received for the bonds by using the present value tables in Appendix A at the end of the text. (Round to the nearest dollar.)

PR 14-4A Entries for bonds payable and installment note transactions — OBJ. 3, 4

✔ 3. $64,317,346

General Ledger

SHOW ME HOW

The following transactions were completed by Winklevoss Inc., whose fiscal year is the calendar year:

2016

July 1. Issued $74,000,000 of 20-year, 11% callable bonds dated July 1, 2016, at a market (effective) rate of 13%, receiving cash of $63,532,267. Interest is payable semiannually on December 31 and June 30.

Oct. 1. Borrowed $200,000 by issuing a six-year, 6% installment note to Nicks Bank. The note requires annual payments of $40,673, with the first payment occurring on September 30, 2017.

Dec. 31. Accrued $3,000 of interest on the installment note. The interest is payable on the date of the next installment note payment.

31. Paid the semiannual interest on the bonds. The bond discount amortization of $261,693 is combined with the semiannual interest payment.

31. Closed the interest expense account.

2017

June 30. Paid the semiannual interest on the bonds. The bond discount amortization of $261,693 is combined with the semiannual interest payment.

Sept. 30. Paid the annual payment on the note, which consisted of interest of $12,000 and principal of $28,673.

Dec. 31. Accrued $2,570 of interest on the installment note. The interest is payable on the date of the next installment note payment.

31. Paid the semiannual interest on the bonds. The bond discount amortization of $261,693 is combined with the semiannual interest payment.

31. Closed the interest expense account.

2018

June 30. Recorded the redemption of the bonds, which were called at 98. The balance in the bond discount account is $9,420,961 after payment of interest and amortization of discount have been recorded. (Record the redemption only.)

Sept. 30. Paid the second annual payment on the note, which consisted of interest of $10,280 and principal of $30,393.

Instructions

1. Journalize the entries to record the foregoing transactions. Round all amounts to the nearest dollar.
2. Indicate the amount of the interest expense in (a) 2016 and (b) 2017.
3. Determine the carrying amount of the bonds as of December 31, 2017.

Appendix 1 and Appendix 2

PR 14-5A Bond discount, entries for bonds payable transactions, interest method of amortizing bond discount

✔ 3. $1,199,083

On July 1, 2016, Merideth Industries Inc. issued $28,500,000 of 10-year, 8% bonds at a market (effective) interest rate of 9%, receiving cash of $26,646,292. Interest on the bonds is payable semiannually on December 31 and June 30. The fiscal year of the company is the calendar year.

Instructions

1. Journalize the entry to record the amount of cash proceeds from the issuance of the bonds.
2. Journalize the entries to record the following:
   a. The first semiannual interest payment on December 31, 2016, and the amortization of the bond discount, using the interest method. (Round to the nearest dollar.)
   b. The interest payment on June 30, 2017, and the amortization of the bond discount, using the interest method. (Round to the nearest dollar.)
3. Determine the total interest expense for 2016.

Appendix 1 and Appendix 2

PR 14-6A Bond premium, entries for bonds payable transactions, interest method of amortizing bond premium

✔ 3. $2,669,887

Saverin, Inc. produces and sells outdoor equipment. On July 1, 2016, Saverin, Inc. issued $62,500,000 of 10-year, 9% bonds at a market (effective) interest rate of 8%, receiving cash of $66,747,178. Interest on the bonds is payable semiannually on December 31 and June 30. The fiscal year of the company is the calendar year.

Instructions

1. Journalize the entry to record the amount of cash proceeds from the issuance of the bonds.
2. Journalize the entries to record the following:
   a. The first semiannual interest payment on December 31, 2016, and the amortization of the bond premium, using the interest method. (Round to the nearest dollar.)
   b. The interest payment on June 30, 2017, and the amortization of the bond premium, using the interest method. (Round to the nearest dollar.)
3. Determine the total interest expense for 2016.

Problems: Series B

PR 14-1B Effect of financing on earnings per share OBJ. 1

✔ 1. Plan 3: $2.84

Three different plans for financing an $80,000,000 corporation are under consideration by its organizers. Under each of the following plans, the securities will be issued at their par or face amount, and the income tax rate is estimated at 40% of income:

	Plan 1	Plan 2	Plan 3
9% Bonds	—	—	$40,000,000
Preferred 5% stock, $25 par	—	$40,000,000	20,000,000
Common stock, $20 par	$80,000,000	40,000,000	20,000,000
Total	$80,000,000	$80,000,000	$80,000,000

Instructions

1. Determine for each plan the earnings per share of common stock, assuming that the income before bond interest and income tax is $10,000,000.
2. Determine for each plan the earnings per share of common stock, assuming that the income before bond interest and income tax is $6,000,000.
3. Discuss the advantages and disadvantages of each plan.

PR 14-2B Bond discount, entries for bonds payable transactions **OBJ. 2, 3**

✔ 3. $2,392,269

General Ledger

SHOW ME HOW

On July 1, 2016, Livingston Corporation, a wholesaler of manufacturing equipment, issued $46,000,000 of 20-year, 10% bonds at a market (effective) interest rate of 11%, receiving cash of $42,309,236. Interest on the bonds is payable semiannually on December 31 and June 30. The fiscal year of the company is the calendar year.

Instructions

1. Journalize the entry to record the amount of cash proceeds from the issuance of the bonds on July 1, 2016.
2. Journalize the entries to record the following:
   a. The first semiannual interest payment on December 31, 2016, and the amortization of the bond discount, using the straight-line method. (Round to the nearest dollar.)
   b. The interest payment on June 30, 2017, and the amortization of the bond discount, using the straight-line method. (Round to the nearest dollar.)
3. Determine the total interest expense for 2016.
4. Will the bond proceeds always be less than the face amount of the bonds when the contract rate is less than the market rate of interest?
5. *(Appendix 1)* Compute the price of $42,309,236 received for the bonds by using the present value tables in Appendix A at the end of the text. (Round to the nearest dollar.)

PR 14-3B Bond premium, entries for bonds payable transactions **OBJ. 2, 3**

✔ 3. $3,494,977

General Ledger

Rodgers Corporation produces and sells football equipment. On July 1, 2016, Rodgers Corporation issued $65,000,000 of 10-year, 12% bonds at a market (effective) interest rate of 10%, receiving cash of $73,100,469. Interest on the bonds is payable semiannually on December 31 and June 30. The fiscal year of the company is the calendar year.

Instructions

1. Journalize the entry to record the amount of cash proceeds from the issuance of the bonds on July 1, 2016.
2. Journalize the entries to record the following:
   a. The first semiannual interest payment on December 31, 2016, and the amortization of the bond premium, using the straight-line method. (Round to the nearest dollar.)
   b. The interest payment on June 30, 2017, and the amortization of the bond premium, using the straight-line method. (Round to the nearest dollar.)
3. Determine the total interest expense for 2016.
4. Will the bond proceeds always be greater than the face amount of the bonds when the contract rate is greater than the market rate of interest?
5. *(Appendix 1)* Compute the price of $73,100,469 received for the bonds by using the present value tables in Appendix A at the end of the text. (Round to the nearest dollar.)

PR 14-4B Entries for bonds payable and installment note transactions **OBJ. 3, 4**

✔ 3. $61,644,484

General Ledger

SHOW ME HOW

The following transactions were completed by Montague Inc., whose fiscal year is the calendar year:

2016

July 1. Issued $55,000,000 of 10-year, 9% callable bonds dated July 1, 2016, at a market (effective) rate of 7%, receiving cash of $62,817,040. Interest is payable semiannually on December 31 and June 30.

Oct. 1. Borrowed $450,000 by issuing a six-year, 8% installment note to Intexicon Bank. The note requires annual payments of $97,342, with the first payment occurring on September 30, 2017.

Dec. 31. Accrued $9,000 of interest on the installment note. The interest is payable on the date of the next installment note payment.

31. Paid the semiannual interest on the bonds. The bond discount amortization of $390,852 is combined with the semiannual interest payment.

31. Closed the interest expense account.

(Continued)

2017

June 30. Paid the semiannual interest on the bonds. The bond discount amortization of $390,852 is combined with the semiannual interest payment.

Sept. 30. Paid the annual payment on the note, which consisted of interest of $36,000 and principal of $61,342.

Dec. 31. Accrued $7,773 of interest on the installment note. The interest is payable on the date of the next installment note payment.

31. Paid the semiannual interest on the bonds. The bond discount amortization of $390,852 is combined with the semiannual interest payment.

31. Closed the interest expense account.

2018

June 30. Recorded the redemption of the bonds, which were called at 103. The balance in the bond premium account is $6,253,632 after payment of interest and amortization of premium have been recorded. (Record the redemption only.)

Sept. 30. Paid the second annual payment on the note, which consisted of interest of $31,093 and principal of $66,249.

Instructions

1. Journalize the entries to record the foregoing transactions.
2. Indicate the amount of the interest expense in (a) 2016 and (b) 2017.
3. Determine the carrying amount of the bonds as of December 31, 2017.

Appendix 1 and Appendix 2

PR 14-5B Bond discount, entries for bonds payable transactions, interest method of amortizing bond discount

✔ 3. $2,327,008

On July 1, 2016, Livingston Corporation, a wholesaler of manufacturing equipment, issued $46,000,000 of 20-year, 10% bonds at a market (effective) interest rate of 11%, receiving cash of $42,309,236. Interest on the bonds is payable semiannually on December 31 and June 30. The fiscal year of the company is the calendar year.

Instructions

1. Journalize the entry to record the amount of cash proceeds from the issuance of the bonds.
2. Journalize the entries to record the following:
   a. The first semiannual interest payment on December 31, 2016, and the amortization of the bond discount, using the interest method. (Round to the nearest dollar.)
   b. The interest payment on June 30, 2017, and the amortization of the bond discount, using the interest method. (Round to the nearest dollar.)
3. Determine the total interest expense for 2016.

Appendix 1 and Appendix 2

PR 14-6B Bond premium, entries for bonds payable transactions, interest method of amortizing bond premium

✔ 3. $3,655,023

Rodgers Corporation produces and sells football equipment. On July 1, 2016, Rodgers Corporation issued $65,000,000 of 10-year, 12% bonds at a market (effective) interest rate of 10%, receiving cash of $73,100,469. Interest on the bonds is payable semiannually on December 31 and June 30. The fiscal year of the company is the calendar year.

Instructions

1. Journalize the entry to record the amount of cash proceeds from the issuance of the bonds.
2. Journalize the entries to record the following:
   a. The first semiannual interest payment on December 31, 2016, and the amortization of the bond premium, using the interest method. (Round to the nearest dollar.)
   b. The interest payment on June 30, 2017, and the amortization of the bond premium, using the interest method. (Round to the nearest dollar.)
3. Determine the total interest expense for 2016.

Cases & Projects

CP 14-1 General Electric bond issuance

General Electric Capital, a division of General Electric, uses long-term debt extensively. In a recent year, GE Capital issued $11 billion in long-term debt to investors, then within days filed legal documents to prepare for another $50 billion long-term debt issue. As a result of the $50 billion filing, the price of the initial $11 billion offering declined (due to higher risk of more debt).

> *Bill Gross, a manager of a bond investment fund, "denounced a 'lack in candor' related to GE's recent debt deal. 'It was the most recent and most egregious example of how bondholders are mistreated.' Gross argued that GE was not forthright when GE Capital recently issued $11 billion in bonds, one of the largest issues ever from a U.S. corporation. What bothered Gross is that three days after the issue the company announced its intention to sell as much as $50 billion in additional debt, warrants, preferred stock, guarantees, letters of credit and promissory notes at some future date."*

In your opinion, did GE Capital act unethically by selling $11 billion of long-term debt without telling those investors that a few days later it would be filing documents to prepare for another $50 billion debt offering?

Source: Jennifer Ablan, "Gross Shakes the Bond Market; GE Calms It, a Bit," *Barron's*, March 25, 2002.

CP 14-2 Ethics and professional conduct in business

Solar Industries develops and produces high-efficiency solar panels. The company has an outstanding $10,000,000, 30-year, 10% bond issue dated July 1, 2011. The bond issue is due June 30, 2040. Some bond indentures require the corporation issuing the bonds to transfer cash to a special cash fund, called a sinking fund, over the life of the bond. Such funds help assure investors that there will be adequate cash to pay the bonds at their maturity date.

The bond indenture requires a bond sinking fund, which has a balance of $1,200,000 as of July 1, 2016. The company is currently experiencing a shortage of funds due to a recent acquisition. Bob Lachgar, the company's treasurer, is considering using the funds from the bond sinking fund to cover payroll and other bills that are coming due at the end of the month. Bob's brother-in-law, a trustee of Solar's sinking fund, has indicated a willingness to allow Bob to use the funds from the sinking fund to temporarily meet the company's cash needs.

Discuss whether Bob's proposal is appropriate.

CP 14-3 Present values

Alex Kelton recently won the jackpot in the Colorado lottery while he was visiting his parents. When he arrived at the lottery office to collect his winnings, he was offered the following three payout options:

a. Receive $100,000,000 in cash today.

b. Receive $25,000,000 today and $9,000,000 per year for eight years, with the first payment being received one year from today.

c. Receive $15,000,000 per year for 10 years, with the first payment being received one year from today.

Assuming that the effective rate of interest is 7%, which payout option should Alex select? Use the present value tables in Appendix A. Explain your answer and provide any necessary supporting calculations.

CP 14-4 Preferred stock vs. bonds

Xentec Inc. has decided to expand its operations to owning and operating golf courses. The following is an excerpt from a conversation between the chief executive officer, Peter Kilgallon, and the vice president of finance, Dan Baron:

Peter: Dan, have you given any thought to how we're going to manage the acquisition of Sweeping Bluff Golf Course?

Dan: Well, the two basic options, as I see it, are to issue either preferred stock or bonds. The equity market is a little depressed right now. The rumor is that the Federal Reserve Bank's going to increase the interest rates either this month or next.

Peter: Yes, I've heard the rumor. The problem is that we can't wait around to see what's going to happen. We'll have to move on this next week if we want any chance to complete the acquisition of Sweeping Bluff Golf Course.

Dan: Well, the bond market is strong right now. Maybe we should issue debt this time around.

Peter: That's what I would have guessed as well. Sweeping Bluff Golf Course's financial statements look pretty good, except for the volatility of its income and cash flows. But that's characteristic of the industry.

Discuss the advantages and disadvantages of issuing preferred stock versus bonds.

CP 14-5 Financing business expansion

You hold a 25% common stock interest in YouOwnIt, a family-owned construction equipment company. Your sister, who is the manager, has proposed an expansion of plant facilities at an expected cost of $26,000,000. Two alternative plans have been suggested as methods of financing the expansion. Each plan is briefly described as follows:

Plan 1. Issue $26,000,000 of 20-year, 8% notes at face amount.

Plan 2. Issue an additional 550,000 shares of $10 par common stock at $20 per share, and $15,000,000 of 20-year, 8% notes at face amount.

The balance sheet as of the end of the previous fiscal year is as follows:

YouOwnIt, Inc.
Balance Sheet
December 31, 2016

Assets	
Current assets	$15,000,000
Property, plant, and equipment	22,500,000
Total assets	$37,500,000
Liabilities and Stockholders' Equity	
Liabilities	$11,250,000
Common stock, $10	4,000,000
Paid-in capital in excess of par	500,000
Retained earnings	21,750,000
Total liabilities and stockholders' equity	$37,500,000

Net income has remained relatively constant over the past several years. The expansion program is expected to increase yearly income before bond interest and income tax from $2,667,000 in the previous year to $5,000,000 for this year. Your sister has asked you, as the company treasurer, to prepare an analysis of each financing plan.

1. Prepare a table indicating the expected earnings per share on the common stock under each plan. Assume an income tax rate of 40%. Round to the nearest cent.
2. a. Discuss the factors that should be considered in evaluating the two plans.

   b. Which plan offers the greater benefit to the present stockholders? Give reasons for your opinion.

CP 14-6 Number of times interest charges are earned

F·A·I

The following financial data (in thousands) were taken from recent financial statements of **Staples, Inc.**:

	Year 3	Year 2	Year 1
Interest expense	$ 173,751	$ 214,824	$ 237,025
Earnings before taxes	1,459,141	1,356,595	1,155,894

1. What is the number of times interest charges are earned for Staples in Year 3, Year 2, and Year 1? (Round your answers to one decimal place.)
2. Evaluate this ratio for Staples.

CHAPTER 16

Statement of Cash Flows

National Beverage Co.

Suppose you were to receive $100 from an event. Would it make a difference what the event was? Yes, it would! If you received $100 for your birthday, then it's a gift. If you received $100 as a result of working part time for a week, then it's the result of your effort. If you received $100 as a loan, then it's money that you will have to pay back in the future. If you received $100 as a result of selling your iPod, then it's the result of selling an asset. Thus, $100 received can be associated with different types of events, and these events have different meanings to you, and different implications for your future. You would much rather receive a $100 gift than take out a $100 loan. Likewise, company stakeholders view inflows and outflows of cash differently, depending on their source.

Companies are required to report information about the events causing a change in cash over a period of time. This information is reported in the statement of cash flows. One such company is **National Beverage**, which is an alternative beverage company, known for its innovative soft drinks, enhanced juices and waters, and fortified powders and supplements. You have probably seen the company's **Shasta** and **Faygo** soft drinks, or **LaCroix**, **Everfresh**, and **Crystal Bay** drinks at your local grocery or convenience store. As with any company, cash is important to National Beverage. Without cash, National Beverage would be unable to expand its brands, distribute its product, support extreme sports, or provide a return for its owners. Thus, its managers are concerned about the sources and uses of cash.

In previous chapters, we have used the income statement, balance sheet, statement of retained earnings, and other information to analyze the effects of management decisions on a business's financial position and operating performance. In this chapter, we focus on the events causing a change in cash by presenting the preparation and use of the statement of cash flows.

Learning Objectives

After studying this chapter, you should be able to: *Example Exercises*

At a Glance 16 Page 764

OBJ 1 Describe the cash flow activities reported in the statement of cash flows.

Reporting Cash Flows

The **statement of cash flows** reports a company's cash inflows and outflows for a period.[1] The statement of cash flows provides useful information about a company's ability to do the following:

- Generate cash from operations
- Maintain and expand its operating capacity
- Meet its financial obligations
- Pay dividends

The statement of cash flows is used by managers in evaluating past operations and in planning future investing and financing activities. It is also used by external users such as investors and creditors to assess a company's profit potential and ability to pay its debt and pay dividends.

Note:
The statement of cash flows reports cash flows from operating, investing, and financing activities.

The statement of cash flows reports three types of cash flow activities, as follows:

1. **Cash flows from operating activities** are the cash flows from transactions that affect the net income of the company.

   Example: Purchase and sale of merchandise by a retailer.

2. **Cash flows from investing activities** are the cash flows from transactions that affect investments in the noncurrent assets of the company.

   Example: Purchase and sale of fixed assets, such as equipment and buildings.

[1] As used in this chapter, *cash* refers to cash and cash equivalents. Examples of cash equivalents include short-term, highly liquid investments, such as money market accounts, bank certificates of deposit, and U.S. Treasury bills.

3. **Cash flows from financing activities** are the cash flows from transactions that affect the debt and equity of the company.

   Example: Issuing or retiring equity and debt securities.

The cash flows are reported in the statement of cash flows as follows:

Cash flows from operating activities	$XXX
Cash flows from investing activities	XXX
Cash flows from financing activities	XXX
Net increase or decrease in cash for the period	$XXX
Cash at the beginning of the period	XXX
Cash at the end of the period	$XXX

The ending cash on the statement of cash flows equals the cash reported on the company's balance sheet at the end of the year.

Exhibit 1 illustrates the sources (increases) and uses (decreases) of cash by each of the three cash flow activities. A *source* of cash causes the cash flow to increase and is called a *cash inflow*. A *use* of cash causes cash flow to decrease and is called *cash outflow*.

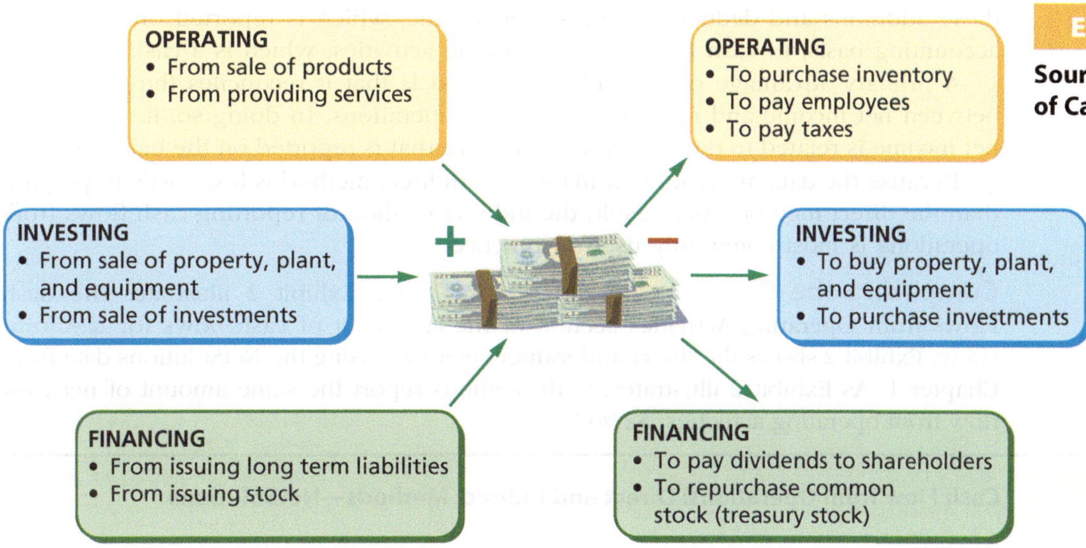

EXHIBIT 1

Sources and Uses of Cash

Cash Flows from Operating Activities

Cash flows from operating activities reports the cash inflows and outflows from a company's day-to-day operations. Companies may select one of two alternative methods for reporting cash flows from operating activities in the statement of cash flows:

- The direct method
- The indirect method

In fiscal 2012, **Google Inc.** generated $16.6 billion in net cash flow from operating activities.

Both methods result in the same amount of cash flows from operating activities. They differ in the way they report cash flows from operating activities.

The Direct Method The **direct method** reports operating cash inflows (receipts) and cash outflows (payments) as follows:

Cash flows from operating activities:		
Cash received from customers		$XXX
Less: Cash payments for merchandise	$XXX	
Cash payments for operating expenses	XXX	
Cash payments for interest	XXX	
Cash payments for income taxes	XXX	XXX
Net cash flow from operating activities		$XXX

The primary operating cash inflow is cash received from customers. The primary operating cash outflows are cash payments for merchandise, operating expenses, interest, and income tax payments. The cash received from operating activities less the cash payments for operating activities is the net cash flow from operating activities.

The primary advantage of the direct method is that it *directly* reports cash receipts and cash payments in the statement of cash flows. Its primary disadvantage is that these data may not be readily available in the accounting records. Thus, the direct method is normally more costly to prepare and, as a result, is used infrequently in practice.

The Indirect Method The **indirect method** reports cash flows from operating activities by beginning with net income and adjusting it for revenues and expenses that do not involve the receipt or payment of cash, as follows:

Cash flows from operating activities:		
Net income	$XXX	
Adjustments to reconcile net income to net cash flow from operating activities	XXX	
Net cash flow from operating activities		$XXX

The adjustments to reconcile net income to net cash flow from operating activities include such items as depreciation and gains or losses on fixed assets. Changes in current operating assets and liabilities such as accounts receivable or accounts payable are also added or deducted, depending on their effect on cash flows. In effect, these additions and deductions adjust net income, which is reported on an accrual accounting basis, to cash flows from operating activities, which is a cash basis.

A primary advantage of the indirect method is that it reconciles the differences between net income and net cash flows from operations. In doing so, it shows how net income is related to the ending cash balance that is reported on the balance sheet.

Because the data are readily available, the indirect method is less costly to prepare than the direct method. As a result, the indirect method of reporting cash flows from operations is most commonly used in practice.

Comparing the Direct and Indirect Methods Exhibit 2 illustrates the Cash Flows from Operating Activities section of the statement of cash flows for **NetSolutions**. Exhibit 2 shows the direct and indirect methods using the NetSolutions data from Chapter 1. As Exhibit 2 illustrates, both methods report the same amount of net cash flow from operating activities, $2,900.

EXHIBIT 2 **Cash Flow from Operations: Direct and Indirect Methods—NetSolutions**

Direct Method

Cash flows from operating activities:	
Cash received from customers	$7,500
Deduct cash payments for expenses and payments to creditors	4,600
Net cash flow from operating activities	$2,900

Indirect Method

Cash flows from operating activities:	
Net income	$3,050
Add increase in accounts payable	400
	$3,450
Deduct increase in supplies	550
Net cash flow from operating activities	$2,900

the same

Business Connection

CASH CRUNCH!

In late 2011, **American Airlines**' deteriorating cash flow situation forced the company to file for bankruptcy. At the time, the airline had generated $235 million in net cash flow from operating activities for the nine-month period ending September 31, 2011, while spending $1.1 billion on additional property, plant, and equipment. The property, plant, and equipment purchases were paid for by issuing additional debt. By Thanksgiving 2011, it became clear that the company's weak net cash flow from operating activities would not be sufficient to pay off the airline's massive debt. On November 29, 2011, the airline filed for bankruptcy. In February 2013, American and **U.S. Airways** announced plans to merge, creating the largest airline in the world.

Source: M. Curriden and N. Posgate, "American Airlines bankruptcy, merger deals were complex, expensive," *Dallas Morning News*, February 17, 2013.

Cash Flows from Investing Activities

Cash flows from investing activities show the cash inflows and outflows related to changes in a company's long-term assets. Cash flows from investing activities are reported on the statement of cash flows as follows:

Cash flows from investing activities:		
Cash inflows from investing activities	$XXX	
Less cash used for investing activities	XXX	
Net cash flows from investing activities		$XXX

Cash inflows from investing activities normally arise from selling fixed assets, investments, and intangible assets. Cash outflows normally include payments to purchase fixed assets, investments, and intangible assets.

Cash Flows from Financing Activities

Cash flows from financing activities show the cash inflows and outflows related to changes in a company's long-term liabilities and stockholders' equity. Cash flows from financing activities are reported on the statement of cash flows as follows:

Cash flows from financing activities:		
Cash inflows from financing activities	$XXX	
Less cash used for financing activities	XXX	
Net cash flow from financing activities		$XXX

In March 2013, U.S. companies in the S&P 500 index were expected to pay $300 billion in dividends to investors during 2013.

Cash inflows from financing activities normally arise from issuing long-term debt or equity securities. For example, issuing bonds, notes payable, preferred stock, and common stock creates cash inflows from financing activities. Cash outflows from financing activities include paying cash dividends, repaying long-term debt, and acquiring treasury stock.

Noncash Investing and Financing Activities

A company may enter into transactions involving investing and financing activities that do not *directly* affect cash. For example, a company may issue common stock to retire long-term debt. Although this transaction does not directly affect cash, it does eliminate future cash payments for interest and for paying the bonds when they mature. Because such transactions *indirectly* affect cash flows, they are reported in a separate section of the statement of cash flows. This section usually appears at the bottom of the statement of cash flows.

Format of the Statement of Cash Flows

The statement of cash flows presents the cash flows generated by, or used for, the three activities previously discussed: operating, investing, and financing. These three activities are always reported in the same order, following the format illustrated in Exhibit 3.

EXHIBIT 3

Format of the Statement of Cash Flows

COMPANY NAME
Statement of Cash Flows
For the Year Ended xxxx

Cash flows from operating activities		
(List of individual items, as illustrated in Exhibit 1)	XXX	
Net cash flows from operating activities		$XXX
Cash flows from investing activities		
(List of individual items, as illustrated in Exhibit 1)	XXX	
Net cash flows from (used for) investing activities		XXX
Cash flows from financing activities		
(List of individual items, as illustrated in Exhibit 1)	XXX	
Net cash flows from (used for) financing activities		XXX
Increase (decrease) in cash		$XXX
Cash at the beginning of the period		XXX
Cash at the end of the period		$XXX
Noncash investing and financing activites		$XXX

Example Exercise 16-1 Classifying Cash Flows OBJ 1

Identify whether each of the following would be reported as an operating, investing, or financing activity in the statement of cash flows:

a. Purchase of patent
b. Payment of cash dividend
c. Disposal of equipment
d. Cash sales
e. Purchase of treasury stock
f. Payment of wages expense

Follow My Example 16-1

a. Investing
b. Financing
c. Investing
d. Operating
e. Financing
f. Operating

Practice Exercises: PE 16-1A, PE 16-1B

No Cash Flow per Share

Cash flow per share is sometimes reported in the financial press. As reported, cash flow per share is normally computed as *cash flow from operations divided by the number of common shares outstanding*. However, such reporting may be misleading because of the following:

- Users may misinterpret cash flow per share as the per-share amount available for dividends. This would not be the case if the cash generated by operations is required for repaying loans or for reinvesting in the business.
- Users may misinterpret cash flow per share as equivalent to (or better than) earnings per share.

For these reasons, the financial statements, including the statement of cash flows, should not report cash flow per share.

OBJ 2 Prepare a statement of cash flows, using the indirect method.

Preparing the Statement of Cash Flows—The Indirect Method

The indirect method of reporting cash flows from operating activities uses the logic that a change in any balance sheet account (including cash) can be analyzed in terms of changes in the other balance sheet accounts. Thus, by analyzing changes in noncash balance sheet accounts, any change in the cash account can be *indirectly* determined.

To illustrate, the accounting equation can be solved for cash as follows:

$$\text{Assets} = \text{Liabilities} + \text{Stockholders' Equity}$$
$$\text{Cash} + \text{Noncash Assets} = \text{Liabilities} + \text{Stockholders' Equity}$$
$$\text{Cash} = \text{Liabilities} + \text{Stockholders' Equity} - \text{Noncash Assets}$$

Therefore, any change in the cash account can be determined by analyzing changes in the liability, stockholders' equity, and noncash asset accounts as follows:

$$\textit{Change} \text{ in Cash} = \textit{Change} \text{ in Liabilities} + \textit{Change} \text{ in Stockholders' Equity} - \textit{Change} \text{ in Noncash Assets}$$

Under the indirect method, there is no order in which the balance sheet accounts must be analyzed. However, net income (or net loss) is the first amount reported on the statement of cash flows. Because net income (or net loss) is a component of any change in Retained Earnings, the first account normally analyzed is Retained Earnings.

To illustrate the indirect method, the income statement and comparative balance sheets for **Rundell Inc.**, shown in Exhibit 4, are used. Ledger accounts and other data supporting the income statement and balance sheet are presented as needed.[2]

EXHIBIT 4

Income Statement and Comparative Balance Sheet

Rundell Inc.
Income Statement
For the Year Ended December 31, 2016

Sales		$1,180,000
Cost of merchandise sold		790,000
Gross profit		$ 390,000
Operating expenses:		
Depreciation expense	$ 7,000	
Other operating expenses	196,000	
Total operating expenses		203,000
Income from operations		$ 187,000
Other income:		
Gain on sale of land	$ 12,000	
Other expense:		
Interest expense	8,000	4,000
Income before income tax		$ 191,000
Income tax expense		83,000
Net income		$ 108,000

Rundell Inc.
Comparative Balance Sheet
December 31, 2016 and 2015

	2016	2015	Increase Decrease*
Assets			
Cash	$ 97,500	$ 26,000	$ 71,500
Accounts receivable (net)	74,000	65,000	9,000
Inventories	172,000	180,000	8,000*
Land	80,000	125,000	45,000*
Building	260,000	200,000	60,000
Accumulated depreciation—building	(65,300)	(58,300)	7,000**
Total assets	$618,200	$537,700	$ 80,500
Liabilities			
Accounts payable (merchandise creditors)	$ 43,500	$ 46,700	$ 3,200*
Accrued expenses payable (operating expenses)	26,500	24,300	2,200
Income taxes payable	7,900	8,400	500*
Dividends payable	14,000	10,000	4,000
Bonds payable	100,000	150,000	50,000*
Total liabilities	$191,900	$239,400	$ 47,500*
Stockholders' Equity			
Common stock ($2 par)	$ 24,000	$ 16,000	$ 8,000
Paid-in capital in excess of par	120,000	80,000	40,000
Retained earnings	282,300	202,300	80,000
Total stockholders' equity	$426,300	$298,300	$128,000
Total liabilities and stockholders' equity	$618,200	$537,700	$ 80,500

**There is a $7,000 increase to Accumulated Depreciation—Building, which is a contra asset account. As a result, the $7,000 increase in this account must be subtracted in summing to the increase in Total assets of $80,500.

[2] An appendix that discusses using a spreadsheet (work sheet) as an aid in assembling data for the statement of cash flows is presented at the end of this chapter. This appendix illustrates the use of this spreadsheet in reporting cash flows from operating activities using the indirect method.

Retained Earnings

The comparative balance sheet for **Rundell Inc.** shows that retained earnings increased $80,000 during the year. The retained earnings account that follows indicates how this change occurred:

Account *Retained Earnings* Account No.

Date		Item	Debit	Credit	Balance Debit	Balance Credit
2016 Jan.	1	Balance				202,300
Dec.	31	Net income		108,000		310,300
	31	Cash dividends	28,000			282,300

The retained earnings account indicates that the $80,000 ($108,000 − $28,000) change resulted from net income of $108,000 and cash dividends of $28,000. The net income of $108,000 is the first amount reported in the Cash Flows from Operating Activities section.

Adjustments to Net Income

The net income of $108,000 reported by **Rundell Inc.** does not equal the cash flows from operating activities for the period. This is because net income is determined using the accrual method of accounting.

Under the accrual method of accounting, revenues and expenses are recorded at different times from when cash is received or paid. For example, merchandise may be sold on account and the cash received at a later date. Likewise, insurance premiums may be paid in the current period but expensed in a following period.

Thus, under the indirect method, adjustments to net income must be made to determine cash flows from operating activities. The typical adjustments to net income are shown in Exhibit 5.[3]

EXHIBIT 5

Adjustments to Net Income (Loss) Using the Indirect Method

		Increase (Decrease)
	Net income (loss)	$ XXX
	Adjustments to reconcile net income to net cash flow from operating activities:	
Step 1	Depreciation of fixed assets	XXX
	Amortization of intangible assets	XXX
Step 2	Losses on disposal of assets	XXX
	Gains on disposal of assets	(XXX)
Step 3	Changes in current operating assets and liabilities:	
	Increases in noncash current operating assets	(XXX)
	Decreases in noncash current operating assets	XXX
	Increases in current operating liabilities	XXX
	Decreases in current operating liabilities	(XXX)
	Net cash flow from operating activities	$ XXX or $(XXX)

Subtract	Add
Increases in accounts receivable	Decreases in accounts receivable
Increases in inventory	Decreases in inventory
Increases in prepaid expenses	Decreases in prepaid expenses
Decreases in accounts payable	Increases in accounts payable
Decreases in accrued expenses payable	Increases in accrued expenses payable
Decreases in income taxes payable	Increases in income taxes payable

[3] Other items that also require adjustments to net income to obtain cash flows from operating activities include amortization of bonds payable discounts (add), losses on debt retirement (add), amortization of bonds payable premiums (deduct), and gains on retirement of debt (deduct).

Net income is normally adjusted to cash flows from operating activities, using the following steps:

- Step 1. Expenses that do not affect cash are added. Such expenses decrease net income but do not involve cash payments and, thus, are added to net income.

  Example: Depreciation of fixed assets and amortization of intangible assets are added to net income.

- Step 2. Losses on the disposal of assets are added and gains on the disposal of assets are deducted. The disposal (sale) of assets is an investing activity rather than an operating activity. However, such losses and gains are reported as part of net income. As a result, any *losses* on disposal of assets are *added* back to net income. Likewise, any *gains* on disposal of assets are *deducted* from net income.

  Example: Land costing $100,000 is sold for $90,000. The loss of $10,000 is added back to net income.

- Step 3. Changes in current operating assets and liabilities are added or deducted as follows:

  - Increases in noncash current operating assets are deducted.
  - Decreases in noncash current operating assets are added.
  - Increases in current operating liabilities are added.
  - Decreases in current operating liabilities are deducted.

  Example: A sale of $10,000 on account increases sales, accounts receivable, and net income by $10,000. However, cash is not affected. Thus, the $10,000 increase in accounts receivable is deducted. Similar adjustments are required for the changes in the other current asset and liability accounts, such as inventory, prepaid expenses, accounts payable, accrued expenses payable, and income taxes payable, as shown in Exhibit 5.

Example Exercise 16-2 Adjustments to Net Income—Indirect Method

OBJ 2

Omni Corporation's accumulated depreciation increased by $12,000, while $3,400 of patent amortization was recognized between balance sheet dates. There were no purchases or sales of depreciable or intangible assets during the year. In addition, the income statement showed a gain of $4,100 from the sale of land. Reconcile Omni's net income of $50,000 to net cash flow from operating activities.

Follow My Example 16-2

Net income	$50,000
Adjustments to reconcile net income to net cash flow from operating activities:	
Depreciation	12,000
Amortization of patents	3,400
Gain from sale of land	(4,100)
Net cash flow from operating activities	$61,300

Practice Exercises: PE 16-2A, PE 16-2B

The Cash Flows from Operating Activities section of **Rundell Inc.'s** statement of cash flows is shown in Exhibit 6.

Rundell's net income of $108,000 is converted to cash flows from operating activities of $100,500 as follows:

Step 1. Add depreciation of $7,000.

EXHIBIT 6

Net Cash Flow From Operating Activities—Indirect Method

	Cash flows from operating activities:		
	Net income	$108,000	
	Adjustments to reconcile net income to net cash flow from operating activities:		
Step 1 →	Depreciation	7,000	
Step 2 →	Gain on sale of land	(12,000)	
	Changes in current operating assets and liabilities:		
Step 3 →	Increase in accounts receivable	(9,000)	
	Decrease in inventories	8,000	
	Decrease in accounts payable	(3,200)	
	Increase in accrued expenses payable	2,200	
	Decrease in income taxes payable	(500)	
	Net cash flow from operating activities		$100,500

Analysis: The comparative balance sheet in Exhibit 4 indicates that Accumulated Depreciation—Building increased by $7,000. The following account indicates that depreciation for the year was $7,000 for the building:

Account *Accumulated Depreciation—Building* Account No.

Date		Item	Debit	Credit	Balance Debit	Balance Credit
2016						
Jan.	1	Balance				58,300
Dec.	31	Depreciation for year		7,000		65,300

Step 2. Deduct the gain on the sale of land of $12,000.
Analysis: The income statement in Exhibit 4 reports a gain of $12,000 from the sale of land. The proceeds, which include the gain, are reported in the Investing section of the statement of cash flows.[4] Thus, the gain of $12,000 is deducted from net income in determining cash flows from operating activities.

Step 3. Add and deduct changes in current operating assets and liabilities excluding cash.
Analysis: The increases and decreases in the current operating asset and current liability accounts excluding cash are as follows:

Accounts	December 31 2016	December 31 2015	Increase Decrease*
Accounts Receivable (net)	$ 74,000	$ 65,000	$9,000
Inventories	172,000	180,000	8,000*
Accounts Payable (merchandise creditors)	43,500	46,700	3,200*
Accrued Expenses Payable (operating expenses)	26,500	24,300	2,200
Income Taxes Payable	7,900	8,400	500*

Accounts receivable (net): The $9,000 increase is deducted from net income. This is because the $9,000 increase in accounts receivable indicates that sales on account were $9,000 more than the cash received from customers. Thus, sales (and net income) includes $9,000 that was not received in cash during the year.

Inventories: The $8,000 decrease is added to net income. This is because the $8,000 decrease in inventories indicates that the cost of merchandise *sold* exceeds the cost of the merchandise *purchased* during the year by $8,000. In other words, the cost of merchandise sold includes $8,000 of goods from inventory that were not purchased (used cash) during the year.

Accounts payable (merchandise creditors): The $3,200 decrease is deducted from net income. This is because a decrease in accounts payable indicates that the cash

[4] The reporting of the proceeds (cash flows) from the sale of land as part of investing activities is discussed later in this chapter.

payments to merchandise creditors exceed the merchandise *purchased on account* by $3,200. Therefore, the cost of merchandise sold is $3,200 less than the cash paid to merchandise creditors during the year.

Accrued expenses payable (operating expenses): The $2,200 increase is added to net income. This is because an increase in accrued expenses payable indicates that operating expenses exceed the cash payments for operating expenses by $2,200. In other words, operating expenses reported on the income statement include $2,200 that did not require a cash outflow during the year.

Income taxes payable: The $500 decrease is deducted from net income. This is because a decrease in income taxes payable indicates that taxes paid exceed the amount of taxes incurred during the year by $500. In other words, the amount reported on the income statement for income tax expense is less than the amount paid by $500.

Example Exercise 16-3 Changes in Current Operating Assets and Liabilities—Indirect Method

OBJ 2

Victor Corporation's current operating assets and liabilities from the company's comparative balance sheet were as follows:

	Dec. 31, 2016	Dec. 31, 2015
Accounts receivable	$ 6,500	$ 4,900
Inventory	12,300	15,000
Accounts payable	4,800	5,200
Dividends payable	5,000	4,000

Adjust Victor's net income of $70,000 for changes in operating assets and liabilities to arrive at cash flows from operating activities.

Follow My Example 16-3

Net income	$70,000
Adjustments to reconcile net income to net cash flow from operating activities:	
Changes in current operating assets and liabilities:	
Increase in accounts receivable	(1,600)
Decrease in inventory	2,700
Decrease in accounts payable	(400)
Net cash flow from operating activities	$70,700

Note: The change in dividends payable impacts the cash paid for dividends, which is disclosed under financing activities.

Practice Exercises: PE 16-3A, PE 16-3B

Using the preceding analyses, Rundell's net income of $108,000 is converted to cash flows from operating activities of $100,500 as shown in Exhibit 6.

Integrity, Objectivity, and Ethics in Business

CREDIT POLICY AND CASH FLOW

Investors frequently use net cash flow from operating activities to assess a company's financial health. If a company is financially healthy, net cash flow from operating activities should be roughly consistent with accrual basis net income. Questions arise, however, when a company's net cash flow from operating activities significantly lags net income. There are two scenarios which can cause this to happen:

- Sales on account are never collected in cash.
- Large cash purchases for inventory are never sold, or sell at a very slow pace.

Both of these scenarios increase net income, without a corresponding increase in net cash flow from operating activities. Prudent investors are often skeptical when they observe these scenarios and tend to avoid these types of investments until the cash flows become clear.

Source: Argersinger, M., "How Companies Fake It (With Cash Flow)," *Daily Finance Investor Center*, July 17, 2011.

Example Exercise 16-4 Cash Flows from Operating Activities—Indirect Method

OBJ 2

Omicron Inc. reported the following data:

Net income	$120,000
Depreciation expense	12,000
Loss on disposal of equipment	15,000
Increase in accounts receivable	5,000
Decrease in accounts payable	2,000

Prepare the Cash Flows from Operating Activities section of the statement of cash flows, using the indirect method.

Follow My Example 16-4

Cash flows from operating activities:		
Net income	$120,000	
Adjustments to reconcile net income to net cash flow from operating activities:		
Depreciation expense	12,000	
Loss on disposal of equipment	15,000	
Changes in current operating assets and liabilities:		
Increase in accounts receivable	(5,000)	
Decrease in accounts payable	(2,000)	
Net cash flow from operating activities		$140,000

Practice Exercises: PE 16-4A, PE 16-4B

Dividends

The retained earnings account of **Rundell Inc.** indicates cash dividends of $28,000 were declared during the year. However, the following dividends payable account indicates that only $24,000 of dividends were paid during the year:

Account *Dividends Payable* Account No.

Date		Item	Debit	Credit	Balance Debit	Balance Credit
2016 Jan.	1	Balance				10,000
	10	Cash paid	10,000		—	—
June	20	Dividends declared		14,000		14,000
July	10	Cash paid	14,000		—	—
Dec.	20	Dividends declared		14,000		14,000

Because dividend payments are a financing activity, the dividend payment of $24,000 is reported in the Financing Activities section of the statement of cash flows, as follows:

Cash flows from financing activities:	
Cash paid for dividends	$24,000

Common Stock

The common stock account of **Rundell Inc.** increased by $8,000, and the paid-in capital in excess of par—common stock account increased by $40,000, as follows:

Account *Common Stock*					Account No.	
					Balance	
Date		Item	Debit	Credit	Debit	Credit
2016 Jan.	1	Balance				16,000
Nov.	1	4,000 shares issued for cash		8,000		24,000

Account *Paid-In Capital in Excess of Par—Common Stock*					Account No.	
					Balance	
Date		Item	Debit	Credit	Debit	Credit
2016 Jan.	1	Balance				80,000
Nov.	1	4,000 shares issued for cash		40,000		120,000

These increases were from issuing 4,000 shares of common stock for $12 per share. This cash inflow is reported in the Financing Activities section as follows:

Cash flows from financing activities:	
Cash received from sale of common stock	$48,000

Bonds Payable

The bonds payable account of **Rundell Inc.** decreased by $50,000, as follows:

Account *Bonds Payable*					Account No.	
					Balance	
Date		Item	Debit	Credit	Debit	Credit
2016 Jan.	1	Balance				150,000
June	1	Retired by payment of cash at face amount	50,000			100,000

This decrease is from retiring the bonds by a cash payment for their face amount. This cash outflow is reported in the Financing Activities section as follows:

Cash flows from financing activities:	
Cash paid to retire bonds payable	$50,000

Building

The building account of **Rundell Inc.** increased by $60,000, and the accumulated depreciation—building account increased by $7,000, as follows:

Account *Building* — Account No.

Date		Item	Debit	Credit	Balance Debit	Balance Credit
2016 Jan.	1	Balance			200,000	
Dec.	27	Purchased for cash	60,000		260,000	

Account *Accumulated Depreciation—Building* — Account No.

Date		Item	Debit	Credit	Balance Debit	Balance Credit
2016 Jan.	1	Balance				58,300
Dec.	31	Depreciation for the year		7,000		65,300

The purchase of a building for cash of $60,000 is reported as an outflow of cash in the Investing Activities section as follows:

Cash flows from investing activities:	
Cash paid for purchase of building	$60,000

The credit in the accumulated depreciation—building account represents depreciation expense for the year. This depreciation expense of $7,000 on the building was added to net income in determining cash flows from operating activities, as reported in Exhibit 6.

Land

The $45,000 decline in the land account of **Rundell Inc.** was from two transactions, as follows:

Account *Land* — Account No.

Date		Item	Debit	Credit	Balance Debit	Balance Credit
2016 Jan.	1	Balance			125,000	
June	8	Sold for $72,000 cash		60,000	65,000	
Oct.	12	Purchased for $15,000 cash	15,000		80,000	

The June 8 transaction is the sale of land with a cost of $60,000 for $72,000 in cash. The $72,000 proceeds from the sale are reported in the Investing Activities section as follows:

Cash flows from investing activities:	
Cash received from sale of land	$72,000

The proceeds of $72,000 include the $12,000 gain on the sale of land and the $60,000 cost (book value) of the land. As shown in Exhibit 6, the $12,000 gain is deducted from net income in the Cash Flows from Operating Activities section. This is so that the $12,000 cash inflow related to the gain is not included twice as a cash inflow.

The October 12 transaction is the purchase of land for cash of $15,000. This transaction is reported as an outflow of cash in the Investing Activities section as follows:

Cash flows from investing activities:	
Cash paid for purchase of land	$15,000

Example Exercise 16-5 Land Transactions on the Statement of Cash Flows

OBJ 2

Alpha Corporation purchased land for $125,000. Later in the year, the company sold a different piece of land with a book value of $165,000 for $200,000. How are the effects of these transactions reported on the statement of cash flows?

Follow My Example 16-5

The gain on the sale of the land is deducted from net income, as follows:

Gain on sale of land	$ (35,000)

The purchase and sale of land is reported as part of cash flows from investing activities, as follows:

Cash received from sale of land	$200,000
Cash paid for purchase of land	(125,000)

Practice Exercises: PE 16-5A, PE 16-5B

Preparing the Statement of Cash Flows

The statement of cash flows for **Rundell Inc.**, using the indirect method, is shown in Exhibit 7. The statement of cash flows indicates that cash increased by $71,500 during the year. The most significant increase in net cash flows ($100,500) was from operating activities. The most significant use of cash ($26,000) was for financing activities. The ending balance of cash on December 31, 2016, is $97,500. This ending cash balance is also reported on the December 31, 2016, balance sheet shown in Exhibit 4.

EXHIBIT 7

Statement of Cash Flows—Indirect Method

Rundell Inc.
Statement of Cash Flows
For the Year Ended December 31, 2016

Cash flows from operating activities:			
Net income..		$108,000	
Adjustments to reconcile net income to net cash flow from operating activities:			
Depreciation		7,000	
Gain on sale of land..................................		(12,000)	
Changes in current operating assets and liabilities:			
Increase in accounts receivable.................		(9,000)	
Decrease in inventories..........................		8,000	
Decrease in accounts payable		(3,200)	
Increase in accrued expenses payable...........		2,200	
Decrease in income taxes payable		(500)	
Net cash flow from operating activities			$100,500
Cash flows from investing activities:			
Cash received from sale of land		$ 72,000	
Less: Cash paid for purchase of land	$15,000		
Cash paid for purchase of building	60,000	75,000	
Net cash flow used for investing activities.............			(3,000)
Cash flows from financing activities:			
Cash received from sale of common stock.............		$ 48,000	
Less: Cash paid to retire bonds payable	$50,000		
Cash paid for dividends..........................	24,000	74,000	
Net cash flow used for financing activities			(26,000)
Increase in cash			$ 71,500
Cash at the beginning of the year..........................			26,000
Cash at the end of the year................................			$ 97,500

OBJ 3 Prepare a statement of cash flows, using the direct method.

Preparing the Statement of Cash Flows—The Direct Method

The direct method reports cash flows from operating activities as follows:

Cash flows from operating activities:		
Cash received from customers		$ XXX
Less: Cash payments for merchandise	$ XXX	
Cash payments for operating expenses	XXX	
Cash payments for interest	XXX	
Cash payments for income taxes	XXX	XXX
Net cash flow from operating activities		$ XXX

The Cash Flows from Investing and Financing Activities sections of the statement of cash flows are exactly the same under both the direct and indirect methods. The amount of net cash flow from operating activities is also the same, but the manner in which it is reported is different.

Under the direct method, the income statement is adjusted to cash flows from operating activities as shown in Exhibit 8.

EXHIBIT 8

Converting Income Statement to Cash Flows from Operating Activities using the Direct Method

Income Statement	Adjusted to	Cash Flows from Operating Activities
Sales	→	Cash received from customers
Cost of merchandise sold	→	Cash payments for merchandise
Operating expenses:		
Depreciation expense	N/A	N/A
Other operating expenses	→	Cash payments for operating expenses
Gain on sale of land	N/A	N/A
Interest expense	→	Cash payments for interest
Income tax expense	→	Cash payments for income taxes
Net income	→	Net cash flow from operating activities

N/A—Not applicable

As shown in Exhibit 8, depreciation expense is not adjusted or reported as part of cash flows from operating activities. This is because deprecation expense does not involve a cash outflow. The gain on the sale of the land is also not adjusted and is not reported as part of cash flows from operating activities. This is because the cash flow from operating activities is determined directly, rather than by reconciling net income. The cash proceeds from the sale of the land are reported as an investing activity.

To illustrate the direct method, the income statement and comparative balance sheet for Rundell Inc., shown in Exhibit 4, are used.

Cash Received from Customers

The income statement (shown in Exhibit 4) of **Rundell Inc.** reports sales of $1,180,000. To determine the cash received from customers, the $1,180,000 is adjusted for any increase or decrease in accounts receivable. The adjustment is summarized in Exhibit 9.

EXHIBIT 9

Determining the Cash Received from Customers

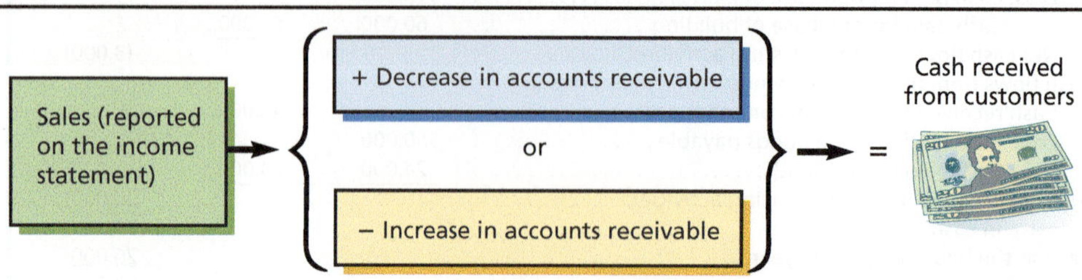

The cash received from customers is $1,171,000, computed as follows:

Sales	$1,180,000
Less increase in accounts receivable	9,000
Cash received from customers	$1,171,000

The increase of $9,000 in accounts receivable (shown in Exhibit 4) during 2016 indicates that sales on account exceeded cash received from customers by $9,000. In other words, sales include $9,000 that did not result in a cash inflow during the year. Thus, $9,000 is deducted from sales to determine the cash received from customers.

Example Exercise 16-6 Cash Received from Customers—Direct Method OBJ 3

Sales reported on the income statement were $350,000. The accounts receivable balance declined $8,000 over the year. Determine the amount of cash received from customers.

Follow My Example 16-6

Sales	$350,000
Add decrease in accounts receivable	8,000
Cash received from customers	$358,000

Practice Exercises: PE 16-6A, PE 16-6B

Cash Payments for Merchandise

The income statement (shown in Exhibit 4) for **Rundell Inc.** reports cost of merchandise sold of $790,000. To determine the cash payments for merchandise, the $790,000 is adjusted for any increases or decreases in inventories and accounts payable. Assuming the accounts payable are owed to merchandise suppliers, the adjustment is summarized in Exhibit 10.

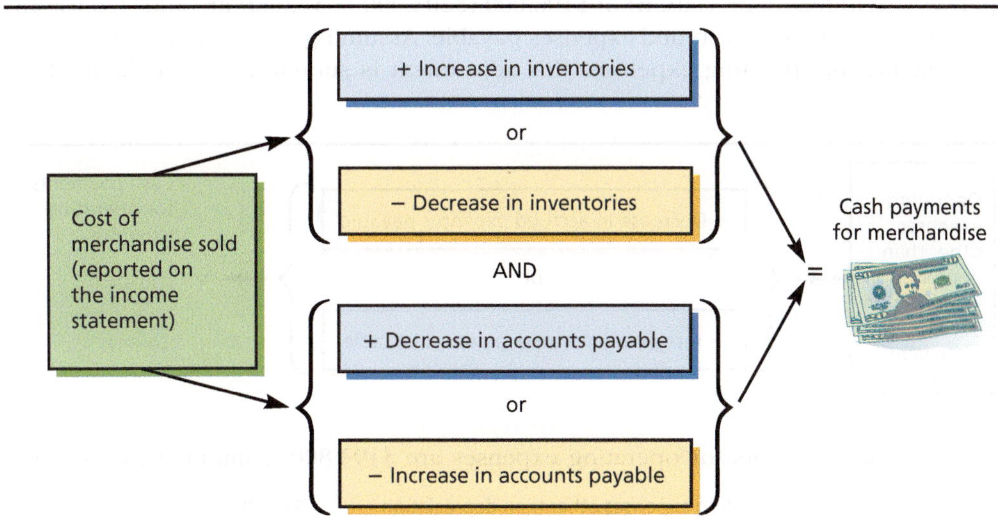

EXHIBIT 10

Determining the Cash Payments for Merchandise

The cash payments for merchandise are $785,200, computed as follows:

Cost of merchandise sold	$790,000
Deduct decrease in inventories	(8,000)
Add decrease in accounts payable	3,200
Cash payments for merchandise	$785,200

The $8,000 decrease in inventories (from Exhibit 4) indicates that the merchandise sold exceeded the cost of the merchandise purchased by $8,000. In other words, the cost of merchandise sold includes $8,000 of goods sold from inventory that did not require a cash outflow during the year. Thus, $8,000 is deducted from the cost of merchandise sold in determining the cash payments for merchandise.

The $3,200 decrease in accounts payable (from Exhibit 4) indicates that cash payments for merchandise were $3,200 more than the purchases on account during 2016. Therefore, $3,200 is added to the cost of merchandise sold in determining the cash payments for merchandise.

Example Exercise 16-7 Cash Payments for Merchandise—Direct Method

OBJ 3

The cost of merchandise sold reported on the income statement was $145,000. The accounts payable balance increased by $4,000, and the inventory balance increased by $9,000 over the year. Determine the amount of cash paid for merchandise.

Follow My Example 16-7

Cost of merchandise sold	$145,000
Add increase in inventories	9,000
Deduct increase in accounts payable	(4,000)
Cash paid for merchandise	$150,000

Practice Exercises: PE 16-7A, PE 16-7B

Cash Payments for Operating Expenses

The income statement for **Rundell Inc.** (from Exhibit 4) reports total operating expenses of $203,000, which includes depreciation expense of $7,000. Because depreciation expense does not require a cash outflow, it is omitted from cash payments for operating expenses.

To determine the cash payments for operating expenses, the other operating expenses (excluding depreciation) of $196,000 ($203,000 − $7,000) are adjusted for any increase or decrease in accrued expenses payable. Assuming that the accrued expenses payable are all operating expenses, this adjustment is summarized in Exhibit 11.

EXHIBIT 11

Determining the Cash Payments for Operating Expenses

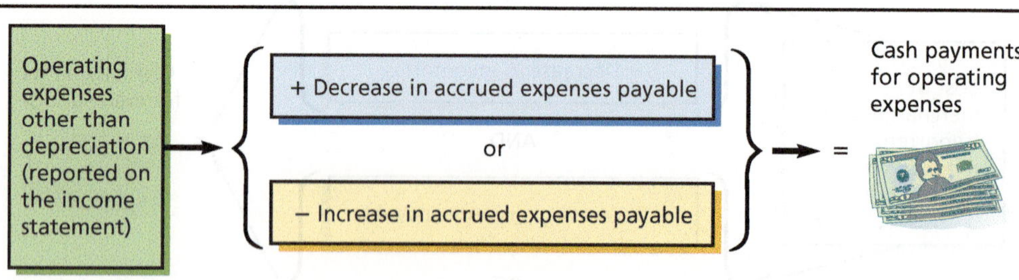

The cash payments for operating expenses are $193,800, computed as follows:

Operating expenses other than depreciation	$196,000
Deduct increase in accrued expenses payable	(2,200)
Cash payments for operating expenses	$193,800

The increase in accrued expenses payable (from Exhibit 4) indicates that the cash payments for operating expenses were $2,200 less than the amount reported for operating expenses during the year. Thus, $2,200 is deducted from the operating expenses in determining the cash payments for operating expenses.

Gain on Sale of Land

The income statement for **Rundell Inc.** (from Exhibit 4) reports a gain of $12,000 on the sale of land. The sale of land is an investing activity. Thus, the proceeds from the sale, which include the gain, are reported as part of the cash flows from investing activities.

Interest Expense

The income statement for **Rundell Inc.** (from Exhibit 4) reports interest expense of $8,000. To determine the cash payments for interest, the $8,000 is adjusted for any increases or decreases in interest payable. The adjustment is summarized in Exhibit 12.

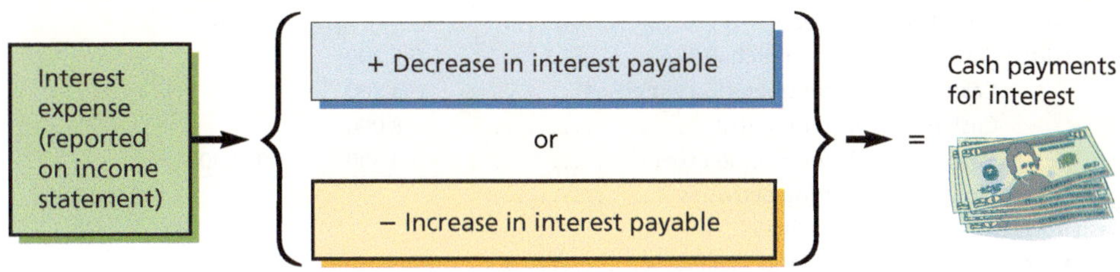

EXHIBIT 12

Determining the Cash Payments for Interest

The comparative balance sheet of Rundell in Exhibit 4 indicates no interest payable. This is because the interest expense on the bonds payable is paid on June 1 and December 31. Because there is no interest payable, no adjustment of the interest expense of $8,000 is necessary.

Cash Payments for Income Taxes

The income statement for **Rundell Inc.** (from Exhibit 3) reports income tax expense of $83,000. To determine the cash payments for income taxes, the $83,000 is adjusted for any increases or decreases in income taxes payable. The adjustment is summarized in Exhibit 13.

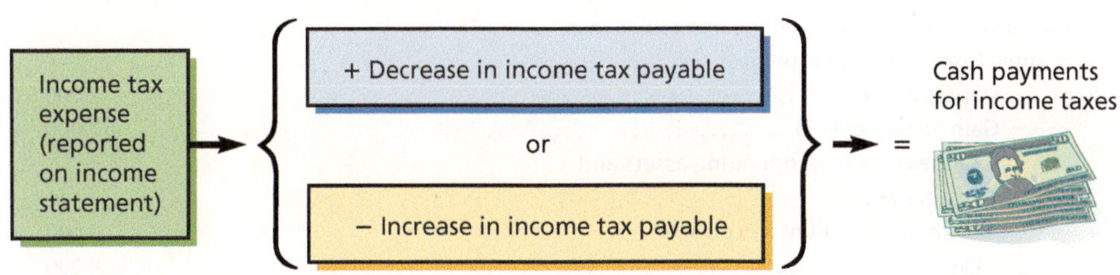

EXHIBIT 13

Determining the Cash Payments for Income Taxes

The cash payments for income taxes are $83,500, computed as follows:

Income tax expense	$83,000
Add decrease in income taxes payable	500
Cash payments for income taxes	$83,500

The $500 decrease in income taxes payable (from Exhibit 4) indicates that the cash payments for income taxes were $500 more than the amount reported for income tax expense during 2016. Thus, $500 is added to the income tax expense in determining the cash payments for income taxes.

Reporting Cash Flows from Operating Activities—Direct Method

The statement of cash flows for **Rundell Inc.**, using the direct method for reporting cash flows from operating activities, is shown in Exhibit 14. The portions of the statement that differ from those prepared under the indirect method are highlighted.

EXHIBIT 14

Statement of Cash Flows—Direct Method

Rundell Inc.
Statement of Cash Flows
For the Year Ended December 31, 2016

Cash flows from operating activities:			
Cash received from customers		$1,171,000	
Deduct: Cash payments for merchandise	$785,200		
Cash payments for operating expenses	193,800		
Cash payments for interest	8,000		
Cash payments for income taxes	83,500	1,070,500	
Net cash flow from operating activities			$100,500
Cash flows from investing activities:			
Cash received from sale of land		$ 72,000	
Less: Cash paid for purchase of land	$ 15,000		
Cash paid for purchase of building	60,000	75,000	
Net cash flow used for investing activities			(3,000)
Cash flows from financing activities:			
Cash received from sale of common stock		$ 48,000	
Less: Cash paid to retire bonds payable	$ 50,000		
Cash paid for dividends	24,000	74,000	
Net cash flow used for financing activities			(26,000)
Increase in cash			$ 71,500
Cash at the beginning of the year			26,000
Cash at the end of the year			$ 97,500
Schedule Reconciling Net Income with Cash Flows from Operating Activities:			
Cash flows from operating activities:			
Net income			$108,000
Adjustments to reconcile net income to net cash flow from operating activities:			
Depreciation			7,000
Gain on sale of land			(12,000)
Changes in current operating assets and liabilities:			
Increase in accounts receivable			(9,000)
Decrease in inventory			8,000
Decrease in accounts payable			(3,200)
Increase in accrued expenses payable			2,200
Decrease in income taxes payable			(500)
Net cash flow from operating activities			$100,500

Exhibit 14 also includes the separate schedule reconciling net income and net cash flow from operating activities. This schedule is included in the statement of cash flows when the direct method is used. This schedule is similar to the Cash Flows from Operating Activities section prepared under the indirect method.

International Connection

IFRS FOR STATEMENT OF CASH FLOWS

The statement of cash flows is required under International Financial Reporting Standards (IFRS). The statement of cash flows under IFRS is similar to that reported under U.S. GAAP in that the statement has separate sections for operating, investing, and financing activities. Like U.S. GAAP, IFRS also allow the use of either the indirect or direct method of reporting cash flows from operating activities. IFRS differ from U.S. GAAP in some minor areas, including:

- Interest paid can be reported as either an operating or a financing activity, while interest received can be reported as either an operating or an investing activity. In contrast, U.S. GAAP reports interest paid or received as an operating activity.
- Dividends paid can be reported as either an operating or a financing activity, while dividends received can be reported as either an operating or an investing activity. In contrast, U.S. GAAP reports dividends paid as a financing activity and dividends received as an operating activity.
- Cash flows to pay taxes are reported as a separate line in the operating activities, in contrast to U.S. GAAP, which does not require a separate line disclosure.

* IFRS are further discussed and illustrated in this chapter and in Appendix D.

Financial Analysis and Interpretation: Free Cash Flow

OBJ 4 Describe and illustrate the use of free cash flow in evaluating a company's cash flow.

F·A·I

A valuable tool for evaluating the cash flows of a business is free cash flow. **Free cash flow** measures the operating cash flow available to a company to use after purchasing the property, plant, and equipment (PP&E) necessary to maintain current productive capacity.[5] It is computed as follows:

Cash flow from operating activities	$XXX
Less: Investments in PP&E needed to maintain current production	XXX
Free cash flow	$XXX

Analysts often use free cash flow, rather than cash flows from operating activities, to measure the financial strength of a business. Industries such as airlines, railroads, and telecommunications companies must invest heavily in new equipment to remain competitive. Such investments can significantly reduce free cash flow. For example, Verizon Communications Inc.'s free cash flow is approximately 51% of the cash flow from operating activities. In contrast, Apple Inc.'s free cash flow is approximately 89% of the cash flow from operating activities.

To illustrate, the cash flow from operating activities for Research in Motion, Inc., maker of BlackBerry® smartphones, was $2,912 million in a recent fiscal year. The statement of cash flows indicated that the cash invested in property, plant, and equipment was $902 million. Assuming that the amount invested in property, plant, and equipment is necessary to maintain productive capacity, free cash flow would be computed as follows (in millions):

Cash flow from operating activities	$2,912
Less: Investments in PP&E needed to maintain current production	902
Free cash flow	$2,010

Research in Motion's free cash flow was 69% of cash flow from operations and more than 10% of sales. Compare this to the calculation of free cash flows for Apple Inc.

[5] Productive capacity is the number of goods the company is currently producing and selling.

(a computer company), The Coca-Cola Company (a beverage company), and Verizon Communications, Inc. (a telecommunications company), that follows (in millions):

	Apple Inc.	The Coca-Cola Company	Verizon Communications, Inc.
Sales	$156,508	$48,017	$115,846
Cash flow from operating activities	50,856	10,645	31,486
Less: Investments in PP&E needed to maintain current production	8,295	2,870	16,175
Free cash flow	$ 42,561	$ 7,775	$ 15,311
Free cash flow as a percentage of cash flow from operations	84%	73%	49%
Free cash flow as a percentage of sales	27%	16%	13%

Positive free cash flow is considered favorable. A company that has free cash flow is able to fund internal growth, retire debt, pay dividends, and benefit from financial flexibility. A company with no free cash flow is unable to maintain current productive capacity. Lack of free cash flow can be an early indicator of liquidity problems. As one analyst notes, "Free cash flow gives the company firepower to reduce debt and ultimately generate consistent, actual income."[6]

Example Exercise 16-8 Free Cash Flow

OBJ 4

Omnicron Inc. reported the following on the company's cash flow statement in 2016 and 2015:

	2016	2015
Net cash flow from operating activities	$140,000	$120,000
Net cash flow used for investing activities	(120,000)	(80,000)
Net cash flow used for financing activities	(20,000)	(32,000)

Seventy-five percent of the net cash flow used for investing activities was used to replace existing capacity.

a. Determine Omnicron's free cash flow.

b. Has Omnicron's free cash flow improved or declined from 2015 to 2016?

Follow My Example 16-8

a.

	2016	2015
Net cash flow from operating activities	$140,000	$120,000
Less: Investments in fixed assets to maintain current production	90,000[1]	60,000[2]
Free cash flow	$ 50,000	$ 60,000

[1] $120,000 × 75%
[2] $80,000 × 75%

b. The change from $60,000 to $50,000 indicates an unfavorable trend.

Practice Exercises: PE 16-8A, PE 16-8B

[6] Jill Krutick, *Fortune*, March 30, 1998, p. 106.

APPENDIX

Spreadsheet (Work Sheet) for Statement of Cash Flows—The Indirect Method

A spreadsheet (work sheet) may be used in preparing the statement of cash flows. However, whether or not a spreadsheet (work sheet) is used, the concepts presented in this chapter are not affected.

The data for **Rundell Inc.**, presented in Exhibit 4 are used as a basis for illustrating the spreadsheet (work sheet) for the indirect method. The steps in preparing this spreadsheet (work sheet), shown in Exhibit 15, are as follows:

- Step 1. List the title of each balance sheet account in the Accounts column.
- Step 2. For each balance sheet account, enter its balance as of December 31, 2015, in the first column and its balance as of December 31, 2016, in the last column. Place the credit balances in parentheses.
- Step 3. Add the December 31, 2015 and 2016 column totals, which should total to zero.
- Step 4. Analyze the change during the year in each noncash account to determine its net increase (decrease) and classify the change as affecting cash flows from operating activities, investing activities, financing activities, or noncash investing and financing activities.
- Step 5. Indicate the effect of the change on cash flows by making entries in the Transactions columns.
- Step 6. After all noncash accounts have been analyzed, enter the net increase (decrease) in cash during the period.
- Step 7. Add the Debit and Credit Transactions columns. The totals should be equal.

Analyzing Accounts

In analyzing the noncash accounts (Step 4), try to determine the type of cash flow activity (operating, investing, or financing) that led to the change in the account. As each noncash account is analyzed, an entry (Step 5) is made on the spreadsheet (work sheet) for the type of cash flow activity that caused the change. After all noncash accounts have been analyzed, an entry (Step 6) is made for the increase (decrease) in cash during the period.

The entries made on the spreadsheet are not posted to the ledger. They are only used in preparing and summarizing the data on the spreadsheet.

The order in which the accounts are analyzed is not important. However, it is more efficient to begin with Retained Earnings and proceed upward in the account listing.

Retained Earnings

The spreadsheet (work sheet) shows a Retained Earnings balance of $202,300 at December 31, 2015, and $282,300 at December 31, 2016. Thus, Retained Earnings increased $80,000 during the year. This increase is from the following:

- Net income of $108,000
- Declaring cash dividends of $28,000

To identify the cash flows from these activities, two entries are made on the spreadsheet.

EXHIBIT 15 End-of-Period Spreadsheet (Work Sheet) for Statement of Cash Flows—Indirect Method

Step 2

	A	B	C	D	E	F	G
1	Rundell Inc.						
2	End-of-Period Spreadsheet (Work Sheet) for Statement of Cash Flows						
3	For the Year Ended December 31, 2016						
4	Accounts	Balance,		Transactions			Balance,
5		Dec. 31, 2015		Debit		Credit	Dec. 31, 2016
6	Cash	26,000	(o)	71,500			97,500
7	Accounts receivable (net)	65,000	(n)	9,000			74,000
8	Inventories	180,000			(m)	8,000	172,000
9	Land	125,000	(k)	15,000	(l)	60,000	80,000
10	Building	200,000	(j)	60,000			260,000
11	Accumulated depreciation—building	(58,300)			(i)	7,000	(65,300)
12	Accounts payable (merchandise creditors)	(46,700)	(h)	3,200			(43,500)
13	Accrued expenses payable (operating expenses)	(24,300)			(g)	2,200	(26,500)
14	Income taxes payable	(8,400)	(f)	500			(7,900)
15	Dividends payable	(10,000)			(e)	4,000	(14,000)
16	Bonds payable	(150,000)	(d)	50,000			(100,000)
17	Common stock	(16,000)			(c)	8,000	(24,000)
18	Paid-in capital in excess of par	(80,000)			(c)	40,000	(120,000)
19	Retained earnings	(202,300)	(b)	28,000	(a)	108,000	(282,300)
20	Totals Step 3 →	0		237,200		237,200	0 ← Step 3
21	Operating activities:						
22	Net income		(a)	108,000			
23	Depreciation of building		(i)	7,000			
24	Gain on sale of land				(l)	12,000	
25	Increase in accounts receivable				(n)	9,000	
26	Decrease in inventories		(m)	8,000			
27	Decrease in accounts payable				(h)	3,200	
28	Increase in accrued expenses payable		(g)	2,200			
29	Decrease in income taxes payable				(f)	500	
30	Investing activities:						
31	Sale of land		(l)	72,000			
32	Purchase of land				(k)	15,000	
33	Purchase of building				(j)	60,000	
34	Financing activities:						
35	Issued common stock		(c)	48,000			
36	Retired bonds payable				(d)	50,000	
37	Declared cash dividends				(b)	28,000	
38	Increase in dividends payable		(e)	4,000			
39	Net increase in cash				(o)	71,500	
40	Totals			249,200		249,200	

Step 1 (rows 6–20)

Steps 4–7

The $108,000 is reported on the statement of cash flows as part of cash flows from operating activities. Thus, an entry is made in the Transactions columns on the spreadsheet, as follows:

		Debit	Credit
(a)	Operating Activities—Net Income	108,000	
	Retained Earnings		108,000

The preceding entry accounts for the net income portion of the change to Retained Earnings. It also identifies the cash flow in the bottom portion of the spreadsheet as related to operating activities.

The $28,000 of dividends is reported as a financing activity on the statement of cash flows. Thus, an entry is made in the Transactions columns on the spreadsheet, as follows:

		Debit	Credit
(b)	Retained Earnings	28,000	
	Financing Activities—Declared Cash Dividends		28,000

The preceding entry accounts for the dividends portion of the change to Retained Earnings. It also identifies the cash flow in the bottom portion of the spreadsheet as related to financing activities. The $28,000 of declared dividends will be adjusted later for the actual amount of cash dividends paid during the year.

Other Accounts

The entries for the other noncash accounts are made in the spreadsheet in a manner similar to entries (a) and (b). A summary of these entries follows:

		Debit	Credit
(c)	Financing Activities—Issued Common Stock	48,000	
	Common Stock		8,000
	Paid-In Capital in Excess of Par—Common Stock		40,000
(d)	Bonds Payable	50,000	
	Financing Activities—Retired Bonds Payable		50,000
(e)	Financing Activities—Increase in Dividends Payable	4,000	
	Dividends Payable		4,000
(f)	Income Taxes Payable	500	
	Operating Activities—Decrease in Income Taxes Payable		500
(g)	Operating Activities—Increase in Accrued Expenses Payable	2,200	
	Accrued Expenses Payable		2,200
(h)	Accounts Payable	3,200	
	Operating Activities—Decrease in Accounts Payable		3,200
(i)	Operating Activities—Depreciation of Building	7,000	
	Accumulated Depreciation—Building		7,000
(j)	Building	60,000	
	Investing Activities—Purchase of Building		60,000
(k)	Land	15,000	
	Investing Activities—Purchase of Land		15,000
(l)	Investing Activities—Sale of Land	72,000	
	Operating Activities—Gain on Sale of Land		12,000
	Land		60,000
(m)	Operating Activities—Decrease in Inventories	8,000	
	Inventories		8,000
(n)	Accounts Receivable	9,000	
	Operating Activities—Increase in Accounts Receivable		9,000
(o)	Cash	71,500	
	Net Increase in Cash		71,500

After all the balance sheet accounts are analyzed and the entries made on the spreadsheet (work sheet), all the operating, investing, and financing activities are identified in the bottom portion of the spreadsheet. The accuracy of the entries is verified by totaling the Debit and Credit Transactions columns. The totals of the columns should be equal.

Preparing the Statement of Cash Flows

The statement of cash flows prepared from the spreadsheet is identical to the statement in Exhibit 7. The data for the three sections of the statement are obtained from the bottom portion of the spreadsheet.

At a Glance 16

OBJ 1 Describe the cash flow activities reported in the statement of cash flows.

Key Points The statement of cash flows reports cash receipts and cash payments by three types of activities: operating activities, investing activities, and financing activities. Cash flows from operating activities reports the cash inflows and outflows from a company's day-to-day operations. Cash flows from investing activities reports the cash inflows and outflows related to changes in a company's long-term assets. Cash flows from financing activities reports the cash inflows and outflows related to changes in a company's long-term liabilities and stockholders' equity. Investing and financing for a business may be affected by transactions that do not involve cash. The effect of such transactions should be reported in a separate schedule accompanying the statement of cash flows.

Learning Outcome	Example Exercises	Practice Exercises
• Classify transactions that either provide or use cash into either operating, investing, or financing activities.	**EE16-1**	**PE16-1A, 16-1B**

OBJ 2 Prepare a statement of cash flows, using the indirect method.

Key Points The indirect method reports cash flows from operating activities by adjusting net income for revenues and expenses that do not involve the receipt or payment of cash. Noncash expenses such as depreciation are added back to net income. Gains and losses on the disposal of assets are added to or deducted from net income. Changes in current operating assets and liabilities are added to or subtracted from net income, depending on their effect on cash. Cash flows from investing activities and cash flows from financing activities are reported below cash flows from operating activities in the statement of cash flows.

Learning Outcomes	Example Exercises	Practice Exercises
• Determine cash flows from operating activities under the indirect method by adjusting net income for noncash expenses and gains and losses from asset disposals.	**EE16-2**	**PE16-2A, 16-2B**
• Determine cash flows from operating activities under the indirect method by adjusting net income for changes in current operating assets and liabilities.	**EE16-3**	**PE16-3A, 16-3B**
• Prepare the Cash Flows from Operating Activities section of the statement of cash flows, using the indirect method.	**EE16-4**	**PE16-4A, 16-4B**
• Prepare the Cash Flows from Investing Activities and Cash Flows from Financing Activities sections of the statement of cash flows.	**EE16-5**	**PE16-5A, 16-5B**

OBJ 3 Prepare a statement of cash flows, using the direct method.

Key Points The amount of cash flows from operating activities is the same under both the direct and indirect methods, but the manner in which cash flows operating activities is reported is different. The direct method reports cash flows from operating activities by major classes of operating cash receipts and cash payments. The difference between the major classes of total operating cash receipts and total operating cash payments is the net cash flow from operating activities. The Cash Flows from Investing and Financing Activities sections of the statement are the same under both the direct and indirect methods.

Learning Outcome	Example Exercises	Practice Exercises
• Prepare the cash flows from operating activities section of the statement of cash flows under the direct method.	**EE16-6** **EE16-7**	**PE16-6A, 16-6B** **PE16-7A, 16-7B**

OBJ 4 Describe and illustrate the use of free cash flow in evaluating a company's cash flow.

Key Points Free cash flow measures the operating cash flow available for company use after purchasing the fixed assets that are necessary to maintain current productive capacity. It is calculated by subtracting these fixed asset purchases from net cash flow from operating activities. A company with strong free cash flow is able to fund internal growth, retire debt, pay dividends, and enjoy financial flexibility. A company with weak free cash flow has much less financial flexibility.

Learning Outcomes	Example Exercises	Practice Exercises
• Describe free cash flow.		
• Calculate and evaluate free cash flow.	**EE16-8**	**PE16-8A, 16-8B**

Key Terms

cash flow per share (744)
cash flows from financing activities (741)
cash flows from investing activities (740)
cash flows from operating activities (740)
direct method (741)
free cash flow (759)
indirect method (742)
statement of cash flows (740)

Illustrative Problem

The comparative balance sheet of Dowling Company for December 31, 2016 and 2015, is as follows:

Dowling Company
Comparative Balance Sheet
December 31, 2016 and 2015

	2016	2015
Assets		
Cash	$ 140,350	$ 95,900
Accounts receivable (net)	95,300	102,300
Inventories	165,200	157,900
Prepaid expenses	6,240	5,860
Investments (long-term)	35,700	84,700
Land	75,000	90,000
Buildings	375,000	260,000
Accumulated depreciation—buildings	(71,300)	(58,300)
Machinery and equipment	428,300	428,300
Accumulated depreciation—machinery and equipment	(148,500)	(138,000)
Patents	58,000	65,000
Total assets	$1,159,290	$1,093,660
Liabilities and Stockholders' Equity		
Accounts payable (merchandise creditors)	$ 43,500	$ 46,700
Accrued expenses payable (operating expenses)	14,000	12,500
Income taxes payable	7,900	8,400
Dividends payable	14,000	10,000
Mortgage note payable, due 2023	40,000	0
Bonds payable	150,000	250,000
Common stock, $30 par	450,000	375,000
Excess of issue price over par—common stock	66,250	41,250
Retained earnings	373,640	349,810
Total liabilities and stockholders' equity	$1,159,290	$1,093,660

The income statement for Dowling Company follows:

Dowling Company
Income Statement
For the Year Ended December 31, 2016

Sales		$1,100,000
Cost of merchandise sold		710,000
Gross profit		$ 390,000
Operating expenses:		
Depreciation expense	$ 23,500	
Patent amortization	7,000	
Other operating expenses	196,000	
Total operating expenses		226,500
Income from operations		$ 163,500
Other income:		
Gain on sale of investments	$ 11,000	
Other expense:		
Interest expense	26,000	(15,000)
Income before income tax		$ 148,500
Income tax expense		50,000
Net income		$ 98,500

An examination of the accounting records revealed the following additional information applicable to 2016:

a. Land costing $15,000 was sold for $15,000.

b. A mortgage note was issued for $40,000.

c. A building costing $115,000 was constructed.

d. 2,500 shares of common stock were issued at $40 in exchange for the bonds payable.

e. Cash dividends declared were $74,670.

Instructions

1. Prepare a statement of cash flows, using the indirect method of reporting cash flows from operating activities.
2. Prepare a statement of cash flows, using the direct method of reporting cash flows from operating activities.

Solution

1.

Dowling Company
Statement of Cash Flows—Indirect Method
For the Year Ended December 31, 2016

Cash flows from operating activities:			
Net income		$ 98,500	
Adjustments to reconcile net income to net cash flow from operating activities:			
Depreciation		23,500	
Amortization of patents		7,000	
Gain on sale of investments		(11,000)	
Changes in current operating assets and liabilities:			
Decrease in accounts receivable		7,000	
Increase in inventories		(7,300)	
Increase in prepaid expenses		(380)	
Decrease in accounts payable		(3,200)	
Increase in accrued expenses payable		1,500	
Decrease in income taxes payable		(500)	
Net cash flow from operating activities			$115,120
Cash flows from investing activities:			
Cash received from sale of:			
Investments	$60,000[1]		
Land	15,000	$ 75,000	
Less: Cash paid for construction of building		115,000	
Net cash flow used for investing activities			(40,000)
Cash flows from financing activities:			
Cash received from issuing mortgage note payable		$ 40,000	
Less: Cash paid for dividends		70,670[2]	
Net cash flow used for financing activities			(30,670)
Increase in cash			$ 44,450
Cash at the beginning of the year			95,900
Cash at the end of the year			$140,350

Schedule of Noncash Investing and Financing Activities:

Issued common stock to retire bonds payable	$100,000

[1] $60,000 = $11,000 gain + $49,000 (decrease in investments)

[2] $70,670 = $74,670 − $4,000 (increase in dividends)

2.

Dowling Company Statement of Cash Flows—Direct Method For the Year Ended December 31, 2016			
Cash flows from operating activities:			
Cash received from customers[1]		$1,107,000	
Deduct: Cash paid for merchandise[2]	$720,500		
Cash paid for operating expenses[3]	194,880		
Cash paid for interest expense	26,000		
Cash paid for income tax[4]	50,500	991,880	
Net cash flow from operating activities			$115,120
Cash flows from investing activities:			
Cash received from sale of:			
Investments	$ 60,000[5]		
Land	15,000	$ 75,000	
Less: Cash paid for construction of building		115,000	
Net cash flow used for investing activities			(40,000)
Cash flows from financing activities:			
Cash received from issuing mortgage note payable		$ 40,000	
Less: Cash paid for dividends[6]		70,670	
Net cash flow used for financing activities			(30,670)
Increase in cash			$ 44,450
Cash at the beginning of the year			95,900
Cash at the end of the year			$140,350
Schedule of Noncash Investing and Financing Activities:			
Issued common stock to retire bonds payable			$100,000
Schedule Reconciling Net Income with Cash Flows from Operating Activities[7]			

Computations:

[1]$1,100,000 + $7,000 = $1,107,000
[2]$710,000 + $3,200 + $7,300 = $720,500
[3]$196,000 + $380 − $1,500 = $194,880
[4]$50,000 + $500 = $50,500
[5]$60,000 = $11,000 gain + $49,000 (decrease in investments)
[6]$74,670 + $10,000 − $14,000 = $70,670
[7]The content of this schedule is the same as the Operating Activities section of part (1) of this solution and is not reproduced here for the sake of brevity.

Discussion Questions

1. What is the principal disadvantage of the direct method of reporting cash flows from operating activities?
2. What are the major advantages of the indirect method of reporting cash flows from operating activities?
3. A corporation issued $2,000,000 of common stock in exchange for $2,000,000 of fixed assets. Where would this transaction be reported on the statement of cash flows?
4. A retail business, using the accrual method of accounting, owed merchandise creditors (accounts payable) $320,000 at the beginning of the year and $350,000 at the end of the year. How would the $30,000 increase be used to adjust net income in determining the amount of cash flows from operating activities by the indirect method? Explain.

5. If salaries payable was $100,000 at the beginning of the year and $75,000 at the end of the year, should $25,000 decrease be added to or deducted from income to determine the amount of cash flows from operating activities by the indirect method? Explain.

6. A long-term investment in bonds with a cost of $500,000 was sold for $600,000 cash. (a) What was the gain or loss on the sale? (b) What was the effect of the transaction on cash flows? (c) How should the transaction be reported on the statement of cash flows if cash flows from operating activities are reported by the indirect method?

7. A corporation issued $2,000,000 of 20-year bonds for cash at 98. How would the transaction be reported on the statement of cash flows?

8. Fully depreciated equipment costing $50,000 was discarded. What was the effect of the transaction on cash flows if (a) $15,000 cash is received for the equipment, (b) no cash is received for the equipment?

9. For the current year, Packers Company decided to switch from the indirect method to the direct method for reporting cash flows from operating activities on the statement of cash flows. Will the change cause the amount of net cash flow from operating activities to be larger, smaller, or the same as if the indirect method had been used? Explain.

10. Name five common major classes of operating cash receipts or operating cash payments presented on the statement of cash flows when the cash flows from operating activities are reported by the direct method.

Practice Exercises

EE 16-1 p. 744

SHOW ME HOW

PE 16-1A Classifying cash flows

OBJ. 1

Identify whether each of the following would be reported as an operating, investing, or financing activity on the statement of cash flows:

a. Repurchase of common stock
b. Cash received from customers
c. Payment of accounts payable
d. Retirement of bonds payable
e. Purchase of equipment
f. Purchase of inventory for cash

EE 16-1 p. 744

SHOW ME HOW

PE 16-1B Classifying cash flows

OBJ. 1

Identify whether each of the following would be reported as an operating, investing, or financing activity on the statement of cash flows:

a. Purchase of investments
b. Disposal of equipment
c. Payment for selling expenses
d. Collection of accounts receivable
e. Cash sales
f. Issuance of bonds payable

EE 16-2 p. 747

SHOW ME HOW

PE 16-2A Adjustments to net income—indirect method

OBJ. 2

Pearl Corporation's accumulated depreciation—furniture account increased by $8,400, while $3,080 of patent amortization was recognized between balance sheet dates. There were no purchases or sales of depreciable or intangible assets during the year. In addition, the income statement showed a loss of $4,480 from the sale of land. Reconcile a net income of $120,400 to net cash flow from operating activities.

EE 16-2 p. 747

SHOW ME HOW

PE 16-2B Adjustments to net income—indirect method

OBJ. 2

Ya Wen Corporation's accumulated depreciation—equipment account increased by $8,750, while $3,250 of patent amortization was recognized between balance sheet dates. There were no purchases or sales of depreciable or intangible assets during the year. In addition, the income statement showed a gain of $18,750 from the sale of investments. Reconcile a net income of $175,000 to net cash flow from operating activities.

EE 16-3 p. 749 **PE 16-3A Changes in current operating assets and liabilities—indirect method** OBJ. 2

SHOW ME HOW

Alpenrose Corporation's comparative balance sheet for current assets and liabilities was as follows:

	Dec. 31, 2016	Dec. 31, 2015
Accounts receivable	$27,000	$32,400
Inventory	18,000	15,480
Accounts payable	16,200	14,220
Dividends payable	49,500	53,100

Adjust net income of $207,000 for changes in operating assets and liabilities to arrive at net cash flow from operating activities.

EE 16-3 p. 749 **PE 16-3B Changes in current operating assets and liabilities—indirect method** OBJ. 2

SHOW ME HOW

Huluduey Corporation's comparative balance sheet for current assets and liabilities was as follows:

	Dec. 31, 2016	Dec. 31, 2015
Accounts receivable	$18,000	$14,400
Inventory	34,800	29,700
Accounts payable	27,600	20,700
Dividends payable	8,400	10,800

Adjust net income of $160,000 for changes in operating assets and liabilities to arrive at net cash flow from operating activities.

EE 16-4 p. 750 **PE 16-4A Cash flows from operating activities—indirect method** OBJ. 2

SHOW ME HOW

Pettygrove Inc. reported the following data:

Net income	$405,000
Depreciation expense	45,000
Gain on disposal of equipment	36,900
Decrease in accounts receivable	25,200
Decrease in accounts payable	6,480

Prepare the Cash Flows from Operating Activities section of the statement of cash flows, using the indirect method.

EE 16-4 p. 750 **PE 16-4B Cash flows from operating activities—indirect method** OBJ. 2

SHOW ME HOW

Staley Inc. reported the following data:

Net income	$280,000
Depreciation expense	48,000
Loss on disposal of equipment	19,520
Increase in accounts receivable	17,280
Increase in accounts payable	8,960

Prepare the Cash Flows from Operating Activities section of the statement of cash flows, using the indirect method.

EE 16-5 p. 753 **PE 16-5A Land transactions on the statement of cash flows** OBJ. 2

SHOW ME HOW

Milo Corporation purchased land for $540,000. Later in the year, the company sold a different piece of land with a book value of $270,000 for $180,000. How are the effects of these transactions reported on the statement of cash flows?

SHOW ME HOW

EE 16-5 p. 753

PE 16-5B Land transactions on the statement of cash flows **OBJ. 2**

IZ Corporation purchased land for $400,000. Later in the year, the company sold a different piece of land with a book value of $200,000 for $240,000. How are the effects of these transactions reported on the statement of cash flows?

SHOW ME HOW

EE 16-6 p. 755

PE 16-6A Cash received from customers—direct method **OBJ. 3**

Sales reported on the income statement were $480,000. The accounts receivable balance increased $54,000 over the year. Determine the amount of cash received from customers.

SHOW ME HOW

EE 16-6 p. 755

PE 16-6B Cash received from customers—direct method **OBJ. 3**

Sales reported on the income statement were $112,000. The accounts receivable balance decreased $10,500 over the year. Determine the amount of cash received from customers.

SHOW ME HOW

EE 16-7 p. 756

PE 16-7A Cash payments for merchandise—direct method **OBJ. 3**

The cost of merchandise sold reported on the income statement was $770,000. The accounts payable balance decreased $44,000, and the inventory balance decreased by $66,000 over the year. Determine the amount of cash paid for merchandise.

SHOW ME HOW

EE 16-7 p. 756

PE 16-7B Cash payments for merchandise—direct method **OBJ. 3**

The cost of merchandise sold reported on the income statement was $240,000. The accounts payable balance increased $12,000, and the inventory balance increased by $19,200 over the year. Determine the amount of cash paid for merchandise.

SHOW ME HOW

EE 16-8 p. 760

F·A·I

PE 16-8A Free cash flow **OBJ. 4**

McMahon Inc. reported the following on the company's statement of cash flows in 2016 and 2015:

	2016	2015
Net cash flow from operating activities	$ 294,000	$ 280,000
Net cash flow used for investing activities	(224,000)	(252,000)
Net cash flow used for financing activities	(63,000)	(42,000)

Seventy percent of the net cash flow used for investing activities was used to replace existing capacity.

a. Determine McMahon's free cash flow for both years.

b. Has McMahon's free cash flow improved or declined from 2015 to 2016?

SHOW ME HOW

EE 16-8 p. 760

F·A·I

PE 16-8B Free cash flow **OBJ. 4**

Dillin Inc. reported the following on the company's statement of cash flows in 2016 and 2015:

	2016	2015
Net cash flow from operating activities	$476,000	$455,000
Net cash flow used for investing activities	(427,000)	(378,000)
Net cash flow used for financing activities	(42,000)	(58,800)

Eighty percent of the net cash flow used for investing activities was used to replace existing capacity.

a. Determine Dillin's free cash flow for both years.

b. Has Dillin's free cash flow improved or declined from 2015 to 2016?

Exercises

EX 16-1 Cash flows from operating activities—net loss

OBJ. 1

On its income statement for a recent year, United Continental Holdings, Inc., the parent company of United Airlines, reported a net *loss* of $723 million from operations. On its statement of cash flows, it reported $935 million of cash flows from operating activities.

Explain this apparent contradiction between the loss and the positive cash flows.

EX 16-2 Effect of transactions on cash flows

OBJ. 1

✔ a. Cash payment, $525,000

State the effect (cash receipt or payment and amount) of each of the following transactions, considered individually, on cash flows:

a. Retired $500,000 of bonds, on which there was $5,000 of unamortized discount, for $525,000.
b. Sold 6,000 shares of $20 par common stock for $30 per share.
c. Sold equipment with a book value of $98,200 for $117,500.
d. Purchased land for $322,000 cash.
e. Purchased a building by paying $75,000 cash and issuing a $62,500 mortgage note payable.
f. Sold a new issue of $300,000 of bonds at 101.
g. Purchased 2,500 shares of $40 par common stock as treasury stock at $50 per share.
h. Paid dividends of $2.00 per share. There were 50,000 shares issued and 10,000 shares of treasury stock.

EX 16-3 Classifying cash flows

OBJ. 1

Identify the type of cash flow activity for each of the following events (operating, investing, or financing):

a. Net income
b. Paid cash dividends
c. Issued common stock
d. Issued bonds
e. Redeemed bonds
f. Sold long-term investments
g. Purchased treasury stock
h. Sold equipment
i. Issued preferred stock
j. Purchased buildings
k. Purchased patents

EX 16-4 Cash flows from operating activities—indirect method

OBJ. 2

Indicate whether each of the following would be added to or deducted from net income in determining net cash flow from operating activities by the indirect method:

a. Decrease in merchandise inventory
b. Increase in accounts receivable
c. Increase in accounts payable
d. Loss on retirement of long-term debt
e. Depreciation of fixed assets
f. Decrease in notes receivable due in 60 days from customers
g. Increase in salaries payable
h. Decrease in prepaid expenses
i. Amortization of patent
j. Increase in notes payable due in 120 days to vendors
k. Gain on disposal of fixed assets

EX 16-5 Cash flows from operating activities—indirect method **OBJ. 1, 2**

✔ Net cash flow from operating activities, $417,600

SHOW ME HOW

The net income reported on the income statement for the current year was $400,000. Depreciation recorded on store equipment for the year amounted to $16,000. Balances of the current asset and current liability accounts at the beginning and end of the year are as follows:

	End of Year	Beginning of Year
Cash	$41,600	$38,400
Accounts receivable (net)	30,400	28,000
Merchandise inventory	40,000	44,000
Prepaid expenses	4,800	3,600
Accounts payable (merchandise creditors)	40,000	36,000
Wages payable	21,200	24,000

a. Prepare the Cash Flows from Operating Activities section of the statement of cash flows, using the indirect method.

b. Briefly explain why net cash flow from operating activities is different than net income.

EX 16-6 Cash flows from operating activities—indirect method **OBJ. 1, 2**

✔ Net cash flow from operating activities, $394,400

SHOW ME HOW

The net income reported on the income statement for the current year was $320,000. Depreciation recorded on equipment and a building amounted to $96,000 for the year. Balances of the current asset and current liability accounts at the beginning and end of the year are as follows:

	End of Year	Beginning of Year
Cash	$ 89,600	$ 96,000
Accounts receivable (net)	112,000	118,400
Inventories	224,000	200,000
Prepaid expenses	12,800	14,400
Accounts payable (merchandise creditors)	96,000	104,000
Salaries payable	16,000	13,600

a. Prepare the Cash Flows from Operating Activities section of the statement of cash flows, using the indirect method.

b. If the direct method had been used, would the net cash flow from operating activities have been the same? Explain.

EX 16-7 Cash flows from operating activities—indirect method **OBJ. 1, 2**

✔ Net cash flow from operating activities, $525,410

SHOW ME HOW

The income statement disclosed the following items for 2016:

Depreciation expense	$ 57,600
Gain on disposal of equipment	33,600
Net income	508,000

Balances of the current assets and current liability accounts changed between December 31, 2015, and December 31, 2016, as follows:

	Increase (Decrease)
Accounts receivable	$8,960
Inventory	(5,120)
Prepaid insurance	(1,920)
Accounts payable	(6,080)
Income taxes payable	1,410
Dividends payable	2,200

a. Prepare the Cash Flows from Operating Activities section of the statement of cash flows, using the indirect method.

b. Briefly explain why net cash flows from operating activities is different than net income.

SHOW ME HOW

EX 16-8 Determining cash payments to stockholders **OBJ. 2**

The board of directors declared cash dividends totaling $585,000 during the current year. The comparative balance sheet indicates dividends payable of $167,625 at the beginning of the year and $146,250 at the end of the year. What was the amount of cash payments to stockholders during the year?

EX 16-9 Reporting changes in equipment on statement of cash flows **OBJ. 2**

An analysis of the general ledger accounts indicates that office equipment, which cost $202,500 and on which accumulated depreciation totaled $84,375 on the date of sale, was sold for $101,250 during the year. Using this information, indicate the items to be reported on the statement of cash flows.

EX 16-10 Reporting changes in equipment on statement of cash flows **OBJ. 2**

An analysis of the general ledger accounts indicates that delivery equipment, which cost $80,000 and on which accumulated depreciation totaled $36,000 on the date of sale, was sold for $37,200 during the year. Using this information, indicate the items to be reported on the statement of cash flows.

EX 16-11 Reporting land transactions on statement of cash flows **OBJ. 2**

On the basis of the details of the following fixed asset account, indicate the items to be reported on the statement of cash flows:

ACCOUNT ***Land*** **ACCOUNT NO.**

Date		Item	Debit	Credit	Balance Debit	Balance Credit
2016						
Jan.	1	Balance			868,000	
Mar.	12	Purchased for cash	104,300		972,300	
Oct.	4	Sold for $95,550		63,840	908,460	

EX 16-12 Reporting stockholders' equity items on statement of cash flows **OBJ. 2**

On the basis of the following stockholders' equity accounts, indicate the items, exclusive of net income, to be reported on the statement of cash flows. There were no unpaid dividends at either the beginning or the end of the year.

ACCOUNT ***Common Stock, $40 par*** **ACCOUNT NO.**

Date		Item	Debit	Credit	Balance Debit	Balance Credit
2016						
Jan.	1	Balance, 120,000 shares				4,800,000
Apr.	2	30,000 shares issued for cash		1,200,000		6,000,000
June	30	4,400-share stock dividend		176,000		6,176,000

ACCOUNT ***Paid-In Capital in Excess of Par—Common Stock*** **ACCOUNT NO.**

Date		Item	Debit	Credit	Balance Debit	Balance Credit
2016						
Jan.	1	Balance				360,000
Apr.	2	30,000 shares issued for cash		720,000		1,080,000
June	30	Stock dividend		114,400		1,194,400

ACCOUNT *Retained Earnings* ACCOUNT NO.

Date		Item	Debit	Credit	Balance	
					Debit	Credit
2016						
Jan.	1	Balance				2,000,000
June	30	Stock dividend	290,440			1,709,560
Dec.	30	Cash dividend	463,200			1,246,360
	31	Net income		1,440,000		2,686,360

EX 16-13 Reporting land acquisition for cash and mortgage note on statement of cash flows **OBJ. 2**

On the basis of the details of the following fixed asset account, indicate the items to be reported on the statement of cash flows:

ACCOUNT *Land* ACCOUNT NO.

Date		Item	Debit	Credit	Balance	
					Debit	Credit
2016						
Jan.	1	Balance			156,000	
Feb.	10	Purchased for cash	246,000		402,000	
Nov.	20	Purchased with long-term mortgage note	324,000		726,000	

EX 16-14 Reporting issuance and retirement of long-term debt **OBJ. 2**

On the basis of the details of the following bonds payable and related discount accounts, indicate the items to be reported in the Financing Activities section of the statement of cash flows, assuming no gain or loss on retiring the bonds:

ACCOUNT *Bonds Payable* ACCOUNT NO.

Date		Item	Debit	Credit	Balance	
					Debit	Credit
2016						
Jan.	1	Balance				750,000
	2	Retire bonds	150,000			600,000
June	30	Issue bonds		450,000		1,050,000

ACCOUNT *Discount on Bonds Payable* ACCOUNT NO.

Date		Item	Debit	Credit	Balance	
					Debit	Credit
2016						
Jan.	1	Balance			33,750	
	2	Retire bonds		12,000	21,750	
June	30	Issue bonds	30,000		51,750	
Dec.	31	Amortize discount		2,625	49,125	

✔ Net income, $341,770

SHOW ME HOW

EX 16-15 Determining net income from net cash flow from operating activities OBJ. 2

Curwen Inc. reported net cash flow from operating activities of $357,500 on its statement of cash flows for the year ended December 31, 2016. The following information was reported in the Cash Flows from Operating Activities section of the statement of cash flows, using the indirect method:

Decrease in income taxes payable	$ 7,700
Decrease in inventories	19,140
Depreciation	29,480
Gain on sale of investments	13,200
Increase in accounts payable	5,280
Increase in prepaid expenses	2,970
Increase in accounts receivable	14,300

a. Determine the net income reported by Curwen Inc. for the year ended December 31, 2016.

b. Briefly explain why Curwen's net income is different than net cash flow from operating activities.

✔ Net cash flow from operating activities, $42,174

EX 16-16 Cash flows from operating activities—indirect method OBJ. 2

Selected data derived from the income statement and balance sheet of National Beverage Co. for a recent year are as follows:

Income statement data (in thousands):	
Net earnings (loss)	$43,993
Losses on inventory write-down and fixed assets	7
Depreciation expense	10,174
Stock-based compensation expense (noncash)	290
Balance sheet data (in thousands):	
Increase in accounts receivable	5,679
Increase in inventory	7,509
Decrease in prepaid expenses	2,239
Decrease in accounts payable and other current liabilities	1,341

a. Prepare the Cash Flows from Operating Activities section of the statement of cash flows, using the indirect method for National Beverage Co.

b. Interpret your results in part (a).

✔ Net cash flow from operating activities, $150

SHOW ME HOW

EX 16-17 Statement of cash flows—indirect method OBJ. 2

The comparative balance sheet of Pelican Joe Industries Inc. for December 31, 2016 and 2015, is as follows:

	Dec. 31, 2016	Dec. 31, 2015
Assets		
Cash	$ 490	$ 160
Accounts receivable (net)	280	200
Inventories	175	110
Land	400	450
Equipment	225	175
Accumulated depreciation—equipment	(60)	(30)
Total assets	$1,510	$1,065
Liabilities and Stockholders' Equity		
Accounts payable (merchandise creditors)	$ 175	$ 160
Dividends payable	30	—
Common stock, $10 par	100	50
Paid-in capital: Excess of issue price over par—common stock	250	125
Retained earnings	955	730
Total liabilities and stockholders' equity	$1,510	$1,065

The following additional information is taken from the records:

1. Land was sold for $125.
2. Equipment was acquired for cash.
3. There were no disposals of equipment during the year.
4. The common stock was issued for cash.
5. There was a $325 credit to Retained Earnings for net income.
6. There was an $100 debit to Retained Earnings for cash dividends declared.

a. Prepare a statement of cash flows, using the indirect method of presenting cash flows from operating activities.

b. Was Pelican Joe Industries Inc. net cash flow from operations more or less than net income? What is the source of this difference?

EX 16-18 Statement of cash flows—indirect method

OBJ. 2

List the errors you find in the following statement of cash flows. The cash balance at the beginning of the year was $240,000. All other amounts are correct, except the cash balance at the end of the year.

Shasta Inc.
Statement of Cash Flows
For the Year Ended December 31, 2016

Cash flows from operating activities:			
Net income		$360,000	
Adjustments to reconcile net income to net cash flow from operating activities:			
Depreciation		100,800	
Gain on sale of investments		17,280	
Changes in current operating assets and liabilities:			
Increase in accounts receivable		27,360	
Increase in inventories		(36,000)	
Increase in accounts payable		(3,600)	
Decrease in accrued expenses payable		(2,400)	
Net cash flow from operating activities			$463,440
Cash flows from investing activities:			
Cash received from sale of investments		$240,000	
Less: Cash paid for purchase of land	$259,200		
Cash paid for purchase of equipment	432,000	691,200	
Net cash flow used for investing activities			(415,200)
Cash flows from financing activities:			
Cash received from sale of common stock		$312,000	
Cash paid for dividends		132,000	
Net cash flow from financing activities			180,000
Increase in cash			$ 47,760
Cash at the end of the year			192,240
Cash at the beginning of the year			$240,000

EX 16-19 Cash flows from operating activities—direct method

OBJ. 3

✔ a. $801,900

The cash flows from operating activities are reported by the direct method on the statement of cash flows. Determine the following:

a. If sales for the current year were $753,500 and accounts receivable decreased by $48,400 during the year, what was the amount of cash received from customers?

b. If income tax expense for the current year was $50,600 and income tax payable decreased by $5,500 during the year, what was the amount of cash payments for income taxes?

c. Briefly explain why the cash received from customers in (a) is different than sales.

EX 16-20 Cash paid for merchandise purchases — OBJ. 3

The cost of merchandise sold for Kohl's Corporation for a recent year was $11,625 million. The balance sheet showed the following current account balances (in millions):

	Balance, End of Year	Balance, Beginning of Year
Merchandise inventories	$3,199	$3,036
Accounts payable	1,233	1,138

Determine the amount of cash payments for merchandise.

EX 16-21 Determining selected amounts for cash flows from operating activities—direct method — OBJ. 3

✔ a. $1,025,800

Selected data taken from the accounting records of Ginis Inc. for the current year ended December 31 are as follows:

	Balance, December 31	Balance, January 1
Accrued expenses payable (operating expenses)	$ 12,650	$ 14,030
Accounts payable (merchandise creditors)	96,140	105,800
Inventories	178,020	193,430
Prepaid expenses	7,360	8,970

During the current year, the cost of merchandise sold was $1,031,550, and the operating expenses other than depreciation were $179,400. The direct method is used for presenting the cash flows from operating activities on the statement of cash flows.

Determine the amount reported on the statement of cash flows for (a) cash payments for merchandise and (b) cash payments for operating expenses.

EX 16-22 Cash flows from operating activities—direct method — OBJ. 3

✔ Net cash flow from operating activities, $96,040

The income statement of Booker T Industries Inc. for the current year ended June 30 is as follows:

Sales		$511,000
Cost of merchandise sold		290,500
Gross profit		$220,500
Operating expenses:		
Depreciation expense	$ 39,200	
Other operating expenses	105,000	
Total operating expenses		144,200
Income before income tax		$ 76,300
Income tax expense		21,700
Net income		$ 54,600

Changes in the balances of selected accounts from the beginning to the end of the current year are as follows:

	Increase (Decrease)
Accounts receivable (net)	($11,760)
Inventories	3,920
Prepaid expenses	(3,780)
Accounts payable (merchandise creditors)	(7,980)
Accrued expenses payable (operating expenses)	1,260
Income tax payable	(2,660)

a. Prepare the Cash Flows from Operating Activities section of the statement of cash flows, using the direct method.

b. What does the direct method show about a company's cash flows from operating activities that is not shown using the indirect method?

✔ Net cash flow from operating activities, $123,860

EX 16-23 Cash flows from operating activities—direct method **OBJ. 3**

The income statement for Rhino Company for the current year ended June 30 and balances of selected accounts at the beginning and the end of the year are as follows:

Sales		$445,500
Cost of merchandise sold		154,000
Gross profit		$291,500
Operating expenses:		
Depreciation expense	$ 38,500	
Other operating expenses	115,280	
Total operating expenses		153,780
Income before income tax		$137,720
Income tax expense		39,600
Net income		$ 98,120

	End of Year	Beginning of Year
Accounts receivable (net)	$36,300	$31,240
Inventories	92,400	80,300
Prepaid expenses	14,520	15,840
Accounts payable (merchandise creditors)	67,540	62,700
Accrued expenses payable (operating expenses)	19,140	20,900
Income tax payable	4,400	4,400

Prepare the Cash Flows from Operating Activities section of the statement of cash flows, using the direct method.

EX 16-24 Free cash flow **OBJ. 4**

F·A·I

SHOW ME HOW

Sweeter Enterprises Inc. has cash flows from operating activities of $539,000. Cash flows used for investments in property, plant, and equipment totaled $210,000, of which 75% of this investment was used to replace existing capacity.

a. Determine the free cash flow for Sweeter Enterprises Inc.

b. How might a lender use free cash flow to determine whether or not to give Sweeter Enterprises Inc. a loan?

EX 16-25 Free cash flow **OBJ. 4**

F·A·I

The financial statements for Nike, Inc., are provided in Appendix C at the end of the text.

a. Determine the free cash flow for the most recent fiscal year. Assume that 90% of the additions to property, plant, and equipment were used to maintain productive capacity. Round to the nearest thousand dollars.

b. How might a lender use free cash flow to determine whether or not to give Nike, Inc., a loan?

c. Would you feel comfortable giving Nike a loan, based on the free cash flow calculated in (a)?

EX 16-26 Free cash flow **OBJ. 4**

F·A·I

Lovato Motors Inc. has cash flows from operating activities of $720,000. Cash flows used for investments in property, plant, and equipment totaled $440,000, of which 85% of this investment was used to replace existing capacity.

Determine the free cash flow for Lovato Motors Inc.

Problems: Series A

PR 16-1A Statement of cash flows—indirect method

OBJ. 2

✔ Net cash flow from operating activities, $143,540

SHOW ME HOW

The comparative balance sheet of Cromme Inc. for December 31, 2016 and 2015, is shown as follows:

	Dec. 31, 2016	Dec. 31, 2015
Assets		
Cash	$ 625,760	$ 585,920
Accounts receivable (net)	227,840	208,960
Inventories	641,760	617,120
Investments	0	240,000
Land	328,000	0
Equipment	705,120	553,120
Accumulated depreciation—equipment	(166,400)	(148,000)
Total assets	$2,362,080	$2,057,120
Liabilities and Stockholders' Equity		
Accounts payable (merchandise creditors)	$ 424,480	$ 404,960
Accrued expenses payable (operating expenses)	42,240	52,640
Dividends payable	24,000	19,200
Common stock, $4 par	150,000	100,000
Paid-in capital: Excess of issue price over par—common stock	417,500	280,000
Retained earnings	1,303,860	1,200,320
Total liabilities and stockholders' equity	$2,362,080	$2,057,120

Additional data obtained from an examination of the accounts in the ledger for 2016 are as follows:

a. The investments were sold for $280,000 cash.

b. Equipment and land were acquired for cash.

c. There were no disposals of equipment during the year.

d. The common stock was issued for cash.

e. There was a $199,540 credit to Retained Earnings for net income.

f. There was a $96,000 debit to Retained Earnings for cash dividends declared.

Instructions

Prepare a statement of cash flows, using the indirect method of presenting cash flows from operating activities.

PR 16-2A Statement of cash flows—indirect method

OBJ. 2

✔ Net cash flow from operating activities, $419,200

SHOW ME HOW

The comparative balance sheet of Del Ray Enterprises Inc. at December 31, 2016 and 2015, is as follows:

	Dec. 31, 2016	Dec. 31, 2015
Assets		
Cash	$ 146,600	$ 179,800
Accounts receivable (net)	224,600	242,000
Merchandise inventory	321,600	299,200
Prepaid expenses	13,400	9,600
Equipment	655,000	537,000
Accumulated depreciation—equipment	(170,800)	(132,200)
Total assets	$1,190,400	$1,135,400
Liabilities and Stockholders' Equity		
Accounts payable (merchandise creditors)	$ 250,200	$ 237,600
Mortgage note payable	0	336,000
Common stock, $10 par	74,000	24,000
Paid-in capital: Excess of issue price over par—common stock	470,000	320,000
Retained earnings	396,200	217,800
Total liabilities and stockholders' equity	$1,190,400	$1,135,400

Additional data obtained from the income statement and from an examination of the accounts in the ledger for 2016 are as follows:

a. Net income, $332,000

b. Depreciation reported on the income statement, $83,400

c. Equipment was purchased at a cost of $162,800 and fully depreciated equipment costing $44,800 was discarded, with no salvage realized.

d. The mortgage note payable was not due until 2018 but the terms permitted earlier payment without penalty.

e. 10,000 shares of common stock were issued at $20 for cash.

f. Cash dividends declared and paid, $153,600

Instructions

Prepare a statement of cash flows, using the indirect method of presenting cash flows from operating activities.

PR 16-3A Statement of cash flows—indirect method **OBJ. 2**

✔ Net cash flow from operating activities, $(169,600)

The comparative balance sheet of Whitman Co. at December 31, 2016 and 2015, is as follows:

	Dec. 31, 2016	Dec. 31, 2015
Assets		
Cash	$ 918,000	$ 964,800
Accounts receivable (net)	828,900	761,940
Inventories	1,268,460	1,162,980
Prepaid expenses	29,340	35,100
Land	315,900	479,700
Buildings	1,462,500	900,900
Accumulated depreciation—buildings	(408,600)	(382,320)
Equipment	512,280	454,680
Accumulated depreciation—equipment	(141,300)	(158,760)
Total assets	$4,785,480	$4,219,020
Liabilities and Stockholders' Equity		
Accounts payable (merchandise creditors)	$ 922,500	$ 958,320
Bonds payable	270,000	0
Common stock, $25 par	317,000	117,000
Paid-in capital: Excess of issue price over par—common stock	758,000	558,000
Retained earnings	2,517,980	2,585,700
Total liabilities and stockholders' equity	$4,785,480	$4,219,020

The noncurrent asset, noncurrent liability, and stockholders' equity accounts for 2016 are as follows:

ACCOUNT *Land* ACCOUNT NO.

Date		Item	Debit	Credit	Balance Debit	Balance Credit
2016						
Jan.	1	Balance			479,700	
Apr.	20	Realized $151,200 cash from sale		163,800	315,900	

ACCOUNT *Buildings* ACCOUNT NO.

Date		Item	Debit	Credit	Balance Debit	Balance Credit
2016						
Jan.	1	Balance			900,900	
Apr.	20	Acquired for cash	561,600		1,462,500	

(Continued)

ACCOUNT ***Accumulated Depreciation—Buildings*** **ACCOUNT NO.**

Date		Item	Debit	Credit	Balance Debit	Balance Credit
2016						
Jan.	1	Balance				382,320
Dec.	31	Depreciation for year		26,280		408,600

ACCOUNT ***Equipment*** **ACCOUNT NO.**

Date		Item	Debit	Credit	Balance Debit	Balance Credit
2016						
Jan.	1	Balance			454,680	
	26	Discarded, no salvage		46,800	407,880	
Aug.	11	Purchased for cash	104,400		512,280	

ACCOUNT ***Accumulated Depreciation—Equipment*** **ACCOUNT NO.**

Date		Item	Debit	Credit	Balance Debit	Balance Credit
2016						
Jan.	1	Balance				158,760
	26	Equipment discarded	46,800			111,960
Dec.	31	Depreciation for year		29,340		141,300

ACCOUNT ***Bonds Payable*** **ACCOUNT NO.**

Date		Item	Debit	Credit	Balance Debit	Balance Credit
2016						
May	1	Issued 20-year bonds		270,000		270,000

ACCOUNT ***Common Stock, $25 par*** **ACCOUNT NO.**

Date		Item	Debit	Credit	Balance Debit	Balance Credit
2016						
Jan.	1	Balance				117,000
Dec.	7	Issued 8,000 shares of common stock for $50 per share		200,000		317,000

ACCOUNT ***Paid-In Capital in Excess of Par—Common Stock*** **ACCOUNT NO.**

Date		Item	Debit	Credit	Balance Debit	Balance Credit
2016						
Jan.	1	Balance				558,000
Dec.	7	Issued 8,000 shares of common stock for $50 per share		200,000		758,000

ACCOUNT *Retained Earnings*						ACCOUNT NO.
					Balance	
Date		Item	Debit	Credit	Debit	Credit
2016						
Jan.	1	Balance				2,585,700
Dec.	31	Net loss	35,320			2,550,380
	31	Cash dividends	32,400			2,517,980

Instructions

Prepare a statement of cash flows, using the indirect method of presenting cash flows from operating activities.

✔ Net cash flow from operating activities, $293,600

General Ledger

SHOW ME HOW

PR 16-4A Statement of cash flows—direct method **OBJ. 3**

The comparative balance sheet of Canace Products Inc. for December 31, 2016 and 2015, is as follows:

	Dec. 31, 2016	Dec. 31, 2015
Assets		
Cash	$ 643,400	$ 679,400
Accounts receivable (net)	566,800	547,400
Inventories	1,011,000	982,800
Investments	0	240,000
Land	520,000	0
Equipment	880,000	680,000
Accumulated depreciation	(244,400)	(200,400)
Total assets	$3,376,800	$2,929,200
Liabilities and Stockholders' Equity		
Accounts payable (merchandise creditors)	$ 771,800	$ 748,400
Accrued expenses payable (operating expenses)	63,400	70,800
Dividends payable	8,800	6,400
Common stock, $2 par	56,000	32,000
Paid-in capital: Excess of issue price over par—common stock	408,000	192,000
Retained earnings	2,068,800	1,879,600
Total liabilities and stockholders' equity	$3,376,800	$2,929,200

The income statement for the year ended December 31, 2016, is as follows:

Sales		$5,980,000
Cost of merchandise sold		2,452,000
Gross profit		$3,528,000
Operating expenses:		
Depreciation expense	$ 44,000	
Other operating expenses	3,100,000	
Total operating expenses		3,144,000
Operating income		$ 384,000
Other expense:		
Loss on sale of investments		(64,000)
Income before income tax		$ 320,000
Income tax expense		102,800
Net income		$ 217,200

Additional data obtained from an examination of the accounts in the ledger for 2016 are as follows:

a. Equipment and land were acquired for cash.

b. There were no disposals of equipment during the year.

(Continued)

c. The investments were sold for $176,000 cash.

d. The common stock was issued for cash.

e. There was a $28,000 debit to Retained Earnings for cash dividends declared.

Instructions

Prepare a statement of cash flows, using the direct method of presenting cash flows from operating activities.

PR 16-5A Statement of cash flows—direct method applied to PR 16-1A OBJ. 3

✔ Net cash flow from operating activities, $143,540

The comparative balance sheet of Cromme Inc. for December 31, 2016 and 2015, is as follows:

	Dec. 31, 2016	Dec. 31, 2015
Assets		
Cash	$ 625,760	$ 585,920
Accounts receivable (net)	227,840	208,960
Inventories	641,760	617,120
Investments	0	240,000
Land	328,000	0
Equipment	705,120	553,120
Accumulated depreciation—equipment	(166,400)	(148,000)
Total assets	$2,362,080	$2,057,120
Liabilities and Stockholders' Equity		
Accounts payable (merchandise creditors)	$ 424,480	$ 404,960
Accrued expenses payable (operating expenses)	42,240	52,640
Dividends payable	24,000	19,200
Common stock, $2 par	150,000	100,000
Paid-in capital: Excess of issue price over par—common stock	417,500	280,000
Retained earnings	1,303,860	1,200,320
Total liabilities and stockholders' equity	$2,362,080	$2,057,120

The income statement for the year ended December 31, 2016, is as follows:

Sales		$5,372,559
Cost of merchandise sold		3,306,190
Gross profit		$2,066,369
Operating expenses:		
Depreciation expense	$ 18,400	
Other operating expenses	1,755,402	
Total operating expenses		1,773,802
Operating income		$ 292,567
Other income:		
Gain on sale of investments		40,000
Income before income tax		$ 332,567
Income tax expense		133,027
Net income		$ 199,540

Additional data obtained from an examination of the accounts in the ledger for 2016 are as follows:

a. The investments were sold for $280,000 cash.

b. Equipment and land were acquired for cash.

c. There were no disposals of equipment during the year.

d. The common stock was issued for cash.

e. There was a $96,000 debit to Retained Earnings for cash dividends declared.

Instructions

Prepare a statement of cash flows, using the direct method of presenting cash flows from operating activities.

Problems: Series B

PR 16-1B Statement of cash flows—indirect method

OBJ. 2

✔ Net cash flow from operating activities, $154,260

SHOW ME HOW

The comparative balance sheet of Merrick Equipment Co. for December 31, 2016 and 2015, is as follows:

	Dec. 31, 2016	Dec. 31, 2015
Assets		
Cash	$ 70,720	$ 47,940
Accounts receivable (net)	207,230	188,190
Inventories	298,520	289,850
Investments	0	102,000
Land	295,800	0
Equipment	438,600	358,020
Accumulated depreciation—equipment	(99,110)	(84,320)
Total assets	$1,211,760	$901,680
Liabilities and Stockholders' Equity		
Accounts payable (merchandise creditors)	$ 205,700	$194,140
Accrued expenses payable (operating expenses)	30,600	26,860
Dividends payable	25,500	20,400
Common stock, $1 par	202,000	102,000
Paid-in capital: Excess of issue price over par—common stock	354,000	204,000
Retained earnings	393,960	354,280
Total liabilities and stockholders' equity	$1,211,760	$901,680

Additional data obtained from an examination of the accounts in the ledger for 2016 are as follows:

a. Equipment and land were acquired for cash.

b. There were no disposals of equipment during the year.

c. The investments were sold for $91,800 cash.

d. The common stock was issued for cash.

e. There was a $141,680 credit to Retained Earnings for net income.

f. There was a $102,000 debit to Retained Earnings for cash dividends declared.

Instructions

Prepare a statement of cash flows, using the indirect method of presenting cash flows from operating activities.

PR 16-2B Statement of cash flows—indirect method

OBJ. 2

✔ Net cash flow from operating activities, $561,400

SHOW ME HOW

The comparative balance sheet of Harris Industries Inc. at December 31, 2016 and 2015, is as follows:

	Dec. 31, 2016	Dec. 31, 2015
Assets		
Cash	$ 443,240	$ 360,920
Accounts receivable (net)	665,280	592,200
Inventories	887,880	1,022,560
Prepaid expenses	31,640	25,200
Land	302,400	302,400
Buildings	1,713,600	1,134,000
Accumulated depreciation—buildings	(466,200)	(414,540)
Machinery and equipment	781,200	781,200
Accumulated depreciation—machinery and equipment	(214,200)	(191,520)
Patents	106,960	112,000
Total assets	$4,251,800	$3,724,420

(Continued)

Liabilities and Stockholders' Equity		
Accounts payable (merchandise creditors)	$ 837,480	$ 927,080
Dividends payable	32,760	25,200
Salaries payable	78,960	87,080
Mortgage note payable, due 2017	224,000	0
Bonds payable	0	390,000
Common stock, $5 par	200,400	50,400
Paid-in capital: Excess of issue price over par—common stock	366,000	126,000
Retained earnings	2,512,200	2,118,660
Total liabilities and stockholders' equity	$4,251,800	$3,724,420

An examination of the income statement and the accounting records revealed the following additional information applicable to 2016:

a. Net income, $524,580.

b. Depreciation expense reported on the income statement: buildings, $51,660; machinery and equipment, $22,680.

c. Patent amortization reported on the income statement, $5,040.

d. A building was constructed for $579,600.

e. A mortgage note for $224,000 was issued for cash.

f. 30,000 shares of common stock were issued at $13 in exchange for the bonds payable.

g. Cash dividends declared, $131,040.

Instructions

Prepare a statement of cash flows, using the indirect method of presenting cash flows from operating activities.

PR 16-3B Statement of cash flows—indirect method

OBJ. 2

✔ Net cash flow from operating activities, $162,800

The comparative balance sheet of Coulson, Inc. at December 31, 2016 and 2015, is as follows:

	Dec. 31, 2016	Dec. 31, 2015
Assets		
Cash	$ 300,600	$ 337,800
Accounts receivable (net)	704,400	609,600
Inventories	918,600	865,800
Prepaid expenses	18,600	26,400
Land	990,000	1,386,000
Buildings	1,980,000	990,000
Accumulated depreciation—buildings	(397,200)	(366,000)
Equipment	660,600	529,800
Accumulated depreciation—equipment	(133,200)	(162,000)
Total assets	$5,042,400	$4,217,400
Liabilities and Stockholders' Equity		
Accounts payable (merchandise creditors)	$ 594,000	$ 631,200
Income taxes payable	26,400	21,600
Bonds payable	330,000	0
Common stock, $20 par	320,000	180,000
Paid-in capital: Excess of issue price over par—common stock	950,000	810,000
Retained earnings	2,822,000	2,574,600
Total liabilities and stockholders' equity	$5,042,400	$4,217,400

The noncurrent asset, noncurrent liability, and stockholders' equity accounts for 2016 are as follows:

ACCOUNT *Land* ACCOUNT NO.

Date		Item	Debit	Credit	Balance Debit	Balance Credit
2016						
Jan.	1	Balance			1,386,000	
Apr.	20	Realized $456,000 cash from sale		396,000	990,000	

ACCOUNT *Buildings* ACCOUNT NO.

Date		Item	Debit	Credit	Balance Debit	Balance Credit
2016						
Jan.	1	Balance			990,000	
Apr.	20	Acquired for cash	990,000		1,980,000	

ACCOUNT *Accumulated Depreciation—Buildings* ACCOUNT NO.

Date		Item	Debit	Credit	Balance Debit	Balance Credit
2016						
Jan.	1	Balance				366,000
Dec.	31	Depreciation for year		31,200		397,200

ACCOUNT *Equipment* ACCOUNT NO.

Date		Item	Debit	Credit	Balance Debit	Balance Credit
2016						
Jan.	1	Balance			529,800	
	26	Discarded, no salvage		66,000	463,800	
Aug.	11	Purchased for cash	196,800		660,600	

ACCOUNT *Accumulated Depreciation—Equipment* ACCOUNT NO.

Date		Item	Debit	Credit	Balance Debit	Balance Credit
2016						
Jan.	1	Balance				162,000
	26	Equipment discarded	66,000			96,000
Dec.	31	Depreciation for year		37,200		133,200

ACCOUNT *Bonds Payable* ACCOUNT NO.

Date		Item	Debit	Credit	Balance Debit	Balance Credit
2016						
May	1	Issued 20-year bonds		330,000		330,000

(Continued)

ACCOUNT ***Common Stock, $20 par*** **ACCOUNT NO.**

Date		Item	Debit	Credit	Balance	
					Debit	**Credit**
2016						
Jan.	1	Balance				180,000
Dec.	7	Issued 7,000 shares of common stock for $40 per share		140,000		320,000

ACCOUNT ***Paid-In Capital in Excess of Par—Common Stock*** **ACCOUNT NO.**

Date		Item	Debit	Credit	Balance	
					Debit	**Credit**
2016						
Jan.	1	Balance				810,000
Dec.	7	Issued 7,000 shares of common stock for $40 per share		140,000		950,000

ACCOUNT ***Retained Earnings*** **ACCOUNT NO.**

Date		Item	Debit	Credit	Balance	
					Debit	**Credit**
2016						
Jan.	1	Balance				2,574,600
Dec.	31	Net income		326,600		2,901,200
	31	Cash dividends	79,200			2,822,000

Instructions

Prepare a statement of cash flows, using the indirect method of presenting cash flows from operating activities.

PR 16-4B Statement of cash flows—direct method **OBJ. 3**

✔ Net cash flow from operating activities, $509,220

General Ledger

SHOW ME HOW

The comparative balance sheet of Martinez Inc. for December 31, 2016 and 2015, is as follows:

	Dec. 31, 2016	Dec. 31, 2015
Assets		
Cash	$ 661,920	$ 683,100
Accounts receivable (net)	992,640	914,400
Inventories	1,394,400	1,363,800
Investments	0	432,000
Land	960,000	0
Equipment	1,224,000	984,000
Accumulated depreciation—equipment	(481,500)	(368,400)
Total assets	$4,751,460	$4,008,900
Liabilities and Stockholders' Equity		
Accounts payable (merchandise creditors)	$1,080,000	$ 966,600
Accrued expenses payable (operating expenses)	67,800	79,200
Dividends payable	100,800	91,200
Common stock, $5 par	130,000	30,000
Paid-in capital: Excess of issue price over par—common stock	950,000	450,000
Retained earnings	2,422,860	2,391,900
Total liabilities and stockholders' equity	$4,751,460	$4,008,900

The income statement for the year ended December 31, 2016, is as follows:

Sales		$4,512,000
Cost of merchandise sold		2,352,000
Gross profit		$2,160,000
Operating expenses:		
Depreciation expense	$ 113,100	
Other operating expenses	1,344,840	
Total operating expenses		1,457,940
Operating income		$ 702,060
Other income:		
Gain on sale of investments		156,000
Income before income tax		$ 858,060
Income tax expense		299,100
Net income		$ 558,960

Additional data obtained from an examination of the accounts in the ledger for 2016 are as follows:

a. Equipment and land were acquired for cash.

b. There were no disposals of equipment during the year.

c. The investments were sold for $588,000 cash.

d. The common stock was issued for cash.

e. There was a $528,000 debit to Retained Earnings for cash dividends declared.

Instructions

Prepare a statement of cash flows, using the direct method of presenting cash flows from operating activities.

PR 16-5B Statement of cash flows—direct method applied to PR 16-1B OBJ. 3

✔ Net cash flow from operating activities, $154,260

The comparative balance sheet of Merrick Equipment Co. for Dec. 31, 2016 and 2015, is:

	Dec. 31, 2016	Dec. 31, 2015
Assets		
Cash	$ 70,720	$ 47,940
Accounts receivable (net)	207,230	188,190
Inventories	298,520	289,850
Investments	0	102,000
Land	295,800	0
Equipment	438,600	358,020
Accumulated depreciation—equipment	(99,110)	(84,320)
Total assets	$1,211,760	$ 901,680
Liabilities and Stockholders' Equity		
Accounts payable (merchandise creditors)	$ 205,700	$ 194,140
Accrued expenses payable (operating expenses)	30,600	26,860
Dividends payable	25,500	20,400
Common stock, $1 par	202,000	102,000
Paid-in capital: Excess of issue price over par—common stock	354,000	204,000
Retained earnings	393,960	354,280
Total liabilities and stockholders' equity	$1,211,760	$ 901,680

(Continued)

The income statement for the year ended December 31, 2016, is as follows:

Sales		$2,023,898
Cost of merchandise sold		1,245,476
Gross profit		$ 778,422
Operating expenses:		
Depreciation expense	$ 14,790	
Other operating expenses	517,299	
Total operating expenses		532,089
Operating income		$ 246,333
Other expenses:		
Loss on sale of investments		(10,200)
Income before income tax		$ 236,133
Income tax expense		94,453
Net income		$ 141,680

Additional data obtained from an examination of the accounts in the ledger for 2016 are as follows:

a. Equipment and land were acquired for cash.

b. There were no disposals of equipment during the year.

c. The investments were sold for $91,800 cash.

d. The common stock was issued for cash.

e. There was a $102,000 debit to Retained Earnings for cash dividends declared.

Instructions

Prepare a statement of cash flows, using the direct method of presenting cash flows from operating activities.

Cases & Projects

CP 16-1 Ethics and professional conduct in business

Lucas Hunter, president of Simmons Industries Inc., believes that reporting operating cash flow per share on the income statement would be a useful addition to the company's just completed financial statements. The following discussion took place between Lucas Hunter and Simmons' controller, John Jameson, in January, after the close of the fiscal year:

Lucas: I've been reviewing our financial statements for the last year. I am disappointed that our net income per share has dropped by 10% from last year. This won't look good to our shareholders. Is there anything we can do about this?

John: What do you mean? The past is the past, and the numbers are in. There isn't much that can be done about it. Our financial statements were prepared according to generally accepted accounting principles, and I don't see much leeway for significant change at this point.

Lucas: No, no. I'm not suggesting that we "cook the books." But look at the cash flow from operating activities on the statement of cash flows. The cash flow from operating activities has increased by 20%. This is very good news—and, I might add, useful information. The higher cash flow from operating activities will give our creditors comfort.

John: Well, the cash flow from operating activities is on the statement of cash flows, so I guess users will be able to see the improved cash flow figures there.

Lucas: This is true, but somehow I feel that this information should be given a much higher profile. I don't like this information being "buried" in the statement of cash flows. You know as well as I do that many users will focus on the income statement. Therefore, I think we ought to include an operating cash flow per share number on the face of the income statement—someplace under the earnings per share number. In this way, users will get the complete picture of our operating performance. Yes, our earnings per share dropped this year, but our cash flow from operating activities improved! And all the information is in one place where users can see and compare the figures. What do you think?

John: I've never really thought about it like that before. I guess we could put the operating cash flow per share on the income statement, under the earnings per share. Users would really benefit from this disclosure. Thanks for the idea—I'll start working on it.

Lucas: Glad to be of service.

How would you interpret this situation? Is John behaving in an ethical and professional manner?

CP 16-2 Using the statement of cash flows

You are considering an investment in a new start-up company, Giraffe Inc., an Internet service provider. A review of the company's financial statements reveals a negative retained earnings. In addition, it appears as though the company has been running a negative cash flow from operating activities since the company's inception.

How is the company staying in business under these circumstances? Could this be a good investment?

CP 16-3 Analysis of statement of cash flows

Dillip Lachgar is the president and majority shareholder of Argon Inc., a small retail store chain. Recently, Dillip submitted a loan application for Argon Inc. to Compound Bank. It called for a $600,000, 9%, 10-year loan to help finance the construction of a building and the purchase of store equipment, costing a total of $750,000. This will enable Argon Inc. to open a store in the town of Compound. Land for this purpose was acquired last year. The bank's loan officer requested a statement of cash flows in addition to the most recent income statement, balance sheet, and retained earnings statement that Dillip had submitted with the loan application.

As a close family friend, Dillip asked you to prepare a statement of cash flows. From the records provided, you prepared the following statement:

Argon Inc.
Statement of Cash Flows
For the Year Ended December 31, 2016

Cash flows from operating activities:		
Net income	$ 300,000	
Adjustments to reconcile net income to net cash flow from operating activities:		
Depreciation	84,000	
Gain on sale of investments	(30,000)	
Changes in current operating assets and liabilities:		
Decrease in accounts receivable	21,000	
Increase in inventories	(42,000)	
Increase in accounts payable	30,000	
Decrease in accrued expenses payable	(6,000)	
Net cash flow from operating activities		$ 357,000
Cash flows from investing activities:		
Cash received from investments sold	$ 180,000	
Less: Cash paid for purchase of store equipment	(120,000)	
Net cash flow from investing activities		60,000
Cash flows from financing activities:		
Cash paid for dividends	$ (126,000)	
Net cash flow used for financing activities		(126,000)
Increase in cash		$ 291,000
Cash at the beginning of the year		108,000
Cash at the end of the year		$ 399,000

Schedule of Noncash Financing and Investing Activities:

Issued common stock for land	$ 240,000

(Continued)

After reviewing the statement, Dillip telephoned you and commented, "Are you sure this statement is right?" Dillip then raised the following questions:

1. "How can depreciation be a cash flow?"
2. "Issuing common stock for the land is listed in a separate schedule. This transaction has nothing to do with cash! Shouldn't this transaction be eliminated from the statement?"
3. "How can the gain on the sale of investments be a deduction from net income in determining the cash flow from operating activities?"
4. "Why does the bank need this statement anyway? They can compute the increase in cash from the balance sheets for the last two years."

After jotting down Dillip's questions, you assured him that this statement was "right." But to alleviate Dillip's concern, you arranged a meeting for the following day.

a. How would you respond to each of Dillip's questions?

b. Do you think that the statement of cash flows enhances the chances of Argon Inc. receiving the loan? Discuss.

CP 16-4 Analysis of cash flow from operations

The Commercial Division of Tidewater Inc. provided the following information on its cash flow from operations:

Net income	$ 945,000
Increase in accounts receivable	(1,134,000)
Increase in inventory	(1,260,000)
Decrease in accounts payable	(189,000)
Depreciation	210,000
Cash flow from operating activities	$(1,428,000)

The manager of the Commercial Division provided the accompanying memo with this report:

From: Senior Vice President, Commercial Division

I am pleased to report that we had earnings of $945,000 over the last period. This resulted in a return on invested capital of 8%, which is near our targets for this division. I have been aggressive in building the revenue volume in the division. As a result, I am happy to report that we have increased the number of new credit card customers as a result of an aggressive marketing campaign. In addition, we have found some excellent merchandise opportunities. Some of our suppliers have made some of their apparel merchandise available at a deep discount. We have purchased as much of these goods as possible in order to improve profitability. I'm also happy to report that our vendor payment problems have improved. We are nearly caught up on our overdue payables balances.

Comment on the senior vice president's memo in light of the cash flow information.

CP 16-5 Statement of cash flows

F·A·I

Internet Project

Group Project

This activity will require two teams to retrieve cash flow statement information from the Internet. One team is to obtain the most recent year's statement of cash flows for **Johnson & Johnson**, and the other team the most recent year's statement of cash flows for **JetBlue Airways Corp.**

The statement of cash flows is included as part of the annual report information that is a required disclosure to the Securities and Exchange Commission (SEC). SEC documents can be retrieved using the EdgarScan™ service at www.sec.gov/edgar/searchedgar/companysearch.html.

To obtain annual report information, key in a company name in the appropriate space. EdgarScan will list the reports available to you for the company you've selected. Select the most recent annual report filing, identified as a 10-K or 10-K405. EdgarScan provides an outline of the report, including the separate financial statements. You can double-click the income statement and balance sheet for the selected company into an Excel™ spreadsheet for further analysis.

As a group, compare the two statements of cash flows.

a. How are Johnson & Johnson and JetBlue Airways Corp. similar or different regarding cash flows?

b. Compute and compare the free cash flow for each company, assuming additions to property, plant, and equipment replace current capacity.

MICHAEL WEBER/IMAGEBROKER/GLOW IMAGES

CHAPTER 17

Financial Statement Analysis

Nike, Inc.

"Just do it." These three words identify one of the most recognizable brands in the world, **Nike**. While this phrase inspires athletes to "compete and achieve their potential," it also defines the company.

Nike began in 1964 as a partnership between University of Oregon track coach Bill Bowerman and one of his former student-athletes, Phil Knight. The two began by selling shoes imported from Japan out of the back of Knight's car to athletes at track and field events. As sales grew, the company opened retail outlets, calling itself **Blue Ribbon Sports**. The company also began to develop its own shoes. In 1971, the company commissioned a graphic design student at Portland State University to develop the swoosh logo for a fee of $35. In 1978, the company changed its name to Nike, and in 1980, it sold its first shares of stock to the public.

Nike would have been a great company to invest in at the time. If you had invested in Nike's common stock back in 1990, you would have paid $5.00 per share. As of April 2011, Nike's stock was worth $109.23 per share. Unfortunately, you can't invest using hindsight.

How can you select companies in which to invest? Like any significant purchase, you should do some research to guide your investment decision. If you were buying a car, for example, you might go to **Edmunds.com** to obtain reviews, ratings, prices, specifications, options, and fuel economies to evaluate different vehicles. In selecting companies to invest in, you can use financial analysis to gain insight into a company's past performance and future prospects. This chapter describes and illustrates common financial data that can be analyzed to assist you in making investment decisions such as whether or not to invest in Nike's stock.

Source: www.nikebiz.com/.

Learning Objectives

After studying this chapter, you should be able to: *Example Exercises*

		Example Exercises
OBJ 1	**Describe basic financial statement analytical methods.**	
	Basic Analytical Methods	
	Horizontal Analysis	EE 17-1
	Vertical Analysis	EE 17-2
	Common-Sized Statements	
	Other Analytical Measures	
OBJ 2	**Use financial statement analysis to assess the solvency of a business.**	
	Liquidity and Solvency Analysis	
	Current Position Analysis	EE 17-3
	Accounts Receivable Analysis	EE 17-4
	Inventory Analysis	EE 17-5
	Ratio of Fixed Assets to Long-Term Liabilities	
	Ratio of Liabilities to Stockholders' Equity	EE 17-6
	Number of Times Interest Charges Are Earned	EE 17-7
OBJ 3	**Use financial statement analysis to assess the profitability of a business.**	
	Profitability Analysis	
	Ratio of Sales to Assets	EE 17-8
	Rate Earned on Total Assets	EE 17-9
	Rate Earned on Stockholders' Equity	
	Rate Earned on Common Stockholders' Equity	EE 17-10
	Earnings per Share on Common Stock	
	Price-Earnings Ratio	EE 17-11
	Divdends per Share	
	Divdend Yield	
	Summary of Analytical Measures	
OBJ 4	**Describe the contents of corporate annual reports.**	
	Corporate Annual Reports	
	Management Discussion and Analysis	
	Report on Internal Control	
	Report on Fairness of the Financial Statements	

At a Glance 17 Page 821

OBJ 1 Describe basic financial statement analytical methods.

Basic Analytical Methods

Users analyze a company's financial statements using a variety of analytical methods. Three such methods are:

- Horizontal analysis
- Vertical analysis
- Common-sized statements

Horizontal Analysis

The analysis of increases and decreases in the amount and percentage of comparative financial statement items is called **horizontal analysis**. Each item on the most recent statement is compared with the same item on one or more earlier statements in terms of the following:

- *Amount* of increase or decrease
- *Percent* of increase or decrease

When comparing statements, the earlier statement is normally used as the base year for computing increases and decreases.

Exhibit 1 illustrates horizontal analysis for the December 31, 2016 and 2015, balance sheets of **Lincoln Company**. In Exhibit 1, the December 31, 2015, balance sheet (the earliest year presented) is used as the base year.

Exhibit 1 indicates that total assets decreased by $91,000 (7.4%), liabilities decreased by $133,000 (30.0%), and stockholders' equity increased by $42,000 (5.3%). Since the long-term investments account decreased by $82,500, it appears that most of the decrease in long-term liabilities of $100,000 was achieved through the sale of long-term investments.

EXHIBIT 1

Comparative Balance Sheet—Horizontal Analysis

Lincoln Company
Comparative Balance Sheet
December 31, 2016 and 2015

	Dec. 31, 2016	Dec. 31, 2015	Increase (Decrease) Amount	Increase (Decrease) Percent
Assets				
Current assets	$ 550,000	$ 533,000	$ 17,000	3.2%
Long-term investments	95,000	177,500	(82,500)	(46.5%)
Property, plant, and equipment (net)	444,500	470,000	(25,500)	(5.4%)
Intangible assets	50,000	50,000	—	—
Total assets	$1,139,500	$1,230,500	$ (91,000)	(7.4%)
Liabilities				
Current liabilities	$ 210,000	$ 243,000	$ (33,000)	(13.6%)
Long-term liabilities	100,000	200,000	(100,000)	(50.0%)
Total liabilities	$ 310,000	$ 443,000	$(133,000)	(30.0%)
Stockholders' Equity				
Preferred 6% stock, $100 par	$ 150,000	$ 150,000	—	—
Common stock, $10 par	500,000	500,000	—	—
Retained earnings	179,500	137,500	$ 42,000	30.5%
Total stockholders' equity	$ 829,500	$ 787,500	$ 42,000	5.3%
Total liabilities and stockholders' equity	$1,139,500	$1,230,500	$ (91,000)	(7.4%)

The balance sheets in Exhibit 1 may be expanded or supported by a separate schedule that includes the individual asset and liability accounts. For example, Exhibit 2 is a supporting schedule of **Lincoln Company**'s current asset accounts.

EXHIBIT 2

Comparative Schedule of Current Assets—Horizontal Analysis

Lincoln Company
Comparative Schedule of Current Assets
December 31, 2016 and 2015

	Dec. 31, 2016	Dec. 31, 2015	Increase (Decrease) Amount	Increase (Decrease) Percent
Cash	$ 90,500	$ 64,700	$ 25,800	39.9%
Temporary investments	75,000	60,000	15,000	25.0%
Accounts receivable (net)	115,000	120,000	(5,000)	(4.2%)
Inventories	264,000	283,000	(19,000)	(6.7%)
Prepaid expenses	5,500	5,300	200	3.8%
Total current assets	$550,000	$533,000	$ 17,000	3.2%

Exhibit 2 indicates that while cash and temporary investments increased, accounts receivable and inventories decreased. The decrease in accounts receivable could be caused by improved collection policies, which would increase cash. The decrease in inventories could be caused by increased sales.

Exhibit 3 illustrates horizontal analysis for the 2016 and 2015 income statements of **Lincoln Company**. Exhibit 3 indicates an increase in sales of $298,000, or 24.8%. However, the percentage increase in sales of 24.8% was accompanied by an even greater percentage increase in the cost of goods (merchandise) sold of 27.2%.[1] Thus, gross profit increased by only 19.7% rather than by the 24.0% increase in sales.

EXHIBIT 3

Comparative Income Statement—Horizontal Analysis

Lincoln Company
Comparative Income Statement
For the Years Ended December 31, 2016 and 2015

			Increase (Decrease)	
	2016	**2015**	**Amount**	**Percent**
Sales	$1,498,000	$1,200,000	$298,000	24.8%
Cost of goods sold	1,043,000	820,000	223,000	27.2%
Gross profit	$ 455,000	$ 380,000	$ 75,000	19.7%
Selling expenses	$ 191,000	$ 147,000	$ 44,000	29.9%
Administrative expenses	104,000	97,400	6,600	6.8%
Total operating expenses	$ 295,000	$ 244,400	$ 50,600	20.7%
Income from operations	$ 160,000	$ 135,600	$ 24,400	18.0%
Other income	8,500	11,000	(2,500)	(22.7%)
	$ 168,500	$ 146,600	$ 21,900	14.9%
Other expense (interest)	6,000	12,000	(6,000)	(50.0%)
Income before income tax	$ 162,500	$ 134,600	$ 27,900	20.7%
Income tax expense	71,500	58,100	13,400	23.1%
Net income	$ 91,000	$ 76,500	$ 14,500	19.0%

Exhibit 3 also indicates that selling expenses increased by 29.9%. Thus, the 24.8% increases in sales could have been caused by an advertising campaign, which increased selling expenses. Administrative expenses increased by only 6.8%, total operating expenses increased by 20.7%, and income from operations increased by 18.0%. Interest expense decreased by 50.0%. This decrease was probably caused by the 50.0% decrease in long-term liabilities (Exhibit 1). Overall, net income increased by 19.0%, a favorable result.

Exhibit 4 illustrates horizontal analysis for the 2016 and 2015 retained earnings statements of **Lincoln Company**. Exhibit 4 indicates that retained earnings increased by 30.5% for the year. The increase is due to net income of $91,000 for the year, less dividends of $49,000.

EXHIBIT 4

Comparative Retained Earnings Statement—Horizontal Analysis

Lincoln Company
Comparative Retained Earnings Statement
For the Years Ended December 31, 2016 and 2015

			Increase (Decrease)	
	2016	**2015**	**Amount**	**Percent**
Retained earnings, January 1	$137,500	$100,000	$37,500	37.5%
Net income for the year	91,000	76,500	14,500	19.0%
Total	$228,500	$176,500	$52,000	29.5%
Dividends:				
On preferred stock	$ 9,000	$ 9,000	—	—
On common stock	40,000	30,000	$10,000	33.3%
Total	$ 49,000	$ 39,000	$10,000	25.6%
Retained earnings, December 31	$179,500	$137,500	$42,000	30.5%

[1] The term *cost of goods sold* is often used in practice in place of *cost of merchandise sold*. Such usage is followed in this chapter.

Example Exercise 17-1 Horizontal Analysis

OBJ 1

The comparative cash and accounts receivable balances for a company follow:

	Dec. 31, 2016	Dec. 31, 2015
Cash	$62,500	$50,000
Accounts receivable (net)	74,400	80,000

Based on this information, what is the amount and percentage of increase or decrease that would be shown on a balance sheet with horizontal analysis?

Follow My Example 17-1

Cash	$12,500 increase ($62,500 – $50,000), or 25%
Accounts receivable	$5,600 decrease ($74,400 – $80,000), or (7%)

Practice Exercises: PE 17-1A, PE 17-1B

Vertical Analysis

The percentage analysis of the relationship of each component in a financial statement to a total within the statement is called **vertical analysis**. Although vertical analysis is applied to a single statement, it may be applied on the same statement over time. This enhances the analysis by showing how the percentages of each item have changed over time.

In vertical analysis of the balance sheet, the percentages are computed as follows:

- Each asset item is stated as a percent of the total assets.
- Each liability and stockholders' equity item is stated as a percent of the total liabilities and stockholders' equity.

Exhibit 5 illustrates the vertical analysis of the December 31, 2016 and 2015, balance sheets of **Lincoln Company**. Exhibit 5 indicates that current assets have increased from 43.3% to 48.3% of total assets. Long-term investments decreased from 14.4% to 8.3% of total assets. Stockholders' equity increased from 64.0% to 72.8%, with a comparable decrease in liabilities.

EXHIBIT 5

Comparative Balance Sheet—Vertical Analysis

Lincoln Company
Comparative Balance Sheet
December 31, 2016 and 2015

	Dec. 31, 2016		Dec. 31, 2015	
	Amount	**Percent**	**Amount**	**Percent**
Assets				
Current assets	$ 550,000	48.3%	$ 533,000	43.3%
Long-term investments	95,000	8.3	177,500	14.4
Property, plant, and equipment (net)	444,500	39.0	470,000	38.2
Intangible assets	50,000	4.4	50,000	4.1
Total assets	$1,139,500	100.0%	$1,230,500	100.0%
Liabilities				
Current liabilities	$ 210,000	18.4%	$ 243,000	19.7%
Long-term liabilities	100,000	8.8	200,000	16.3
Total liabilities	$ 310,000	27.2%	$ 443,000	36.0%
Stockholders' Equity				
Preferred 6% stock, $100 par	$ 150,000	13.2%	$ 150,000	12.2%
Common stock, $10 par	500,000	43.9	500,000	40.6
Retained earnings	179,500	15.7	137,500	11.2
Total stockholders' equity	$ 829,500	72.8%	$ 787,500	64.0%
Total liabilities and stockholders' equity	$1,139,500	100.0%	$1,230,500	100.0%

In a vertical analysis of the income statement, each item is stated as a percent of sales. Exhibit 6 illustrates the vertical analysis of the 2016 and 2015 income statements of **Lincoln Company**.

EXHIBIT 6

Comparative Income Statement—Vertical Analysis

Lincoln Company
Comparative Income Statement
For the Years Ended December 31, 2016 and 2015

	2016		2015	
	Amount	Percent	Amount	Percent
Sales	$1,498,000	100.0%	$1,200,000	100.0%
Cost of goods sold	1,043,000	69.6	820,000	68.3
Gross profit	$ 455,000	30.4%	$ 380,000	31.7%
Selling expenses	$ 191,000	12.8%	$ 147,000	12.3%
Administrative expenses	104,000	6.9	97,400	8.1
Total operating expenses	$ 295,000	19.7%	$ 244,400	20.4%
Income from operations	$ 160,000	10.7%	$ 135,600	11.3%
Other income	8,500	0.6	11,000	0.9
	$ 168,500	11.3%	$ 146,600	12.2%
Other expense (interest)	6,000	0.4	12,000	1.0
Income before income tax	$ 162,500	10.9%	$ 134,600	11.2%
Income tax expense	71,500	4.8	58,100	4.8
Net income	$ 91,000	6.1%	$ 76,500	6.4%

Exhibit 6 indicates a decrease in the gross profit rate from 31.7% in 2015 to 30.4% in 2016. Although this is only a 1.3 percentage point (31.7% – 30.4%) decrease, in dollars of potential gross profit, it represents a decrease of $19,474 (1.3% × $1,498,000) based on 2016 sales. Thus, a small percentage decrease can have a large dollar effect.

Example Exercise 17-2 Vertical Analysis

OBJ 1

Income statement information for Lee Corporation follows:

Sales	$100,000
Cost of goods sold	65,000
Gross profit	$ 35,000

Prepare a vertical analysis of the income statement for Lee Corporation.

Follow My Example 17-2

	Amount	Percentage	
Sales	$100,000	100%	($100,000 ÷ $100,000)
Cost of goods sold	65,000	65	($65,000 ÷ $100,000)
Gross profit	$ 35,000	35%	($35,000 ÷ $100,000)

Practice Exercises: PE 17-2A, PE 17-2B

Common-Sized Statements

In a **common-sized statement**, all items are expressed as percentages, with no dollar amounts shown. Common-sized statements are often useful for comparing one company with another or for comparing a company with industry averages.

Exhibit 7 illustrates common-sized income statements for **Lincoln Company** and Madison Corporation. Exhibit 7 indicates that Lincoln has a slightly higher rate of gross profit (30.4%) than Madison (30.0%). However, Lincoln has a higher percentage of selling expenses (12.8%) and administrative expenses (6.9%) than does Madison (11.5% and 4.1%). As a result, the income from operations of Lincoln (10.7%) is less than that of Madison (14.4%).

EXHIBIT 7

Common-Sized Income Statements

	Lincoln Company	Madison Corporation
Sales	100.0%	100.0%
Cost of goods sold	69.6	70.0
Gross profit	30.4%	30.0%
Selling expenses	12.8%	11.5%
Administrative expenses	6.9	4.1
Total operating expenses	19.7%	15.6%
Income from operations	10.7%	14.4%
Other income	0.6	0.6
	11.3%	15.0%
Other expense (interest)	0.4	0.5
Income before income tax	10.9%	14.5%
Income tax expense	4.8	5.5
Net income	6.1%	9.0%

The unfavorable difference of 3.7 (14.4% – 10.7%) percentage points in income from operations would concern the managers and other stakeholders of Lincoln. The underlying causes of the difference should be investigated and possibly corrected. For example, Lincoln may decide to outsource some of its administrative duties so that its administrative expenses are more comparative to that of Madison.

Other Analytical Measures

Other relationships may be expressed in ratios and percentages. Often, these relationships are compared within the same statement and, thus, are a type of vertical analysis. Comparing these items with items from earlier periods is a type of horizontal analysis.

Analytical measures are not a definitive conclusion. They are only guides in evaluating financial and operating data. Many other factors, such as trends in the industry and general economic conditions, should also be considered when analyzing a company.

Liquidity and Solvency Analysis

OBJ 2 Use financial statement analysis to assess the solvency of a business.

All users of financial statements are interested in the ability of a company to do the following:

- Maintain liquidity and solvency
- Earn income, called **profitability**

The ability of a company to convert assets into cash is called **liquidity**, while the ability of a company to pay its debts is called **solvency**. Liquidity, solvency, and profitability are interrelated. For example, a company that cannot convert assets into cash may have difficulty taking advantage of profitable courses of action requiring immediate cash outlays. Likewise, a company that cannot pay its debts will have difficulty obtaining credit. A lack of credit will, in turn, limit the company's ability to purchase merchandise or expand operations, which decreases its profitability.

Liquidity and solvency are normally assessed using the following:

- Current position analysis
  - Working capital
  - Current ratio
  - Quick ratio
- Accounts receivable analysis
  - Accounts receivable turnover
  - Number of days' sales in receivables
- Inventory analysis
  - Inventory turnover
  - Number of days' sales in inventory
- The ratio of fixed assets to long-term liabilities
- The ratio of liabilities to stockholders' equity
- The number of times interest charges are earned

One popular printed source for industry ratios is *Annual Statement Studies* from Risk Management Association. Online analysis is available from Zacks Investment Research site at www.zacks.com.

The Lincoln Company financial statements presented earlier are used to illustrate the preceding analyses.

Current Position Analysis

A company's ability to pay its current liabilities is called **current position analysis.** It is a solvency measure of special interest to short-term creditors and includes the computation and analysis of the following:

- Working capital
- Current ratio
- Quick ratio

Working Capital A company's **working capital** is computed as follows:

Working Capital = Current Assets − Current Liabilities

To illustrate, the working capital for **Lincoln Company** for 2016 and 2015 is computed as follows:

	2016	2015
Current assets	$550,000	$533,000
Less current liabilities	210,000	243,000
Working capital	$340,000	$290,000

The working capital is used to evaluate a company's ability to pay current liabilities. A company's working capital is often monitored monthly, quarterly, or yearly by creditors and other debtors. However, it is difficult to use working capital to compare companies of different sizes. For example, working capital of $250,000 may be adequate for a local hardware store, but it would be inadequate for The Home Depot.

Current Ratio The **current ratio**, sometimes called the *working capital ratio*, is computed as follows:

$$\text{Current Ratio} = \frac{\text{Current Assets}}{\text{Current Liabilities}}$$

To illustrate, the current ratio for **Lincoln Company** is computed as follows:

	2016	2015
Current assets	$550,000	$533,000
Current liabilities	$210,000	$243,000
Current ratio	2.6 ($550,000 ÷ $210,000)	2.2 ($533,000 ÷ $243,000)

The current ratio is a more reliable indicator of a company's ability to pay its current liabilities than is working capital, and it is much easier to compare across companies. To illustrate, assume that as of December 31, 2016, the working capital of a competitor is much greater than $340,000, but its current ratio is only 1.3. Considering these facts alone, Lincoln, with its current ratio of 2.6, is in a more favorable position to obtain short-term credit than the competitor, which has the greater amount of working capital.

Quick Ratio One limitation of working capital and the current ratio is that they do not consider the types of current assets a company has and how easily they can be turned in to cash. Because of this, two companies may have the same working capital and current ratios but differ significantly in their ability to pay their current liabilities.

To illustrate, the current assets and liabilities for **Lincoln Company** and Jefferson Corporation as of December 31, 2016, are as follows:

	Lincoln Company	Jefferson Corporation
Current assets:		
Cash	$ 90,500	$ 45,500
Temporary investments	75,000	25,000
Accounts receivable (net)	115,000	90,000
Inventories	264,000	380,000
Prepaid expenses	5,500	9,500
Total current assets	$550,000	$550,000
Total current assets	$550,000	$550,000
Less current liabilities	210,000	210,000
Working capital	$340,000	$340,000
Current ratio ($550,000 ÷ $210,000)	2.6	2.6

Lincoln and Jefferson both have a working capital of $340,000 and current ratios of 2.6. Jefferson, however, has more of its current assets in inventories. These inventories must be sold and the receivables collected before all the current liabilities can be paid. This takes time. In addition, if the market for its product declines, Jefferson may have difficulty selling its inventory. This, in turn, could impair its ability to pay its current liabilities.

In contrast, Lincoln's current assets contain more cash, temporary investments, and accounts receivable, which can easily be converted to cash. Thus, Lincoln is in a stronger current position than Jefferson to pay its current liabilities.

A ratio that measures the "instant" debt-paying ability of a company is the **quick ratio**, sometimes called the *acid-test ratio*. The quick ratio is computed as follows:

$$\text{Quick Ratio} = \frac{\text{Quick Assets}}{\text{Current Liabilities}}$$

Quick assets are cash and other current assets that can be easily converted to cash. Quick assets normally include cash, temporary investments, and receivables but exclude inventories and prepaid assets.

To illustrate, the quick ratio for **Lincoln Company** is computed as follows:

	2016	2015
Quick assets:		
Cash	$ 90,500	$ 64,700
Temporary investments	75,000	60,000
Accounts receivable (net)	115,000	120,000
Total quick assets	$280,500	$244,700
Current liabilities	$210,000	$243,000
Quick ratio	1.3 ($280,500 ÷ $210,000)	1.0 ($244,700 ÷ $243,000)

Example Exercise 17-3 Current Position Analysis OBJ 2

The following items are reported on a company's balance sheet:

Cash	$300,000
Temporary investments	100,000
Accounts receivable (net)	200,000
Inventory	200,000
Accounts payable	400,000

Determine (a) the current ratio and (b) the quick ratio.

Follow My Example 17-3

a. Current Ratio = Current Assets ÷ Current Liabilities
= ($300,000 + $100,000 + $200,000 + $200,000) ÷ $400,000
= 2.0

b. Quick Ratio = Quick Assets ÷ Current Liabilities
= ($300,000 + $100,000 + $200,000) ÷ $400,000
= 1.5

Practice Exercises: PE 17-3A, PE 17-3B

Accounts Receivable Analysis

A company's ability to collect its accounts receivable is called **accounts receivable analysis**. It includes the computation and analysis of the following:

- Accounts receivable turnover
- Number of days' sales in receivables

Collecting accounts receivable as quickly as possible improves a company's liquidity. In addition, the cash collected from receivables may be used to improve or expand operations. Quick collection of receivables also reduces the risk of uncollectible accounts.

Accounts Receivable Turnover The **accounts receivable turnover** is computed as follows:

$$\text{Accounts Receivable Turnover} = \frac{\text{Sales}^{2}}{\text{Average Accounts Receivable}}$$

To illustrate, the accounts receivable turnover for **Lincoln Company** for 2016 and 2015 is computed as follows. Lincoln's accounts receivable balance at the beginning of 2015 is $140,000.

	2016	2015
Sales	$1,498,000	$1,200,000
Accounts receivable (net):		
Beginning of year	$ 120,000	$ 140,000
End of year	115,000	120,000
Total	$ 235,000	$ 260,000
Average accounts receivable	$117,500 ($235,000 ÷ 2)	$130,000 ($260,000 ÷ 2)
Accounts receivable turnover	12.7 ($1,498,000 ÷ $117,500)	9.2 ($1,200,000 ÷ $130,000)

The increase in Lincoln's accounts receivable turnover from 9.2 to 12.7 indicates that the collection of receivables has improved during 2016. This may be due to a change in how credit is granted, collection practices, or both.

[2] If known, *credit* sales should be used in the numerator. Because credit sales are not normally known by external users, we use sales in the numerator.

For Lincoln, the average accounts receivable was computed using the accounts receivable balance at the beginning and the end of the year. When sales are seasonal and, thus, vary throughout the year, monthly balances of receivables are often used. Also, if sales on account include notes receivable as well as accounts receivable, notes and accounts receivable are normally combined for analysis.

Number of Days' Sales in Receivables The **number of days' sales in receivables** is computed as follows:

$$\text{Number of Days' Sales in Receivables} = \frac{\text{Average Accounts Receivable}}{\text{Average Daily Sales}}$$

where

$$\text{Average Daily Sales} = \frac{\text{Sales}}{\text{365 days}}$$

To illustrate, the number of days' sales in receivables for **Lincoln Company** is computed as follows:

	2016	2015
Average accounts receivable	$117,500 ($235,000 ÷ 2)	$130,000 ($260,000 ÷ 2)
Average daily sales	$4,104 ($1,498,000 ÷ 365)	$3,288 ($1,200,000 ÷ 365)
Number of days' sales in receivables	28.6 ($117,500 ÷ $4,104)	39.5 ($130,000 ÷ $3,288)

The number of days' sales in receivables is an estimate of the time (in days) that the accounts receivable have been outstanding. The number of days' sales in receivables is often compared with a company's credit terms to evaluate the efficiency of the collection of receivables.

To illustrate, if Lincoln's credit terms are 2/10, n/30, then Lincoln was very *inefficient* in collecting receivables in 2015. In other words, receivables should have been collected in 30 days or less but were being collected in 39.5 days. Although collections improved during 2016 to 28.6 days, there is probably still room for improvement. On the other hand, if Lincoln's credit terms are n/45, then there is probably little room for improving collections.

Example Exercise 17-4 Accounts Receivable Analysis

OBJ 2

A company reports the following:

Sales	$960,000
Average accounts receivable (net)	48,000

Determine (a) the accounts receivable turnover and (b) the number of days' sales in receivables. Round to one decimal place.

Follow My Example 17-4

a. Accounts Receivable Turnover = Sales ÷ Average Accounts Receivable
= $960,000 ÷ $48,000
= 20.0

b. Number of Days' Sales in Receivables = Average Accounts Receivable ÷ Average Daily Sales
= $48,000 ÷ ($960,000 ÷ 365) = $48,000 ÷ $2,630
= 18.3 days

Practice Exercises: PE 17-4A, PE 17-4B

Inventory Analysis

A company's ability to manage its inventory effectively is evaluated using **inventory analysis**. It includes the computation and analysis of the following:

- Inventory turnover
- Number of days' sales in inventory

Excess inventory decreases liquidity by tying up funds (cash) in inventory. In addition, excess inventory increases insurance expense, property taxes, storage costs, and other related expenses. These expenses further reduce funds that could be used elsewhere to improve or expand operations.

Excess inventory also increases the risk of losses because of price declines or obsolescence of the inventory. On the other hand, a company should keep enough inventory in stock so that it doesn't lose sales because of lack of inventory.

Inventory Turnover The **inventory turnover** is computed as follows:

$$\text{Inventory Turnover} = \frac{\text{Cost of Goods Sold}}{\text{Average Inventory}}$$

To illustrate, the inventory turnover for **Lincoln Company** for 2016 and 2015 is computed as follows. Lincoln's inventory balance at the beginning of 2015 is $311,000.

	2016	2015
Cost of goods sold	$1,043,000	$820,000
Inventories:		
Beginning of year	$ 283,000	$311,000
End of year	264,000	283,000
Total	$ 547,000	$594,000
Average inventory	$273,500 ($547,000 ÷ 2)	$297,000 ($594,000 ÷ 2)
Inventory turnover	3.8 ($1,043,000 ÷ $273,500)	2.8 ($820,000 ÷ $297,000)

The increase in Lincoln's inventory turnover from 2.8 to 3.8 indicates that the management of inventory has improved in 2016. The inventory turnover improved because of an increase in the cost of goods sold, which indicates more sales and a decrease in the average inventories.

What is considered a good inventory turnover varies by type of inventory, companies, and industries. For example, grocery stores have a higher inventory turnover than jewelers or furniture stores. Likewise, within a grocery store, perishable foods have a higher turnover than the soaps and cleansers.

Number of Days' Sales in Inventory The **number of days' sales in inventory** is computed as follows:

$$\text{Number of Days' Sales in Inventory} = \frac{\text{Average Inventory}}{\text{Average Daily Cost of Goods Sold}}$$

where

$$\text{Average Daily Cost of Goods Sold} = \frac{\text{Cost of Goods Sold}}{\text{365 days}}$$

To illustrate, the number of days' sales in inventory for **Lincoln Company** is computed as follows:

	2016	2015
Average inventory	$273,500 ($547,000 ÷ 2)	$297,000 ($594,000 ÷ 2)
Average daily cost of goods sold	$2,858 ($1,043,000 ÷ 365)	$2,247 ($820,000 ÷ 365)
Number of days' sales in inventory	95.7 ($273,500 ÷ $2,858)	132.2 ($297,000 ÷ $2,247)

The number of days' sales in inventory is a rough measure of the length of time it takes to purchase, sell, and replace the inventory. Lincoln's number of days' sales in inventory improved from 132.2 days to 95.7 days during 2016. This is a major improvement in managing inventory.

Example Exercise 17-5 Inventory Analysis OBJ 2

A company reports the following:

Cost of goods sold	$560,000
Average inventory	112,000

Determine (a) the inventory turnover and (b) the number of days' sales in inventory. Round to one decimal place.

Follow My Example 17-5

a. Inventory Turnover = Cost of Goods Sold ÷ Average Inventory
= $560,000 ÷ $112,000
= 5.0

b. Number of Days' Sales in Inventory = Average Inventory ÷ Average Daily Cost of Goods Sold
= $112,000 ÷ ($560,000 ÷ 365) = $112,000 ÷ $1,534
= 73.0 days

Practice Exercises: PE 17-5A, PE 17-5B

Ratio of Fixed Assets to Long-Term Liabilities

The **ratio of fixed assets to long-term liabilities** provides a measure of whether noteholders or bondholders will be paid. Because fixed assets are often pledged as security for long-term notes and bonds, it is computed as follows:

$$\text{Ratio of Fixed Assets to Long-Term Liabilities} = \frac{\text{Fixed Assets (net)}}{\text{Long-Term Liabilities}}$$

To illustrate, the ratio of fixed assets to long-term liabilities for **Lincoln Company** is computed as follows:

	2016	2015
Fixed assets (net)	$444,500	$470,000
Long-term liabilities	$100,000	$200,000
Ratio of fixed assets to long-term liabilities	4.4 ($444,500 ÷ $100,000)	2.4 ($470,000 ÷ $200,000)

During 2016, Lincoln's ratio of fixed assets to long-term liabilities increased from 2.4 to 4.4. This increase was due primarily to Lincoln paying off one-half of its long-term liabilities in 2016.

Ratio of Liabilities to Stockholders' Equity

The **ratio of liabilities to stockholders' equity** measures how much of the company is financed by debt and equity. It is computed as follows:

$$\text{Ratio of Liabilities to Stockholders' Equity} = \frac{\text{Total Liabilities}}{\text{Total Stockholders' Equity}}$$

To illustrate, the ratio of liabilities to stockholders' equity for **Lincoln Company** is computed as follows:

	2016	2015
Total liabilities	$310,000	$443,000
Total stockholders' equity	$829,500	$787,500
Ratio of liabilities to stockholders' equity	0.4 ($310,000 ÷ $829,500)	0.6 ($443,000 ÷ $787,500)

Lincoln's ratio of liabilities to stockholders' equity decreased from 0.6 to 0.4 during 2016. This is an improvement and indicates that Lincoln's creditors have an adequate margin of safety.

Example Exercise 17-6 Long-Term Solvency Analysis

OBJ 2

The following information was taken from Acme Company's balance sheet:

Fixed assets (net)	$1,400,000
Long-term liabilities	400,000
Total liabilities	560,000
Total stockholders' equity	1,400,000

Determine the company's (a) ratio of fixed assets to long-term liabilities and (b) ratio of liabilities to total stockholders' equity.

Follow My Example 17-6

a. Ratio of Fixed Assets to Long-Term Liabilities = Fixed Assets ÷ Long-Term Liabilities
= $1,400,000 ÷ $400,000
= 3.5

b. Ratio of Liabilities to Total Stockholders' Equity = Total Liabilities ÷ Total Stockholders' Equity
= $560,000 ÷ $1,400,000
= 0.4

Practice Exercises: PE 17-6A, PE 17-6B

Number of Times Interest Charges Are Earned

The **number of times interest charges are earned**, sometimes called the *fixed charge coverage ratio*, measures the risk that interest payments will not be made if earnings decrease. It is computed as follows:

$$\text{Number of Times Interest Charges Are Earned} = \frac{\text{Income Before Income Tax} + \text{Interest Expense}}{\text{Interest Expense}}$$

Interest expense is paid before income taxes. In other words, interest expense is deducted in determining taxable income and, thus, income tax. For this reason, income *before taxes* is used in computing the number of times interest charges are earned.

The *higher* the ratio the more likely interest payments will be paid if earnings decrease. To illustrate, the number of times interest charges are earned for **Lincoln Company** is computed as follows:

	2016	2015
Income before income tax	$162,500	$134,600
Add interest expense	6,000	12,000
Amount available to pay interest	$168,500	$146,600
Number of times interest charges are earned	28.1 ($168,500 ÷ $6,000)	12.2 ($146,600 ÷ $12,000)

The number of times interest charges are earned improved from 12.2 to 28.1 during 2016. This indicates that Lincoln has sufficient earnings to pay interest expense.

The number of times interest charges are earned can be adapted for use with dividends on preferred stock. In this case, the *number of times preferred dividends are earned* is computed as follows:

$$\text{Number of Times Preferred Dividends Are Earned} = \frac{\text{Net Income}}{\text{Preferred Dividends}}$$

Since dividends are paid after taxes, net income is used in computing the number of times preferred dividends are earned. The *higher* the ratio, the more likely preferred dividend payments will be paid if earnings decrease.

Example Exercise 17-7 Times Interest Charges Are Earned OBJ 2

A company reports the following:

Income before income tax	$250,000
Interest expense	100,000

Determine the number of times interest charges are earned.

Follow My Example 17-7

Number of Times Interest Charges Are Earned = (Income Before Income Tax + Interest Expense) ÷ Interest Expense
= ($250,000 + $100,000) ÷ $100,000
= 3.5

Practice Exercises: PE 17-7A, PE 17-7B

Profitability Analysis

OBJ 3 Use financial statement analysis to assess the profitability of a business.

Profitability analysis focuses on the ability of a company to earn profits. This ability is reflected in the company's operating results, as reported in its income statement. The ability to earn profits also depends on the assets the company has available for use in its operations, as reported in its balance sheet. Thus, income statement and balance sheet relationships are often used in evaluating profitability.

Common profitability analyses include the following:

- Ratio of sales to assets
- Rate earned on total assets
- Rate earned on stockholders' equity
- Rate earned on common stockholders' equity
- Earnings per share on common stock
- Price-earnings ratio
- Dividends per share
- Dividend yield

Note: **Profitability analysis focuses on the relationship between operating results and the resources available to a business.**

Ratio of Sales to Assets

The **ratio of sales to assets** measures how effectively a company uses its assets. It is computed as follows:

$$\text{Ratio of Sales to Assets} = \frac{\text{Sales}}{\text{Average Total Assets (excluding long-term investments)}}$$

Note that any long-term investments are excluded in computing the ratio of sales to assets. This is because long-term investments are unrelated to normal operations and sales.

To illustrate, the ratio of sales to assets for **Lincoln Company** is computed as follows. Total assets (excluding long-term investments) are $1,010,000 at the beginning of 2015.

	2016	2015
Sales	$1,498,000	$1,200,000
Total assets (excluding long-term investments):		
Beginning of year	$1,053,000*	$1,010,000
End of year	1,044,500**	1,053,000*
Total	$2,097,500	$2,063,000
Average total assets	$1,048,750 ($2,097,500 ÷ 2)	$1,031,500 ($2,063,000 ÷ 2)
Ratio of sales to assets	1.4 ($1,498,000 ÷ $1,048,750)	1.2 ($1,200,000 ÷ $1,031,500)

*($1,230,500 – $177,500)
**($1,139,500 – $95,000)

For Lincoln, the average total assets was computed using total assets (excluding long-term investments) at the beginning and end of the year. The average total assets could also be based on monthly or quarterly averages.

The ratio of sales to assets indicates that Lincoln's use of its operating assets has improved in 2016. This was primarily due to the increase in sales in 2016.

Example Exercise 17-8 Sales to Assets OBJ 3

A company reports the following:

Sales	$2,250,000
Average total assets	1,500,000

Determine the ratio of sales to assets.

Follow My Example 17-8

Ratio of Sales to Assets = Sales ÷ Average Total Assets
= $2,250,000 ÷ $1,500,000
= 1.5

Practice Exercises: PE 17-8A, PE 17-8B

Rate Earned on Total Assets

The **rate earned on total assets** measures the profitability of total assets, without considering how the assets are financed. In other words, this rate is not affected by the portion of assets financed by creditors or stockholders. It is computed as follows:

$$\text{Rate Earned on Total Assets} = \frac{\text{Net Income} + \text{Interest Expense}}{\text{Average Total Assets}}$$

The rate earned on total assets is computed by adding interest expense to net income. By adding interest expense to net income, the effect of whether the assets are financed by creditors (debt) or stockholders (equity) is eliminated. Because net income includes any income earned from long-term investments, the average total assets includes long-term investments as well as the net operating assets.

To illustrate, the rate earned on total assets by **Lincoln Company** is computed as follows. Total assets are $1,187,500 at the beginning of 2015.

	2016	2015
Net income	$ 91,000	$ 76,500
Plus interest expense	6,000	12,000
Total	$ 97,000	$ 88,500
Total assets:		
Beginning of year	$1,230,500	$1,187,500
End of year	1,139,500	1,230,500
Total	$2,370,000	$2,418,000
Average total assets	$1,185,000 ($2,370,000 ÷ 2)	$1,209,000 ($2,418,000 ÷ 2)
Rate earned on total assets	8.2% ($97,000 ÷ $1,185,000)	7.3% ($88,500 ÷ $1,209,000)

The rate earned on total assets improved from 7.3% to 8.2% during 2016.

The *rate earned on operating assets* is sometimes computed when there are large amounts of nonoperating income and expense. It is computed as follows:

$$\text{Rate Earned on Operating Assets} = \frac{\text{Income from Operations}}{\text{Average Operating Assets}}$$

Because Lincoln Company does not have a significant amount of nonoperating income and expense, the rate earned on operating assets is not illustrated.

Example Exercise 17-9 Rate Earned on Total Assets

OBJ 3

A company reports the following income statement and balance sheet information for the current year:

Net income	$ 125,000
Interest expense	25,000
Average total assets	2,000,000

Determine the rate earned on total assets.

Follow My Example 17-9

Rate Earned on Total Assets = (Net Income + Interest Expense) ÷ Average Total Assets
= ($125,000 + $25,000) ÷ $2,000,000
= $150,000 ÷ $2,000,000
= 7.5%

Practice Exercises: PE 17-9A, PE 17-9B

Rate Earned on Stockholders' Equity

The **rate earned on stockholders' equity** measures the rate of income earned on the amount invested by the stockholders. It is computed as follows:

$$\text{Rate Earned on Stockholders' Equity} = \frac{\text{Net Income}}{\text{Average Total Stockholders' Equity}}$$

To illustrate, the rate earned on stockholders' equity for **Lincoln Company** is computed as follows. Total stockholders' equity is $750,000 at the beginning of 2015.

	2016	2015
Net income	$ 91,000	$ 76,500
Stockholders' equity:		
Beginning of year	$ 787,500	$ 750,000
End of year	829,500	787,500
Total	$1,617,000	$1,537,500
Average stockholders' equity	$808,500 ($1,617,000 ÷ 2)	$768,750 ($1,537,500 ÷ 2)
Rate earned on stockholders' equity	11.3% ($91,000 ÷ $808,500)	10.0% ($76,500 ÷ $768,750)

The rate earned on stockholders' equity improved from 10.0% to 11.3% during 2016.

Leverage involves using debt to increase the return on an investment. The rate earned on stockholders' equity is normally higher than the rate earned on total assets. This is because of the effect of leverage.

For **Lincoln Company**, the effect of leverage for 2016 is 3.1% and for 2015 is 2.7% computed as follows:

	2016	2015
Rate earned on stockholders' equity	11.3%	10.0%
Less rate earned on total assets	8.2	7.3
Effect of leverage	3.1%	2.7%

Exhibit 8 shows the 2016 and 2015 effects of leverage for Lincoln.

Rate Earned on Common Stockholders' Equity

The **rate earned on common stockholders' equity** measures the rate of profits earned on the amount invested by the common stockholders. It is computed as follows:

$$\text{Rate Earned on Common Stockholders' Equity} = \frac{\text{Net Income} - \text{Preferred Dividends}}{\text{Average Common Stockholders' Equity}}$$

EXHIBIT 8

Effect of Leverage

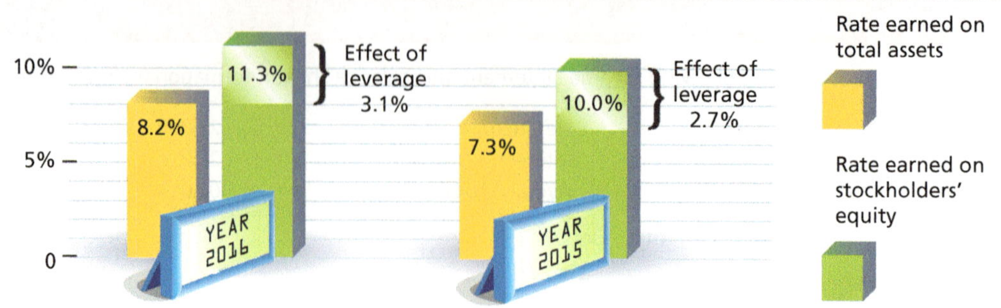

Because preferred stockholders rank ahead of the common stockholders in their claim on earnings, any preferred dividends are subtracted from net income in computing the rate earned on common stockholders' equity.

Lincoln Company had $150,000 of 6% preferred stock outstanding on December 31, 2016 and 2015. Thus, preferred dividends of $9,000 ($150,000 × 6%) are deducted from net income. Lincoln's common stockholders' equity is determined as follows:

	December 31		
	2016	**2015**	**2014**
Common stock, $10 par	$500,000	$500,000	$500,000
Retained earnings	179,500	137,500	100,000
Common stockholders' equity	$679,500	$637,500	$600,000

The retained earnings on December 31, 2014, of $100,000 is the same as the retained earnings on January 1, 2015, as shown in Lincoln's retained earnings statement in Exhibit 4.

Using this information, the rate earned on common stockholders' equity for Lincoln is computed as follows:

	2016	**2015**
Net income	$ 91,000	$ 76,500
Less preferred dividends	9,000	9,000
Total	$ 82,000	$ 67,500
Common stockholders' equity:		
Beginning of year	$ 637,500	$ 600,000
End of year	679,500*	637,500**
Total	$1,317,000	$1,237,500
Average common stockholders' equity	$658,500 ($1,317,000 ÷ 2)	$618,750 ($1,237,500 ÷ 2)
Rate earned on common stockholders' equity	12.5% ($82,000 ÷ $658,500)	10.9% ($67,500 ÷ $618,750)

*($829,500 – $150,000)
**($787,500 – $150,000)

Lincoln's rate earned on common stockholders' equity improved from 10.9% to 12.5% in 2016. This rate differs from the rates earned by Lincoln on total assets and stockholders' equity, which follow:

	2016	**2015**
Rate earned on total assets	8.2%	7.3%
Rate earned on stockholders' equity	11.3%	10.0%
Rate earned on common stockholders' equity	12.5%	10.9%

These rates differ because of leverage, as discussed in the preceding section.

Example Exercise 17-10 Common Stockholders' Profitability Analysis

OBJ 3

A company reports the following:

Net income	$ 125,000
Preferred dividends	5,000
Average stockholders' equity	1,000,000
Average common stockholders' equity	800,000

Determine (a) the rate earned on stockholders' equity and (b) the rate earned on common stockholders' equity.

Follow My Example 17-10

a. Rate Earned on Stockholders' Equity = Net Income ÷ Average Stockholders' Equity
= $125,000 ÷ $1,000,000
= 12.5%

b. Rate Earned on Common Stockholders' Equity = (Net Income – Preferred Dividends) ÷ Average Common Stockholders' Equity
= ($125,000 – $5,000) ÷ $800,000
= 15%

Practice Exercises: PE 17-10A, PE 17-10B

Earnings per Share on Common Stock

Earnings per share (EPS) on common stock measures the share of profits that are earned by a share of common stock. Earnings per share must be reported in the income statement. As a result, earnings per share (EPS) is often reported in the financial press. It is computed as follows:

$$\text{Earnings per Share (EPS) on Common Stock} = \frac{\text{Net Income} - \text{Preferred Dividends}}{\text{Shares of Common Stock Outstanding}}$$

When preferred and common stock are outstanding, preferred dividends are subtracted from net income to determine the income related to the common shares.

To illustrate, the earnings per share (EPS) of common stock for **Lincoln Company** is computed as follows:

	2016	2015
Net income	$91,000	$76,500
Preferred dividends	9,000	9,000
Total	$82,000	$67,500
Shares of common stock outstanding	50,000	50,000
Earnings per share on common stock	$1.64 ($82,000 ÷ 50,000)	$1.35 ($67,500 ÷ 50,000)

Lincoln had $150,000 of 6% preferred stock outstanding on December 31, 2016 and 2015. Thus, preferred dividends of $9,000 ($150,000 x 6%) are deducted from net income in computing earnings per share on common stock.

Lincoln did not issue any additional shares of common stock in 2016. If Lincoln had issued additional shares in 2016, a weighted average of common shares outstanding during the year would have been used.

Lincoln's earnings per share (EPS) on common stock improved from $1.35 to $1.64 during 2016.

Lincoln Company has a simple capital structure with only common stock and preferred stock outstanding. Many corporations, however, have complex capital structures with various types of equity securities outstanding, such as convertible preferred stock,

stock options, and stock warrants. In such cases, the possible effects of such securities on the shares of common stock outstanding are considered in reporting earnings per share. These possible effects are reported separately as *earnings per common share assuming dilution* or *diluted earnings per share*. This topic is described and illustrated in advanced accounting courses and textbooks.

Price-Earnings Ratio

The **price-earnings (P/E) ratio** on common stock measures a company's future earnings prospects. It is often quoted in the financial press and is computed as follows:

$$\text{Price-Earnings (P/E) Ratio} = \frac{\text{Market Price per Share of Common Stock}}{\text{Earnings per Share on Common Stock}}$$

To illustrate, the price-earnings (P/E) ratio for **Lincoln Company** is computed as follows:

	2016	2015
Market price per share of common stock	$41.00	$27.00
Earnings per share on common stock	$1.64	$1.35
Price-earnings ratio on common stock	25 ($41 ÷ $1.64)	20 ($27 ÷ $1.35)

The price-earnings ratio improved from 20 to 25 during 2016. In other words, a share of common stock of Lincoln was selling for 20 times earnings per share at the end of 2015. At the end of 2016, the common stock was selling for 25 times earnings per share. This indicates that the market expects Lincoln to experience favorable earnings in the future.

Example Exercise 17-11 Earnings per Share and Price-Earnings Ratio

OBJ 3

A company reports the following:

Net income	$250,000
Preferred dividends	$15,000
Shares of common stock outstanding	20,000
Market price per share of common stock	$35.25

a. Determine the company's earnings per share on common stock.

b. Determine the company's price-earnings ratio. Round to one decimal place.

Follow My Example 17-11

a. Earnings per Share on Common Stock = (Net Income – Preferred Dividends) ÷ Shares of Common Stock Outstanding
= ($250,000 – $15,000) ÷ 20,000
= $11.75

b. Price-Earnings Ratio = Market Price per Share of Common Stock ÷ Earnings per Share on Common Stock
= $35.25 ÷ $11.75
= 3.0

Practice Exercises: PE 17-11A, PE 17-11B

Dividends per Share

Dividends per share measures the extent to which earnings are being distributed to common shareholders. It is computed as follows:

$$\text{Dividends per Share} = \frac{\text{Dividends on Common Stock}}{\text{Shares of Common Stock Outstanding}}$$

To illustrate, the dividends per share for **Lincoln Company** are computed as follows:

	2016	2015
Dividends on common stock	$40,000	$30,000
Shares of common stock outstanding	50,000	50,000
Dividends per share of common stock	$0.80 ($40,000 ÷ 50,000)	$0.60 ($30,000 ÷ 50,000)

The dividends per share of common stock increased from $0.60 to $0.80 during 2016.

Dividends per share are often reported with earnings per share. Comparing the two per-share amounts indicates the extent to which earnings are being retained for use in operations. To illustrate, the dividends and earnings per share for **Lincoln Company** are shown in Exhibit 9.

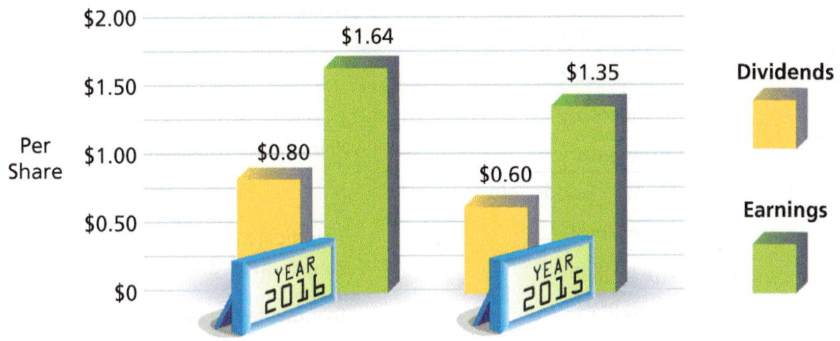

EXHIBIT 9

Dividends and Earnings per Share of Common Stock

Dividend Yield

The **dividend yield** on common stock measures the rate of return to common stockholders from cash dividends. It is of special interest to investors whose objective is to earn revenue (dividends) from their investment. It is computed as follows:

$$\text{Dividend Yield} = \frac{\text{Dividends per Share of Common Stock}}{\text{Market Price per Share of Common Stock}}$$

To illustrate, the dividend yield for **Lincoln Company** is computed as follows:

	2016	2015
Dividends per share of common stock	$0.80	$0.60
Market price per share of common stock	$41.00	$27.00
Dividend yield on common stock	2.0% ($0.80 ÷ $41)	2.2% ($0.60 ÷ $27)

The dividend yield declined slightly from 2.2% to 2.0% in 2016. This decline was primarily due to the increase in the market price of Lincoln's common stock.

The dividends per share, dividend yield, and P/E ratio of a common stock are normally quoted on the daily listing of stock prices in *The Wall Street Journal* and on **Yahoo!**'s finance Web site.

Summary of Analytical Measures

Exhibit 10 shows a summary of the solvency and profitability measures discussed in this chapter. The type of industry and the company's operations usually affect which measures are used. In many cases, additional measures are used for a specific industry. For example, airlines use *revenue per passenger mile* and *cost per available seat* as profitability measures. Likewise, hotels use *occupancy rates* as a profitability measure.

The analytical measures shown in Exhibit 10 are a useful starting point for analyzing a company's solvency and profitability. However, they are not a substitute for sound judgment. For example, the general economic and business environment should always be considered in analyzing a company's future prospects. In addition, any trends and interrelationships among the measures should be carefully studied.

EXHIBIT 10 Summary of Analytical Measures

Group	Measure	Method of Computation	Use
Liquidity and Solvency Measures	Working Capital	Current Assets − Current Liabilities	To indicate the ability to meet currently maturing obligations (measures solvency)
	Current Ratio	Current Assets / Current Liabilities	(same as above)
	Quick Ratio	Quick Assets / Current Liabilities	To indicate instant debt-paying ability (measures solvency)
	Accounts Receivable Turnover	Sales / Average Accounts Receivable	To assess the efficiency in collecting receivables and in the management of credit (measures liquidity)
	Numbers of Days' Sales in Receivables	Average Accounts Receivable / Average Daily Sales	(same as above)
	Inventory Turnover	Cost of Goods Sold / Average Inventory	To assess the efficiency in the management of inventory (measures liquidity)
	Number of Days' Sales in Inventory	Average Inventory / Average Daily Cost of Goods Sold	(same as above)
	Ratio of Fixed Assets to Long-Term Liabilities	Fixed Assets (net) / Long-Term Liabilities	To indicate the margin of safety to long-term creditors (measures solvency)
	Ratio of Liabilities to Stockholders' Equity	Total Liabilities / Total Stockholders' Equity	To indicate the margin of safety to creditors (measures solvency)
	Number of Times Interest Charges Are Earned	Income Before Income Tax + Interest Expense / Interest Expense	To assess the risk to debtholders in terms of number of times interest charges were earned (measures solvency)
	Number of Times Preferred Dividends Are Earned	Net Income / Preferred Dividends	To assess the risk to preferred stockholders in terms of the number of times preferred dividends were earned (measures solvency)
Profitability Measures	Ratio of Sales to Assets	Sales / Average Total Assets (excluding long-term investments)	To assess the effectiveness in the use of assets
	Rate Earned on Total Assets	Net Income + Interest Expense / Average Total Assets	To assess the profitability of the assets
	Rate Earned on Stockholders' Equity	Net Income / Average Total Stockholders' Equity	To assess the profitability of the investment by stockholders
	Rate Earned on Common Stockholders' Equity	Net Income − Preferred Dividends / Average Common Stockholders' Equity	To assess the profitability of the investment by common stockholders
	Earnings per Share (EPS) on Common Stock	Net Income − Preferred Dividends / Shares of Common Stock Outstanding	(same as above)
	Price-Earnings (P/E) Ratio	Market Price per Share of Common Stock / Earnings per Share on Common Stock	To indicate future earnings prospects, based on the relationship between market value of common stock and earnings
	Dividends per Share	Dividends on Common Stock / Shares of Common Stock Outstanding	To indicate the extent to which earnings are being distributed to common stockholders
	Dividend Yield	Dividends per Share of Common Stock / Market Price per Share of Common Stock	To indicate the rate of return to common stockholders in terms of dividends

Integrity, Objectivity, and Ethics in Business

CHARACTERISTICS OF FINANCIAL STATEMENT FRAUD

Each year the Association of Certified Fraud Examiners conducts a worldwide survey examining the characteristics of corporate fraud. The most recent study found that:

- 43.3% of frauds were detected by a tip from an employee or someone close to the company;
- Frauds committed by owners and executives tended to be much larger than those caused by employees;
- Most people who are caught committing fraud are first time offenders with clean employment histories; and
- In 81% of the cases, the person committing the fraud displayed one or more behavioral red flags such as living beyond their means, financial difficulties, and excessive control issues.

Fraud examiners can use these trends to help them narrow their focus when searching for fraud.

Source: 2012 Report to the Nations, Association of Certified Fraud Examiners, 2012.

Corporate Annual Reports

OBJ 4 Describe the contents of corporate annual reports.

Public corporations issue annual reports summarizing their operating activities for the past year and plans for the future. Such annual reports include the financial statements and the accompanying notes. In addition, annual reports normally include the following sections:

- Management discussion and analysis
- Report on internal control
- Report on fairness of the financial statements

IFRS See Appendix D for more information.

Management Discussion and Analysis

Management's Discussion and Analysis (MD&A) is required in annual reports filed with the Securities and Exchange Commission. It includes management's analysis of current operations and its plans for the future. Typical items included in the MD&A are as follows:

- Management's analysis and explanations of any significant changes between the current and prior years' financial statements.
- Important accounting principles or policies that could affect interpretation of the financial statements, including the effect of changes in accounting principles or the adoption of new accounting principles.
- Management's assessment of the company's liquidity and the availability of capital to the company.
- Significant risk exposures that might affect the company.
- Any "off-balance-sheet" arrangements such as leases not included directly in the financial statements. Such arrangements are discussed in advanced accounting courses and textbooks.

Report on Internal Control

The Sarbanes-Oxley Act of 2002 requires a report on internal control by management. The report states management's responsibility for establishing and maintaining internal control. In addition, management's assessment of the effectiveness of internal controls over financial reporting is included in the report.

Sarbanes-Oxley also requires a public accounting firm to verify management's conclusions on internal control. Thus, two reports on internal control, one by management and one by a public accounting firm, are included in the annual report. In some situations, these may be combined into a single report on internal control.

Report on Fairness of the Financial Statements

All publicly held corporations are required to have an independent audit (examination) of their financial statements. The Certified Public Accounting (CPA) firm that conducts the audit renders an opinion, called the *Report of Independent Registered Public Accounting Firm*, on the fairness of the statements.

An opinion stating that the financial statements present fairly the financial position, results of operations, and cash flows of the company is said to be an *unqualified opinion*, sometimes called a *clean opinion*. Any report other than an unqualified opinion raises a "red flag" for financial statement users and requires further investigation as to its cause.

The annual report of Nike Inc. is shown in Appendix C. The Nike report includes the financial statements as well as the MD&A Report on Internal Control and the Report on Fairness of the Financial Statements.

Integrity, Objectivity, and Ethics in Business

BUY LOW, SELL HIGH

Research analysts work for banks, brokerages, or other financial institutions. Their job is to estimate the value of a company's common stock by reviewing and evaluating the company's business model, strategic plan, and financial performance. Based on this analysis, the analyst develops an estimate of a stock's value, which is called its *fundamental value*. Analysts then advise their clients to "buy" or "sell" a company's stock based on the following guidelines:

Current market price is greater than fundamental value	Sell
Current market price is lower than fundamental value	Buy

If analysts are doing their job well, their clients will enjoy large returns by buying stocks at low prices and selling them at high prices.

APPENDIX

Unusual Items on the Income Statement

Generally accepted accounting principles require that unusual items be reported separately on the income statement. This is because such items do not occur frequently and are typically unrelated to current operations. Without separate reporting of these items, users of the financial statements might be misled about current and future operations.

Unusual items on the income statement are classified as one of the following:

- Affecting the *current period* income statement
- Affecting a *prior period* income statement

Unusual Items Affecting the Current Period's Income Statement

Unusual items affecting the current period's income statement include the following:

- Discontinued operations
- Extraordinary items

These items are reported separately on the income statement for any period in which they occur.

Discontinued Operations A company may discontinue a component of its operations by selling or abandoning the component's operations. For example, a retailer might decide to sell its product only online and, thus, discontinue selling its merchandise at its retail outlets (stores).

If the discontinued component is (1) the result of a strategic shift and (2) has a major effect on the entity's operations and financial results, any gain or loss on discontinued operations is reported on the income statement as a *Gain (or loss) from discontinued operations.* It is reported immediately following *Income from continuing operations.*

To illustrate, assume that Jones Corporation produces and sells electrical products, hardware supplies, and lawn equipment. Because of a lack of profits, Jones discontinues its electrical products operation and sells the remaining inventory and other assets at a loss of $100,000. Exhibit 11 illustrates the reporting of the loss on discontinued operations.[3]

EXHIBIT 11

Unusual Items in the Income Statement

Jones Corporation Income Statement For the Year Ended December 31, 2016	
Sales	$12,350,000
Cost of merchandise sold	5,800,000
Gross profit	$ 6,550,000
Selling and administrative expenses	5,240,000
Income from continuing operations before income tax	$ 1,310,000
Income tax expense	620,000
Income from continuing operations	$ 690,000
Loss on discontinued operations	100,000
Income before extraordinary items	$ 590,000
Extraordinary items:	
Gain on condemnation of land	150,000
Net income	$ 740,000

In addition, a note to the financial statements should describe the operations sold, including the date operations were discontinued, and details about the assets, liabilities, income, and expenses of the discontinued component.

Extraordinary Items An **extraordinary item** is defined as an event or a transaction that has both of the following characteristics:

- Unusual in nature
- Infrequent in occurrence

Gains and losses from natural disasters such as floods, earthquakes, and fires are normally reported as extraordinary items, provided that they occur infrequently. Gains or losses from land or buildings taken (condemned) for public use are also reported as extraordinary items.

Any gain or loss from extraordinary items is reported on the income statement as *Gain (or loss) from extraordinary item.* It is reported immediately following *Income from continuing operations* and any *Gain (or loss) on discontinued operations.*

To illustrate, assume that land owned by Jones Corporation was taken for public use (condemned) by the local government. The condemnation of the land resulted in a gain of $150,000. Exhibit 11 illustrates the reporting of the extraordinary gain.[4,5]

[3] The gain or loss on discontinued operations is reported net of any tax effects. To simplify, the tax effects are not specifically identified in Exhibit 11.

[4] The gain or loss on extraordinary operations is reported net of any tax effects.

[5] At the time of this writing, the Financial Accounting Standards Board had released an exposure draft, which proposes eliminating extraordinary items as a separate line item on the income statement. The outcome of this proposal was uncertain at the time of this writing.

Reporting Earnings per Share Earnings per common share should be reported separately for discontinued operations and extraordinary items. To illustrate, a partial income statement for Jones Corporation is shown in Exhibit 12. The company has 200,000 shares of common stock outstanding.

Exhibit 12 reports earnings per common share for income from continuing operations, discontinued operations, and extraordinary items. However, only earnings per share for income from continuing operations and net income are required by generally accepted accounting principles. The other per-share amounts may be presented in the notes to the financial statements.

EXHIBIT 12

Income Statement with Earnings per Share

Jones Corporation Income Statement For the Year Ended December 31, 2016	
Earnings per common share:	
Income from continuing operations	$3.45
Loss on discontinued operations	0.50
Income before extraordinary items	$2.95
Extraordinary items:	
Gain on condemnation of land	0.75
Net income	$3.70

Unusual Items Affecting the Prior Period's Income Statement

An unusual item may occur that affects a prior period's income statement. Two such items are as follows:

- Errors in applying generally accepted accounting principles
- Changes from one generally accepted accounting principle to another

If an error is discovered in a prior period's financial statement, the prior-period statement and all following statements are restated and thus corrected.

A company may change from one generally accepted accounting principle to another. In this case, the prior-period financial statements are restated as if the new accounting principle had always been used.[5]

For both of the preceding items, the current-period earnings are not affected. That is, only the earnings reported in prior periods are restated. However, because the prior earnings are restated, the beginning balance of Retained Earnings may also have to be restated. This, in turn, may cause the restatement of other balance sheet accounts. Illustrations of these types of adjustments and restatements are provided in advanced accounting courses.

[5] Changes from one acceptable depreciation method to another acceptable depreciation method are an exception to this general rule and are to be treated prospectively as a change in estimate, as discussed in Chapter 10.

At a Glance 17

OBJ 1 Describe basic financial statement analytical methods.

Key Points The basic financial statements provide much of the information users need to make economic decisions. Analytical procedures are used to compare items on a current financial statement with related items on earlier statements, or to examine relationships within a financial statement.

Learning Outcomes	Example Exercises	Practice Exercises
• Prepare a vertical analysis from a company's financial statements.	**EE17-1**	**PE17-1A, 17-1B**
• Prepare a horizontal analysis from a company's financial statements.	**EE17-2**	**PE17-2A, 17-2B**
• Prepare common-sized financial statements.		

OBJ 2 Use financial statement analysis to assess the solvency of a business.

Key Points All users of financial statements are interested in the ability of a business to convert assets into cash (liquidity), pay its debts (solvency), and earn income (profitability). Liquidity, solvency, and profitability are interrelated. Liquidity and solvency are normally assessed by examining the following: current position analysis, accounts receivable analysis, inventory analysis, the ratio of fixed assets to long-term liabilities, the ratio of liabilities to stockholders' equity, and the number of times interest charges are earned.

Learning Outcomes	Example Exercises	Practice Exercises
• Determine working capital.		
• Compute and interpret the current ratio.	**EE17-3**	**PE17-3A, 17-3B**
• Compute and interpret the quick ratio.	**EE17-3**	**PE17-3A, 17-3B**
• Compute and interpret accounts receivable turnover.	**EE17-4**	**PE17-4A, 17-4B**
• Compute and interpret the number of days' sales in receivables.	**EE17-4**	**PE17-4A, 17-4B**
• Compute and interpret inventory turnover.	**EE17-5**	**PE17-5A, 17-5B**
• Compute and interpret the number of days' sales in inventory.	**EE17-5**	**PE17-5A, 17-5B**
• Compute and interpret the ratio of fixed assets to long-term liabilities.	**EE17-6**	**PE17-6A, 17-6B**
• Compute and interpret the ratio of liabilities to stockholders' equity.	**EE17-6**	**PE17-6A, 17-6B**
• Compute and interpret the number of times interest charges are earned.	**EE17-7**	**PE17-7A, 17-7B**

OBJ 3 Use financial statement analysis to assess the profitability of a business.

Key Points Profitability analysis focuses on the ability of a company to earn profits. This ability is reflected in the company's operating results as reported on the income statement and resources available as reported on the balance sheet. Major analyses include the ratio of sales to assets, the rate earned on total assets, the rate earned on stockholders' equity, the rate earned on common stockholders' equity, earnings per share on common stock, the price-earnings ratio, dividends per share, and dividend yield.

Learning Outcomes	Example Exercises	Practice Exercises
• Compute and interpret the ratio of sales to assets.	EE17-8	PE17-8A, 17-8B
• Compute and interpret the rate earned on total assets.	EE17-9	PE17-9A, 17-9B
• Compute and interpret the rate earned on stockholders' equity.	EE17-10	PE17-10A, 17-10B
• Compute and interpret the rate earned on common stockholders' equity.	EE17-10	PE17-10A, 17-10B
• Compute and interpret the earnings per share on common stock.	EE17-11	PE17-11A, 17-11B
• Compute and interpret the price-earnings ratio.	EE17-11	PE17-11A, 17-11B
• Compute and interpret the dividends per share and dividend yield.		
• Describe the uses and limitations of analytical measures.		

OBJ 4 Describe the contents of corporate annual reports.

Key Points Corporations normally issue annual reports to their stockholders and other interested parties. Such reports summarize the corporation's operating activities for the past year and plans for the future.

Learning Outcome	Example Exercises	Practice Exercises
• Describe the elements of a corporate annual report.		

Key Terms

accounts receivable analysis (804)
accounts receivable turnover (804)
common-sized statement (800)
current position analysis (802)
current ratio (802)
dividend yield (815)
dividends per share (814)
earnings per share (EPS) on common stock (813)
extraordinary item (819)
horizontal analysis (796)
inventory analysis (806)
inventory turnover (806)
leverage (811)
liquidity (801)
Management's Discussion and Analysis (MD&A) (817)
number of days' sales in inventory (806)
number of days' sales in receivables (805)
number of times interest charges are earned (808)
price-earnings (P/E) ratio (814)
profitability (801)
quick assets (803)
quick ratio (803)
rate earned on common stockholders' equity (811)
rate earned on stockholders' equity (811)
rate earned on total assets (810)
ratio of fixed assets to long-term liabilities (807)
ratio of liabilities to stockholders' equity (807)
ratio of sales to assets (809)
solvency (801)
vertical analysis (799)
working capital (802)

Illustrative Problem

Rainbow Paint Co.'s comparative financial statements for the years ending December 31, 2016 and 2015, are as follows. The market price of Rainbow Paint Co.'s common stock was $25 on December 31, 2016, and $30 on December 31, 2015.

Rainbow Paint Co.
Comparative Income Statement
For the Years Ended December 31, 2016 and 2015

	2016	2015
Sales	$5,000,000	$3,200,000
Cost of goods sold	3,400,000	2,080,000
Gross profit	$1,600,000	$1,120,000
Selling expenses	$ 650,000	$ 464,000
Administrative expenses	325,000	224,000
Total operating expenses	$ 975,000	$ 688,000
Income from operations	$ 625,000	$ 432,000
Other income	25,000	19,200
	$ 650,000	$ 451,200
Other expense (interest)	105,000	64,000
Income before income tax	$ 545,000	$ 387,200
Income tax expense	300,000	176,000
Net income	$ 245,000	$ 211,200

Rainbow Paint Co.
Comparative Retained Earnings Statement
For the Years Ended December 31, 2016 and 2015

	2016	2015
Retained earnings, January 1	$723,000	$581,800
Add net income for year	245,000	211,200
Total	$968,000	$793,000
Deduct dividends:		
On preferred stock	$ 40,000	$ 40,000
On common stock	45,000	30,000
Total	$ 85,000	$ 70,000
Retained earnings, December 31	$883,000	$723,000

Rainbow Paint Co. Comparative Balance Sheet December 31, 2016 and 2015		
	Dec. 31, 2016	Dec. 31, 2015
Assets		
Current assets:		
Cash	$ 175,000	$ 125,000
Temporary investments	150,000	50,000
Accounts receivable (net)	425,000	325,000
Inventories	720,000	480,000
Prepaid expenses	30,000	20,000
Total current assets	$1,500,000	$1,000,000
Long-term investments	250,000	225,000
Property, plant, and equipment (net)	2,093,000	1,948,000
Total assets	$3,843,000	$3,173,000
Liabilities		
Current liabilities	$ 750,000	$ 650,000
Long-term liabilities:		
Mortgage note payable, 10%, due 2017	$ 410,000	—
Bonds payable, 8%, due 2020	800,000	$ 800,000
Total long-term liabilities	$1,210,000	$ 800,000
Total liabilities	$1,960,000	$1,450,000
Stockholders' Equity		
Preferred 8% stock, $100 par	$ 500,000	$ 500,000
Common stock, $10 par	500,000	500,000
Retained earnings	883,000	723,000
Total stockholders' equity	$1,883,000	$1,723,000
Total liabilities and stockholders' equity	$3,843,000	$3,173,000

Instructions

Determine the following measures for 2016:

1. Working capital
2. Current ratio
3. Quick ratio
4. Accounts receivable turnover
5. Number of days' sales in receivables
6. Inventory turnover
7. Number of days' sales in inventory
8. Ratio of fixed assets to long-term liabilities
9. Ratio of liabilities to stockholders' equity
10. Number of times interest charges are earned
11. Number of times preferred dividends are earned
12. Ratio of sales to assets
13. Rate earned on total assets
14. Rate earned on stockholders' equity

15. Rate earned on common stockholders' equity
16. Earnings per share on common stock
17. Price-earnings ratio
18. Dividends per share
19. Dividend yield

Solution

(Ratios are rounded to the nearest single digit after the decimal point.)

1. Working capital: $750,000
   $1,500,000 – $750,000
2. Current ratio: 2.0
   $1,500,000 ÷ $750,000
3. Quick ratio: 1.0
   $750,000 ÷ $750,000
4. Accounts receivable turnover: 13.3
   $5,000,000 ÷ [($425,000 + $325,000) ÷ 2]
5. Number of days' sales in receivables: 27.4 days
   $5,000,000 ÷ 365 days = $13,699
   $375,000 ÷ $13,699
6. Inventory turnover: 5.7
   $3,400,000 ÷ [($720,000 + $480,000) ÷ 2]
7. Number of days' sales in inventory: 64.4 days
   $3,400,000 ÷ 365 days = $9,315
   $600,000 ÷ $9,315
8. Ratio of fixed assets to long-term liabilities: 1.7
   $2,093,000 ÷ $1,210,000
9. Ratio of liabilities to stockholders' equity: 1.0
   $1,960,000 ÷ $1,883,000
10. Number of times interest charges are earned: 6.2
    ($545,000 + $105,000) ÷ $105,000
11. Number of times preferred dividends are earned: 6.1
    $245,000 ÷ $40,000
12. Ratio of sales to assets: 1.5
    $5,000,000 ÷ [($3,593,000 + $2,948,000) ÷ 2]
13. Rate earned on total assets: 10.0%
    ($245,000 + $105,000) ÷ [($3,843,000 + $3,173,000) ÷ 2]
14. Rate earned on stockholders' equity: 13.6%
    $245,000 ÷ [($1,883,000 + $1,723,000) ÷ 2]
15. Rate earned on common stockholders' equity: 15.7%
    ($245,000 – $40,000) ÷ [($1,383,000 + $1,223,000) ÷ 2]
16. Earnings per share on common stock: $4.10
    ($245,000 – $40,000) ÷ 50,000 shares
17. Price-earnings ratio: 6.1
    $25 ÷ $4.10
18. Dividends per share: $0.90
    $45,000 ÷ 50,000 shares
19. Dividend yield: 3.6%
    $0.90 ÷ $25

Discussion Questions

1. What is the difference between horizontal and vertical analysis of financial statements?
2. What is the advantage of using comparative statements for financial analysis rather than statements for a single date or period?
3. The current year's amount of net income (after income tax) is 25% larger than that of the preceding year. Does this indicate an improved operating performance? Discuss.
4. How would the current and quick ratios of a service business compare?
5. a. Why is it advantageous to have a high inventory turnover?
   b. Is it possible to have a high inventory turnover and a high number of days' sales in inventory? Discuss.
6. What do the following data taken from a comparative balance sheet indicate about the company's ability to borrow additional funds on a long-term basis in the current year as compared to the preceding year?

	Current Year	Preceding Year
Fixed assets (net)	$1,260,000	$1,360,000
Total long-term liabilities	300,000	400,000

7. a. How does the rate earned on total assets differ from the rate earned on stockholders' equity?
   b. Which ratio is normally higher? Explain.
8. **Kroger**, a grocery store, recently had a price-earnings ratio of 13.7, while the average price-earnings ratio in the grocery store industry was 22.5. What might explain this difference?
9. The dividend yield of **Suburban Propane** was 7.7% in a recent year, and the dividend yield of **Google** was 0% in the same year. What might explain the difference between these ratios?
10. Describe two reports provided by independent auditors in the annual report to shareholders.

Practice Exercises

EE 17-1 p. 799 **PE 17-1A Horizontal analysis** **OBJ. 1**

SHOW ME HOW

The comparative temporary investments and inventory balances of a company follow.

	Current Year	Previous Year
Temporary investments	$59,280	$52,000
Inventory	70,680	76,000

Based on this information, what is the amount and percentage of increase or decrease that would be shown in a balance sheet with horizontal analysis?

EE 17-1 p. 799 **PE 17-1B Horizontal analysis** **OBJ. 1**

SHOW ME HOW

The comparative accounts payable and long-term debt balances for a company follow.

	Current Year	Previous Year
Accounts payable	$111,000	$100,000
Long-term debt	132,680	124,000

Based on this information, what is the amount and percentage of increase or decrease that would be shown in a balance sheet with horizontal analysis?

SHOW ME HOW

EE 17-2 p. 800

PE 17-2A Vertical analysis

OBJ. 1

Income statement information for Axiom Corporation follows:

Sales	$725,000
Cost of goods sold	391,500
Gross profit	333,500

Prepare a vertical analysis of the income statement for Axiom Corporation.

SHOW ME HOW

EE 17-2 p. 800

PE 17-2B Vertical analysis

OBJ. 1

Income statement information for Einsworth Corporation follows:

Sales	$1,200,000
Cost of goods sold	780,000
Gross profit	420,000

Prepare a vertical analysis of the income statement for Einsworth Corporation.

SHOW ME HOW

EE 17-3 p. 804

PE 17-3A Current position analysis

OBJ. 2

The following items are reported on a company's balance sheet:

Cash	$160,000
Marketable securities	75,000
Accounts receivable (net)	65,000
Inventory	140,000
Accounts payable	200,000

Determine (a) the current ratio and (b) the quick ratio. Round to one decimal place.

SHOW ME HOW

EE 17-3 p. 804

PE 17-3B Current position analysis

OBJ. 2

The following items are reported on a company's balance sheet:

Cash	$210,000
Marketable securities	120,000
Accounts receivable (net)	110,000
Inventory	160,000
Accounts payable	200,000

Determine (a) the current ratio and (b) the quick ratio. Round to one decimal place.

SHOW ME HOW

EE 17-4 p. 805

PE 17-4A Accounts receivable analysis

OBJ. 2

A company reports the following:

Sales	$832,000
Average accounts receivable (net)	80,000

Determine (a) the accounts receivable turnover and (b) the number of days' sales in receivables. Round to one decimal place.

SHOW ME HOW

EE 17-4 p. 805

PE 17-4B Accounts receivable analysis

OBJ. 2

A company reports the following:

Sales	$3,150,000
Average accounts receivable (net)	210,000

Determine (a) the accounts receivable turnover and (b) the number of days' sales in receivables. Round to one decimal place.

SHOW ME HOW

EE 17-5 p. 807

PE 17-5A Inventory analysis **OBJ. 2**

A company reports the following:

Cost of goods sold	$630,000
Average inventory	90,000

Determine (a) the inventory turnover and (b) the number of days' sales in inventory. Round to one decimal place.

SHOW ME HOW

EE 17-5 p. 807

PE 17-5B Inventory analysis **OBJ. 2**

A company reports the following:

Cost of goods sold	$435,000
Average inventory	72,500

Determine (a) the inventory turnover and (b) the number of days' sales in inventory. Round to one decimal place.

SHOW ME HOW

EE 17-6 p. 808

PE 17-6A Long-term solvency analysis **OBJ. 2**

The following information was taken from Kellman Company's balance sheet:

Fixed assets (net)	$2,000,000
Long-term liabilities	800,000
Total liabilities	1,000,000
Total stockholders' equity	625,000

Determine the company's (a) ratio of fixed assets to long-term liabilities and (b) ratio of liabilities to stockholders' equity.

SHOW ME HOW

EE 17-6 p. 808

PE 17-6B Long-term solvency analysis **OBJ. 2**

The following information was taken from Charu Company's balance sheet:

Fixed assets (net)	$860,000
Long-term liabilities	200,000
Total liabilities	600,000
Total stockholders' equity	250,000

Determine the company's (a) ratio of fixed assets to long-term liabilities and (b) ratio of liabilities to stockholders' equity.

SHOW ME HOW

EE 17-7 p. 809

PE 17-7A Times interest charges are earned **OBJ. 2**

A company reports the following:

Income before income tax	$4,000,000
Interest expense	400,000

Determine the number of times interest charges are earned.

SHOW ME HOW

EE17-7 p. 809

PE 17-7B Times interest charges are earned **OBJ. 2**

A company reports the following:

Income before income tax	$8,000,000
Interest expense	500,000

Determine the number of times interest charges are earned.

SHOW ME HOW

EE 17-8 p. 810

PE 17-8A Sales to assets **OBJ. 3**

A company reports the following:

Sales	$1,800,000
Average total assets (excluding long-term investments)	1,125,000

Determine the ratio of sales to assets.

EE 17-8 p. 810

SHOW ME HOW

PE 17-8B Sales to assets **OBJ. 3**

A company reports the following:

Sales	$4,400,000
Average total assets (excluding long-term investments)	2,000,000

Determine the ratio of sales to assets.

EE 17-9 p. 811

SHOW ME HOW

PE 17-9A Rate earned on total assets **OBJ. 3**

A company reports the following income statement and balance sheet information for the current year:

Net income	$ 250,000
Interest expense	100,000
Average total assets	2,500,000

Determine the rate earned on total assets.

EE 17-9 p. 811

SHOW ME HOW

PE 17-9B Rate earned on total assets **OBJ. 3**

A company reports the following income statement and balance sheet information for the current year:

Net income	$ 410,000
Interest expense	90,000
Average total assets	5,000,000

Determine the rate earned on total assets.

EE 17-10 p. 813

SHOW ME HOW

PE 17-10A Common stockholders' profitability analysis **OBJ. 3**

A company reports the following:

Net income	$ 375,000
Preferred dividends	75,000
Average stockholders' equity	2,500,000
Average common stockholders' equity	1,875,000

Determine (a) the rate earned on stockholders' equity and (b) the rate earned on common stockholders' equity. Round to one decimal place.

EE 17-10 p. 813

SHOW ME HOW

PE 17-10B Common stockholders' profitability analysis **OBJ. 3**

A company reports the following:

Net income	$1,000,000
Preferred dividends	50,000
Average stockholders' equity	6,250,000
Average common stockholders' equity	3,800,000

Determine (a) the rate earned on stockholders' equity and (b) the rate earned on common stockholders' equity. Round to one decimal place.

EE 17-11 p. 814

SHOW ME HOW

PE 17-11A Earnings per share and price-earnings ratio **OBJ. 3**

A company reports the following:

Net income	$185,000
Preferred dividends	$25,000
Shares of common stock outstanding	100,000
Market price per share of common stock	$20

a. Determine the company's earnings per share on common stock.

b. Determine the company's price-earnings ratio.

EE 17-11 p. 814

SHOW ME HOW

PE 17-11B Earnings per share and price-earnings ratio OBJ. 3

A company reports the following:

Net income	$410,000
Preferred dividends	$60,000
Shares of common stock outstanding	50,000
Market price per share of common stock	$84

a. Determine the company's earnings per share on common stock.

b. Determine the company's price-earnings ratio.

Exercises

✔ a. Current year net income: $175,000; 7.0% of sales

SHOW ME HOW

EX 17-1 Vertical analysis of income statement OBJ. 1

Revenue and expense data for Gresham Inc. for two recent years are as follows:

	Current Year	Previous Year
Sales	$2,500,000	$2,350,000
Cost of goods sold	1,500,000	1,292,500
Selling expenses	300,000	376,000
Administrative expenses	375,000	305,500
Income tax expense	150,000	141,000

a. Prepare an income statement in comparative form, stating each item for both years as a percent of sales. Round to one decimal place.

b. Comment on the significant changes disclosed by the comparative income statement.

✔ a. Current fiscal year income from continuing operations, 13.0% of revenues

EX 17-2 Vertical analysis of income statement OBJ. 1

The following comparative income statement (in thousands of dollars) for the two recent fiscal years was adapted from the annual report of Speedway Motorsports, Inc., owner and operator of several major motor speedways, such as the Atlanta, Texas, and Las Vegas Motor Speedways.

	Current Year	Previous Year
Revenues:		
Admissions	$116,034	$130,239
Event-related revenue	151,562	163,621
NASCAR broadcasting revenue	192,662	185,394
Other operating revenue	29,902	26,951
Total revenue	$490,160	$506,205
Expenses and other:		
Direct expense of events	$101,402	$106,204
NASCAR purse and sanction fees	122,950	120,146
Other direct expenses	18,908	20,352
General and administrative	183,215	241,223
Total expenses and other	$426,475	$487,925
Income from continuing operations	$ 63,685	$ 18,280

a. Prepare a comparative income statement for these two years in vertical form, stating each item as a percent of revenues. Round to one decimal place.

b. Comment on the significant changes.

✔ a. Tannenhill net income: $120,000; 3.0% of sales

SHOW ME HOW

EX 17-3 Common-sized income statement OBJ. 1

Revenue and expense data for the current calendar year for Tannenhill Company and for the electronics industry are as follows. The Tannenhill Company data are expressed in dollars. The electronics industry averages are expressed in percentages.

	Tannenhill Company	Electronics Industry Average
Sales	$4,000,000	100.0%
Cost of goods sold	2,120,000	60.0
Gross profit	$1,880,000	40.0%
Selling expenses	$1,080,000	24.0%
Administrative expenses	640,000	14.0
Total operating expenses	$1,720,000	38.0%
Operating income	$ 160,000	2.0%
Other income	120,000	3.0
	$ 280,000	5.0%
Other expense	80,000	2.0
Income before income tax	$ 200,000	3.0%
Income tax expense	80,000	2.0
Net income	$ 120,000	1.0%

a. Prepare a common-sized income statement comparing the results of operations for Tannenhill Company with the industry average. Round to one decimal place.

b. As far as the data permit, comment on significant relationships revealed by the comparisons.

✔ Retained earnings, Current year, 40.0%

SHOW ME HOW

EX 17-4 Vertical analysis of balance sheet OBJ. 1

Balance sheet data for Novak Company on December 31, the end of two recent fiscal years, follows:

	Current Year	Previous Year
Current assets	$1,300,000	$ 945,000
Property, plant, and equipment	3,000,000	3,150,000
Intangible assets	700,000	405,000
Current liabilities	1,000,000	720,000
Long-term liabilities	1,500,000	1,575,000
Common stock	500,000	495,000
Retained earnings	2,000,000	1,710,000

Prepare a comparative balance sheet for both years, stating each asset as a percent of total assets and each liability and stockholders' equity item as a percent of the total liabilities and stockholders' equity. Round to one decimal place.

✔ a. Net income increase, 80.0%

SHOW ME HOW

EX 17-5 Horizontal analysis of the income statement OBJ. 1

Income statement data for Moreno Company for two recent years ended December 31, are as follows:

	Current Year	Previous Year
Sales	$1,120,000	$1,000,000
Cost of goods sold	971,250	875,000
Gross profit	$ 148,750	$ 125,000
Selling expenses	$ 71,250	$ 62,500
Administrative expenses	56,000	50,000
Total operating expenses	$ 127,250	$ 112,500
Income before income tax	$ 21,500	$ 12,500
Income tax expense	8,000	5,000
Net income	$ 13,500	$ 7,500

a. Prepare a comparative income statement with horizontal analysis, indicating the increase (decrease) for the current year when compared with the previous year. Round to one decimal place.

b. What conclusions can be drawn from the horizontal analysis?

✔ a. Current year working capital, $1,600,000

SHOW ME HOW

EX 17-6 Current position analysis

OBJ. 2

The following data were taken from the balance sheet of Gostkowski Company at the end of two recent fiscal years:

	Current Year	Previous Year
Cash	$ 480,000	$ 392,000
Marketable securities	576,000	411,600
Accounts and notes receivable (net)	384,000	316,400
Inventories	408,000	333,200
Prepaid expenses	552,000	506,800
Total current assets	$2,400,000	$1,960,000
Accounts and notes payable (short-term)	$ 600,000	$ 525,000
Accrued liabilities	200,000	175,000
Total current liabilities	$ 800,000	$ 700,000

a. Determine for each year (1) the working capital, (2) the current ratio, and (3) the quick ratio. Round ratios to one decimal place.

b. What conclusions can be drawn from these data as to the company's ability to meet its currently maturing debts?

✔ a. (1) Current year's current ratio, 1.1

EX 17-7 Current position analysis

OBJ. 2

PepsiCo, Inc., the parent company of Frito-Lay snack foods and Pepsi beverages, had the following current assets and current liabilities at the end of two recent years:

	Current Year (in millions)	Previous Year (in millions)
Cash and cash equivalents	$ 6,297	$4,067
Short-term investments, at cost	322	358
Accounts and notes receivable, net	7,041	6,912
Inventories	3,581	3,827
Prepaid expenses and other current assets	1,479	2,277
Short-term obligations	4,815	6,205
Accounts payable	12,274	11,949

a. Determine the (1) current ratio and (2) quick ratio for both years. Round to one decimal place.

b. What conclusions can you draw from these data?

EX 17-8 Current position analysis

OBJ. 2

The bond indenture for the 10-year, 9% debenture bonds issued January 2, 2015, required working capital of $100,000, a current ratio of 1.5, and a quick ratio of 1.0 at the end of each calendar year until the bonds mature. At December 31, 2016, the three measures were computed as follows:

1. Current assets:		
Cash	$102,000	
Temporary investments	48,000	
Accounts and notes receivable (net)	120,000	
Inventories	36,000	
Prepaid expenses	24,000	
Intangible assets	124,800	
Property, plant, and equipment	55,200	
Total current assets (net)		$510,000
Current liabilities:		
Accounts and short-term notes payable	$ 96,000	
Accrued liabilities	204,000	
Total current liabilities		300,000
Working capital		$210,000
2. Current ratio	1.7	$510,000 ÷ $300,000
3. Quick ratio	1.2	$115,200 ÷ $ 96,000

a. List the errors in the determination of the three measures of current position analysis.

b. Is the company satisfying the terms of the bond indenture?

✔ a. Accounts receivable turnover, 2016, 7.0

SHOW ME HOW

EX 17-9 Accounts receivable analysis OBJ. 2

The following data are taken from the financial statements of Krawcheck Inc. Terms of all sales are 2/10, n/55.

	2016	2015	2014
Accounts receivable, end of year	$ 500,000	$ 475,000	$440,000
Sales on account	3,412,500	2,836,500	

a. For 2015 and 2016, determine (1) the accounts receivable turnover and (2) the number of days' sales in receivables. Round to the nearest dollar and one decimal place.

b. What conclusions can be drawn from these data concerning accounts receivable and credit policies?

EX 17-10 Accounts receivable analysis OBJ. 2

Xavier Stores Company and Lestrade Stores Inc. are large retail department stores. Both companies offer credit to their customers through their own credit card operations. Information from the financial statements for both companies for two recent years is as follows (all numbers are in millions):

	Xavier	Lestrade
Merchandise sales	$8,500,000	$4,585,000
Credit card receivables—beginning	820,000	600,000
Credit card receviables—ending	880,000	710,000

a. Determine the (1) accounts receivable turnover and (2) the number of days' sales in receivables for both companies. Round to one decimal place.

b. Compare the two companies with regard to their credit card policies.

✔ a. Inventory turnover, current year, 7.5

SHOW ME HOW

EX 17-11 Inventory analysis OBJ. 2

The following data were extracted from the income statement of Saleh Inc.:

	Current Year	Previous Year
Sales	$12,750,000	$13,284,000
Beginning inventories	840,000	800,000
Cost of goods sold	6,375,000	7,380,000
Ending inventories	860,000	840,000

a. Determine for each year (1) the inventory turnover and (2) the number of days' sales in inventory. Round to the nearest dollar and one decimal place.

b. What conclusions can be drawn from these data concerning the inventories?

✔ a. Dell inventory turnover, 32.1

EX 17-12 Inventory analysis OBJ. 2

Dell Inc. and **Hewlett-Packard Company (HP)** compete with each other in the personal computer market. Dell's primary strategy is to assemble computers to customer orders, rather than for inventory. Thus, for example, Dell will build and deliver a computer within four days of a customer entering an order on a Web page. Hewlett-Packard, on the other hand, builds some computers prior to receiving an order, then sells from this inventory once an order is received. Selected financial information for both companies from a recent year's financial statements follows (in millions):

	Dell Inc.	Hewlett-Packard Company
Sales	$56,940	$120,357
Cost of goods sold	44,754	92,385
Inventory, beginning of period	1,382	6,317
Inventory, end of period	1,404	7,490

a. Determine for both companies (1) the inventory turnover and (2) the number of days' sales in inventory. Round to one decimal place.

b. Interpret the inventory ratios by considering Dell's and Hewlett-Packard's operating strategies.

EX 17-13 Ratio of liabilities to stockholders' equity and number of times interest charges are earned OBJ. 2

✔ a. Ratio of liabilities to stockholders' equity, current year, 0.9

The following data were taken from the financial statements of Hunter Inc. for December 31 of two recent years:

	Current Year	Previous Year
Accounts payable	$ 924,000	$ 800,000
Current maturities of serial bonds payable	200,000	200,000
Serial bonds payable, 10%, issued 2009, due 2019	1,000,000	1,200,000
Common stock, $10 par value	250,000	250,000
Paid-in capital in excess of par	1,250,000	1,250,000
Retained earnings	860,000	500,000

The income before income tax was $480,000 and $420,000 for the current and previous years, respectively.

a. Determine the ratio of liabilities to stockholders' equity at the end of each year. Round to one decimal place.

b. Determine the number of times the bond interest charges are earned during the year for both years. Round to one decimal place.

c. What conclusions can be drawn from these data as to the company's ability to meet its currently maturing debts?

EX 17-14 Ratio of liabilities to stockholders' equity and number of times interest charges are earned OBJ. 2

✔ a. Hasbro, 1.9

Hasbro and Mattel, Inc., are the two largest toy companies in North America. Condensed liabilities and stockholders' equity from a recent balance sheet are shown for each company as follows (in thousands):

	Hasbro	Mattel
Current liabilities	$ 960,435	$ 1,716,012
Long-term debt	1,396,421	1,100,000
Deferred liabilities	461,152	643,729
Total liabilities	$ 2,818,008	$ 3,459,741
Shareholders' equity:		
Common stock	$ 104,847	$ 441,369
Additional paid in capital	655,943	1,727,682
Retained earnings	3,354,545	3,515,181
Accumulated other comprehensive loss and other equity items	(72,307)	(464,486)
Treasury stock, at cost	(2,535,649)	(2,152,702)
Total stockholders' equity	$ 1,507,379	$ 3,067,044
Total liabilities and stockholders' equity	$ 4,325,387	$ 6,526,785

The income from operations and interest expense from the income statement for each company were as follows (in thousands):

	Hasbro	Mattel
Income from operations (before income tax)	$453,402	$945,045
Interest expense	117,403	88,835

a. Determine the ratio of liabilities to stockholders' equity for both companies. Round to one decimal place.

b. Determine the number of times interest charges are earned for both companies. Round to one decimal place.

c. Interpret the ratio differences between the two companies.

✔ a. Mondelez International, Inc., 1.3

EX 17-15 Ratio of liabilities to stockholders' equity and ratio of fixed assets to long-term liabilities OBJ. 2

Recent balance sheet information for two companies in the food industry, Mondelez International, Inc., and The Hershey Company, is as follows (in thousands of dollars):

	Mondelez	Hershey
Net property, plant, and equipment	$10,010,000	$1,674,071
Current liabilities	14,873,000	1,471,110
Long-term debt	15,574,000	1,530,967
Other long-term liabilities	12,816,000	716,013
Stockholders' equity	32,215,000	1,036,749

a. Determine the ratio of liabilities to stockholders' equity for both companies. Round to one decimal place.

b. Determine the ratio of fixed assets to long-term liabilities for both companies. Round to one decimal place.

c. Interpret the ratio differences between the two companies.

✔ a. YRC Worldwide, 1.5

EX 17-16 Ratio of sales to assets OBJ. 3

Three major segments of the transportation industry are motor carriers, such as YRC Worldwide; railroads, such as Union Pacific; and transportation arrangement services, such as C.H. Robinson Worldwide Inc. Recent financial statement information for these three companies is shown as follows (in thousands of dollars):

	YRC Worldwide	Union Pacific	C.H. Robinson Worldwide Inc.
Sales	$4,334,640	$16,965,000	$9,274,305
Average total assets	2,812,504	42,636,000	1,914,974

a. Determine the ratio of sales to assets for all three companies. Round to one decimal place.

b. Assume that the ratio of sales to assets for each company represents their respective industry segment. Interpret the differences in the ratio of sales to assets in terms of the operating characteristics of each of the respective segments.

✔ a. Rate earned on total assets, 2016, 12.0%

SHOW ME HOW

EX 17-17 Profitability ratios OBJ. 3

The following selected data were taken from the financial statements of Robinson Inc. for December 31, 2016, 2015 and 2014:

	December 31		
	2016	2015	2014
Total assets	$4,800,000	$4,400,000	$4,000,000
Notes payable (8% interest)	2,250,000	2,250,000	2,250,000
Common stock	250,000	250,000	250,000
Preferred 4% stock, $100 par (no change during year)	500,000	500,000	500,000
Retained earnings	1,574,000	1,222,000	750,000

The 2016 net income was $372,000, and the 2015 net income was $492,000. No dividends on common stock were declared between 2014 and 2016.

a. Determine the rate earned on total assets, the rate earned on stockholders' equity, and the rate earned on common stockholders' equity for the years 2015 and 2016. Round to one decimal place.

b. What conclusions can be drawn from these data as to the company's profitability?

EX 17-18 Profitability ratios **OBJ. 3**

✔a. Year 3 rate earned on total assets, 12.2%

Ralph Lauren Corp. sells men's apparel through company-owned retail stores. Recent financial information for Ralph Lauren follows (all numbers in thousands):

	Fiscal Year 3	Fiscal Year 2	
Net income	$567,600	$479,500	
Interest expense	18,300	22,200	
	Fiscal Year 3	**Fiscal Year 2**	**Fiscal Year 1**
Total assets (at end of fiscal year)	$4,981,100	$4,648,900	$4,356,500
Total stockholders' equity (at end of fiscal year)	3,304,700	3,116,600	2,735,100

Assume the apparel industry average rate earned on total assets is 8.0%, and the average rate earned on stockholders' equity is 10.0% for the year ended April 2, Year 3.

a. Determine the rate earned on total assets for Ralph Lauren for fiscal Years 2 and 3. Round to one digit after the decimal place.

b. Determine the rate earned on stockholders' equity for Ralph Lauren for fiscal Years 2 and 3. Round to one decimal place.

c. Evaluate the two-year trend for the profitability ratios determined in (a) and (b).

d. Evaluate Ralph Lauren's profit performance relative to the industry.

EX 17-19 Six measures of solvency or profitability **OBJ. 2, 3**

✔ c. Ratio of sales to assets, 4.2

The following data were taken from the financial statements of Gates Inc. for the current fiscal year. Assuming that long-term investments totaled $3,000,000 throughout the year and that total assets were $7,000,000 at the beginning of the current fiscal year, determine the following: (a) ratio of fixed assets to long-term liabilities, (b) ratio of liabilities to stockholders' equity, (c) ratio of sales to assets, (d) rate earned on total assets, (e) rate earned on stockholders' equity, and (f) rate earned on common stockholders' equity. Round to one decimal place.

Property, plant, and equipment (net)			$ 3,200,000
Liabilities:			
Current liabilities		$1,000,000	
Mortgage note payable, 6%, issued 2005, due 2021		2,000,000	
Total liabilities			$ 3,000,000
Stockholders' equity:			
Preferred $10 stock, $100 par (no change during year)			$ 1,000,000
Common stock, $10 par (no change during year)			2,000,000
Retained earnings:			
Balance, beginning of year	$1,570,000		
Net income	930,000	$2,500,000	
Preferred dividends	$ 100,000		
Common dividends	400,000	500,000	
Balance, end of year			2,000,000
Total stockholders' equity			$ 5,000,000
Sales			$18,900,000
Interest expense			$ 120,000

EX 17-20 Six measures of solvency or profitability **OBJ. 2, 3**

✔ d. Price-earnings ratio, 10.0

The balance sheet for Garcon Inc. at the end of the current fiscal year indicated the following:

Bonds payable, 8% (issued in 2006, due in 2026)	$5,000,000
Preferred $4 stock, $50 par	2,500,000
Common stock, $10 par	5,000,000

Income before income tax was $3,000,000, and income taxes were $1,200,000 for the current year. Cash dividends paid on common stock during the current year totaled $1,200,000. The common stock was selling for $32 per share at the end of the year. Determine each of the following: (a) number of times bond interest charges are earned, (b) number of times preferred dividends are earned, (c) earnings per share on common stock, (d) price-earnings ratio, (e) dividends per share of common stock, and (f) dividend yield. Round to one decimal place, except earnings per share, which should be rounded to two decimal places.

EX 17-21 Earnings per share, price-earnings ratio, dividend yield **OBJ. 3**

✔ b. Price-earnings ratio, 15.0

SHOW ME HOW

The following information was taken from the financial statements of Tolbert Inc. for December 31 of the current fiscal year:

Common stock, $20 par (no change during the year)	$10,000,000
Preferred $4 stock, $40 par (no change during the year)	2,500,000

The net income was $1,750,000 and the declared dividends on the common stock were $1,125,000 for the current year. The market price of the common stock is $45 per share.

For the common stock, determine (a) the earnings per share, (b) the price-earnings ratio, (c) the dividends per share, and (d) the dividend yield. Round to one decimal place, except earnings per share, which should be rounded to two decimal places.

EX 17-22 Price-earnings ratio; dividend yield **OBJ. 3**

The table that follows shows the stock price, earnings per share, and dividends per share for three companies for a recent year:

	Price	Earnings per Share	Dividends per Share
Deere & Co.	$ 86.20	$ 8.71	$2.04
Google	873.32	36.75	0.00
The Coca-Cola Company	39.79	1.97	1.02

a. Determine the price-earnings ratio and dividend yield for the three companies. Round to one decimal place.

b. Explain the differences in these ratios across the three companies.

Appendix

EX 17-23 Earnings per share, extraordinary item

✔ b. Earnings per share on common stock, $7.60

The net income reported on the income statement of Cutler Co. was $4,000,000. There were 500,000 shares of $10 par common stock and 100,000 shares of $2 preferred stock outstanding throughout the current year. The income statement included two extraordinary items: an $800,000 gain from condemnation of land and a $400,000 loss arising from flood damage, both after applicable income tax. Determine the per-share figures for common stock for (a) income before extraordinary items and (b) net income.

Appendix

EX 17-24 Extraordinary item

Assume that the amount of each of the following items is material to the financial statements. Classify each item as either normally recurring (NR) or extraordinary (E).

a. Loss on the disposal of equipment considered to be obsolete because of the development of new technology.

b. Uninsured loss on building due to hurricane damage. The building was purchased by the company in 1910 and had not previously incurred hurricane damage.

c. Gain on sale of land condemned by the local government for a public works project.

d. Uninsured flood loss. (Flood insurance is unavailable because of periodic flooding in the area.)

e. Interest revenue on notes receivable.

f. Uncollectible accounts expense.

g. Loss on sale of investments in stocks and bonds.

Appendix

EX 17-25 Income statement and earnings per share for extraordinary items and discontinued operations

Apex Inc. reports the following for a recent year:

Income from continuing operations before income tax	$1,000,000
Extraordinary property loss from hurricane	$140,000*
Loss from discontinued operations	$240,000*
Weighted average number of shares outstanding	20,000
Applicable tax rate	40%

*Net of any tax effect.

a. Prepare a partial income statement for Apex Inc., beginning with income from continuing operations before income tax.

b. Calculate the earnings per common share for Apex Inc., including per-share amounts for unusual items.

Appendix

EX 17-26 Unusual items

Discuss whether Colston Company correctly reported the following items in the financial statements:

a. In a recent year, the company discovered a clerical error in the prior year's accounting records. As a result, the reported net income for the previous year was overstated by $45,000. The company corrected this error by restating the prior-year financial statements.

b. In a recent year, the company voluntarily changed its method of accounting for long-term construction contracts from the percentage of completion method to the completed contract method. Both methods are acceptable under generally acceptable accounting principles. The cumulative effect of this change was reported as a separate component of income in the current period income statement.

Problems: Series A

PR 17-1A Horizontal analysis of income statement **OBJ. 1**

✔ 1. Sales, 12.5% increase

General Ledger

SHOW ME HOW

For 2016, Clapton Company reported a decline in net income. At the end of the year, S. Hand, the president, is presented with the following condensed comparative income statement:

Clapton Company
Comparative Income Statement
For the Years Ended December 31, 2016 and 2015

	2016	2015
Sales	$6,750,000	$6,000,000
Cost of goods sold	2,480,000	2,000,000
Gross profit	$4,270,000	$4,000,000
Selling expenses	$1,260,000	$1,000,000
Administrative expenses	625,000	500,000
Total operating expenses	$1,885,000	$1,500,000
Income from operations	$2,385,000	$2,500,000
Other income	110,000	100,000
Income before income tax	$2,495,000	$2,600,000
Income tax expense	60,000	50,000
Net income	$2,435,000	$2,550,000

Instructions

1. Prepare a comparative income statement with horizontal analysis for the two-year period, using 2015 as the base year. Round to one decimal place.
2. To the extent the data permit, comment on the significant relationships revealed by the horizontal analysis prepared in (1).

PR 17-2A Vertical analysis of income statement

OBJ. 1

✔ 1. Net income, 2016, 13.0%

General Ledger

For 2016, Indigo Company initiated a sales promotion campaign that included the expenditure of an additional $39,000 for advertising. At the end of the year, Lumi Neer, the president, is presented with the following condensed comparative income statement:

Indigo Company
Comparative Income Statement
For the Years Ended December 31, 2016 and 2015

	2016	2015
Sales	$820,000	$600,000
Cost of goods sold	311,600	240,000
Gross profit	$508,400	$360,000
Selling expenses	$164,000	$108,000
Administrative expenses	57,400	54,000
Total operating expenses	$221,400	$162,000
Income from operations	$287,000	$198,000
Other income	65,600	48,000
Income before income tax	$352,600	$246,000
Income tax expense	246,000	180,000
Net income	$106,600	$ 66,000

Instructions

1. Prepare a comparative income statement for the two-year period, presenting an analysis of each item in relationship to sales for each of the years. Round to one decimal place.
2. To the extent the data permit, comment on the significant relationships revealed by the vertical analysis prepared in (1).

PR 17-3A Effect of transactions on current position analysis

OBJ. 2

✔ 2. c. Current ratio, 2.0

Data pertaining to the current position of Forte Company are as follows:

Cash	$412,500
Marketable securities	187,500
Accounts and notes receivable (net)	300,000
Inventories	700,000
Prepaid expenses	50,000
Accounts payable	200,000
Notes payable (short-term)	250,000
Accrued expenses	300,000

Instructions

1. Compute (a) the working capital, (b) the current ratio, and (c) the quick ratio. Round to one decimal place.

2. List the following captions on a sheet of paper:

Transaction	Working Capital	Current Ratio	Quick Ratio

Compute the working capital, the current ratio, and the quick ratio after each of the following transactions, and record the results in the appropriate columns. *Consider each transaction separately* and assume that only that transaction affects the data given. Round to one decimal place.

a. Sold marketable securities at no gain or loss, $70,000.
b. Paid accounts payable, $125,000.
c. Purchased goods on account, $110,000.
d. Paid notes payable, $100,000.
e. Declared a cash dividend, $150,000.
f. Declared a common stock dividend on common stock, $50,000.
g. Borrowed cash from bank on a long-term note, $225,000.
h. Received cash on account, $125,000.
i. Issued additional shares of stock for cash, $600,000.
j. Paid cash for prepaid expenses, $10,000.

PR 17-4A Nineteen measures of solvency and profitability

OBJ. 2, 3

✔ 5. Number of days' sales in receivables, 36.5

The comparative financial statements of Bettancort Inc. are as follows. The market price of Bettancort Inc. common stock was $71.25 on December 31, 2016.

Bettancort Inc.
Comparative Retained Earnings Statement
For the Years Ended December 31, 2016 and 2015

	2016	2015
Retained earnings, January 1	$2,655,000	$2,400,000
Add net income for year	300,000	280,000
Total	$2,955,000	$2,680,000
Deduct dividends:		
On preferred stock	$ 15,000	$ 15,000
On common stock	10,000	10,000
Total	$ 25,000	$ 25,000
Retained earnings, December 31	$2,930,000	$2,655,000

Bettancort Inc.
Comparative Income Statement
For the Years Ended December 31, 2016 and 2015

	2016	2015
Sales	$1,200,000	$1,000,000
Cost of goods sold	500,000	475,000
Gross profit	$ 700,000	$ 525,000
Selling expenses	$ 240,000	$ 200,000
Administrative expenses	180,000	150,000
Total operating expenses	$ 420,000	$ 350,000
Income from operations	$ 280,000	$ 175,000
Other income	166,000	225,000
	$ 446,000	$ 400,000
Other expense (interest)	66,000	60,000
Income before income tax	$ 380,000	$ 340,000
Income tax expense	80,000	60,000
Net income	$ 300,000	$ 280,000

Bettancort Inc.
Comparative Balance Sheet
December 31, 2016 and 2015

	Dec. 31, 2016	Dec. 31, 2015
Assets		
Current assets:		
Cash	$ 450,000	$ 400,000
Marketable securities	300,000	260,000
Accounts receivable (net)	130,000	110,000
Inventories	67,000	58,000
Prepaid expenses	153,000	139,000
Total current assets	$1,100,000	$ 967,000
Long-term investments	2,350,000	2,200,000
Property, plant, and equipment (net)	1,320,000	1,188,000
Total assets	$4,770,000	$4,355,000
Liabilities		
Current liabilities	$ 440,000	$ 400,000
Long-term liabilities:		
Mortgage note payable, 8%, due 2021	$ 100,000	$ 0
Bonds payable, 5%, due 2017	1,000,000	1,000,000
Total long-term liabilities	$1,100,000	$1,000,000
Total liabilities	$1,540,000	$1,400,000
Stockholders' Equity		
Preferred $0.75 stock, $10 par	$ 200,000	$ 200,000
Common stock, $10 par	100,000	100,000
Retained earnings	2,930,000	2,655,000
Total stockholders' equity	$3,230,000	$2,955,000
Total liabilities and stockholders' equity	$4,770,000	$4,355,000

Instructions

Determine the following measures for 2016, rounding to one decimal place:

1. Working capital
2. Current ratio
3. Quick ratio
4. Accounts receivable turnover
5. Number of days' sales in receivables
6. Inventory turnover
7. Number of days' sales in inventory
8. Ratio of fixed assets to long-term liabilities
9. Ratio of liabilities to stockholders' equity
10. Number of times interest charges are earned
11. Number of times preferred dividends are earned
12. Ratio of sales to assets
13. Rate earned on total assets
14. Rate earned on stockholders' equity
15. Rate earned on common stockholders' equity
16. Earnings per share on common stock
17. Price-earnings ratio
18. Dividends per share of common stock
19. Dividend yield

PR 17-5A Solvency and profitability trend analysis — OBJ. 2, 3

Addai Company has provided the following comparative information:

	2016	2015	2014	2013	2012
Net income	$ 273,406	$ 367,976	$ 631,176	$ 884,000	$ 800,000
Interest expense	616,047	572,003	528,165	495,000	440,000
Income tax expense	31,749	53,560	106,720	160,000	200,000
Total assets (ending balance)	4,417,178	4,124,350	3,732,443	3,338,500	2,750,000
Total stockholders' equity (ending balance)	3,706,557	3,433,152	3,065,176	2,434,000	1,550,000
Average total assets	4,270,764	3,928,396	3,535,472	3,044,250	2,475,000
Average total stockholders' equity	3,569,855	3,249,164	2,749,588	1,992,000	1,150,000

You have been asked to evaluate the historical performance of the company over the last five years.

Selected industry ratios have remained relatively steady at the following levels for the last five years:

	2012–2016
Rate earned on total assets	28%
Rate earned on stockholders' equity	18%
Number of times interest charges are earned	2.7
Ratio of liabilities to stockholders' equity	0.4

Instructions

1. Prepare four line graphs with the ratio on the vertical axis and the years on the horizontal axis for the following four ratios (rounded to one decimal place):
   a. Rate earned on total assets
   b. Rate earned on stockholders' equity
   c. Number of times interest charges are earned
   d. Ratio of liabilities to stockholders' equity

   Display both the company ratio and the industry benchmark on each graph. That is, each graph should have two lines.
2. Prepare an analysis of the graphs in (1).

Problems: Series B

PR 17-1B Horizontal analysis of income statement — OBJ. 1

✔ 1. Sales, 30.0% increase

General Ledger

SHOW ME HOW

For 2016, Macklin Inc. reported a significant increase in net income. At the end of the year, John Mayer, the president, is presented with the following condensed comparative income statement:

Macklin Inc.
Comparative Income Statement
For the Years Ended December 31, 2016 and 2015

	2016	2015
Sales	$910,000	$700,000
Cost of goods sold	441,000	350,000
Gross profit	$469,000	$350,000
Selling expenses	$ 139,150	$115,000
Administrative expenses	99,450	85,000
Total operating expenses	$238,600	$200,000
Income from operations	$230,400	$150,000
Other income	65,000	50,000
Income before income tax	$295,400	$200,000
Income tax expense	65,000	50,000
Net income	$230,400	$150,000

Instructions

1. Prepare a comparative income statement with horizontal analysis for the two-year period, using 2015 as the base year. Round to one decimal place.
2. To the extent the data permit, comment on the significant relationships revealed by the horizontal analysis prepared in (1).

PR 17-2B Vertical analysis of income statement **OBJ. 1**

✔ 1. Net income, 2015, 14.0%

General Ledger

For 2016, Fielder Industries Inc. initiated a sales promotion campaign that included the expenditure of an additional $40,000 for advertising. At the end of the year, Leif Grando, the president, is presented with the following condensed comparative income statement:

Fielder Industries Inc.
Comparative Income Statement
For the Years Ended December 31, 2016 and 2015

	2016	2015
Sales	$1,300,000	$1,180,000
Cost of goods sold	682,500	613,600
Gross profit	$ 617,500	$ 566,400
Selling expenses	$ 260,000	$ 188,800
Adminstrative expenses	169,000	177,000
Total operating expenses	$ 429,000	$ 365,800
Income from operations	$ 188,500	$ 200,600
Other income	78,000	70,800
Income before income tax	$ 266,500	$ 271,400
Income tax expense	117,000	106,200
Net income	$ 149,500	$ 165,200

Instructions

1. Prepare a comparative income statement for the two-year period, presenting an analysis of each item in relationship to sales for each of the years. Round to one decimal place.
2. To the extent the data permit, comment on the significant relationships revealed by the vertical analysis prepared in (1).

PR 17-3B Effect of transactions on current position analysis **OBJ. 2**

✔ 2. g. Quick ratio, 1.6

Data pertaining to the current position of Lucroy Industries Inc. are as follows:

Cash	$ 800,000
Marketable securities	550,000
Accounts and notes receivable (net)	850,000
Inventories	700,000
Prepaid expenses	300,000
Accounts payable	1,200,000
Notes payable (short-term)	700,000
Accrued expenses	100,000

Instructions

1. Compute (a) the working capital, (b) the current ratio, and (c) the quick ratio. Round to one decimal place.
2. List the following captions on a sheet of paper:

Transaction	Working Capital	Current Ratio	Quick Ratio

Compute the working capital, the current ratio, and the quick ratio after each of the following transactions, and record the results in the appropriate columns. *Consider each transaction separately* and assume that only that transaction affects the data given. Round to one decimal place.

a. Sold marketable securities at no gain or loss, $500,000.
b. Paid accounts payable, $287,500.
c. Purchased goods on account, $400,000.
d. Paid notes payable, $125,000.
e. Declared a cash dividend, $325,000.
f. Declared a common stock dividend on common stock, $150,000.
g. Borrowed cash from bank on a long-term note, $1,000,000.
h. Received cash on account, $75,000.
i. Issued additional shares of stock for cash, $2,000,000.
j. Paid cash for prepaid expenses, $200,000.

PR 17-4B Nineteen measures of solvency and profitability — OBJ. 2, 3

✔ 9. Ratio of liabilities to stockholders' equity, 0.4

The comparative financial statements of Stargel Inc. are as follows. The market price of Stargel Inc. common stock was $119.70 on December 31, 2016.

Stargel Inc.
Comparative Retained Earnings Statement
For the Years Ended December 31, 2016 and 2015

	2016	2015
Retained earnings, January 1	$5,375,000	$4,545,000
Add net income for year	900,000	925,000
Total	$6,275,000	$5,470,000
Deduct dividends:		
On preferred stock	$ 45,000	$ 45,000
On common stock	50,000	50,000
Total	$ 95,000	$ 95,000
Retained earnings, December 31	$6,180,000	$5,375,000

Stargel Inc.
Comparative Income Statement
For the Years Ended December 31, 2016 and 2015

	2016	2015
Sales	$10,000,000	$9,400,000
Cost of goods sold	5,350,000	4,950,000
Gross profit	$ 4,650,000	$4,450,000
Selling expenses	$ 2,000,000	$1,880,000
Administrative expenses	1,500,000	1,410,000
Total operating expenses	$ 3,500,000	$3,290,000
Income from operations	$ 1,150,000	$1,160,000
Other income	150,000	140,000
	$ 1,300,000	$1,300,000
Other expense (interest)	170,000	150,000
Income before income tax	$ 1,130,000	$1,150,000
Income tax expense	230,000	225,000
Net income	$ 900,000	$ 925,000

Stargel Inc.
Comparative Balance Sheet
December 31, 2016 and 2015

	Dec. 31, 2016	Dec. 31, 2015
Assets		
Current assets:		
Cash	$ 500,000	$ 400,000
Marketable securities	1,010,000	1,000,000
Accounts receivable (net)	740,000	510,000
Inventories	1,190,000	950,000
Prepaid expenses	250,000	229,000
Total current assets	$3,690,000	$3,089,000
Long-term investments	2,350,000	2,300,000
Property, plant, and equipment (net)	3,740,000	3,366,000
Total assets	$9,780,000	$8,755,000
Liabilities		
Current liabilities	$ 900,000	$ 880,000
Long-term liabilities:		
Mortgage note payable, 8.8%, due 2021	$ 200,000	$ 0
Bonds payable, 9%, due 2017	1,500,000	1,500,000
Total long-term liabilities	$1,700,000	$1,500,000
Total liabilities	$2,600,000	$2,380,000
Stockholders' Equity		
Preferred $0.90 stock, $10 par	$ 500,000	$ 500,000
Common stock, $5 par	500,000	500,000
Retained earnings	6,180,000	5,375,000
Total stockholders' equity	$7,180,000	$6,375,000
Total liabilities and stockholders' equity	$9,780,000	$8,755,000

Instructions

Determine the following measures for 2016, rounding to one decimal place, except per-share amounts, which should be rounded to the nearest penny:

1. Working capital
2. Current ratio
3. Quick ratio
4. Accounts receivable turnover
5. Number of days' sales in receivables
6. Inventory turnover
7. Number of days' sales in inventory
8. Ratio of fixed assets to long-term liabilities
9. Ratio of liabilities to stockholders' equity
10. Number of times interest charges are earned
11. Number of times preferred dividends are earned
12. Ratio of sales to assets
13. Rate earned on total assets
14. Rate earned on stockholders' equity
15. Rate earned on common stockholders' equity
16. Earnings per share on common stock
17. Price-earnings ratio
18. Dividends per share of common stock
19. Dividend yield

PR 17-5B Solvency and profitability trend analysis OBJ. 2, 3

Crosby Company has provided the following comparative information:

	2016	2015	2014	2013	2012
Net income	$ 5,571,720	$ 3,714,480	$ 2,772,000	$ 1,848,000	$ 1,400,000
Interest expense	1,052,060	891,576	768,600	610,000	500,000
Income tax expense	1,225,572	845,222	640,320	441,600	320,000
Total assets (ending balance)	29,378,491	22,598,839	17,120,333	12,588,480	10,152,000
Total stockholders' equity (ending balance)	18,706,200	13,134,480	9,420,000	6,648,000	4,800,000
Average total assets	25,988,665	19,859,586	14,854,406	11,370,240	8,676,000
Average total stockholders' equity	15,920,340	11,277,240	8,034,000	5,724,000	4,100,000

You have been asked to evaluate the historical performance of the company over the last five years.

Selected industry ratios have remained relatively steady at the following levels for the last five years:

	2012–2016
Rate earned on total assets	19%
Rate earned on stockholders' equity	26%
Number of times interest charges are earned	3.4
Ratio of liabilities to stockholders' equity	1.4

Instructions

1. Prepare four line graphs with the ratio on the vertical axis and the years on the horizontal axis for the following four ratios (rounded to one decimal place):
   a. Rate earned on total assets
   b. Rate earned on stockholders' equity
   c. Number of times interest charges are earned
   d. Ratio of liabilities to stockholders' equity

   Display both the company ratio and the industry benchmark on each graph. That is, each graph should have two lines.
2. Prepare an analysis of the graphs in (1).

Nike, Inc., Problem

Financial Statement Analysis

The financial statements for Nike, Inc., are presented in Appendix C at the end of the text. The following additional information (in thousands) is available:

Accounts receivable at May 31, 2010	$ 3,138
Inventories at May 31, 2010	2,715
Total assets at May 31, 2010	14,998
Stockholders' equity at May 31, 2010	9,843

Instructions

1. Determine the following measures for the fiscal years ended May 31, 2013 (fiscal 2012), and May 31, 2012 (fiscal 2011), rounding to one decimal place.
   a. Working capital
   b. Current ratio
   c. Quick ratio
   d. Accounts receivable turnover
   e. Number of days' sales in receivables
   f. Inventory turnover
   g. Number of days' sales in inventory
   h. Ratio of liabilities to stockholders' equity
   i. Ratio of sales to assets

j. Rate earned on total assets, assuming interest expense is $23 million for the year ending May 31, 2013, and $31 million for the year ending May 31, 2012
k. Rate earned on common stockholders' equity
l. Price-earnings ratio, assuming that the market price was $61.66 per share on May 31, 2013, and $53.10 per share on May 31, 2012
m. Percentage relationship of net income to sales

2. What conclusions can be drawn from these analyses?

Cases & Projects

CP 17-1 Analysis of financing corporate growth

Assume that the president of Freeman Industries Inc. made the following statement in the Annual Report to Shareholders:

"The founding family and majority shareholders of the company do not believe in using debt to finance future growth. The founding family learned from hard experience during Prohibition and the Great Depression that debt can cause loss of flexibility and eventual loss of corporate control. The company will not place itself at such risk. As such, all future growth will be financed either by stock sales to the public or by internally generated resources."

As a public shareholder of this company, how would you respond to this policy?

CP 17-2 Receivables and inventory turnover

Rodgers Industries Inc. has completed its fiscal year on December 31. The auditor, Josh McCoy, has approached the CFO, Aaron Mathews, regarding the year-end receivables and inventory levels of Rodgers Industries. The following conversation takes place:

Josh: We are beginning our audit of Rodgers Industries and have prepared ratio analyses to determine if there have been significant changes in operations or financial position. This helps us guide the audit process. This analysis indicates that the inventory turnover has decreased from 5.1 to 2.7, while the accounts receivable turnover has decreased from 11 to 7. Could you explain this change in operations?

Aaron: There is little need for concern. The inventory represents computers that we were unable to sell during the holiday buying season. We are confident, however, that we will be able to sell these computers as we move into the next fiscal year.

Josh: What gives you this confidence?

Aaron: We will increase our advertising and provide some very attractive price concessions to move these machines. We have no choice. Newer technology is already out there, and we have to unload this inventory.

Josh: ... and the receivables?

Aaron: As you may be aware, the company is under tremendous pressure to expand sales and profits. As a result, we lowered our credit standards to our commercial customers so that we would be able to sell products to a broader customer base. As a result of this policy change, we have been able to expand sales by 35%.

Josh: Your responses have not been reassuring to me.

Aaron: I'm a little confused. Assets are good, right? Why don't you look at our current ratio? It has improved, hasn't it? I would think that you would view that very favorably.

Why is Josh concerned about the inventory and accounts receivable turnover ratios and Aaron's responses to them? What action may Josh need to take? How would you respond to Aaron's last comment?

CP 17-3 Vertical analysis

The condensed income statements through income from operations for **Dell Inc.** and **Apple Inc.** for recent fiscal years follow (numbers in millions of dollars):

	Dell Inc.	Apple Inc.
Sales	$56,940	$156,508
Cost of sales	44,754	87,846
Gross profit	$12,186	$68,662
Selling, general, and administrative expenses	$ 8,102	$10,040
Research and development	1,072	3,381
Operating expenses	$ 9,174	$13,421
Income from operations	$ 3,012	$55,241

Prepare comparative common-sized statements, rounding percents to one decimal place. Interpret the analyses.

CP 17-4 Profitability and stockholder ratios

Deere & Co. manufactures and distributes farm and construction machinery that it sells around the world. In addition to its manufacturing operations, Deere & Co.'s credit division loans money to customers to finance the purchase of their farm and construction equipment.

The following information is available for three recent years (in millions except per-share amounts):

	Year 3	Year 2	Year 1
Net income (loss)	$3,064.7	$2,799.9	$1,865.0
Preferred dividends	$0.00	$0.00	$0.00
Interest expense	$782.8	$759.4	$811.4
Shares outstanding for computing earnings per share	397	417	424
Cash dividend per share	$1.79	$1.52	$1.16
Average total assets	$52,237	$45,737	$42,200
Average stockholders' equity	$6,821	$6,545	$5,555
Average stock price per share	$79.27	$80.48	$61.18

1. Calculate the following ratios for each year (Round percentages to one decimal place):
   a. Rate earned on total assets
   b. Rate earned on stockholders' equity
   c. Earnings per share
   d. Dividend yield
   e. Price-earnings ratio
2. What is the ratio of average liabilities to average stockholders' equity for Year 3?
3. Based on these data, evaluate Deere & Co.'s performance.

CP 17-5 Comprehensive profitability and solvency analysis

Marriott International, Inc., and Hyatt Hotels Corporation are two major owners and managers of lodging and resort properties in the United States. Abstracted income statement information for the two companies is as follows for a recent year:

	Marriott (in millions)	Hyatt (in millions)
Operating profit before other expenses and interest	$ 677	$ 39
Other income (expenses)	54	118
Interest expense	(180)	(54)
Income before income taxes	$ 551	$103
Income tax expense	93	37
Net income	$ 458	$ 66

Balance sheet information is as follows:

	Marriott (in millions)	Hyatt (in millions)
Total liabilities	$7,398	$2,125
Total stockholders' equity	1,585	5,118
Total liabilities and stockholders' equity	$8,983	$7,243

The average liabilities, average stockholders' equity, and average total assets were as follows:

	Marriott (in millions)	Hyatt (in millions)
Average total liabilities	$7,095	$2,132
Average total stockholders' equity	1,364	5,067
Average total assets	8,458	7,199

1. Determine the following ratios for both companies (round to one decimal place after the whole percent):
   a. Rate earned on total assets
   b. Rate earned on stockholders' equity
   c. Number of times interest charges are earned
   d. Ratio of liabilities to stockholders' equity
2. Analyze and compare the two companies, using the information in (1).